The 23 Greatest Solo Piano Works

Robert Greenberg, Ph.D.

THE
GREAT
COURSES

PUBLISHED BY:

THE GREAT COURSES
Corporate Headquarters
4840 Westfields Boulevard, Suite 500
Chantilly, Virginia 20151-2299
Phone: 1-800-832-2412
Fax: 703-378-3819
www.thegreatcourses.com

Robert Greenberg, Ph.D.
Music Historian-in-Residence
San Francisco Performances

Professor Robert Greenberg was born in Brooklyn, New York, in 1954 and has lived in the San Francisco Bay Area since 1978. Professor Greenberg received a B.A. in Music, magna cum laude, from Princeton University in 1976. His principal teachers at Princeton were Edward Cone, Daniel Werts, and Carlton Gamer in composition; Claudio Spies and Paul Lansky in analysis; and Jerry Kuderna in piano. In 1984, Professor Greenberg received a Ph.D. in Music Composition, with distinction, from the University of California, Berkeley, where his principal teachers were Andrew Imbrie and Olly Wilson in composition and Richard Felciano in analysis.

Professor Greenberg has composed more than 45 works for a wide variety of instrumental and vocal ensembles. Recent performances of his works have taken place in New York; San Francisco; Chicago; Los Angeles; England; Ireland; Greece; Italy; and the Netherlands, where his *Child's Play* for String Quartet was performed at the Concertgebouw in Amsterdam.

Professor Greenberg has received numerous honors, including three Nicola de Lorenzo Composition Prizes and three Meet The Composer grants. He has received recent commissions from the Koussevitzky Music Foundation in the Library of Congress, the Alexander String Quartet, the San Francisco Contemporary Music Players, the Strata Ensemble, San Francisco Performances, and the XTET ensemble. Professor Greenberg is a board member and an artistic director of COMPOSERS, INC., a composers' collective and production organization based in San Francisco. His music is published by Fallen Leaf Press and CPP/Belwin and is recorded on the Innova label.

Professor Greenberg has performed, taught, and lectured extensively across North America and Europe. He is currently Music Historian-in-Residence with San Francisco Performances, where he has lectured and performed since 1994, and is a faculty member of the Advanced Management Program at the University of Pennsylvania's Wharton School of Business. He has served on the faculties of the University of California, Berkeley; California State University, East Bay; and the San Francisco Conservatory of Music, where he chaired the Department of Music History and Literature from 1989 to 2001 and served as the director of the Adult Extension Division from 1991 to 1996.

Professor Greenberg has lectured for some of the most prestigious musical and arts organizations in the United States, including the San Francisco Symphony (where for 10 years he was host and lecturer for the symphony's nationally acclaimed Discovery Series), the Chautauqua Institution (where he was the Everett Scholar-in-Residence during the 2006 season), the Ravinia Festival, Lincoln Center for the Performing Arts, the Van Cliburn Foundation, the Nasher Sculpture Center, the Dallas Symphony Orchestra, the Hartford Symphony Orchestra, Villa Montalvo, Music@Menlo, and the University of British Columbia (where he was the Dal Grauer Lecturer in September 2006).

In addition, Professor Greenberg is a sought-after lecturer for businesses and business schools and has recently spoken for such diverse organizations as S. C. Johnson, Canadian Pacific, Deutsches Bank, the University of California/Haas School of Business Executive Seminar, the University of Chicago Graduate School of Business, Harvard Business School Publishing, Kaiser Permanente, the Strategos Institute, Quintiles Transnational, the Young Presidents' Organization, the World Presidents' Organization, and the Commonwealth Club of San Francisco. Professor Greenberg has been profiled in *The Wall Street Journal, Inc.* magazine, *The Times* of London, the *Los Angeles Times*, *The Christian Science Monitor*, the *San Francisco Chronicle*, the *San Jose Mercury News*, the University of California alumni magazine, *Princeton Alumni Weekly*, and *Diablo* magazine.

For many years, Professor Greenberg was the resident composer and music historian for NPR's *Weekend All Things Considered*; he currently plays that role on NPR's *Weekend Edition, Sunday* with Liane Hansen. In February 2003, Maine's *Bangor Daily News* referred to Professor Greenberg as the Elvis of music history and appreciation, an appraisal that has given him more pleasure than any other.

Professor Greenberg's other Great Courses include *The 30 Greatest Orchestral Works; How to Listen to and Understand Great Music, 3rd Edition; Concert Masterworks; Bach and the High Baroque; The Symphonies of Beethoven; How to Listen to and Understand Opera;* the *Great Masters* series; *The Operas of Mozart; The Life and Operas of Verdi; The Symphony; The Chamber Music of Mozart; Beethoven's Piano Sonatas; The Concerto; Understanding the Fundamentals of Music;* and *The Music of Richard Wagner.* ■

Table of Contents

Table of Contents

Table of Contents

SUPPLEMENTAL MATERIAL

The 23 Greatest Solo Piano Works

Scope:

The *23 Greatest Solo Piano Works* is a guide through more than 200 years of keyboard music, and in 24 lectures, it will give you the knowledge and insight to enjoy and appreciate the stunningly diverse literature of piano music. In addition to the study of the music, the course digs deeply into the artistic and social environments that shaped the music itself, shedding light on what inspired these great works and how they were created.

Beginning with the towering figures of Bach, Mozart, and Beethoven, the course moves on to the piano music of such great 19th-century masters as Chopin, Schumann, Liszt, Brahms, and Rachmaninoff and finally to visionary modernists including Scriabin, Debussy, Copland, and Prokofiev.

While all of the works featured in this course are worthy of being called among the "greatest," there are—admittedly—many other "greatest solo works for the piano" that could have been addressed in this course. The selections were governed by three basic ground rules.

- The works included have stood the test of time, meaning that they are part of the standard piano repertoire—works that can be heard in concert, works that have been published, works that are readily available on recordings.

- A single composer is represented by a maximum of two major works. This is in order to fulfill a larger goal of the course, which is to explore a stylistically and historically varied body of some of the greatest works ever written for piano, works that offer the collateral advantage of illustrating the development of the piano as an instrument and pianistic technique as a skill.

- Sets of works published together count as a single work. The only exception to this is the two lectures that focus on Debussy: "The Sunken Cathedral," from his first book of *Préludes*, and another on the remainder of Debussy's *Préludes*, Book One. (Given his incredible innovations as both a composer and as a composer for the piano, this bit of Debussy worship is entirely appropriate.)

The principal backstory of this course is the technological development of the piano and the concurrent evolution of piano music that exploited its developing capabilities. Parallel with the unfolding of the musical repertoire, you will follow the technological development of the piano, from the German-built pianos manufactured by Gottfried Silbermann in the 1730s to the modern grand pianos built by Steinway and Sons in the 1870s.

This, therefore, is not just a course about music played on the piano but one about music written specifically for the piano by composers who were, not coincidentally, among the greatest pianists who ever lived—composers who exploited the instrument's ever-growing dynamic range, touch, and sonority.

The nature of piano music coevolved with piano technology. Consequently, the technical and expressive content of the music surveyed in this course vary depending on the nature of the pianos available to the composers. For example, it would never have occurred to Mozart—whose piano spanned five octaves—to use the upper and lower notes available on a modern piano, which spans seven-plus octaves. In addition, the double escapement mechanism, pioneered in the 1820s, made fast, repeated notes possible and allowed Liszt to create a sort of piano music that could never have been played on earlier pianos. Debussy used the resonance and overtones of the modern grand piano to create shimmering—otherworldly musical environments that would likewise have been unthinkable on earlier pianos.

A particularly exciting feature of the course is the performance of custom-recorded musical examples by three concert pianists who performed and recorded them at The Great Courses studio. Their appearance in the course provides the opportunity to discuss the significant differences between a talented pianist and the true concert pianist, who is a supremely (one might say ruthlessly) disciplined professional. Like being a champion athlete, being a professional pianist requires strength, conditioning, technique, commitment, precision, mental toughness, and a fiercely competitive spirit.

The course is strengthened and enriched by the wonderful performances of three concert pianists: Magdalina Melkonyan, Woobin Park, and Eun Joo Chung.

For the most part, the works featured in this course appear in chronological order. However, this course is not conceived as a single, sequential unit of 24 lectures. The course can be consumed as a single entity, Lectures 1 through 24, or as a compendium of discrete lectures to be enjoyed in any order one chooses.

Three lectures (9, 11, and 16) stand somewhat apart from the others. Discussed in these lectures is the extraordinarily innovative pianism of the three composers who, more than any others, defined the piano as we understand it today: Frédéric Chopin, Franz Liszt, and Claude Debussy. These lectures do focus on a single work or set of works—respectively, Chopin's Ballade in G Minor, Liszt's *Years of Pilgrimage*, and Debussy's *Préludes*, Book One—but they examine their composers' revolutionary pianism as much as the music itself.

By the end of the course, you will have come to see that a piano is a one-person orchestra. From the keyboard music of Johann Sebastian Bach through the piano music of Mozart, Beethoven, Schubert, Chopin, Liszt, Schumann, Brahms, Mussorgsky, Rachmaninoff, Debussy, Scriabin, Albéniz, Ravel, Copland, Prokofiev, and hundreds of other composer old and new, the repertoire of the piano spans a historical and expressive depth far beyond that of any other single instrument. ∎

Piano Starts Here!
Lecture 1

In this course, Lectures 2 through 23 will each deal with a single work or a set of works published together. Lectures 9, 11, and 16 stand somewhat apart from the others. These three lectures are dedicated to discussing the extraordinarily innovative pianism of the three composers who, more than any others, defined the piano as we understand it today: Frédéric Chopin, Franz Liszt, and Claude Debussy. While these lectures focus on a single work or set of works, they will examine their composers' revolutionary pianism as much as the music itself.

The Composers and the Piano

- A "concert pianist" is a professional pianist who makes his or her living playing concerts. (A "concert" is a live performance during which people pay good money to hear a professional pianist play.) This course features three concert pianists, who will provide custom-recorded musical examples: Magdalina Melkonyan, Woobin Park, and Eun Joo Chung.

- In this course, 19 different composers are represented, and every one of those 19 composers was a competent pianist. Of the 19, 11 were world-class concert players: Bach, Mozart, Beethoven, Chopin, Liszt, Anton Rubinstein, Brahms, Isaac Albéniz, Alexander Scriabin, Rachmaninoff, and Prokofiev; 5 were accomplished professionals: Felix Mendelssohn, Robert Schumann, Claude Debussy, Maurice Ravel, and Aaron Copland; and 3 were—at the very least—passably competent: Franz Schubert, Modest Mussorgsky, and Antonín Dvořák. Of all these composers, the only one who didn't initially train as a keyboard player was Dvořák.

- This is not just a course about music played on the piano but about music written specifically for the piano by composers who were, in most cases, among the greatest pianists who ever lived.

The harpsichord, a keyboard musical instrument, led to the invention of the piano.

- The exception is Johann Sebastian Bach, who had a checkered relationship with the piano. Bach—who lived from 1685 to 1750—was, without any doubt, the greatest keyboard player of his time. His main axes were the organ and the harpsichord. The piano was still in its techno-infancy when Bach got to know it, and overall, he was not particularly impressed.

- The two works by Bach included in this survey—Book One of *The Well-Tempered Clavier* and the *Goldberg Variations*—were originally performed on the harpsichord. However, for more than 200 years, these works have been, much more often than not, played on the piano. Given their performance history, it can be asserted that Bach's *The Well-Tempered Clavier* and *Goldberg Variations* are piano as well as harpsichord works, and as such, they must be numbered as being among the greatest piano works ever composed and, thus, deserve a place in this course.

- To a not-insignificant degree, this will also be a course about the piano, an instrument that changed tremendously over the first 170 years of its existence. The 9-foot-long, 1,000-pound concert grand piano that today is considered the "standard" concert instrument came into existence well after the lives and careers of Mozart, Beethoven, Schubert, Chopin, and Schumann.

- Invented around 1700 by a Florence-based harpsichord builder named Bartolomeo Cristofori, the piano was an evolving technology until the 1870s, when the modern concert grand came into existence. Thus, the nature of piano music coevolved with the piano. Consequently, the technical and expressive content of the music surveyed in this course will vary depending on the nature of the pianos available to the composers.

The Harpsichord and the Early Piano

- The harpsichord was invented around the year 1400. By 1700, harpsichords were as ubiquitous as electric keyboards are today. A harpsichord is a mechanical harp, a wing-shaped instrument in which the strings of a horizontally set harp are plucked from a keyboard.

- When a harpsichord key is pressed, it levers upward a slat of wood called a jack. Mounted on the jack is a pick that is made from either a quill or a piece of hardened leather. The plectrum "plucks" a string as it rises past it. When the key is released, the jack-and-plectrum assembly falls back into place by gravity. A small hinge folds the plectrum assembly upward, and thus, it passes the string without replucking it, at which point a damper stops the vibration of the string.

- The nature of a harpsichord's action precludes it from getting progressively louder and softer or of **accenting**—that is, making some **notes** louder than others. Pushing down harder on the keys of a harpsichord will not make the instrument play louder; all that will do is create a wooden thump.

- The loudness of a harpsichord is not determined by the speed with which the plectrum moves, but by the actual mass of the plectrum itself. The mass of the plectrum is built into a harpsichord; it's not something that can be modified during a performance. Therefore, a harpsichord is incapable of **graded dynamics**—of getting progressively louder or softer.

- For many members of the 17th-century Italian musical community—a community increasingly enamored of the lyric expressivity of opera on one hand and the violin on the other—the limitations of the harpsichord became increasingly problematic.

- The inventor of genius who solved the harpsichord problem (and in doing so became the Hewlett, Packard, Wozniak, and Jobs of baroque era instrumental innovation) was Bartolomeo Cristofori, who was born in Padua in 1655.

- In around 1688, Cristofori was hired by Prince Ferdinando de'Medici of Florence to maintain the family's harpsichords and build new ones. In 1700, Cristofori built an instrument that sought to address the **dynamic** shortcomings of the harpsichord that employed leather-covered "hammers" to strike—rather than a plectrum to pluck—the strings.

- For this instrument, Cristofori created an entirely new sort of action, one that varied the speed of the hammers (and, therefore, the loudness of the strike) depending on how hard a key was pressed. Cristofori called the instrument a *gravicembalo col pian e fort*, meaning a "big harpsichord with soft (*pian*) and loud (*fort*)," a "pianoforte," a "soft-loud."

- Initially, Cristofori considered his *gravicembalo col pian e fort* to be a modified harpsichord. It took both Cristofori and the musical community around him roughly 25 years to realize that he had, in reality, invented an entirely new instrument, one capable of an entirely new degree of expressive nuance.

- When Cristofori died in 1731 at the age of 76, his "pianoforte" was just starting to catch on. The following year, 1732, saw the publication of the first music composed specifically for the piano: 12 **sonatas** by the Italian composer Ludovico Giustini.

- It was also in 1732 that a German organ and harpsichord builder named Gottfried Silbermann built his first piano. Silbermann's early pianos were copies of Cristofori's design. However, over time, and thanks in no small part to the feedback Silbermann received from a local keyboard player and composer named Johann Sebastian Bach, Silbermann's pianos became known as the most reliable and playable on the market. So dominant did Silbermann's pianos become that by the late 18th century, he was being credited with having invented the thing.

- We can forgive Beethoven his chauvinism, because Gottfried Silbermann was—directly and indirectly—responsible for basic design of most of the pianos Haydn, Mozart, and Beethoven played in their lifetimes.

- One of Gottfried Silbermann's most important pupils was his nephew Johann Andreas Silbermann (1712–1783), whose workshop was in Strasbourg, in northeastern France. Among his apprentices was a young wizard named Andreas Stein (1728–1792), who went on to create what is now known as the "Viennese action" and was accordingly the principal designer of what today is generically called the "Viennese fortepiano," the five-octave instrument for which Haydn, Mozart, and the young Beethoven composed.

- Andreas Stein founded a piano-building dynasty. His daughter Nanette (1769–1833) was a skilled piano builder. Nanette continued the family business after her father died under her married name of Streicher. The Streicher company built pianos for Beethoven and went on to play an instrumental role in the development of the piano across the 19th century. The firm—run to the end by the Streicher family—remained in business until 1894.

- Over the course of these lectures, you will learn about the technological history of the piano, from the German-built pianos manufactured by Gottfried Silbermann in the 1730s to the modern grands built by Steinway & Sons in the 1870s. However, because this is a course about piano music and not piano technology, all of the musical examples will be played on a modern Steinway.

Important Terms

accent: The emphasis of certain notes over others.

dynamics: Degrees of loudness—e.g., piano (quiet), forte (loud)—indicated in a musical score.

graded dynamics: Markings used to indicate a progressive increase in loudness or softness, respectively, crescendo (getting louder) or decrescendo/diminuendo (getting softer/quieter).

note: A sound with three properties: a single, singable fundamental frequency; timbre; and duration.

sonata: Piece of music, typically in three or four movements, composed for a piano (piano sonata) or a piano plus one instrument (violin sonata, for instance).

Piano Starts Here!
Lecture 1—Transcript

Welcome to the *23 Greatest Solo Piano Works*. The is Lecture 1. It is entitled Piano Starts Here!

The lies we tell. Oh, the little white lies we tell, purposely or not. From the tiniest exaggeration to the most outrageous whopper, it would seem to be human nature to stretch the truth. The examples are endless. "The check is in the mail." "No, those pants don't make your butt look big." "Your table will be ready in just a minute, ma'am." "It's not the money, it's the principle." "This won't hurt a bit." "Hey, really, I was just kidding."

Please, let's add to this inglorious list one of my favorites: "So-and-so is a concert pianist." A concert pianist. There are two possible applications of the phrase "concert pianist." One of them is correct and one of them is not correct.

Let's start with the correct one. A "concert pianist" is a professional pianist who makes his or her living playing concerts, a concert in this case being a live performance during which people pay good cash money to hear a professional pianist play. That definition of "concert pianist" does not, unfortunately, include the locally known music major who teaches piano to the neighborhood kids, plays at church on Sundays and performs Beethoven's "Für Elise" at rotary club meetings. [**Piano performance:** Beethoven, *Für Elise.*]

Neither does the correct definition of "concert pianist" include my own beloved paternal grandmother, who graduated from The New York Institute of Musical Art (later renamed The Juilliard School) in 1916, who gave piano lessons in the borough of Queens for 50 years and who played Mozart piano sonatas at Hadassah meetings. [**Piano performance:** Mozart, Piano Sonata in C Major, K. 545.]

In fact, a genuine concert pianist is as different from my grandmother as an Olympic gymnast is from you or me. Let's run with this Olympic analogy for a moment. When the American swimmer Michael Phelps won his

22nd Olympic medal in August of 2012, he became far and away the most decorated Olympian ever. Phelps's success was a function of strength, conditioning, technique, commitment, precision, mental toughness, and a fiercely competitive spirit, sustained over a period of 20 years, from the age of seven—when he started swimming—to the age of 27, when he presumably retired from competitive swimming.

That sounds like a concert pianist, only not as impressive. Let's hear an example of pianistic strength, conditioning and technique: Franz Liszt's depiction of inferno, from a piece entitled "After Reading Dante," contained in the second volume of a set of works called *Years of Pilgrimage*.

[**Piano performance:** Liszt, *Années de pèlerinage*, Year Two: Italy, "After Reading Dante."]

Like a champion swimmer, a professional pianist also needs strength, conditioning, technique, commitment, precision, mental toughness, and a fiercely competitive spirit. But more than any swimmer, a concert pianist requires, in addition, artistry, memory, the finest nuance of motor control, deep theoretical understanding and historical knowledge, superior intellect, and the fearlessness of a Nepalese Gurkha. Yes, fearlessness. Try sitting down at a piano in front of 1,000 people and playing from memory for 90 minutes, without error, without lapse, and with total emotional, intellectual, and physical control. You must be fearless.

Michael Phelps's career, brilliant though it was, spanned just 20 years. Longish for an athlete, but a mere beginning for a professional pianist. You see, professional pianists are expected to keep getting better. They are expected to become ever more technically accomplished; they are expected to learn and memorize ever more music; they are expected to become ever better interpreters of the music they perform. Professional pianists are expected to mature, whereas professional athletes are expected to retire. Barring arthritis or dementia, pianists can continue to concertize into their 70s and beyond: Claude Frank continued to concertize into his early 80s; Vladimir Horowitz made his triumphant return to the Russian stage in 1986, at the age of 83; Artur Rubinstein retired at the age of 89.

By comparison, these pianists make my favorite living pianist, Maurizio Pollini, look like a kid, at age 70.

Our Pianists

We are blessed in this course to have the services of three concert pianists, who will provide for us custom-recorded musical examples: Magdalina Melkonyan, Woobin Park, and Eun Joo Chung. Let us use the life and career of Dr. Magdalina Melkonyan as an object lesson of what it takes to become a concert pianist.

Dr. Melkonyan was born in Yerevan, the capital city of the Republic of Armenia, in 1980. She began her piano lessons at the age of six on a piano originally bought for her older brother. Oh my friends, this is one of the oldest stories in the book: An instrument bought for an older sibling is, instead, devoured whole by a younger one. Let's hear it for having an instrument in the house while the kids grow up, and not waiting for one of them to show some interest before acquiring a piano. Without the physical presence of the instrument, the interest might never develop.

Magdalina's talent was immediately apparent. At the age of seven she began attending specialized music schools, and at 10 she performed Edvard Grieg's finger-busting piano concerto with the Armenian Philharmonic Orchestra.

A word: I don't care how talented you are, you don't get from the starting block to the Grieg concerto in three years without working your patootie off. Dr. Melkonyan's first teacher, whom she admits to having disliked as a child, she now is eternally grateful towards. This teacher was a strict disciplinarian. Magdalina had to practice four to five hours a day, before and after school and in doing so, like all *über*-talented child dancers, athletes, and musicians, she sacrificed the sort of activities "normal" children take for granted. In her case, it paid off, and by the age of 15, she was competing in—and winning—the sorts of piano competitions that are the springboards to a professional career.

Competitions. Competitions are a hateful necessity. They are hateful because they presume to judge players on the most subjective of all things: artistic merit and interpretive content. Michael Phelps had no such interpretive challenge. He merely had to arrive at point B before any other swimmer did. Yet competitions are necessary for pianists because they help to separate potential professionals from the pack and teach those potential professionals how to conquer their nerves. Nerves, yes, nerves. If you think performing in front of an ordinary audience is hard, try playing Chopin or Rachmaninoff for 45 minutes in front of a panel of judges, each of whom is looking for any excuse, technical or artistic, to mark you down, down, and further down.

In 2001, Dr. Melkonyan and her family moved to the United States. She attended Catholic University for a year before moving on the University of Maryland, where she studied with Larissa Dedova. She received a Master of Music with honors in piano performance in 2006 and a DMA, or Doctor of Musical Arts in 2010, also with honors, in piano performance.

In the world of academic performing degrees, a DMA in piano performance from a major institution is equivalent, in medicine, to a degree in neurosurgery; it's the top of the heap, the toughest of the tough, the best of the best. To achieve such a thing, you must continue to practice four to five (or six or seven) hours a day. You must concertize tirelessly. You must read literature and go to art museums and travel and live a real life because that's the only way you will be able to understand and therefore interpret the music you perform. As an interpreter, you are on your own. Unlike an orchestral player, a solo pianist does not have (or want) a conductor to tell her how to play. Then, having graduated, you must grow your career even as you begin your adulthood. Bless her, Magdalina Melkonyan has thus far pulled it off: She is married and raising two little boys; she teaches and has an international concert career that has nowhere to go but up, provided that she still practices every day; continues to learn new repertoire, and is willing to make the sort of sacrifices and take the sorts of risks her career demands.

Yes, risks. As a pianist you are singularly exposed; you are not buried inside a section like an orchestral player. Every time a concert pianist sits down to perform, she puts her rear end not just on a bench but on the line: There is nowhere to hide, no one to follow, no one else to supply the bass line or middle voices, no one else to determine the expressive message of the music. My friends, you must do it all by yourself. We hear Magdalina Melkonyan perform the final two minutes of "Tarantella" from Franz Liszt's *Years of Pilgrimage*. [**Piano performance:** Liszt, *Années de pèlerinage*, Year Two: Italy, "Tarantella."]

Our Composers and the Piano

Nineteen different composers are represented in this course. Every one of those 19 composers was a competent pianist. As an aside: I am often asked why such a disproportionately large number of composers and conductors began their music lives as pianists. My answer is that to be a composer or a conductor, one needs to hear music in a non-parochial manner. For example, when a flute player listens to an orchestra perform, the first thing that flute player does is listen to the flutes. Ditto a trumpet player, a 'cellist, or a violinist.

A pianist, on the other hand, will hear the orchestra as a holistic entity, one possessed of a foreground, middle ground, and background, because that is how they are accustomed to hearing and playing music at a piano. The three-dimensionality with which pianists hear music predisposes them towards both composing and conducting, crafts that demand their practitioners perceive music holistically. Now obviously, this is not to say that all composers and conductors started their musical lives as pianists. But for every non-pianist conductor like Arturo Toscanini who was trained as a 'cellist, and Gustavo Dudamel, who trained as a violinist, there is a host of conductors—for example, George Solti, Leonard Bernstein, Zubin Mehta, George Szell, Fritz Reiner, Herbert von Karajan, Andre Previn, James Levine, Seiji Ozawa, and Michael Tilson-Thomas—who trained as pianists. The same holds true for composers, and thus it is a fact that many of the greatest composers of the last 300 years were also among the greatest keyboard players of their time, including Johann Sebastian Bach and Wolfgang Mozart; Ludwig van Beethoven and Johannes Brahms; Frédéric Chopin and Franz Liszt; and the Sergeis, Rachmaninoff and Prokofiev, to name just a few.

Back, then, to the statement that every one of the 19 composers represented in this course was a competent pianist. Of those nineteen, 11 were world-class concert players: Bach, Mozart, Beethoven, Chopin, Liszt, Anton Rubinstein, Brahms, Isaac Albéniz, Alexander Scriabin, Rachmaninoff, and Prokofiev. Five were accomplished professionals: Felix Mendelssohn, Robert Schumann, Claude Debussy, Maurice Ravel, and Aaron Copland; and three were—at the very least—passably competent: Franz Schubert, Modest Mussorgsky, and Antonin Dvořák. Of all these composers, the only one who didn't initially train as a keyboard player was Dvořák. So, this is not just a course about music played on the piano, but about music written specifically for the piano by composers who were, in most cases, among the greatest pianists who ever lived.

The exception here is Johann Sebastian Bach, who had, frankly, a checkered relationship with the piano. Bach, who lived from 1685 to 1750, was, without any doubt, the greatest keyboard player of his time. His main axes were the organ the harpsichord. The piano was still in its techno-infancy when Bach got to know it, and overall, he was not particularly impressed. The two works by Bach included in this survey—book one of *The Well-Tempered Clavier* and the *Goldberg Variations*—were originally performed on the harpsichord, an instrument we'll talk about in just a few minutes. However, for the past 200-plus years, these works have, much more often than not, been played on the piano. From *The Well-Tempered* Clavier, Book One, we hear Prelude No. 5 in D Major, which sounds just fine on a modern piano! **[Piano performance:** Bach, *The Well-Tempered Clavier*, Book One, Prelude No. 5 in D Major.]

Given their performance history over the last 200-plus years, I have no problem whatsoever asserting that Bach's *The Well-Tempered Clavier* and *Goldberg Variations* are piano as well as harpsichord works. As such, they must be numbered as being among the greatest piano works ever composed and thus deserve a place in this course. Purists might quibble, but not to include Bach in this course would have been a fatal omission. Besides, purists can be—as we are all, sadly, aware—whiners and bores.

The Piano: A Changing Technology

To a not-insignificant degree, this will also be a course about the piano itself, an instrument that changed tremendously over the first 170 years of its existence. The nine-foot-long, 1,000-pound concert grand piano that today is considered the standard concert instrument came into existence well after the lives and careers of Mozart, Beethoven, Schubert, Chopin, and Schumann. Invented around 1700 by a Florence-based harpsichord builder named Bartolomeo Cristofori, the piano was an evolving technology until the 1870s, when the modern concert grand came into existence.

Thus, the nature of piano music coevolved with the piano. For example, it would never have occurred to Mozart—whose piano spanned five octaves—to use the upper and lower notes available on a modern piano, which spans seven-plus octaves. Consequently, the technical and expressive content of the music surveyed in this course will vary depending upon the nature of the pianos available to the composers.

The Harpsichord and the Early Piano

The harpsichord was invented around the year 1400. By 1700, harpsichords were as ubiquitous as, heaven help us, electric keyboards are today. A harpsichord is a mechanical harp, a wing-shaped instrument in which the strings of a horizontally set harp are plucked from a keyboard. In Dutch, such an instrument is called *klavecimbel*; in French, a *clavecin*; in German, a *cembalo*; in Italian, a *clavicembalo*.

When a harpsichord key is pressed, it levers upwards a slat of wood called a jack. Mounted on the jack is a pick, which is made from either a quill or a piece of hardened leather. The plectrum plucks a string as it rises past it. When the key is released, the jack-and-plectrum assembly falls back into place by gravity. A small hinge folds the plectrum assembly upwards and thus it passes the string without re-plucking it, at which point a damper stops the vibration of the string.

The nature of a harpsichord's action precludes it from getting progressively louder and softer or of accenting, that is, making some notes louder than others. Pushing down harder on the keys of a harpsichord will not make the instrument play louder; all that will do is create a wooden thump. You see, the harpsichord's loudness is not determined by the speed with which the plectrum moves, but by the actual mass of the plectrum itself. Obviously, the mass of the plectrum is built into a harpsichord; it's not something that can be modified during a performance. We say then that a harpsichord is incapable of graded dynamics: of getting progressively louder or softer.

For many members of the 17th -century Italian musical community—a community increasingly enamored of the lyric expressivity of opera on one hand and the violin on the other—the limitations of the harpsichord became increasingly problematic. The Italian composer Giovanni Casini spoke for many when he wrote that music should consist of "the speech of the heart, now with the delicate touch of an angel, now with the violent eruptions of passion. [Regrettably], the harpsichord cannot fulfill all the expressions of human sentiment."

The inventor of genius who solved the "harpsichord problem" (and in doing so became the Hewlett, the Packard, the Wozniak, and the Jobs of baroque-era instrumental innovation) was Bartolomeo Cristofori. Cristofori was born in Padua in 1655. In 1688 or so, he was hired by Prince Ferdinand de'Medici of Florence to maintain the family's harpsichords and build new ones. In 1700, Cristofori built an instrument that sought to address the dynamic shortcomings of the harpsichord. It was an instrument that employed leather-covered hammers to strike—rather than a plectrum to pluck—the strings. For this instrument, Cristofori created an entirely new sort of action, one that varied the speed of the hammers (and therefore, the loudness of the strike) depending upon how hard a key was pressed. Cristofori called the instrument a *gravicembalo col pian e fort*, meaning a b"ig harpsichord with soft (*pian*) and loud (*fort*)," a "pianoforte," a "soft-loud." Initially, Cristofori considered his *gravicembalo col pian e fort* to be a modified harpsichord. It took both Cristofori and the musical community around him roughly 25 years to realize that he had, in reality, invented an entirely new instrument, one capable of an entirely new degree of expressive nuance.

When Cristofori died in 1731 at the age of 76, his pianoforte—his "soft and loud"—was just starting to catch on. The following year, 1732, saw the publication of the first music composed specifically for the piano: 12 sonatas by the Italian composer Ludovico Giustini.

It was also in 1732 that a German organ and harpsichord builder named Gottfried Silbermann built his first piano. Silbermann's early pianos were straight-up copies of Cristofori's design. However, over time and thanks in no small part to the feedback Silbermann received from a local keyboard player and composer named Johann Sebastian Bach, Silbermann's pianos became known as the most reliable and playable on the market. So dominant did Silbermann's pianos become that by the late 18th century, he was being credited with having invented the thing!

Writes Edwin Good:

> For a long time, Germans and Austrians—Beethoven among them—thought the piano had been invented by [Silbermann], a German. Beethoven at one point [went] on a crusade to substitute musical terms for the conventional Italian ones, and published some of his later works as for the *hammerklavier* ("hammer-keyboard"), rather than for the Italian *pianoforte*. He thought the instrument, being a good German invention, out to have a good, solid German name.

We can forgive Beethoven his chauvinism, because Gottfried Silbermann was directly and indirectly responsible for basic design of the pianos Haydn, Mozart, and Beethoven played in their lifetimes. One of Gottfried Silbermann's most important pupils was his nephew Johann Andreas Silbermann (who lived from 1712–1783). Johann Andreas's workshop was in Strasbourg, in northeastern France. Among his apprentices was a young wizard named Andreas Stein (1728–1792). It was Stein who went on to create what is now known as the Viennese action and was accordingly the principal designer of what today is generically called the Viennese fortepiano, the five-octave instrument for which Haydn, Mozart, and the young Beethoven composed.

Andreas Stein founded a piano-building dynasty. His daughter Nanette, who lived from 1769–1833, was herself a skilled piano builder. Nanette continued the family business after her father died under her married name of Streicher. The Streicher Company built pianos for Beethoven, and went on to play an instrumental role (pun intended) in the development of the piano across the 19th century. Johannes Brahms, for example, owned a Streicher. The firm, run to the end by the Streicher family, remained in business until 1894.

Over the course of these lectures, we will fill out the technological history of the piano, from the German-built pianos manufactured by Gottfried Silbermann in the 1730s to the modern grands built by Steinway & Sons in the 1870s. However, as this is a course about piano music and not piano technology, will hear all of our musical examples played on a modern Steinway. Let's hear an example of what such a piano can do: the brilliant, dancing, knuckle-cracking, finger-busting conclusion of Isaac Albéniz's *Iberia* of 1908, the final minute and a half of a movement entitled *Eritaña*.
[**Piano performance:** Albéniz, *Iberia*, "Eritaña."]

Dang, that's amazingly good piano music!

What's So Special about the Number 23?

Oh, the magic of the number 23! There are 23 chromosomes in a human sperm or egg; Julius Caesar was reportedly stabbed 23 times by his homies in the Roman Senate. Hey, the number 23 is sacred in Discordianism, a religion based on the worship of the Eris, the Greek goddess of chaos. We read in no less impeccable a source—that being Wikipedia—that "[Discordianism] was founded circa 1958–1959 after the publication of its first holy book - the *Principia Discordia* - written by Malaclypse the Younger and Omar Khayyam Ravenhurst after a series of shared, [drug-induced] hallucinations at a bowling alley [in Whittier, California]."

OK. I could go on but I won't because, in truth, there is nothing special about the number 23, except that in a 24-lecture course, 23 is the number of lectures that will follow the introductory lecture in which we are presently ensconced. So I suggest that from here on out we just let this numeric stuff go!

Selection Criteria and Ground Rules

Whatever the number of works examined in this survey, there are obviously many other "greatest solo piano works" that could have been addressed. Grieve though we might for those un-chosen work, let us be consoled by the fact that every piece we will discuss in this course is a winner.

Aside from my numerous appeals to my fortune-telling magic 8-ball (Question: "Should I feature Schumann's *Carnival* or *Kreisleriana*?" Answer: "Signs point to yes.") my selections were governed by three basic criteria/ground rules. They are …

One: All the works have to have stood the test of time, meaning that they have to be part of the standard piano repertoire. Works that can be heard in concert; works that have been published; works that are readily available on recordings.

Ground rule/criterion number two: A single composer can be represented by a maximum of two major works. Yes, I am well aware of the fact that this entire course could easily consist only of works by Beethoven, or Chopin, or Schumann, or Liszt, or Debussy. But that would not fulfill the larger goal of the course. That goal is to explore a stylistically and historically varied body of some of the greatest works ever written for piano, works that offer the collateral advantage of illustrating the development of the piano as an instrument and pianistic technique as a skill.

Three: Sets of works published together (for example, Chopin's 24 Preludes published together as Op. 28) count as a single work. The only exception to this will occur in Lectures 16 and 17. Lecture 16 will focus on Claude Debussy's "The Sunken Cathedral" from his first book of *Préludes*. Lecture 17 will then focus on the remainder of Debussy's *Préludes*, Book One. Given his incredible innovations as both a composer and as a composer for the piano, this bit of Debussy worship is entirely appropriate. We begin the Debussy love-fest here and now. Magdalina Melkonyan plays *Prélude No. XII* from Debussy's first book of *Préludes* of 1910, a piece entitled "Minstrels." [**Piano performance:** Debussy, *Prélude no. XII*, entire prelude.]

Temporal Spread of Works

At the time of this recording we find ourselves more than one-eighth of the way through the 21st century. The music of the 20th century is now the music of a previous century. And despite the fact that there is no shortage of great and worthy solo piano music composed during the 20th century, very little is represented in this course, and not a single work composed after 1942.

We rightfully ask: Why so few? The answer: because of fear, greed, short-sightedness and sometimes pure venality. Not mine, but rather, that of the legal eagles and publishing houses that guard the estates of living and recently deceased composers with a drooling ferocity that makes Cerberus the three-headed dog from Hades look like the Taco Bell Chihuahua by comparison.

Here's the scoop. Music remains under copyright until 75 years after the death of its composer. Yes, some composer's estates and publishers do allow us to license their music for use, which is the reason why the piano music of Rachmaninoff, Prokofiev, and Copland is featured in this course. But others are virtually impossible to work with, and consequently this course does not include piano music by Charles Ives, Béla Bartók, and Olivier Messiaen, to name but a worthy few.

To my mind, this is all completely counterintuitive: We'd think that featuring a composer in a survey like this one would be considered a good thing by a composer's estate. But in their desire to "preserve the sanctity" of and "maximize the profits" from a composer's work, the guard dogs fend off all but the wealthiest licensees, and we are all the poorer for it. If someone out there knows how to change this, I'd sure love to hear about it. But until that day comes, we're just going to have to wait out those 75 years. Our consolation is that there is always more Chopin!

The Overall Structure of This Course

Lectures 2–23 will each deal with a single work or a set of works published together. Lecture 24 stands apart, for reasons to be revealed when we get there. For the most part, the featured works (or sets of works) will appear in chronological order. However, this course is not conceived as a single, sequential unit of 24 lectures. Rather, each of the twenty-three "repertoire lectures" is a self-standing entity. Consequently, the course can be consumed as a single entity, Lectures 1–24, or as a compendium of discrete lectures to be enjoyed in any order one chooses.

One last bit of preliminary business. Lectures 9, 11, and 16 stand somewhat apart from the others. These three lectures are dedicated to discussing the extraordinarily innovative pianism of the three composers who, more than any others, defined the piano as we understand it today: Frédéric Chopin, Franz Liszt, and Claude Debussy. So while these lectures do focus on a single work or set of works—respectively, Chopin's Ballade in G Minor, Liszt's *Years of Pilgrimage*, and Debussy's *Préludes*, Book One—they will examine their composers' revolutionary pianism as much as the music itself. Onward!

Thank you.

J. S. Bach—*The Well-Tempered Clavier*, Book One
Lecture 2

Johann Sebastian Bach's *The Well-Tempered Clavier* remains the single most influential and pedagogically important keyboard work ever composed. It was *The Well-Tempered Clavier* that kept Bach's name alive during the decades of obscurity that followed his death in 1750. Throughout the second half of the 18th century and well into the 19th century—what we've come to refer to as the classical period and the romantic era—*The Well-Tempered Clavier* was considered to be the basic manual for keyboard training for players of all ages.

Introduction to *The Well-Tempered Clavier*

- On March 2, 1783, an article appeared in a German periodical called "C. F. Cramer's Magazine of Music," which was written by an organist named Christian Gottlob Neefe. In 1781, Neefe had been appointed court organist for the Rhineland city of Bonn, at which time he took on as a student a 10-year-old local named Ludwig van Beethoven.

- Wolfgang Mozart was introduced to *The Well-Tempered Clavier* by his Viennese patron Baron Gottfried van Swieten in 1783. It was an introduction that changed Mozart's life. Mozart immediately arranged five of Bach's **fugues** for two violins, viola, and bass, catalogued as Köchel 405. Frédéric Chopin was weaned on both books of *The Well-Tempered Clavier*—all 48 preludes and fugues.

- What is referred to as *The Well-Tempered Clavier* is actually two separate sets of compositions, known as Book One and Book Two. Each book contains 24 sets of paired preludes and fugues: one prelude and fugue in each **major** and each **minor key**.

- Book One is a mix-and-match collection that evolved from a series of preludes that Bach compiled for his son Wilhelm Friedemann in 1720. In 1722, he went public with a collection of 24 preludes and fugues. Between 1738 and 1742, Bach composed a second set of "24 new preludes and fugues," which was issued as Book Two.

- That Bach intended both books of *The Well-Tempered Clavier* to be performed on a range of keyboard instruments is evident from his own title: He did not call the piece "The Well-Tempered Harpsichord" but, rather, "The Well-Tempered Clavier," meaning quite generically "The Well-Tempered Keyboard."

The Nature of the High Baroque Aesthetic

- The period of time we refer to as the baroque era—from 1600 to 1750—saw the beginnings of modern science, as the "natural philosophers" of the age sought to catalog the wonders of the physical world and understand their workings through deductive method and not supernatural explanation. It was the era of Hume, Locke, Descartes, and Leibniz—of Galileo, Kepler, Malthus, and Newton.

- Typical of his time, Newton's work was a blend of religious faith and hard science. He believed that beneath the seeming random chaos of the visible universe there existed stable, systemic order—the hand of god, a universal operating system.

- At its essence, a fugue investigates and catalogs the musical properties and capabilities of its **theme**, a specially designed **melody** called a **subject**. In a fugue, the subject is examined from various angles by repeating it in different keys and in different voices. By definition, a fugue is a **polyphonic** construct—that is, a work for two or more simultaneous melodic parts of equal importance.

- No matter how simple or brain-numbingly complex it may be, a fugue will always feature three basic structural elements: an **exposition**, a series of subject restatements, and a series of transitions between those restatements called episodes.

- The exposition is the first part of any fugue, during which the fugue subject is stated successively in each constituent part until all of the parts have entered. In the exposition of Bach's Fugue no. 2 in

C Minor from Book One of *The Well-Tempered Clavier*, the fugue is cast for three voices.

Johann Sebastian Bach (1685–1750) is one of the most celebrated baroque-era composers to have ever lived.

- Following the exposition, a fugue will feature any number of subject restatements in various different keys. These restatements are preceded by transitions called episodes, which are typically built from bits and pieces of the subject and are tasked with modulating to the key of the next restatement.

- Every tuning system is based on the primacy of the octave. An octave is the sonic relationship created when one object vibrates twice as fast as another. An octave is a sonic manifestation of the simplest of ratios—a 1:2 ratio.

- As every possible **pitch** that exists within the span of a single octave is duplicated in octaves above and below it, every pitch system will divide the octave into a series of smaller **intervals**, which are then duplicated in upper and lower octaves.

- Since the first ancient Greek music theorists fired up their writing styli in order to codify Western musical practice as it then existed, the interval of a perfect fifth has been that musical entity used to divide the octave into discrete pitches.

- After the octave, the next most consonant is a sonic manifestation of a 2:3 ratio, an interval called a perfect fifth. This collection of seven pitches became known as the Pythagorean collection. The tuning system that creates the Pythagorean collection is called "just intonation."

- Just intonation served the needs of Western music quite nicely until the 15th century, at which point growing expressive demands led to an across-the-board rethinking of Western pitch resources and tuning. After rising through five more pitches, each a perfect fifth above the last, the 13th pitch was the same as the first pitch.

- After much experimentation, a system called "well-tempered tuning" came into use during the 17th century. A well-tempered tuning is one in which all of the fifths are tempered almost the same.

- By the 1850s, equal temperament had become the standard and remains so to this day. In equal temperament, each of the fifths is tempered to exactly same degree. Instead of representing a "pure" 2:3 ratio, equally tempered fifths are all 2/100s of a **semitone** flat.

Bach's Influences

- Bach was powerfully influenced by the work of the organist, theorist, and Lutheran religious philosopher Andreas Werckmeister (1645–1706). Werckmeister—who experimented widely with tunings and actually coined the phrase "well-tempered"—believed that scriptural authority justified his technical theories. Like Werckmeister, Bach believed that music of every kind—religious and secular—was an audible manifestation of God's presence and perfection.

- The three principal musical styles of the high baroque were the so-called Italian style, French style, and German style. The Italian style was preconditioned by the vocality of opera. An example is the exposition of Fugue no. 3 in C-**sharp** Major. Fugue no. 7 in E-**flat** Major employs another such Italianate subject.

- The French style was best known for its highly embellished melody lines and dance rhythms. In addition, French baroque keyboard music was well known for something called the *style brisé*, which means the "broken style," in which **chords** are broken, or strummed, in a manner derived from the strumming of lute music. An example is the opening of Prelude no. 8 in E-flat Minor.

- The German style was characterized by compositional rigor: polyphonic intricacy, harmonic complexity, and thematic concision. For example, Fugue no. 4 in C-sharp Minor—set for five voices—features a diamond-hard subject of stunning brevity.

- Brief though it is, the subject that drives this fugue is also programmatic. Its four pitches describe the four parts of the cross: The first pitch, a C-sharp, depicts the left-hand horizontal beam. The next two pitches, a B-sharp and an E, are the lowest and highest; they depict the vertical beam. Finally, the last pitch, a D-sharp, depicts the right-hand horizontal beam:

- In German notation, the letter "B" represents the pitch B-flat and the letter "H" represents the pitch B **natural**. By designing his C-sharp minor fugue subject as he did, Bach made explicit his own identification with the cross and Christ's suffering on the cross.

Bach's Encyclopedic Works
- Bach's encyclopedic works include both books of *The Well-Tempered Clavier*, the *Brandenburg Concertos*, the *Goldberg Variations*, *The Art of the Fugue*, and many others. The preludes in Book One of *The Well-Tempered Clavier* constitute, all by themselves, a virtual encyclopedia of old and new keyboard genres and compositional techniques.

- Preludes nos. 3, 13, and 15 are two-part inventions. As an example, listen to the first half of Prelude no. 13 in F-sharp Major. Preludes nos. 9, 18, 19, 23, and 24 are three-part inventions. As an example, listen to the first half of Prelude no. 18 in G-sharp Minor.

- Preludes 2, 3, 5, 6, and 21 are cast as toccatas. The word "toccata" comes from the Italian *toccare*, which means "to touch." Any piece thus named is a fast, virtuoso work that puts a performer's dexterity and "touch" in high relief. As an example, listen to the toccata that is Prelude no. 5 in D Major.

- Listen to the opening of the gorgeous and powerfully moving Prelude no. 4 in C-sharp Minor. The technique with which Bach brings 8 of the 24 fugues to their climax is referred to as climactic thematic saturation through stretto.

- The word "stretto" is the past participle of the Italian noun *stringere*, which means "to tighten or squeeze." In a fugue, a stretto is a squeezing together of appearances of the fugue subject. Stretti typically appear at or near the end of a fugue, where, by overlapping the subject with itself, a climactic degree of thematic saturation is achieved. For example, listen to the subject of Fugue no. 1 in C Major. The stretto that brings this fugue to its climax appears seven **measures** before the fugue concludes.

Important Terms

chord: Simultaneous sounding of three or more different pitches.

exposition: The first part of a sonata form, during which the principal themes are introduced.

flat: Accidental (sign/symbol) placed to the left of a note indicating that the pitch should be lowered by a semitone.

fugue: Important baroque musical procedure in which a theme (or subject) is developed by means of various contrapuntal techniques.

interval: Distance between two pitches, e.g., C–G (upward) equals a fifth.

key: Collection of pitches that relate to a specific major or minor mode.

major: Modern term for Ionian mode; characterized by an intervallic profile of whole tone–whole tone–semitone–whole tone–whole tone–whole tone–semitone (symbolized as: T–T–S | T–T–T–S).

measure: Metric unit; space between two bar lines.

melody: Any succession of pitches.

minor: Modern term for Aeolian mode; characterized by an intervallic profile of whole tone–semitone–whole tone–whole tone–semitone–whole tone–whole tone (symbolized as T–S–T | T–S–T–T).

natural: Accidental (sign/symbol) placed to the left of a note, indicating that the note should not be sharpened or flattened; a white key on a keyboard.

pitch: A sound with two properties: a single, singable fundamental frequency and timbre.

polyphonic texture/polyphony: Texture consisting of two or more simultaneous melody lines of equal importance.

semitone: Smallest interval in Western music; on the keyboard, the distance between a black key and a white key, as well as B–C and E–F.

sharp: Accidental (sign/symbol) placed to the left of a note, indicating that the pitch should be raised by a semitone.

subject: The theme of a fugue.

theme: Primary musical subject matter in a given section of music.

J.S. Bach—The *Well-Tempered Clavier*, Book One
Lecture 2—Transcript

Welcome back to *The 23 Greatest Solo Piano Works*. This is Lecture 2. It is entitled J.S. Bach—*The Well-Tempered Clavier*, Book One.

On March 2, 1783, an article appeared in a periodical called *C. F. Cramer's Magazine of Music*, an article written by an organist named Christian Gottlob Neefe. Two years before, in 1781, Neefe had been appointed court organist for the city of Bonn, at which time he took on as a student a 10-year-old local named Ludwig van Beethoven. Neefe's article was intended to introduce his young charge to the larger German musical community. He wrote, in part:

> Louis van Beethoven is a boy of very promising talent. He plays the piano in a very finished manner, reads at sight and plays *The Well-Tempered Clavier* of Sebastian Bach. Those who are familiar with this collection of Preludes and Fugues in every key—which one could practically call [the "ultimate"] of our art—will understand the significance of this.

The "ultimate of our art." While Neefe made that statement in 1783, before the composition of any of the piano works featured in this course, his appraisal still holds: Johann Sebastian Bach's *The Well-Tempered Clavier* remains the single most influential and pedagogically important keyboard work ever composed.

It was *The Well-Tempered Clavier* that kept Bach's name alive during the decades of obscurity that followed his death in 1750. Throughout the second half of the 18th century and well into the 19th century, *The Well-Tempered Clavier* was considered to be the basic manual for keyboard training.

Wolfgang Mozart was introduced to *The Well-Tempered Clavier* by his Viennese patron, Baron Gottfried van Swieten, in 1783. It was an introduction that changed Mozart's life. Mozart immediately arranged five of Bach's fugues for strings, a work catalogued as Köchel 405. Mozart played *The Well-Tempered Clavier* constantly, to the pleasure of his wife Constanze, who loved it. In a letter dated April 12, 1783, Mozart wrote:

When Constanze heard the fugues, she fell hopelessly in love with them. She now wants to hear nothing but fugues. As she has often heard me play fugues, she asked me if I'd ever written any down, and when I said no, she told me off. She didn't stop begging me until I'd written [one] down for her and that's how 'it' all came about."

The "it" Mozart refers to is the polyphonic intensity and complexity that crept into his later music, inspired, without any doubt, by the music of Johann Sebastian Bach. Frédéric Chopin was weaned on both books of *The Well-Tempered Clavier* (48 preludes and fugues in all) and "carried the works by heart for the rest of his life." In the 1830s, Robert Schumann referred to *The Well-Tempered Clavier* as "the pianist's daily bread."

When the unmanned *Voyager* space explorer was launched in 1977, it carried a recording of a prelude and fugue from *The Well-Tempered Clavier*. Speaking for myself, I can think of few, if any, earthly constructs more likely to arouse the interest and envy of extraterrestrials than *The Well-Tempered Clavier* of Bach.

What is referred to as *The Well-Tempered Clavier* is actually two separate sets of compositions: Book One and Book Two. Each book contains 24 sets of preludes and fugues, one prelude and fugue in each major and minor key.

Book One is a mix-and-match collection that evolved from a series of preludes that Bach compiled for his son Wilhelm Friedemann in 1720. Over the next two years Bach extended and added to the collection, until, in 1722, he went public with an album of 24 preludes and fugues. Book One of *The Well-Tempered Clavier* proved to be so popular that between 1738 and 1742 Bach composed a second set of 24 new preludes and fugues, which was issued as Book Two.

That Bach intended both books of *The Well-Tempered Clavier* to be performed on a range of keyboard instruments is evident from his title: He did not call the piece *The Well-Tempered Harpsichord* but rather *The Well-Tempered Clavier*, meaning quite generically "the well-tempered keyboard."

Our Approach to *The Well-Tempered Clavier*

We will approach the first book of *The Well-Tempered Clavier* from three mutually reinforcing angles. First, we will address the nature of Bach's High (or late) baroque aesthetic, and in doing so come to understand *The Well-Tempered Clavier* as being representative of the intellectual and musical currents of its time. Second, we will define what is meant by a "well-tempered keyboard" and thus come to understand Bach's tuning system as a cutting-edge practical technology. Third, we will discuss Bach as a musical synthesist of encyclopedic tendencies, as a composer whose musical voice represents a synthesis of the dominant musical styles and genres of his time. Along the way, we will define what constitutes a prelude and a fugue and have an opportunity to sample roughly half of the 24 preludes and fugues that make up Book One of *The Well-Tempered Clavier*.

The Nature of the High Baroque Aesthetic

My friends, the period of time we so casually refer to as the baroque era—from 1600–1750—saw the beginnings of modern science, as the natural philosophers of the age sought to catalog the wonders of the physical world and understand their workings through deductive method and not supernatural explanation. It was the era of Hume, of Locke, Descartes, and Leibniz; of Galileo, Kepler, Malthus, and Newton.

Typical of his time, Newton's work was a blend of religious faith and hard science. He believed that beneath the seeming random chaos of the visible universe there existed stable, systemic order—literally, the hand of God, the universal operating system. baroque artistic design mirrors this attempt to reconcile surface complexity with underlying order and control. We talk, then, about the paradoxical duality of baroque art, art in which exuberant expression is tempered by intellectual control. In baroque art and architecture, we are witness to a riot of visual detail, a metaphor for the complexity of the visible universe. However, this visual exuberance is made coherent through symmetry, a metaphor for divine meaning and order. Nowhere is this baroque duality more apparent than in the music of the age, in which expressive exuberance and surface detail (lots of notes, almost all the time) are held in check by rock-steady rhythms and systemic harmonic control.

Fugue

Fugue is the single most representative instrumental musical form (or "procedure") to emerge from the baroque era: a manifestation of the baroque predilection for codification and scientific investigation as well as the baroque duality of exuberance and control!

At its essence, a fugue investigates and catalogs the musical properties and capabilities of its theme, a specially designed melody called a "subject". In a fugue, the subject is examined from various angles by repeating it in different keys and in different voices; by fragmenting it; by overlapping it with itself; by turning it upside down; by stretching it out and compressing it, and so forth.

By definition, a fugue is a polyphonic construct: that is, a work for two or more simultaneous melodic parts of equal importance. However, the exuberant melodic interplay of a fugue is carefully controlled by a rock-steady beat, clock-regular harmonic rhythm, and a time-honored structural ritual that allows an informed listener to follow its progress.

You see, no matter how simple or brain-numbingly complex it may be, a fugue will always feature three basic structural elements: an exposition, a series of subject restatements, and series of transitions between those restatements called episodes.

The exposition is the first part of any fugue, during which the fugue subject is stated successively in each part until all the parts have entered. Let's hear the Exposition of Bach's Fugue No. 2 in C Minor from Book One of *The Well-Tempered Clavier*. The fugue is cast for three voices. The subject will appear first in the middle, or alto voice; then in the top or soprano voice; then lastly in the lowest or bass voice. [**Piano demonstration:** Bach, *The Well-Tempered Clavier*, Book One, Fugue No. 2 in C Minor.]

Following the exposition, a fugue will feature a number of subject restatements in various different keys. These restatements are preceded by transitions called episodes, which are typically built from bits and pieces of the subject and are tasked with modulating to the key of the next restatement.

Let's listen to the C-minor fugue in its entirety. I will identify its structural elements as they appear: its exposition, five subject restatements and five episodes. [**Piano performance:** Bach, *The Well-Tempered Clavier,* Book One, Fugue No. 2 in C Minor.]

By preceding each of the fugues in *The Well-Tempered Clavier* with a prelude, Bach raises the duality of exuberance and control to a structural level. A fugue, by its investigative nature and with its ritual structure, can be perceived as the most controlled of all baroque-era musical procedures. Conversely, the preludes are for the most part freely exuberant pieces during which pretty much anything goes. Let's hear the prelude that precedes the C-minor fugue: a prelude based on keyboard figuration and a harmonic progression rather than on a thematic melody, a piece as free in form as the fugue that follows it is controlled and ritualized. [**Piano performance:** Bach, *The Well-Tempered Clavier,* Book One, Prelude No. 2 in C Minor.]

Tuning In

A proper discussion of tuning systems is at once among the most fascinating, complicated, and ultimately confusing of all musical discussions, except, perhaps, the precise nature of Justin Bieber's talent. Nevertheless, we must tackle this gnarliest of musical subjects if we are to understand the magnitude of Bach's accomplishment in *The Well-Tempered Clavier*. So please, bear with me.

The Octave

Every tuning system on this planet is based on the primacy of the octave. What we call an octave is the sonic relationship created when one object vibrates twice as fast as another. For example, the string that vibrates as middle C on a modern grand piano runs about 40 inches in length. [**Piano demonstration.**] A string exactly one-half that length, 20 inches, vibrates twice as fast. We perceive the sound the smaller string creates as being an octave higher than the string twice its length. So here's middle C followed by the pitch an octave higher. [**Piano demonstration.**] When played simultaneously, these two pitches blend into a single sound; they are entirely consonant with one another. [**Piano demonstration.**] An octave is a sonic manifestation of that simplest of ratios, a 1:2 ratio.

We perceive pitches an octave apart as being duplicates of one another: higher or lower versions of the same pitch. Please, back to the original statement: Every tuning system on this planet is based on the primacy of the octave. As every possible pitch that exists within the span of a single octave is duplicated in octaves above and below it, every pitch system on this planet will divide the octave into a series of smaller intervals, which are then duplicated in upper and lower octaves.

The Perfect Fifth

Since the first ancient Greek music theorists codified musical practice as it then existed, the interval of a perfect fifth has been that musical entity used to divide the octave into discrete pitches. I'll explain. After the octave, the next most consonant interval is a sonic manifestation of a 2:3 ratio, an interval called a perfect fifth. [**Piano demonstration.**] The perfect fifth in a non-duplicating interval. Moving up and down by perfect fifths, you will get a different pitch every time: [**Piano demonstration.**] Ancient Greek music theorists discovered that the seven-pitch scales (or modes) in common use at the time could be explained via the perfect fifth. These theorists discovered that if you start with a pitch: [**Piano demonstration.**] And then stack six perfect fifths above that starting pitch: [**Piano demonstration.**]

And then place those seven pitches all within the span of single octave, you get what are essentially the white keys on a modern piano, which includes what today are called the Major and Minor scales. This collection of seven pitches became known as the Pythagorean collection. The tuning system that creates the Pythagorean collection is called just intonation.

Just intonation served the needs of Western music quite nicely until around the beginning of the 15th century, at which point growing expressive demands led to an across-the-board rethinking of Western pitch resources and tuning. The theorists and aestheticians of the time went back to the acoustical drawing board and continued to stack perfect fifths one upon the next, building upon the seven-pitch Pythagorean collection. In doing so, they made a stunning discovery: After rising through five more pitches, each a perfect fifth above the last, the 13th pitch was the same as the first pitch!

Let's do it. Starting on a low C, let us move through what is called the circle of fifths, through 12 different pitches before we arrive smack-dab back to where we began, on a C. **[Piano demonstration.]** Cool, huh? And neat as a pin: after hearing 12 successive perfect fifths, we arrived on a C perfectly in tune with the C from which we departed. **[Piano demonstration.]**

But I cheated. I played that circle of fifths using a tuning system in which the fifths have been altered, or tempered. If I had moved upwards through a series of pure 2:3 sonic ratios, the 13th pitch would have been an eighth of a tone sharper than the one on which we began.

For the musicians and theorists of the 16th and 17th centuries, the promise of an octave divided into twelve discrete pitches was irresistible. (Oh, the mystery of the dozen! There are 12 hours in the am and in the pm; there are twelve months in a year; 12 tribes in ancient Israel; 12 apostles; 12 ribs in the human body.)

The solution was to temper, or shrink, some (or all) of these fifths so that when incorporated into a single octave, the 13th pitch would be in tune with the first. After much experimentation, a system called well-tempered tuning came into use during the 17th century. A well-tempered tuning is one in which all of the fifths are tempered almost the same. The minute differences in tuning imbued keys with differences in character that we, today, do not hear in our equal-tempered tuning.

Yes, by the 1850s, equal temperament had become the standard and remains so to this day. In equal temperament, each of the fifths is tempered to exactly the same degree. Instead of representing a "pure" 2:3 ratio, equally tempered fifths are all 2/100's of a semitone flat.

Back to Bach

The tired cliché is that Bach created *The Well-Tempered Clavier* in order to demonstrate the technical capabilities of well-tempered tuning," meaning that he created the piece in order to demonstrate a practical technology. In fact, the opposite is true: For Bach, well-temperament was not an end unto itself but a means to an end, a tuning system that allowed him to utilize and explore all 12 major and all 12 minor keys.

My friends, there was also a spiritual aspect to Bach's embrace of well-temperament. In this, Bach was powerfully influenced by the work of the organist, theorist, and Lutheran religious philosopher Andreas Werckmeister (who lived from 1645–1706). Werckmeister, who experimented widely with tunings and personally coined the phrase "well tempered," believed that scriptural authority justified his technical theories. Werckmeister claimed that music was itself a metaphysical construct, "a creation of God, through which we may have a foretaste of the harmony of heaven."

For Johann Sebastian Bach, Andreas Werckmeister's ideas were mother's milk. Like Werckmeister, Bach believed that music of every kind, religious and secular, was an audible manifestation of God's presence and perfection. For Bach, well-tempered tuning became a practical tool for exploring, ever more completely, the nuances of God's own voice.

Bach as Synthesist and Encylopedist

With its dazzling variety of musical styles and compositional techniques, Book One of *The Well-Tempered Clavier* is a perfect example of Bach as a synthesist, an encylopedist, and as a historical universalist! We will define and demonstrate all of this with music. The three principal musical styles of the high baroque were the so-called Italian style, the French style, and the German style.

The Italian style was preconditioned by the vocality of opera, by melodic grace and memorability. The lilting subject of the fugue in C-sharp major is a brilliant example of the sort of memorable, tune-like thematic melody characteristic of the Italian style: **[Piano demonstration.]** Let's hear the exposition of Fugue No. 3 in C-sharp Major: **[Piano performance:** Bach, *The Well-Tempered* Clavier, Book One, Fugue No. 3 in C-sharp Major.**]**

Fugue No. 7 in E-flat major employs another such Italianate subject, a subject that goes like this. [**Piano demonstration.**] Its Italian-styled subject notwithstanding, this fugue, in its polyphonic intensity and harmonic complexity, is all Bach all the time. Let's hear it in its entirety. [**Piano performance:** Bach, *The Well-Tempered* Clavier, Book One, Fugue No. 7 in E-flat Major.]

The French style was best known for its highly embellished melody lines and dance rhythms. In addition, French baroque keyboard music was well known for something called the *style brisé*, which means the "broken style," a style of playing in which chord are broken, or strummed, in a manner derived from the strumming of lute music.

Let's hear the opening of Prelude no. 8 in E-flat Minor. With its highly embellished melody line; its strummed, *style brisé* chords; and its sarabande-like character (a sarabande is a slow, triple-meter dance), this is keyboard music clearly inspired by the French style. [**Piano performance:** Bach, *The Well-Tempered* Clavier, Book One, Prelude No. 8 in E-flat Minor.]

The German style was characterized by compositional rigor: polyphonic intricacy, harmonic complexity, and thematic concision. For example, Fugue No. 4 in C-sharp Minor, set for five voices, features a diamond-hard subject of stunning brevity. [**Piano demonstration.**]

From a purely musical point of view, Bach's subject is not so much a fully realized thematic melody as a building block, a building block that only becomes a fully realized musical idea over the developmental course of the fugue. This sort of theme, and the process of development it undergoes, is typical of German music and the German style. We hear the exposition of Bach's Fugue No. 4 in C-sharp Minor. [**Piano performance:** Bach, *The Well-Tempered* Clavier, Book One, Fugue No. 4 in C-sharp Minor.]

Brief though it is, the subject that drives this fugue is also programmatic. Its four pitches describe the four parts of the cross. The first pitch, a C-sharp, depicts the left-hand horizontal beam. [**Piano demonstration.**] The next two pitches, a B-sharp and an E, are the lowest and highest. They depict the vertical beam. [**Piano demonstration.**] Finally, the last pitch, a D-sharp, depicts the right-hand horizontal beam. [**Piano demonstration.**] All together. [**Piano demonstration.**]

Bach's extra-musical symbolism goes still deeper yet. Check it out: In German notation, the letter B represents the pitch B-flat and the letter H represents the pitch B-natural. So, in German notation, it is possible to spell out the name Bach in four pitches. [**Piano demonstration.**] That, my friends, is an exact transposition of Bach's cruciform fugue subject. Again, the Bach motif, the one that spells out his name. [**Piano demonstration.**] And the fugue subject. [**Piano demonstration.**] By designing his C-sharp Minor fugue subject as he did, Bach made explicit his own identification with the cross and Christ's suffering on the cross.

Bach had a proclivity to compose sets of works that synthesized the prevalent styles of his day, sets that employed a wide variety of contemporary and archaic compositional genres and techniques—works that typically milked every last drop of musical juice from their thematic materials. Such encyclopedic works include both books of *The Well-Tempered Clavier*, the *Brandenburg Concerti*, the *Goldberg Variations*, the *Art of the Fugue*, the B-minor Mass, and many, many others.

The preludes in Book One of *The Well-Tempered Clavier* constitute, all by themselves, a virtual encyclopedia of keyboard genres and compositional techniques. For example, preludes numbers 3, 13, and 15 are two-part inventions. As an example, let's hear the first half of Prelude No. 13 in F-sharp Major. [**Piano performance:** Bach, *The Well-Tempered* Clavier, Book One, Prelude No. 13 in F-sharp Major.] Preludes numbers 9, 18, 19, 23, and 24 are three-part inventions. As an example, here's the first half of the Prelude No. 18 in G-sharp Minor. [**Piano performance:** Bach, *The Well-Tempered* Clavier, Book One, Prelude No. 18 in G-sharp Minor.] Preludes 2, 3, 5, 6, and 21 are toccatas. For our info: the word "toccata" comes from the Italian *toccare*, which means "to touch." Any piece thus named is a fast, virtuoso work that puts a performer's dexterity and touch in highest relief. As an example, let's hear the toccata that is Prelude No. 5 in D Major. [**Piano performance:** Bach, *The Well-Tempered* Clavier, Book One, Prelude No. 5 in D Major.]

Other preludes employ the French *style brisé*; we'll examine one such prelude at the conclusion of this lecture. Finally, a number of preludes are simply superb and penetrating works of keyboard art, works that could easily stand alone on any recital program I would include in this group preludes numbers 4, 7, 10, 12, and 23. Let's hear the opening of the gorgeous and powerfully moving Prelude No. 4 in C-sharp Minor. [**Piano performance:** Bach, *The Well-Tempered* Clavier, Book One, Prelude No. 4 in C-sharp Minor.]

A Comparison

We conclude by comparing the very first and last works in Book One of *The Well-Tempered* Clavier: Prelude No. 1 in C-major and Fugue No. 12 in B-minor. By doing so, we will observe something of the amazing artistic range traversed by *The Well-Tempered Clavier*. The Prelude No. 1 in C Major is a piece known to anyone who ever studied the piano. [**Piano demonstration.**]

As a prelude, this one in C Major does not just precede the Fugue in C Major; it introduces the entire first book of *The Well-Tempered Clavier*. It does so in a manner that would appear to be the Acme of simplicity. Employing the arpeggiated strumming of the *style brisé*, the prelude lacks any sort of thematic melody. Instead, it consists entirely of a gorgeously subtle harmonic progression, the well-tempered system at work. Fugue No. 24 in B Minor is cast for four voices. We're going to hear its exposition, during which I want us be aware of the following three points.

One: The particularly spacious fugue subject features a series of meticulously phrased falling intervals. The subject contains every one of the 12 chromatic pitches. [**Piano demonstration.**] Point two: This is music in which the rise-and-fall of its long, sighing, singing, chromatic melody lines must be presented with the greatest possible clarity. Point three: A truly spectacular degree of harmonic dissonance marks the exposition (and the fugue as a whole) as the constituent chromatic voices stack one atop the next. There are moments when this fugue sounds as if it had been written during the late 19th or early 20th century. [**Piano performance:** Bach, *The Well-Tempered* Clavier, Book One, Fugue No. 24 in B Minor.]

In terms of both its compositional and expressive substance, this B-minor fugue is the antithesis of the Prelude in C Major. The prelude, with its *style brisé* figuration, evokes the past. The fugue, with its astonishing chromaticism and pathos, evokes the distant future of the late 19th and early 20th centuries. The prelude is music suited equally to a harpsichord or a piano. The fugue—with its slow tempo and sustained, legato cantabile expressive substance—is much more suited to a piano, with its graded dynamic capabilities and its increased resonance.

The Fugue in B Minor, which runs over six minutes in performance, is a fitting conclusion to Book One of *The Well-Tempered Clavier*: It looks forward to a new expressive world, one in which the piano will come to be the dominant keyboard instrument.

Thank you.

J. S. Bach—*Goldberg Variations*
Lecture 3

The *Goldberg Variations* was conceived as a harpsichord piece. Nevertheless, that fact has not prevented it from becoming a mainstay of the piano repertoire, recorded by many of the greatest pianists of the last 70 years. Typical of Bach, the individual variations within the *Goldberg Variations* display an encyclopedic variety of keyboard genres and compositional techniques. There are dances, canons, toccatas, an invention, a fugue, a French overture, and a quodlibet. This riot of compositional diversity notwithstanding, the *Goldberg Variations*—as a total work of art—constitutes perhaps the single most radical example of the high baroque's obsession with unity, order, and control.

The Theme

- The *Goldberg Variations* consist of a theme, which Bach calls an "aria" (or an "air"), followed by 30 variations and then a reprise of the theme. Despite the fact that the *Goldberg Variations* consists of 32 separate **movements**, we do not actually perceive the work as consisting of 32 separate movements. Rather, we perceive a series of concentric groups of variations, which create, on both the smallest and largest **scales**, a series of apparent "departures" and "returns."

- The 30 variations of the *Goldberg Variations* consist of a series of concentric groupings, or cycles, of variations. At the smallest micro level are the four phrases within each of the 30 variations—120 phrases in all. At the miniature level are the variations themselves—30 in number. At the midi level, Bach groups the variations into sets of three, thus creating 10 larger cycles. At the macro level, Bach divides the variations into two distinct sets of 15 variations. Finally, at the universal level, the entire work stands as a universal cycle—a life cycle—a unified singularity.

- At every level—from the micro to miniature to midi to macro—the *Goldberg Variations* resonates with the baroque belief that the complexity of the visible universe was controlled and given order by the singularity: God.

- The key to understanding the amazing, expressive, spiritual, and metaphysical power of the *Goldberg Variations* is an awareness of the concentric formal cycles that make up the piece and how they interact and combine to create a whole that is infinitely greater than the sum of its 32 parts.

- Typical of a baroque-era variations work, the theme of the *Goldberg Variations* is not a **tune**—that is, a memorable melody—but, rather, a bass line and the harmonies supported by that bass line. Such a work is variously called a passacaglia, or a chaconne, or a ground bass.

- The *a–a–b–b* phrase structure articulated by this bass line represents the most ubiquitous musical structure of the baroque era: binary dance form. Each variation will feature the same bass line outlining the same binary dance form, and as a result, over the course of the piece, we will hear the same 32-measure-long bass line 32 times, one after the other. Bach's great compositional challenge is to overcome the potentially numbing regularity of the repeated bass line and create diversity and variety around it.

- Bach chose to set this first thematic iteration of the bass line as a sarabande, which is a slow, three-step dance of Spanish origin. Bach's sarabande is exquisite and diaphanous, one that strikes a perfect balance between the physicality of dance and the lyricism of song.

- In the opening phrase *a* of the theme, there is a temptation to call the melody of the sarabande the "theme," but the melody is not the theme; the theme is the bass line and phrase structure beneath the sarabande melody. In actuality, the sarabande is the first outward manifestation of the bass line, harmonies, and phrase structure—which are, collectively, the theme.

The Concentric Cycles

- In regard to the concentric, interactive cycles that make up the *Goldberg Variations*, the micro cycle consists of the four symmetrical phrases of the thematic bass line: *a–a–b–b*. The miniature cycle consists of the entire thematic bass line, repeated 32 times in succession. The midi cycle divides the 30 variations into 10 groups of three variations—that is, 10 trinities. At the macro level, Bach divides the *Goldberg Variations* exactly in half.

Bach's title for the keyboard piece we know as the *Goldberg Variations* is quite instrument-specific: "Aria with Diverse Variations for Cembalo" (meaning harpsichord).

- If listeners are to perceive a structural division halfway through the *Goldberg Variations*, two things must happen: Variation 15 will have to sound like an ending of some sort, and variation 16 will have to sound like a new beginning—which is exactly what happens.

- The opening *a* section of variation 16 has a moderate **tempo**, sweeping scales, and long-short rhythms, all of which combine to create a majestic, pompous mood. Any musically aware European living in 1741 would have immediately recognized this music as being in the character of a French **overture**, a ubiquitous baroque genre invented in the 1650s in order to welcome the king, Louis XIV to the theater. The sweeping majesty and pomp that characterize the opening of a French overture were intended to reflect the magnificence of the king himself.

The Trinities

- There are 10 variational trinities in the *Goldberg Variations*—from trinity 1 (which consists of variations 1, 2, and 3) through trinity 10 (which consists of the final three variations, numbers 28, 29, and 30). Each of these trinities is a self-contained structural unit.

- The first variation of each trinity—with the exception of variation 16—is a character piece, which means that they are primarily dances. Variation 16, which begins trinity 6, is a French overture. These character pieces are melodically conceived, which means that they feature clear thematic melodies.

- Variation 7 initiates trinity 3 and is a loure, or a moderately slow dance of French origin in compound duple (6/8) **meter**. Bach's loure has a graceful, courtly elegance and is highly embellished in what is considered the French style. Keep in mind that every variation is built on the same cyclically repeated bass line.

- With one exception, the second variation of each trinity is a toccata, which is a fast, virtuosic work that puts a performer's dexterity in highest relief. The toccatas in the *Goldberg Variations* are harmonically conceived, which means that they consist of harmonic progressions outlined by virtuosic keyboard figuration.

The Canons

- With one exception, each of the 10 trinities concludes with a canon, which is a piece of strict imitative polyphony in which one or more voices follow a lead voice at some interval of time. (Think of *Row, Row, Row Your Boat*.)

- If the trinities are the musical heart of the *Goldberg Variations*, then the canons are collectively the spiritual soul of the trinities. These are canons with a twist; in each successive canon, the following voice begins another step further away from the leading voice.

- Variation 3 offers the first canon. It is a canon at the unison, which means that the following voice "sings" exactly the same pitches as the leading voice. With one exception, the canons are presented in the upper two voices while accompanied below by embellished versions of the bass line.

- Variation 6 concludes the second trinity. It is a canon at the second, meaning that the following voice begins a step above the leading voice.

- The third canon, variation 9, is a canon at the third, because the following voice appears three notes above the leader. The fourth canon, variation 12, is a canon at the fourth; the fifth canon is a canon at the fifth, and so on, through the ninth canon, which is a canon at the ninth. Variation 30, the variation that concludes the 10th and final trinity, is special.

- Because of the ever-growing intervallic distance between the leader and the follower, each of the canons will be characterized by a different level of **dissonance**. Over the years, this has rendered them ripe for all sorts of numerical, allegorical, and metaphysical discussion. Given Bach's proclivity toward numerical symbolism, such discussions are entirely appropriately.

- The canon at the fifth, variation 15, is the variation that brings the first half of the *Goldberg Variations* to its conclusion, the variation that immediately precedes the French overture that is variation 16. Bach does a number of things in variation 15 that make it very special.

- First, variation 15 is set in minor—specifically, G minor. It is the first variation in the *Goldberg Variations* to be so set. Combined with its slow tempo, the minor **mode** imbues this variation with a sense of quiet profundity and mystery.

- Second, variation 15 is not just a canon at the fifth, in which the following voice begins a perfect fifth above the leading voice; it is also a canon in **inversion**, meaning that the following voice is a mirror image of the leading voice.

- The third thing that makes this canon special is the overwhelming musical and spiritual importance attached to the interval of a fifth. Bach's well-tempered tuning system—like the modern equal-tempered system—is based on a circle of perfect fifths. The primal power of the perfect fifth carried with it a huge degree of spiritual significance for the baroque musical community. Thus, the perfect fifth was perceived as a metaphor for "the absolute concord which is God."

- The 10th and final trinity—variations 28, 29, and 30—breaks the pattern established in the earlier nine trinities. Bach wants to create the maximum degree of momentum going into the 30th and final variation, and he does this by preceding that final variation with not just one but two toccatas.

- The 30th and final variation is not a canon but, rather, a quodlibet—a medley of popular tunes. The upper two voices of this variation incorporate two contemporary popular songs, *I've Not Been with You for So Long* and *Kraut und Rüben* (meaning "Cabbage and Beets").

- Following the jolly 30th variation, the opening sarabande returns exactly as heard at the beginning of the piece—except it doesn't sound the same. That is because we now hear within it an implicit world of possibilities and experience we could not have perceived at the beginning of the piece. We are older and wiser now, and the serenity and sense of a circle closed we hear in the reprise reflect the serenity and closure one might feel looking back at a life well lived.

Important Terms

dissonance: A musical entity or state of instability that seeks resolution to consonance.

inversion: Loosely applied to indicate a reversal in melodic direction. Harmonic inversion is a situation in which a chord tone other than the root is in the bass.

meter: Group of beats organized in a regular rhythmic pattern and notated in music as a time signature.

mode: A type of pitch collection (or scale).

movement: Independent section within a larger work.

overture: Music preceding an opera or play, often played as an independent concert piece.

scale: All the pitches inside a given octave, arranged stepwise so that there is no duplication. The names of the chords built on the scale steps are: tonic, supertonic, mediant, subdominant, dominant, submediant, and leading tone.

tempo: Relative speed of a passage of music.

tune: Generally singable, memorable melody with a clear sense of beginning, middle, and end.

J. S. Bach—*Goldberg Variations*
Lecture 3—Transcript

We return to *The 23 Greatest Solo Piano Works*. This is Lecture 3. It is entitled J.S. Bach—*Goldberg Variations*.

The *New Grove Dictionary of Music and Musicians* is the single most comprehensive music reference in existence. My 1980 edition consists of 20 volumes running to roughly 17,000 pages. Altogether, the various articles in the *New Grove Dictionary* on the Bach family of musicians run 112 pages. This means that 0.66 percent of the *New Grove*—which covers virtually every conceivable aspect of world music, music history, and music theory—that one out of every 151 pages is dedicated to the members of a single family of musicians. Altogether, some 86 members of the Bach clan are listed, from Vitus Bach—Johann Sebastian's great-great grandfather, who lived from around 1527 to 1577—to Wilhelm Friedrich Ernst Bach, who lived from 1759 to 1845.

These Bach family musicians ran the gamut from country fiddlers and town pipers to church organists and cantors; from court musicians to *Kapellmeisters*; from the humblest of musicians—great-great grandfather Vitus was a baker with a local rep as a mandolin player—to world renown: Bach's son Johann Christian (or J. C.) was a jet-setting composer of Italian-style opera who lived much of his professional life in London and numbered among his friends King George III, Queen Charlotte, and, even more importantly (as far as we're concerned), Wolfgang Mozart. Yes, yes! According to the *New Grove Dictionary*, "[J. C. Bach's compositional] style, which was largely derived from Italian opera, was the most important single influence on Mozart."

A whopping 14 members of the Bach clan had compositional careers distinguished enough to earn them individual articles in *New Grove*. Along with Johann Sebastian himself, these include two of his uncles, three cousins, four of his sons, and his grandson Wilhelm Friedrich Ernst, who, according to New Grove, died childless and was the last of the Bach family line. With the exception of Bach's sons Carl Philipp Emanuel and Johann Christian—who had international careers—the other Bachs with their own articles in

Grove were, overwhelmingly, trained as church organists and Lutheran music directors (or "cantors").

Johann Sebastian's career hardly differed from those of his fellow organists and cantors. He never travelled outside of his native Germany. In fact, the positions he held never took him outside of a small area in central East Germany. Those positions ranged from that of church organist, court organist and court music director, to the music director of the St. Thomas Church in Leipzig, a job he held from 1723 at the age of 38 until his death in 1750, age 65.

For our information, the good *Herren* of Leipzig did not want to hire Bach, and did so only grudgingly when their first three choices for the job—Georg Philipp Telemann, Christoph Graupner, and Johann Friedrich Fasch—all turned the job down. One of the rocket scientists on the search committee—a municipal councilor, no less—complained that since none of the best men wanted the job, Leipzig would have to make do with a mediocrity. Bach was no happier with his job in Leipzig than Leipzig was with Bach, and until advancing age took him out of contention, he did his darnedest to find another position, but without success.

One of the upshots of Bach's professional unhappiness was that he began spending more and more time on outside projects, projects that ranged from taking on the directorship of the University of Leipzig's *Collegium Musicum* to consulting on organ construction and repair to composing esoteric works of extraordinary complexity, works considered by most of Bach's contemporaries to be hopelessly "artificial" in expressive content and "archaic" in musical style. These works include the B Minor Mass, completed in 1749, *The Musical Offering* of 1747, *The Art of the Fugue* of 1745, and the *Goldberg Variations* of 1741.

Instrumentation and a Confession

Bach's own title for the keyboard piece we know as the *Goldberg Variations* is quite instrument-specific.It reads: "Aria with Diverse Variations for Cembalo" (meaning harpsichord). The *Goldberg Variations* was conceived as a harpsichord piece; Johann Sebastian Bach himself has told us so.

Nevertheless, that fact has not prevented the Goldbergs from becoming a mainstay of the piano repertoire, recorded by many of the greatest pianists of the last 70 years, from Rosalyn Tureck, Peter Serkin, and Charles Rosen to Andras Schiff, Daniel Barenboim, Murray Perahia, and, of course, Glenn Gould.

The *Goldberg Variations* is—by every measure—a thrillingly virtuosic work, one that demands a nuanced approach to dynamics (meaning relative loudness and softness), a full range of articulation (from the smoothest *legato cantabile* to ear-popping *martellato*), and a full range of timbral quality (from sonorous roundness to pin-point staccato). Oops. Dynamic nuance, a full range of articulation, and varied timbre? Those are all things you can do on a piano, but not on a harpsichord.

I confess: Accustomed as I am to the brilliant, Technicolor, graceful, and subtly shaded piano recordings of Barenboim, Schiff, and Gould, even the best harpsichord performances sound monochromatic to my ears. In this, sadly, I must agree with the great English conductor Sir Thomas Beecham, who likened the sound of the harpsichord to "two skeletons copulating on a tin roof." Bach's original intentions notwithstanding, the *Goldberg Variations* is a much better piano piece than it is a harpsichord piece.

Gestation

Writing in 1802—more than 60 years after the *Goldberg Variations* was composed—Bach's first biographer Johann Nikolaus Forkel described how the piece came to be composed. In the two centuries-plus that has passed since, much doubt has been cast on Forkel's version of events. However, in the spirit of never letting the possible facts get in the way of a great story, I offer up Forkel's account. Lacking any other explanation for the creation of the Goldbergs, Forkel's is as good as any. The story revolves around a wealthy Count named Hermann Carl von Kaiserling. According to Forkel:

> The count once remarked to Bach that he would like to have a few keyboard piece for his musician [Johann Gottlieb] Goldberg, pieces so gentle and somewhat merry that the Count could be a bit cheered up by them during his sleepless nights. Bach thought he could

best fulfill this with the variations. The Count thenceforth referred to them only as his variations. He could not get enough of them, and for a long time, whenever sleepless nights came, he would say, "Dear Goldberg, do play me one of my variations." Bach was perhaps never rewarded so well for one of his compositions as for these. The count bestowed on him a gold beaker filled with a hundred Louis d'or.

A "Louis d'or" was a French gold coin with the French king's portrait on the obverse. According to the Bach scholar Christoph Wolff writing in the year 2000, 100 Louis d'ors was the equivalent of 360,000 dollars. Yes; that's a lot of money!

The *Goldberg Variations* is one of the few works by Bach to be published in his lifetime, issued by Balthasar Schmid of Nuremburg. The original published title page reads in part: "*Klavierübung* [meaning keyboard exercise], consisting of an aria with diverse variations for harpsichord with two manuals [or two keyboards]. Composed for connoisseurs, for the refreshment of their spirits, by Johann Sebastian Bach, Kapellmeister and Director of Choral Music in Leipzig."

The *Goldberg Variations*: Questions and Answers

The Goldbergs consist of a theme—which Bach calls an aria (or an "air")—followed by 30 variations and then a reprise of the theme. Pretty straightforward, yes? But in reality, straightforward it is not. In fact, the *Goldberg Variations* has inspired more downright wacky discourse than pretty much any other musical work, with the possible exception of John Lennon's "I Am the Walrus." Behind all the *Goldberg*-inspired discourse is a seemingly inexplicable dichotomy, a dichotomy best described by framing it as a question. Here it is: How can a piece of music that consists entirely of 32 discrete miniatures—a theme, 30 variations, and a reprise of the theme— manage to project the incredible degree of expressive power, unity, and sheer drama that the *Goldberg Variations* does indeed project? It is the answer to that question that will drive our examination of the piece. We begin with a grand statement, one we will flesh out over the remainder of this lecture.

Despite the fact that the *Goldberg Variations* consists on paper of 32 separate movements, we do not actually perceive the work as consisting of 32 separate movements. Rather, we perceive a series of concentric groups of variations. These concentric groups of variations create, on both the smallest and largest scales, a series of apparent departures and returns. It is, my friends, entirely miraculous.

Let us begin fleshing out that statement immediately. Like a giant musical bulls-eye, the 30 variations of the *Goldberg Variations* consist of a series of concentric groupings (or cycles) of variations. At the smallest micro level are the four phrases within each of the 30 variations, 120 phrases in all. At the miniature level are the variations themselves, 30 in number. At the midi level, Bach groups the variations into sets of three, thus creating 10 larger cycles. At the macro level Bach divides the variations into two distinct sets of 15 variations. Finally, at the universal level, the entire work stands as a universal cycle, a life cycle, a unified singularity.

The ratios between these concentric cycles is most revealing. One-hundred-twenty phrases divided by 30 variations equals four. Thirty variations divided by 10 groups of 3 variations equals three. Thirty variations divided by two groups of 15 equals two. Finally, the holistic singularity of the entire group equals one. From micro to miniature to midi to macro, from four to three to two to one, from the many to the singularity. At every level, the *Goldberg Variations* resonates with the baroque belief that the complexity of the visible universe was controlled and given order by the singularity: by the hand, by the breath, by the voice of God.

That is exactly why numerological analysis of Bach's music is not specious mumbo jumbo. As a man of his time, Bach believed that music was a sonic manifestation of God's voice, of the beauty and order that lay behind the complexity of the visible world. For the natural philosophers (meaning the scientists) of the baroque era, from Galileo to Kepler to Harvey to Isaac Newton, numbers and ratios held mystical meaning. They were the passwords through which the workings of God's universe could be divined, understood, and explored. For Bach, such numerological constructs were not games incidental to his art, but intrinsic elements of his compositional process, as important as pitch and rhythm.

Thus, the single key to understanding the amazing expressive, spiritual, and metaphysical power of the *Goldberg Variations* is an awareness of the concentric formal cycles that make up the piece and how they interact and combine to create a whole that is a gazillion times greater than the sum of its 32 parts. Our job, then, will be to identify these concentric cycles, and in doing so, get a glimpse of the metaphysical and spiritual unity these mutually reinforcing cycles create.

The Theme

Typical of a baroque era variations work, the theme of the Goldbergs is not a tune—that is, a memorable melody—but rather, a bass line and the harmonies supported by that bass line. Such a work is variously called a passacaglia, or a chaconne, or a ground bass. I will play this thematic bass line on the piano, and while I do, I will point out its four phrases as each begins: A-A-B-B. Each of these phrases is exactly the same number of measure in length. **[Piano demonstration.]**

The A-A-B-B phrase structure articulated by this bass line represents the most ubiquitous musical structure of the baroque era, something called binary dance form. Each variation will feature the same bass line outlining the same binary dance form, and as a result, over the course of the piece, we will hear the same 32-measure-long bass line 32 times, one after the other. Bach's great compositional challenge is to overcome the potentially numbing regularity of the repeated bass line and create diversity and variety around it.

Bach chose to set this first, thematic iteration of the bass line as a sarabande. A sarabande is a slow, three-step dance of Spanish origin. Bach's sarabande is exquisite and diaphanous, one that strikes a perfect balance between the physicality of dance and the lyricism of song. Let's hear the opening A of the theme. [**Piano performance:** Bach, *Goldberg Variations*, Aria.]

There is a temptation to call the melody of this sarabande the theme. But the melody is not the theme; the theme is the bass line and phrase structure beneath the sarabande melody. In actuality, the sarabande is a sort of ur-variation, the first outward manifestation of the bass line, harmonies, and phrase structure which are, collectively, the theme.

The Concentric Cycles Revisited

Let us now discuss the nature of the concentric, interactive cycles that make up the Goldbergs. As previously observed, the micro cycle consists of the four symmetrical phrases of the thematic bass line: A-A-B-B. The miniature cycle consists of the entire thematic bass line, repeated 32 times in succession. The midi cycle divides the 30 variations into 10 groups of three variations, that is, ten trinities (yes, like the holy trinity). At the macro level Bach divides the Goldberg's exactly in half.

Let's start with this macro division. If we as listeners are to perceive a structural division halfway through the *Goldberg Variations*, two things must happen: Variation 15 will have to sound like an ending of some sort and Variation 16 will have to sound like a beginning. This is, indeed, exactly what happens. We'll tackle Variation 15 in a bit; for now, let's examine Variation 16 and the new beginning it represents.

Let's hear the opening A section of Variation 16, and let us be aware of its moderate tempo, sweeping scales, and long-short rhythms, all of which combine to create a majestic, pompous (as in pomp-filled) mood. [**Piano performance:** Bach, *Goldberg Variations*, Variation 16.]

Any musically aware European living in 1741 would have immediately recognized that music as being in the character of a French overture, a ubiquitous baroque genre invented in the 1650s in order to welcome the king— Louis XIV his very self—to the theater. The sweeping majesty and pomp that characterize the opening of a French overture were intended to reflect the magnificence of the king himself. Bach pulls no punches here: Under the heading Variation 16 at the top of the page he writes the word "Overture." And thus does this 16th variation most explicitly begin the second half of *The Goldberg Variations*.

The Trinities

There are 10 variational trinities in the *Goldberg Variations*. From trinity number one (which consists of variations one, two, and three) through trinity number 10, which consists of the final three variations, number 28, 29, and 30, each of these trinities is a self contained structural unit.

With but one exception, the first variation of each trinity is a character piece, primarily dances although, as we just observed, Variation 16—which begins trinity number 6—is a French Overture. These character pieces are melodically conceived, which means that they feature clear thematic melodies.

Let's sample Variation 7, which initiates trinity number 3. Variation 7 is a loure: a moderately slow dance of French origin in compound duple (6/8) meter. Bach's loure has a graceful, courtly elegance and is highly embellished in what is considered the French style. We hear the opening A section. Variation 7: [**Piano performance:** Bach, *Goldberg Variations*, Variation 7.]

A reminder, lest we forget: Every variation is built on the same, cyclically repeated bass line. With but one exception, the second variation of each trinity is a toccata. The word "toccata" comes from the Italian verb *toccare*, which means "to touch." Any piece thus entitled will be a fast, virtuosic work that puts a performer's dexterity in highest relief. The toccatas here in the *Goldberg Variations* are harmonically conceived, which means that they consist of harmonic progressions outlined by virtuosic keyboard figuration.Let's hear Variation 8, the toccata which follows the loure we sampled moments ago. We hear both phrases A and B of the toccata. [**Piano performance:** Bach, *Goldberg Variations*, Variation 8.]

The Canons

With but one exception, each of the 10 trinities concludes with a canon. A canon is a piece of strict imitative polyphony in which one or more voices follow a lead voice at some interval of time. Think "Row, Row, Row Your Boat" and "Frere Jacques." My friends, if the trinities are the musical heart of the Goldbergs, then the canons are collectively the spiritual soul of the trinities. You see, these are canons with a twist, as in each successive canon, the following voice begins another step further away from the leading voice.

I'll explain. Variation number 3 offers up the first canon. It is a canon at the unison, which means that the following voice sings exactly the same pitches as the leading voice. Let's just hear the two voices of the canon, and let's be aware that the follower articulates exactly the same pitches as the leader. [**Piano performance:** Bach, *Goldberg Variations*, Variation 3.]

For our information: With but one exception, the canons are presented in the upper two voices while accompanied below by embellished versions of the bass line. Here's what all three voices of Variation 3 sound like. [**Piano performance:** Bach, *Goldberg Variations*, Variation 3.] Variation 6 concludes the second trinity. It is a canon at the second, meaning that the following voice begins a step above the leading voice. Listen, here is the leading voice. [**Piano demonstration.**] And here's the following voice, pitched a step higher. [**Piano demonstration.**]

Here's what the first phrase of Variation 6—the canon at the second—sounds like with its accompanimental bass line added. [**Piano performance:** Bach, *Goldberg Variations*, Variation 6.] The third canon—Variation 9—is a canon at the third, as the following voice appears three notes above the leader. The fourth canon—Variation 12—is a canon at the fourth, the fifth canon a canon at the fifth, and so on, through the ninth canon, which is a canon at the ninth. Variation 30—the variation that concludes the 10th and final trinity—is a most special critter about which we'll talk in a moment. In his book, *Bach and the Dance of God*, the English musicologist Wilfrid Mellers describes the nature of the trinities this way:

> The dance pieces start from the earth; the toccatas spring from the physical excitation of virtuosity. [The toccatas] thus provide a transition to the canons which, always vocal in [conception], tend to negate meter and therefore the temporal sense. In their level of impersonal flow, the canons approach a metaphysical rather than a physical state of being.

Because of the ever-growing intervallic distance between the leader and the follower, each of the canons will be characterized by a different level of dissonance. Over the years, this has rendered them ripe for all sorts of numerical, allegorical, and metaphysical discussion. Given Bach's proclivity towards numerical symbolism, such discussions are entirely appropriate. For example, the canon at the unison—Variation 3—has been credited with representing "the unity, the one, All-Oneness, individuality and non-duality, an archetype and attribute of God."

The canon at a second is credited as representing "the dissonance of the other." Conversely, the canon at the third is understood to represent the consonance of divine union: "The Father precedes the Son; the unity of Father and Son is the *Vinculum Amoris*, and this constitutes the holy ghost, the Third."

And so forth. This sort of numerological symbolism has been ascribed to each canon one through nine.

Let us address one more canon, the canon at the fifth that is Variation 15. This is the variation that brings the first half of *The Goldbergs* to its conclusion, the variation that immediately precedes the French Overture that is Variation 16.

Bach does a number of things in Variation 15 that make it very special. First: Variation 15 is set in minor, G Minor, specifically. It is the first variation in the *Goldbergs* to be set in a minor key. Combined with its slow tempo, the minor mode imbues this variation with a sense of quiet profundity and mystery. Let's hear just the opening. [**Piano performance:** Bach, *Goldberg Variations*, Variation 15.] We're talking about those things that make Variation 15 special. The second thing is that Variation 15 is not just a canon at the fifth, in which the following voice begins a perfect fifth above the leading voice; it is also a canon in inversion, meaning that the following voice is a mirror image of the leading voice! I would demonstrate by playing the two canonic voices as heard at the very beginning of the variation. [**Piano demonstration.**] Things are going in opposite directions, and that's special.

The third thing that makes this canon special is the overwhelming musical and spiritual importance attached to the interval of a fifth. Bach's well-tempered tuning system—like our modern, equal-tempered system—is based on a circle of perfect fifths. The primal power of the perfect fifth carries with it a huge degree of spiritual significance for the baroque musical community. Thus, the perfect fifth was perceived as a metaphor for "the absolute concord which is God." We hear Variation 15 in its entirety. [**Piano performance:** Bach, *Goldberg Variations*, Variation 15.]

The Final Trinity

The 10th and final trinity—Variations 28, 29, and 30—breaks the pattern established in the earlier nine trinities. Bach wants to create the maximum degree of momentum going into the 30th and final variation, and this he does by preceding that final variation with not just one but two toccatas. The 30th and final variation is not a canon but rather, a quodlibet: a medley of popular tunes. The upper two voices of this variation incorporate two contemporary popular songs, one entitled "I've Not Been With You For So Long" and the other "*Kraut und Rüben*"—meaning "Cabbage and Beets." The words to "Cabbage and Beets" are worth noting:

> Cabbage and beets
> Drove me away;
> Had my mother cooked me meat
> I might have longer stayed.

The inclusion of this song in the quodlibet has led some to speculate that the cabbage and beets represent, in Bach's own mind, his variations, and that had he only cooked more meat (that is, had his game plan for the piece been less esoteric), we, the listeners, might have stuck around long enough to hear this final variation. If this is true, Bach needn't have worried. We always stick around for the Goldbergs. Here it is, Variation 30, the quodlibet. [**Piano performance:** Bach, *Goldberg Variations*, Variation 30.]

The Da Capo

Following the jolly 30th variation, the opening sarabande returns exactly as heard at the beginning of the piece, except it doesn't sound the same. That is because we now hear within it an implicit world of possibilities and experience we could not have perceived at the beginning of the piece. We are older and wiser now, and the serenity and sense of a circle closed we hear in the reprise reflect the serenity and closure one might feel looking back at a life well lived. The Da Capo. [**Piano performance:** Bach, *Goldberg Variations*, Da Capo.]

Typical of Bach, the individual variations display an encyclopedic variety of keyboard genres and compositional techniques. There are dances, canons, toccatas, an invention, a fugue, a French Overture and a quodlibet. This riot of compositional diversity notwithstanding, the *Goldberg Variations* —as a total work of art—constitutes perhaps the single most radical example of the high baroque's obsession with unity, order, and control. It is a singular work.

Bach and the Piano

Johann Sebastian Bach was an entrepreneur par excellence. Along with his many professional (and domestic) responsibilities, Bach ran an instrument rental business, sold instruments on a commission basis, and sold books and music. Given the opportunity, Bach might have peddled George Foreman grills as well; hey, a guy's got to feed his family.

Of all Bach's entrepreneurial side jobs, the one for which he was uniquely qualified was as an organ consultant, as a designer and tester of organs. It was in this capacity that Bach came to work with the organ designer and builder Gottfried Silbermann (who lived from 1683–1753), who was one of the greatest organ builders of the baroque era.

In 1732, Silbermann built his first piano, based on the designs of Bartolomeo Cristofori, who had invented the piano around 1700. By building instruments of quality and by putting his considerable prestige behind those instruments, Silbermann became a major player in promoting what was then a very new technology. Gottfried Silbermann was a proud, oversensitive, and uncompromising man who met his match in Johann Sebastian Bach. Having built his first two pianos, Silbermann invited Bach to take one for a test drive. Bach's friend, the organist and composer Johann Friedrich Agricola, described what happened:

> [Bach] admired its tone; but he complained that it was too weak in the high register and [that its action was] too hard to play. This was taken greatly amiss by Mr. Silbermann, who could not bear to have

any fault found in his handiworks. He was therefore angry with Bach for a long time. And yet his conscience told him that Bach was not wrong. He therefore decided—to his great credit—not to deliver any more of these instruments, but instead to eliminate the faults Bach had observed. He worked for many years on this. Silbermann showed one of these later instruments to Bach, and received, in return, complete approval from him.

Bach's approval was genuine, and late in life he went on to act as a sales agent for Silbermann's pianos. While Bach never personally embraced the piano, his feedback was—if you'll excuse me—instrumental to its evolution and popularization. You see, Silbermann's nephew and apprentice Johann Andreas Silbermann taught Johann Andreas Stein, who perfected the so-called Viennese action used in the pianos played by Haydn, Mozart, and Beethoven. Other of Silbermann's students migrated to England and created the so-called English action. The English action went on to be modified and improved by Sébastian Érard in Paris and became the basis for the action used in all grand pianos today. So even if Bach didn't personally like the piano, his input played a major role in its evolution.

Thank you.

Mozart—Piano Sonata in C Minor, K. 457
Lecture 4

Wolfgang Amadeus Mozart's creative predisposition toward lyric music informed every aspect of his compositional voice, including his choice of piano over the harpsichord. Mozart's style of keyboard playing was learned at the harpsichord—a minimum of extraneous movement, play from the wrist, sit centered at the keyboard—but his mature keyboard music is piano music. Mozart's Piano Sonata in C Minor, K. 457, could not be successfully performed on a harpsichord; rather, this is music conceived of and composed for the piano.

Mozart's Piano Sonatas

- Mozart composed 19 "piano" sonatas. The first—set in C major and catalogued as Köchel 279—was composed in 1774, when Mozart was 18 years old. The last, in D major, K. 576, was composed in 1788. It remains a matter of debate as to whether the first five of these sonatas—composed in 1774 and 1775—were composed for the harpsichord or the piano.

- It's probably a safe bet to say that they were composed to be played on either instrument. However, starting with the Sonata no. 6 in D Major, K. 284—composed in 1775—the remainder of the sonatas were clearly composed for the piano.

- The classical keyboard sonata, of which Mozart's are presumably representative, is a typically three-movement construct in which the first movement is a moderate-to-fast **sonata form**, the second movement a lyric respite from the dramatic rigors of the first, followed by a fast third movement, more often than not cast as a **rondo**.

- While we in the 21ˢᵗ century perceive Mozart as being a mainstream exponent of the **classical** style, Mozart's contemporaries certainly did not. Mozart's mature works were considered by his contemporaries to be unnecessarily difficult to perform and just plain too long.

- For example, Mozart's Piano Sonata in C Minor of 1784 runs 561 measures without its repeats. Most of Haydn's piano sonatas run from between 300 to 400 measures in length; even Haydn's massive (for him) Piano Sonata in E-flat Major of 1794 runs 450 measures, 111 measures shorter than Mozart's.

- The truth is, there's nothing typically "classical" about Mozart's mature music, so if we want to find solo piano music equal in dramatic scope and length to Mozart's C Minor Sonata, we will have to look

Wolfgang Amadeus Mozart (1756–1791) is often celebrated as one of the greatest composers of Western music.

forward to Ludwig van Beethoven, whose own groundbreaking Piano Sonata in C Minor—also known as the *Pathétique*, composed in 1798—runs 582 measures, the same length as Mozart's.

- Mozart single-handedly turned the piano sonata from a small-scale genre intended for amateur amusement into a large-scale, virtuosic genre. When compared to the massive piano sonatas of the 19th century—starting with Beethoven's—Mozart's might seem relatively understated. But comparing Mozart's piano sonatas to those of the 19th century is a fool's exercise; instead, we should be comparing Mozart's piano sonatas with those of his own contemporaries.

- Only then will we realize that it was Mozart who began the process of enlarging the scale, virtuosity, and artistic importance of the piano sonata. Mozart's piano sonatas were Beethoven's essential models, just as Beethoven's sonatas became the essential models for Schubert, Schumann, Liszt, and Brahms.

Movement One: Sonata Form

- Sonata form is a **musical form** in which multiple contrasting themes—typically two—are introduced in a section called the exposition. Materials presented in the exposition are then "developed" in a section called the **development**. The themes return in their original order in a section called the **recapitulation**. Finally, a **coda** will usually bring such a movement to its conclusion.

- Typical of Mozart, theme 1 of his Piano Sonata in C Minor features an embarrassment of melodic riches. It consists of three distinct parts, any one of which would have been adequate for the rather "thriftier" Haydn or Beethoven to build an entire theme.

- Part 1 of Mozart's theme consists of the alternation of two contrasting elements. The first of these elements—that musical idea that initiates the sonata—was very familiar to Mozart's audience. Mozart opens with a boldly rising arpeggio (that is, a "broken harmony") played in octaves, a gesture that was universally known as a "Mannheim rocket"—an opening musical gambit that was made cliché by the house composers for the Mannheim court orchestra, which was considered, between roughly 1740 to 1780, to be the greatest orchestra in Europe.

- The "rocket" was a gesture that Mozart would use to striking effect in the opening of the fourth movement of his Symphony in G Minor of 1788. Beethoven used a Mannheim rocket to begin his Piano Sonata no. 1 in F Minor of 1795, calculating that a "rocket" would be a most conspicuous way to begin his first published piano sonata.

- In the first part of Mozart's theme 1, the rising, frankly ithyphallic rocket alternates with a quiet, trilling phrase of more feminine quality. The first part of theme 1 is where Mozart lays out—in its first eight measures—the expressive extremes of the movement. The second part of theme 1 features drooping, deathly, descending **chromatic** lines over a throbbing tremolo in the bass.

- There are many resemblances—expressive, spiritual, and musical—between Mozart's Piano Sonata in C Minor and Beethoven's Piano Sonata in C Minor of 1798. One of the more obvious resemblances between the two pieces is the second part of Mozart's theme 1 and Beethoven's movement 1, theme 1.

- Mozart's thematic phrase consists of *descending* chromatic lines heard over a throbbing tremolo in the bass. Beethoven's theme 1 consists of *ascending* chromatic lines heard over a throbbing tremolo in the bass. The third part of Mozart's theme 1 combines melodic material drawn from part 1 with the throbbing accompaniment of part 2.

- After a brief modulating bridge, theme 2—set in E-flat major—begins. Like theme 1, it is a theme of extraordinary melodic variety cast in three parts. The first part of theme 2 features a lilting, graceful tune set against an undulating, broken-chord accompaniment in the pianist's left hand.

- This sort of accompaniment, which is ubiquitous in classical-era keyboard music, is called an Alberti bass, named for the Italian composer Domenico Alberti, who did not invent but popularized it.

- The second part of Mozart's theme 2 constitutes a free variation of the first part and is cast as a dialogue between the treble and bass of the piano. Finally, the third part of theme 2 recalls theme 1, as dramatic, rising chromatic octaves alternate with scurrying scales and arpeggios.

- The recapitulation of Mozart's first movement contains the following main sections: theme 1, modulating bridge, theme 2, **cadence** material, and finally the coda that brings the movement to its conclusion.

- As you listen to this, be aware of the nature of Mozart's keyboard writing: With its powerful use of octaves, its accompanimental tremolos, its graded dynamics (meaning getting louder and softer), and its stark contrasts between loud and soft, this is pure piano music.

Movement Two: Rondo Form

- Rondo is a musical form or process in which a principal theme—the rondo theme—is stated and then returns periodically, like a refrain, after various contrasting episodes. The rondo theme is the A section in a musical structure that can be schematicized as A–B–A–C–A plus a coda.

- Both the contrasting B and C sections of the movement feature lush, lyric themes as well, and the two returns of the rondo theme see the theme embellished. The overall effect of the movement is one of constantly changing, expressively rich thematic melody.

- The second movement of Beethoven's Piano Sonata in C Minor is also structured as a rondo, A–B–A–C–A plus coda. Both Beethoven's rondo theme and Mozart's second contrasting episode are set in A-flat major.

Movement Three

- This is a spectacular movement. Structurally, it is an odd duck: Some sources consider it a rondo, others a sonata form, and still others as a hybrid called rondo-sonata. The movement features three sharply contrasting themes and virtually no transitional passages to soften the impact of those contrasts.

- The schizoaffective first theme, theme A, is cast in two spectacularly contrasting parts. The first part, quiet and melancholy, sees a series of drooping, syncopated **motives** heard over the simplest of accompaniments. This part is followed by the loud, manic second part of the theme, which twice pulls up short and stops completely after a series of explosive dissonances. This music, in turns, is hyper-agitated, explosively dissonant, disoriented, and melancholy.

- A single **harmony** effects the "transition" (if we can really call it that) to theme B, which, though initially set in E-flat major (an ostensibly more upbeat key), is filled with a terrific sense of urgency—in part due to the constant fluctuation between "piano" (soft) and "forte" (loud) that we hear throughout the theme.

- The final thematic element, theme C, is a despairing little melody consisting almost entirely of weepy little semitones. Theme C features the same sorts of explosive dissonances and silences first heard in theme A.

- Rather surprisingly, given its relative brevity compared to themes A and B, it is this quietly despairing theme C that is tasked with concluding the movement. Theme C is followed by the movement- and sonata-ending coda.

- If we had to schematicize this third and final movement, the schematic would be A–B–A–C–B^1–A–C plus coda—which is sort of random. As such, Mozart's idiosyncratic approach to large-scale form becomes a basic part of this movement's expressive message. Without the familiar structural landmarks provided by familiar musical forms, listeners cannot anticipate events, which significantly magnifies the movement's dark expressive power. Such a purposely alien formal landscape is antithetical to the classical style and looks forward not just to the music of Beethoven, but even beyond—to the highly personalized formal structures of the 19th and 20th centuries.

Important Terms

cadence: A harmonic or melodic formula that occurs at the end of a phrase, section, or composition and conveys a momentary or permanent conclusion—in other words, a musical punctuation mark.

chromatic: A pitch that lies outside of whatever key area presently anchors a passage.

classical: Designation given to works of art of the 17th and 18th centuries, characterized by clear lines and balanced form.

coda: The closing few measures of a composition; usually not a part of the main theme groups of the standard form of a composition but a finishing theme added to the end to give the composition closure.

development: The second large part of a sonata form movement, during which the themes are developed in a generally unstable harmonic environment.

harmony: The musical art (and science) of manipulating simultaneous pitches.

motive: Brief succession of pitches from which a melody grows through the processes of repetition, sequence, and transformation.

musical form: The manner in which a given movement of music is structured.

recapitulation: The third large part of a sonata form movement, during which the themes return in their original order.

rondo form: A classical-era form that sees a principal theme (the rondo theme) return like a refrain after various contrasting episodes.

sonata form: A classical-era formal process posited on the introduction, development, recapitulation, and reconciliation of multiple contrasting themes.

Mozart—Piano Sonata in C Minor, K. 457
Lecture 4—Transcript

We return to *The 23 Greatest Solo Piano Works*. This is Lecture 4, and it is entitled Mozart—Piano Sonata in C Minor, K. 457.

Of all the stunned reactions to the child Mozart's amazing talent, my personal favorite is that of Niccolò Jommelli. Jommelli was a well-known Italian composer who was, at the time he first heard Mozart, court composer for Duke Karl Eugen of *Württemberg* in southwest Germany. As an Italian living in Germany, Jommelli had a certain understandable chauvinism when it came to Italian culture versus German culture. Thus, his encounter with the seven-year-old Mozart left him shaken when he admitted that "it was amazing and hardly believable that a child of German birth could be such a musical genius and so intelligent and passionate!" Believe it, bub.

Jommelli heard Mozart perform sometime in September of 1763, soon after the Mozart family had embarked on their nearly three-and-a-half year tour that has come to be known as the grand journey. It was the tour that created the Mozart legend and established Mozart as the child prodigy by whom we measure prodigies to this day. If the performance Jommelli attended was typical, it would have been a cross between a circus side show and a music recital. An advertisement written by Mozart's father for just such a production reads, in part, as follows:

> The boy will also play a concerto on the violin, accompany symphonies on the [harpsichord], completely cover the keyboard of the [harpsichord], and play on the cloth as well as though he had the keyboard under his eyes; he will accurately name from a distance any notes that may be sounded for him either singly or in chords, on the [harpsichord] or on every imaginable instrument including bells, glasses, and clocks. Lastly, he will improvise out of his head, not only on the harpsichord but also on an organ.

The ad copy Mozart's father prepared for a performance in London on June 5, 1764 (Mozart would have been eight years old) crosses the line into hucksterism:

Master Mozart of seven years of age, prodigy of nature; taking the opportunity of representing to the Public the greatest prodigy that Europe or Human Nature has to boast of. Everybody will be astonished to hear a Child of so tender [an] age play the harpsichord in such perfection—it surmounts all [that is] fantastic, and is hard to express which is more astonishing, his execution upon the harpsichord playing at Sight, or his own composition.

One of the many things we can take away from these advertisements is that the child Mozart's primary keyboard instrument was the harpsichord. The Mozart family owned a big one, one that had been built sometime around 1750 by Christian Ernst Friederici of Gera, in central East Germany.

Mozart and the Piano

So, Mozart grew up playing the harpsichord. We do not know when Mozart first played a piano. Here are a few things we do know. Up until the 1770s, pianos were still considered a novelty. They were expensive to build and most variable in quality. They were also scarce: It is likely that at the time Mozart was born in 1756 there was only one piano in his hometown of Salzburg, an instrument built by Andreas Stein and owned by the Archbishop.

We know that Johann Christian Bach—the 11th and youngest son of Johann Sebastian Bach—gave "the world's first piano recital in London in 1768." We know that the nine-year-old Mozart hung out extensively with J. C. Bach while the Mozart family lived in London in 1764 and 1765, so we suspect that the eight- or nine-year-old Mozart might have played his first piano there, in the English capitol.We know, thanks to an article in a contemporary journal called Schubart's "German Chronicle." that Mozart performed on a piano in the Munich home of one "Herr Albert" in early 1775.

We know that by 1777—by the age of 21—Mozart was thoroughly familiar with the piano. In October of 1777, he visited the workshop of Andreas Stein in the German city of Augsburg and was blown away by the pianos he played. He wrote a long letter to his father in which he described Stein's pianos at length and, in doing so, revealed his own knowledge of and fascination with this still-new instrument. We quote the letter in brief part:

I shall begin with Stein's pianofortes. Before I had seen any of his make, Späth's claviers had always been my favorites. But now I much prefer Stein's, for they damp ever so much better than [Späth's] instruments.

In whatever way I touch the keys, the tone never jars; in a word, it is always even. It is true that he does not sell a pianoforte of this kind for less than three hundred gulden, but the trouble and the labor which Stein puts into the making of it cannot be paid for. His instruments have this special advantage over others [in] that they are made with escape action. Only one maker in a hundred bothers about this. But without an escapement it is impossible to avoid jangling and vibration after the note is struck. [And] he guarantees that the sounding-board will neither break nor split.

Back, then, to what we know. We know that by the time Mozart wrote the just-quoted letter—October of 1777—he had made the switch from harpsichord to the piano. Of this switch the eminent American music scholar Nathan Broder writes:

By the end of 1777, Mozart found pianos wherever he went; and the reports of his contemporaries combined with information yielded by [his manuscripts] leave no doubt that all the [keyboard] works from that time on must have been intended for the piano. Mozart's mature piano style, to be sure, contains many elements that started life in answer to the needs of an instrument with plucked strings [meaning the harpsichord]; but its most characteristic elements are those [made possible by an instrument that employed] hammers instead of quills. Thus embellishments, being no longer needed to emphasize particular tones, tend to disappear; the melodic line acquires a more flowing, song-like character, and sustained tones appear more frequently and are used with greater effect.

Broder touches on a key issue here. Mozart's adoption of the piano was not just a matter of a young dude being attracted to a new technology. Oh no, it's much more than that, because for Mozart, the piano and his innately lyric proclivities as a composer went together like the proverbial horse and

71

carriage. The keyboard scholar Conrad Wolff points out that "there is no doubt that the melodic style of Mozart's [mature] keyboard works is indeed operatic and generally vocal. In particular, the 'aria' character of the slow movements of his sonatas has been recognized by many."

Let's hear the theme of the second movement rondo from Mozart's Piano Sonata in C Minor, K. 457, and let us be aware that this nuanced, lyric, vocally conceived music could not be successfully performed on a harpsichord. Rather, this is music conceived of and composed for the piano. [**Piano performance:** Piano Sonata in C Minor, K. 457, movement 2.] Mozart's creative predisposition towards lyric music informed every aspect of his compositional voice, including his choice of piano over the harpsichord. Yes, Mozart's style of keyboard playing was learned at the harpsichord—a minimum of extraneous movement, play from the wrist, sit centered at the keyboard—but his mature keyboard music is piano music.

So, we know that from the time Mozart settled permanently in Vienna in 1781 until his death 10 years later, the piano was his keyboard instrument of choice. We know that Mozart used a piano at his first public concert after having settled in Vienna, on April 3, 1781. Finally, we know that Mozart bought a piano of his own sometime between late 1782 and 1784, a piano built by Anton Walter of Vienna based on a design by Andreas Stein. That piano can be seen (and occasionally even heard) in the Mozart Museum in Salzburg.

Mozart's Piano Sonatas

All told, Mozart composed 19 so-called piano sonatas. The first—set in C Major and catalogued as Köchel 279—was composed in 1774, when Mozart was 18 years old. The last, in D Major, K. 576, was composed in 1788. It remains a matter of debate as to whether the first five of these sonatas— composed in 1774 and 1775—were composed for the harpsichord or the piano. It's probably a safe bet to say that they were composed to be played on either instrument. However, starting with the Sonata No. 6 in D Major, K. 284 —composed in 1775—the remainder of the sonatas were clearly composed for the piano.

The classical keyboard sonata, of which Mozart's are presumably representative, is typically a three-movement construct in which the first movement is a moderate-to-fast sonata form, the second movement a lyric respite from the dramatic rigors of the first, followed by a fast third movement, more often than not cast as a rondo.

Moments ago I asserted that Mozart's piano sonatas are presumably representative of the classical piano sonata. In reality, they are not representative at all. While we here in the 21st century perceive Mozart as being a mainstream exponent of the classical style, Mozart's contemporaries certainly did not. Oh no: For them, his music was considered "too consistently 'artful,'" a euphemism for "over-written and overly complicated." Mozart's mature works were considered by his contemporaries to be unnecessarily difficult to perform and just plain too long, containing "too many notes, dear Mozart, too many notes."

For example, Mozart's Piano Sonata in C Minor of 1784, which we will tackle in just a moment, runs 561 measures without its repeats. Most of Haydn's piano sonatas run from between 300 to 400 measures in length; even Haydn's massive (for him) Piano Sonata in E-flat major of 1794 runs but 450 measures, 111 measures shorter than Mozart's. The truth is, there's nothing typically classical about Mozart's mature music, so if we want to find solo piano music equal in dramatic scope and length to Mozart's C Minor Sonata, we will have to look forward to the bad boy from Bonn, Ludwig van Beethoven, whose own groundbreaking Piano Sonata in C Minor—composed in 1798 and also known as the "Pathétique"—runs 582 measures, the same length as Mozart's.

Please, don't get me started on this Mozart versus Beethoven thing. OK, I'm started. I wish I had a dollar for every time I've heard someone say that "Mozart's expressively milquetoast music is utterly inferior to Beethoven's." I'd change all those dollars into pennies and I'd put 'em up the nose of the next person to say it!

Some points to consider. One: Beethoven stood in awe of Mozart as he stood in awe of only two other people, living or dead: his paternal grandfather Ludwig, for whom he was named, and Johann Sebastian Bach. Two: In terms of expressive content, length and complexity Mozart's music pushed pretty much every panic button it could in the ears of his contemporary audience. Three: Had Mozart lived long enough to be affected by the revolutionary currents that so influenced Beethoven, there's no telling where his music might have gone. Four: Had Beethoven died, as Mozart did, at the age of 35, he (Beethoven) would never have composed most of the music for which he is famous, including his symphonies nos. 4 through 9, his piano concerti nos. 4 and 5, his violin concerto, his opera *Fidelio*, his middle and late string quartets, the *Missa Solemnis*; you get the picture.

In fact, Mozart singlehandedly turned the piano sonata from a small-scale genre intended for amateur amusement into a large-scale, virtuosic genre. When compared to the massive piano sonatas of the 19th century, starting, of course, with Beethoven's, Mozart's may seem relatively understated by comparison. But comparing Mozart's piano sonatas to those of the 19th century is a fool's exercise; instead we should be comparing Mozart's piano sonatas with those of his own contemporaries. Only then will we realize that it was Mozart himself who began the process of enlarging the scale, virtuosity, and artistic importance of the piano sonata. It is a fact: Mozart's piano sonatas were Beethoven's essential models, just as Beethoven's sonatas became the essential models for Schubert, Schumann, Liszt, and Brahms. Thank you. I'm done now.

Piano Sonata in C Minor, K. 457

Scale, virtuosity, expressive extremes, and idiosyncratic pianism: Mozart's C Minor has got it all!

Movement One: Sonata Form

Sonata Form is a musical form in which multiple contrasting themes— typically two in number—are introduced in a section called the exposition. Materials presented in the exposition are then developed in a section called, logically enough, the development. The themes return in their original order a section called the recapitulation. Finally, a coda will usually bring such a movement to its conclusion.

Exposition. Let's hear Mozart's theme 1 in its all its dark, heroic, C Minor glory before we talk about it. [**Piano performance:** Mozart, Piano Sonata in C Minor, K. 457, movement 1, theme 1.] Typical of Mozart, this theme features an embarrassment of melodic riches. It consists of three distinct parts, any one of which would have been adequate for the rather thriftier Haydn or Beethoven to build an entire theme.

Part one of Mozart's theme consists of the alternation of two contrasting elements. Mozart opens with a boldly rising arpeggio (that is, a broken harmony) played in octaves, a gesture that was universally known as a "Mannheim rocket." [**Piano demonstration.**] As we would correctly gather from its name, this opening musical gambit was made cliché by the house composers for the Mannheim Court Orchestra, which was considered , between roughly 1740 to 1780, to be the greatest orchestra in Europe. The rocket was a gesture that Mozart would use to striking effect in the opening of fourth movement of his Symphony in G Minor of 1788. [**Piano demonstration.**] Beethoven used a Mannheim rocket to begin his Piano Sonata No. 1 in F Minor of 1795, calculating that a rocket would be a most conspicuous way to begin his first published piano sonata. [**Piano demonstration.**]

Back to the first part of Mozart's theme 1. The rising, frankly ithyphallic (look it up!) rocket alternates with a quiet, trilling phrase of more feminine quality. Let's hear the first part of theme 1, this alternation between loud rockets and quieter, more lyric phrases, and let us be exceedingly aware that Mozart is laying out—right here, in its first eight measures—the expressive extremes of the movement. [**Piano performance:** Mozart, Piano Sonata in C Minor, K. 457, movement 1.] The second part of theme 1 features drooping, deathly, descending chromatic lines over a throbbing tremolo in the bass. [**Piano performance:** Mozart, Piano Sonata in C Minor, K. 457, movement 1.] Let's hear that again. [**Piano performance:** Mozart, Piano Sonata in C Minor, K. 457, movement 1.]

My friends, we will be neither the first nor the last to observe the resemblances—expressive, spiritual, and musical—between Mozart's Piano Sonata in C Minor and Beethoven's Piano Sonata in C Minor of 1798, also known as the "Pathétique." I would suggest that Beethoven could have played Mozart's C Minor Sonata with his hands tied behind his back, and

I've no doubt that Mozart would have been fascinated by Beethoven's sonata had he lived long enough to know it. One of the more obvious resemblances between the two pieces is this second part of Mozart's theme 1 and Beethoven's movement 1, theme 1. Again, here's Mozart's thematic phrase: consisting of descending chromatic lines heard over a throbbing tremolo in the bass. [**Piano performance:** Mozart, Piano Sonata in C Minor, K. 457, movement 1.]

Here's Beethoven's theme 1 from the first movement, which consists of ascending chromatic lines heard over a throbbing tremolo in the bass: [**Piano performance:** Beethoven, Piano Sonata in C Minor, op. 13, movement 1.] The third part of Mozart's theme 1combines melodic material drawn from part 1 with the throbbing accompaniment of part 2: [**Piano performance:** Mozart, Piano Sonata in C Minor, K. 457, movement 1, theme 3.] Once again, Mozart's theme 1 in its entirety: [**Piano performance:** Mozart, Piano Sonata in C Minor, K. 457, movement 1, theme 1.]

After a brief modulating bridge, theme 2—set in E-flat Major—begins. Like theme 1, it is a theme of extraordinary melodic variety cast in three parts. The first part of theme 2 features a lilting, graceful tune set against an undulating, broken-chord accompaniment in the pianist's left hand. [**Piano demonstration.**] For our information, this sort of accompaniment, which is ubiquitous in classical-era keyboard music, is called an Alberti bass, named for the Italian composer Domenico Alberti, who did not invent it but popularized it. Theme 2, part 1: [**Piano performance:** Mozart, Piano Sonata in C Minor, K. 457, movement 1, theme 2, part 1.]

The second part of Mozart's theme 2 constitutes a free variation of the first part, and is cast as a dialogue between the treble and bass of the piano. [**Piano performance:** Mozart, Piano Sonata in C Minor, K. 457, movement 1, theme 2, part 2.] Finally, the third part of theme 2 recalls theme 1, as dramatic, rising chromatic octaves alternate with scurrying scales and arpeggios. [**Piano performance:** Mozart, Piano Sonata in C Minor, K. 457, movement 1, theme 2, part 3.]

We are going to hear the recapitulation and concluding coma of this first movement. What I'd like us to be most aware of while we listen is the nature of Mozart's keyboard writing: With its powerful use of octaves, its accompanimental tremolos, its graded dynamics (meaning getting louder and softer), and its stark contrasts between loud and soft, this is pure piano music. [**Piano performance:** Mozart, Piano Sonata in C Minor, K. 457, movement 1, recapitulation.] According to Hermann Abert, whose magisterial 1,515 page-biography of Mozart was first published in 1924: "This opening movement [is characterized by a] constant feeling of rebellion and of sinking back, of struggle and renunciation, and ends on a note of somber resignation."

Movement Two: Rondo Form

Rondo is a musical form or process in which a principal theme—the rondo theme—is stated and then returns periodically, like a refrain, after various contrasting episodes. We heard the lyric rondo theme earlier in this lecture. That theme is the large A section in a musical structure that can be schematicized as A-B-A-C-A plus a coda. Both the contrasting B and C sections of the movement feature lush, lyric themes as well, and the two returns of the rondo theme see the theme embellished. The overall effect of the movement is one of constantly changing thematic melody, as expressively rich as a chocolate cheese cake *mit schlag*. The first contrasting episode begins this way. [**Piano performance:** Mozart, Piano Sonata in C Minor, K. 457, movement 2.] The second contrasting episode begins this way. [**Piano performance:** Mozart, Piano Sonata in C Minor, K. 457, movement 2.] We must observe the following. The second movement of Beethoven's Piano Sonata in C Minor, the "Pathétique," is also structured as a rondo, A-B-A-C-A plus coda. Beethoven's rondo theme—set in A-flat Major—begins this way. [**Piano demonstration.**] Mozart's second contrasting episode, set as well in A-flat Major, begins this way. [**Piano demonstration.**] Again, Mozart. [**Piano demonstration.**] Beethoven. [**Piano demonstration.**] As the song says, too close, too close for comfort.

Movement Three

This is a spectacular movement. Structurally, it is an odd duck: Some sources consider it a rondo, others a sonata form, and still others as a hybrid called rondo-sonata. We will be content to simply call it the third movement of Mozart's Piano Sonata in C Minor.

The movement features three sharply contrasting themes and virtually no transitional passages to soften the impact of those contrasts. The schizo-affective first theme—which we will call theme A —is cast in two spectacularly contrasting parts. Part one, quiet and melancholy, sees a series of drooping, syncopated motives heard over the simplest of accompaniments: [**Piano performance:** Mozart, Piano Sonata in C Minor, K. 457, movement 3.] This bit of "gnawing, self torment" (as one writer calls it) is followed by the loud, manic second part of the theme which twice pulls up short and stops completely after a series of explosive dissonances. [**Piano performance:** Mozart, Piano Sonata in C Minor, K. 457, movement 3.] That's crazy music, my friends: in turns hyper-agitated, explosively dissonant, disoriented, and melancholy. A single harmony effects the "transition" (if we can really call it that) to theme B. [**Piano demonstration.**]

Theme B, though initially set in E-flat Major (an ostensibly more upbeat key) is filled with a terrific sense of urgency, in part due to the constant fluctuation between piano and forte, between soft and loud that we hear throughout the theme (yeah, try doing that on a harpsichord!). Here we go, transition chord followed by theme B. [**Piano performance:** Mozart, Piano Sonata in C Minor, K. 457, movement 3.] The final thematic element in this movement, theme C, is a despairing little melody consisting almost entirely of weepy little semitones. [**Piano demonstration.**] Theme C features the same sorts of explosive dissonances and silences first heard in theme A. Theme C. [**Piano performance:** Mozart, Piano Sonata in C Minor, K. 457, movement 3.]

Rather surprisingly—given its relative brevity compared to themes A and B—it is this quietly despairing theme C that is tasked with concluding the movement. Here is that final appearance of theme C, followed by the movement and sonata-ending coda. [**Piano performance:** Mozart, Piano Sonata in C Minor, K. 457, movement 3.]

Now, if we absolutely had to schematicize this third and final movement, the schematic would read A-B-A-C-B¹-A-C plus coda. If that seems sort of random, well, that's because it is sort of random. As such, Mozart's idiosyncratic approach to large-scale form becomes a basic part of this movement's expressive message. Without the familiar structural landmarks provided by familiar musical forms, we—as listeners—cannot anticipate events, which significantly magnifies the movement's dark expressive power. Such a purposely alien formal landscape is antithetical to the classical style, and looks forward not just to the music of Beethoven but even beyond, to the highly personalized formal structures of the 19th and 20th centuries.

An Amazing Story

For over 200 years, it was believed that Mozart's Fantasy in C Minor for Piano, K. 475 was composed as a prelude for the Piano Sonata in C Minor and was thus to be performed in tandem with the sonata. However, the only things that could conclusively prove that the fantasy and the sonata were indeed part of the same piece were Mozart's handwritten manuscripts. But as Mozart's autograph manuscripts were lost, this was a puzzle that was deemed unsolvable. I turn the floor over to Eugene Wolf, a musicologist and Mozart scholar who was, for many years, on the faculty of the University of Pennsylvania in Philadelphia:

> On 31 July 1990, Judith Dibona, accounting manager at Eastern College in St. David's, Pennsylvania, was rummaging through an old safe at Eastern Baptist Theological Seminary in Philadelphia. She had gone to look for documents relating to Eastern College. The safe was rarely opened, and its contents were in disarray. An amateur pianist, DiBona's attention was attracted by two manila envelopes with the notation "Sacred Music" on the outside. Upon opening the packets, DiBona found a bound manuscript labeled "Fantasia and Sonata in C minor" that [she] immediately recognized as containing Mozart's great pair of piano works, K. 475 and 457. [Calls were made.] One of these calls came to the University of Pennsylvania, and I offered my services. However, as I was skeptical that these could be authentic sources, I [set] our appointment as late in the week as possible. This was a move I instantly regretted [when I found out] that the autographs had been missing since 1915. Upon seeing the manuscripts I knew at once that they were in fact [the] autographs. After exactly seventy-five years, the works that many consider Mozart's greatest compositions for piano had again come to light.

Can you imagine? One moment you're standing in St. David's, Pennsylvania, about 15 miles northwest of Philly, and the next you're holding handwritten manuscripts by Mozart? It was the musicological coup of a lifetime. Based upon analysis of the paper types and watermarks, the span of the staves printed on the paper, ink type and color, Wolf correctly concluded that the sonata and the fantasy had been composed as two separate works, works that could be performed together but need not be performed together.

Postscript. The autographs were auctioned at Sotheby's in London on November 21, 1990. The sale price was £880,000, roughly $1.7 million. The manuscripts were bought by a consortium of Austrian cultural institutions, and now reside at the International Mozart Foundation in Salzburg. The proceeds from the sale were used by the Eastern Baptist Theological Seminary to grow its sacred music program. All in all, a perfect ending to an amazing story.

A Piano Lesson

A Viennese physician and music lover named Joseph Frank took twelve lessons from Mozart in 1790. Dr. Frank recalled:

> I found Mozart to be a little man with a broad head and fleshy hands. He received me rather coldly. "Now," he said, "play me something!" I played him a fantasia of his own composition. "Not bad," he said, to my great astonishment, "now I'll play it for you." What a marvel! The piano became a completely different instrument under his fingers. Mozart then made a few observations about the way in which I should play his fantasia. [He then asked:] "Do you play other pieces of my composition?" "Yes, sir" I replied, "your variations on the theme Unser dummer *Pöbel* meint." "Good." [he said], "I will play the piece to you; you will derive more benefit from hearing me than [by] playing it yourself."

Yes, so would we all!

Thank you.

Beethoven—The *Appassionata* Sonata
Lecture 5

Although we are so accustomed to the image of Ludwig van Beethoven the pianist, he actually began his professional musical life as an organist. Beethoven had a frightening propensity to annihilate pianos, but that wasn't because he disliked them; he did it because he wanted to wrest from them the power and sonority he heard and felt as an organist. Among the gaggle of works that were breakaway works for Beethoven is his Piano Sonata in F Minor, Op. 57, also known as the *Appassionata* (which means "passionate"), composed between 1804 and 1806.

Movement 1: Sonata Form

- The first theme is astonishing in its simplicity and dramatic power. It consists of two elements. The first element is a falling, then rising, F-minor harmony, played in both hands two octaves apart. The effect is of something dark and ominous slithering about in some cavernous place.

- The second element of the theme consists of a dismal, imploring figure featuring a trill and followed by an **open cadence** (meaning an unresolved dissonance). Instead of the dissonance being resolved, the first element of the theme is heard again, now a **half step** higher, outlining a G-flat major harmony.

- It concludes with another open cadence—another unresolved dissonance. Instead of the dissonance being resolved, a lengthy closing phrase follows, in which the imploring, trilling figure is heard lower, then higher, each time followed by an ominous half-step motive that sounds like a funeral drum.

- The studied avoidance of any resolution in this closing passage creates a mood of existential frustration, after which an explosive arpeggiated figure leads to yet another unresolved dissonance followed by yet another pause.

- Thus far, this movement has asked a lot of questions—with its unresolved dissonances and pauses—but has yet to provide a single "answer" in the form of a harmonic resolution. And for all of its pounding, no answers are forthcoming during the second half of the theme either, during which the falling/rising F-minor harmony is viciously declaimed by crashing chords.

- The modulating bridge that follows just starts without any resolution to mark the end of theme 1. It's a brief but agitated passage characterized by repeated E-flats, the **dominant** pitch of the approaching new key of theme 2, A-flat major.

- Finally, we hear the first **closed cadence**, the first real resolution in the movement, as the repeated E-flats in the bass ease into an A-flat major chord in preparation for the entrance of theme 2. Initially, theme 2 seems to be everything that theme 1 is not—lyric, graceful, and set in a major key. Stately and regal though theme 2 appears, it is in reality theme 1 in lamb's clothing.

- These themes do not just resemble each other; they are, in truth, two different sides of the same musical personality. Despite the fact that theme 2 begins in A-flat major, it darkens and concludes in A-flat minor, with a long, falling line that descends into the same cavernous depths from which theme 1 emerged. The genius of this second theme is that Beethoven has managed to introduce a gentler, more lyric expressive element into the exposition without sacrificing its essentially tragic nature.

- The descent that concludes theme 2 gives way to a furious cadence theme that just erupts from the piano. The exposition ends, once again, without a resolution—without a defining harmonic event—by simply coming to a pause on two A-flats spaced five octaves apart.

- Beethoven does not call for a repeat of the exposition, and instead, the movement plunges headlong into the development section. By definition, a "development section" is characterized by harmonic instability. The exposition—with all of its unresolved dissonances—was not a pinnacle of harmonic stability itself, but the harmonic irresolution of the exposition is nothing compared to the onslaught of harmonic instability we hear in the development section.

- As the development section nears its conclusion, the rate of **modulation**—that is, of key change—becomes so rapid that our sense of **tonality** is shredded. Diminished seventh chords—the most dissonant harmony in Beethoven's vocabulary—sweep up and down the piano like gale-force winds. Finally, hammering

Ludwig van Beethoven (1770–1827) composed exquisite music in the period between the classical and romantic eras.

groups of three repeated notes—the funeral drum previously observed—drive the harmony back toward the **home key** of F minor for the beginning of the recapitulation.

- Low, throbbing Cs, which go on for two full measures, initiate the recapitulation. We desperately await a resolution to F minor at the beginning of the recapitulation, but we wait in vain. Even as theme 1 begins, the low C continues to thrum away in the bass, robbing us of an unambiguous resolution to F minor. At the beginning of the recapitulation, the harmonic and spiritual frustration fundamental to this movement continues unabated.

- We move next to the second half of the lengthy and magnificent coda that concludes the movement. The second half of the coda begins with an expansion of the stormy, drumming music that brought the development section to its conclusion. It is a windswept passage.

- The final section of the coda—marked *più allegro*, or "faster"—begins with an explosive resolution (finally!) to the home key of F minor. Theme 2 then begins quietly but soon becomes loud and brutally dissonant. Next, violent, gunshot-like groups of three repeated chords climb up and down the piano.

- Finally, theme 1 rises and falls one last time, disappearing into the depths, accompanied by a shivering tremolo. The final six measures of the movement consist solely of the three pitches that make up an F-minor chord. Instead of an unambiguous statement of harmonic conclusion, the music just sort of fizzles out. The effect is frustrating, and while we know that the movement is over, we also know that the "story" is not.

- Whatever Beethoven intended the dark-toned and harmonically ambiguous music of this movement to mean, no one can deny the power of such music to evoke deep metaphorical meaning. The entire sonata is about questions—questions projected by harmonic ambiguity, questions that are never answered. In the end, as will be revealed in the third movement, all that is left is death.

Movement 2: Theme and Variations Form

- The second movement is the eye of the musical hurricane, a desperately needed break between the stormy, hyper-intense outer movements. The theme is a gentle, chorale-like melody structured in two parts, with each part immediately repeated: A–A–B–B.

- This theme and the three variations that follow are all rooted in the key of D-flat major and within the predictable confines of classical **theme and variations form**. As such, this second movement stands in the greatest possible contrast with the expressive turmoil, harmonic instability, and formal idiosyncrasy of the outer movements.

- In this second movement, the coda begins with an abbreviated version of the theme presented in a sort of cubist manner, with each phrase heard in a different register of the piano. The music comes to an open cadence (an unresolved dissonance), and instead of the expected resolution, two diminished seventh chords—those incredibly dissonant harmonies that were used in the opera house to evoke terror—suddenly and unexpectedly appear, the first one pianissimo and the second one fortissimo.

- As for the "expected" resolution, once again, our expectations have been thrown bodily into the Danube. These two diminished sevenths introduce a level of harmonic disruption and expressive darkness equal to that inspired by receiving a registered letter from the IRS. But before we even have a chance to react, a vicious series of diminished seventh chords drill through our crania and obliterate entirely any remaining vestiges of calm that might have still lingered from the second movement.

- Our ears thus wiped clean, the third movement introduction begins, consisting of a quiet, rippling descending line in F minor that slowly but steadily gains momentum.

Movement 3: Sonata Form

- Theme 1 begins with a rising-and-falling sixteenth-note line that in the opera house would represent a storm. Slowly, a series of short-long motives is superimposed over the roiling "storm" music, which eventually come together to create a droopy little melody.

- The modulating bridge that follows is dominated by the storm element of theme 1. Theme 2 is a twitching little theme in C minor, a theme that offers no relief from the relentless darkness of the movement to this point.

- The cadence material the concludes the exposition combines the storm element of theme 1 with explosive, cadential chords and concludes with a huge rising/falling G-flat diminished seventh arpeggio that spans six octaves, nearly the entire width of Beethoven's six-and-a-half-octave piano.

- As per the first movement, there is no exposition repeat in the third movement. However, and most uncharacteristically, Beethoven does indicate that the development section and the recapitulation be repeated, which guarantees that the unrelentingly dark, stormy, and harmonically unstable music of the development section will become the dominant element of the movement.

- The intestine-twisting, heart-stopping coda is cast in four parts. In part 1, the driving cadential music that concluded the recapitulation is whipped into a frenzy by the indication *sempre più allegro*, meaning roughly "faster, faster, faster!"

- The second part of the coda—marked "**presto**," meaning "very fast"—introduces an entirely new theme. Although it is rather late in the game to be introducing new themes, Beethoven wants this ferocious *totentanz*—this "dance of death" in F minor—to be pretty much the last thing we remember when the sonata concludes. The expressive message is that the only answer, in the end, is death.

- From this point, it's a maniacal, careening sprint to the end of the movement. In part 3 of the coda, the storm element of theme 1 screams past with accents on the second **beat** of every measure. Finally, in part 4, a cadential phrase in F minor collapses into the depths of the piano, followed by an explosive series of F-minor chords, which provide the only unambiguous conclusion to a movement in the entire sonata.

Important Terms

beat: Smallest pulse to which we can comfortably move our bodies. *See also* **meter**.

closed cadence: Equivalent to a period or an exclamation mark; such a cadence ends on the tonic and gives a sense of rest and resolution.

dominant: Pitch and chord five pitches above a given tonic pitch/chord. The dominant harmony is the chord most closely related to the tonic chord in a given key; the dominant chord will almost always immediately precede an appearance of the tonic chord.

half step: *See* **semitone**.

home key: Main key of a movement or composition. *See also* **key**.

modulation: The process of changing key during the course of a piece of music.

open cadence: Equivalent to a comma; such a cadence pauses on the dominant harmony without resolving the tonic harmony, creating tension and the need to continue.

presto: Very fast.

theme and variations form: A classical-era formal process that exhibits a systematically varied theme in a series of variations.

tonal/tonality: Sense that one pitch is central to a section of music, as opposed to atonal/atonality.

Beethoven—The *Appassionata* Sonata
Lecture 5—Transcript

Welcome back to *The 23 Greatest Solo Piano Works*. This is Lecture 5. It is entitled Beethoven—The *Appassionata* Sonata.

Ludwig van Beethoven was born and raised in the Rhineland city of Bonn. He was baptized at the Church of St. Remigius on December 17, 1770. Since Catholic parishes required newborns to be baptized within 24 hours of birth, his assumed date of birth is December 16.

Beethoven's paternal grandfather Ludwig, for whom the child was named, was a big man around town: the *kapellmeister*—the chief of musical staff— for the Elector of Cologne, that combination prince and priest who resided in Bonn. Beethoven's mother Maria Magdalena was frail and depressed. She died tragically quite young, at the age of 40, of tuberculosis.

Beethoven's father, Johann van Beethoven, was a singer—a tenor—also in the employ of the elector's court. He was a mediocrity in all things except alcohol consumption, at which he was most accomplished. Disrespected and unrewarded by those he worked for—including his father, the *kapellmeister*—Johann van Beethoven decided that his ticket to fame and fortune would be his prodigiously gifted son, Ludwig.

The lessons began when the child was about five. They were marked by a brutality that scarred him for life. Beethoven biographer Edmund Morris writes:

> Neighbors of the Beethovens recall seeing a small boy "standing in front of the clavier and weeping." He was so short he had to climb a footstool to reach the keys. If he hesitated, his father beat him. When he was allowed off, it was only to have a violin thrust into his hands, or musical theory drummed into his head. There were few days when he was not flogged or locked up in the cellar. Johann also deprived him of sleep, waking him at midnight for more hours of practice.

Alas, Johann van Beethoven's plans to make his son the next Mozart came to naught; there could be only one Mozart. What he did succeed in doing was to make his son hate him, and by association, authority figures in general. According to a psychiatric study of Beethoven written by Edith and Richard Sterba: "An early rebellion against his father laid the foundation for the revolt against every kind of authority which appears in Beethoven with an intensity which can only be described as highly unusual."

Thankfully, the young dude did not hate music. Instead, it became his refuge, his solace, his escape from the misery of his domestic life. And more than any other instrument, it was the organ that provided young Beethoven his happiest place. Well before he turned 10, Beethoven had taken it upon himself to seek out lessons from various organists who worked in Bonn. In the process, he got access to the three pipe organs in town: the one in the electoral chapel, the one at the minorite monastery, and the one in Bonn's towering Romanesque basilica known as the Münster.

In the fall of 1781, the still 10-year-old Beethoven began studying organ and music composition with the newly appointed court organist, a 33-year-old Lutheran from Leipzig named Christian Gottlob Neefe. Neefe introduced Beethoven to the music of Johann Sebastian Bach, and it was love at first hear. Beethoven learned (and memorized) all 48 preludes and fugues from Bach's *The Well-Tempered Clavier* books one and two, and over time mastered Bach's gut-wrenchingly powerful organ music.

Power. Power. That's the feeling you get when you play a big pipe organ. Its huge, all-enveloping sound; its kidney-rattling bass; its orchestral range of sonority and its ability to sustain forever. As it turned out, the pipe organ preconditioned Beethoven's ears and hands for the rest of his life. Till the end of his days, Beethoven sought to capture in his orchestral music the same spacious, multi-layered, bass-heavy muscularity he felt and heard when he played the organ. And to the end of his life, he sought to pull from the piano the same range of color, sonority, and power he felt at the organ.

My friends, we are so accustomed to our image of Beethoven the pianist that it's easy to forget that he began his professional musical life as an organist. His first regular, paid job was as an organist: In February of 1784, the

13-year-old Beethoven was appointed assistant court organist. At 16 he was appointed court organist, which allowed him to wear a sword on his left side. The organ did not just give Beethoven a salary, it gave him status. As one biographer observes: "[Beethoven] would have been a rare teenager if he did not delight in mounting the palace organ loft is all his finery, and letting go with the loudest possible blast from the big pipes."

Now, of course, most people do not have pipe organs in their homes. But they did—in ever increasing numbers—have pianos in their homes. Beethoven played those pianos all the time. But, conditioned as he was by the organ, he didn't play those pianos like the lightweight, harpsichord-derived constructs of balsa wood and dental floss that they were. No; he played them as if they were organs, with often disastrous results. An oft-told story bears retelling. Beethoven's friend, Anton Reicha, related that one evening, when Beethoven was playing a Mozart concerto at court:

> He asked me to turn pages for him. But I was mostly occupied in wrenching out the strings of the pianoforte that had snapped, while the hammers got stuck among the broken strings. Beethoven insisted upon finishing the concerto, and so back and forth I leapt, jerking out a string, disentangling a hammer, turning a page. I worked [much] harder than Beethoven.

Beethoven had a frightening propensity to annihilate pianos. But that wasn't because he disliked them or once saw a piano wink at his mother. No; he did it because he wanted to wrest from them the power and sonority he heard and felt as an organist. When Beethoven was 20, a most perceptive critic named Carl Ludwig Junker heard him play and observed, "his playing is so different from the usual styles of performance that it appears he has attained the height of perfection on which he now stands by a path of his own." And you know what? That he had. Harold Schonberg, for many years the principal music critic for the New York Times writes:

> Beethoven was, in many respects, a self-taught pianist. His instructors were not professional pianists. Professionals, when they teach, instill in their pupils the proper respect for their instrument, and in 99 cases out of a hundred, the instrument ends up being more

important than the music. Quite the reverse is true with Beethoven, who turned out to be a musician first, and a pianist second.

To which we would add, "a musician first, an organist second, and a pianist third."

Vienna

The trip: In November of 1792, Beethoven took the five-day stagecoach from Bonn to the capital city of German music: Vienna. The plan was to study with Haydn for a year or two, pick up some of that high-end Viennese cache, and head back to Dullsville—meaning Bonn—to work as a musical functionary for the elector. The reality: Beethoven's lessons with Haydn were a disaster and Beethoven never set foot in Bonn again. And when his stipend from the elector was cut off, it made not a shred of difference, because Beethoven, almost overnight, had become the darling of the piano-crazed Viennese aristocracy. According to Dieter Hildebrandt, "In Vienna, Beethoven established his fame with three strokes of genius: his impetuous virtuosity at the keyboard, his unprecedented talent for improvisation, and his rudeness, which must have reminded civilized Vienna of that archetypal character of the 18th-century novel, *The Noble Savage*."

Ten years later, in 1802, the not-yet 32-year-old Beethoven was smokin' hot. His first symphony had been publically premiered to great acclaim; his first two piano concerti had been publically performed and published; and his first six string quartets were getting wide circulation. Most tellingly: His name was been uttered alongside that of Haydn and Mozart. What no one could know—because Beethoven made sure that no one knew except his doctors and a few close friends—was that in tiny, agonizing increments, he was losing his hearing.

As we now know, Beethoven's hearing loss was slowly disabling. It began around 1796, when he was in his mid-20s. For years he had good hearing days and bad hearing days, and he was still playing piano publicly (although not very successfully) as late as 1812. By 1818 Beethoven was clinically deaf: completely deaf in his right ear and able to hear only low-frequency sounds in his left.

Beethoven hit a "hearing disability-inspired" emotional wall during the fall of 1802, a few months shy of his 32nd birthday. He was holed up in the Viennese suburb of Heilegenstadt, attempting to finish his second symphony. In a document now known as the Heilegenstadt Testament, he wrote out his will, contemplated suicide and railed against God and humankind for his fate. By late 1802, Beethoven's worst fears would seem to have come to pass: He believed himself to be, once again, abused and alone, as he had been as a child; he was, once again, enraged by the unfairness of God and fate. How would any of us dig our way out of such a physical, emotional, and spiritual hole? How would we deal with such overwhelming frustration and isolation, with ill health, and the prospect of professional disaster?

For Beethoven in late 1802, it was gut-check time; his choice, frankly, was innovate or die. Happily for everyone, he chose to innovate. Inspired equally by the spirit of individual empowerment engendered by the Enlightenment, the heady sense of inevitable change created by the French Revolution, and by the heroic model of Napoleon Bonaparte, Beethoven fashioned for himself a heroic self-image, one that allowed him to funnel his rage, alienation, passion, and imagination into a music the likes of which no one had ever before heard. Central to Beethoven's reinvention was his conviction that his music must be, first and foremost, a vehicle for self-expression. Beethoven's tremendous emotional stress led to a proactive compositional stance, and he emerged from his depression with a vision of himself as a hero struggling with and triumphing over fate itself.

Rebirth

The musical poster child for Beethoven rebirth is his Symphony No. 3—the aptly named *Eroica* or "Heroic Symphony"—composed in 1803 and 1804 and first publically performed in 1805. It is appropriate that *Eroica* should be considered Beethoven's watershed work, given that a symphony was in Beethoven's day the single most important and public artistic declaration a composer could make.

However, there is a gaggle—by my count, six—other works, all written during the same period, that were breakaway works as well: the Violin Sonata in A Major of 1803, also known as the "Kreutzer Sonata"; the Piano

Sonata in C Major of 1804, also known as the "Waldstein Sonata"; the three String Quartets of Op. 59 of 1805 and 1806, also known as the "Razumovsky Quartets," and the Piano Sonata in F Minor composed between 1804 and 1806, also known as the *Appassionata*.

Piano Sonata in F Minor, Op. 57, *Appassionata*

Appassionata means "passionate." It's an awful nickname, one that has nothing to do with the true spirit of the piece. I would suggest three much more appropriate nicknames: the tragic, the ominous, and the unresolved.

Movement I: Sonata Form

The first theme is astonishing in its simplicity and dramatic power. It consists of two elements. Element one is a falling, then rising F Minor harmony, played in both hands two octaves apart. The effect is of something dark and ominous slithering about in some cavernous place. [**Piano performance:** Beethoven, Sonata No. 23 in F Minor, op. 57, movement 1.]

The second element of the theme consists of a dismal, imploring figure featuring a trill and followed by an open cadence (meaning an unresolved dissonance). [**Piano performance:** Beethoven, Sonata No. 23 in F Minor, op. 57, movement 1.] And then, silence. Does the dissonance resolve? No it does not. Instead, element 1 of the theme is heard again, now a half-step higher, outlining a G-flat Major harmony. It concludes with another open cadence, another unresolved dissonance. [**Piano performance:** Beethoven, Sonata No. 23 in F Minor, op. 57, movement 1.]

Is this dissonance resolved? No, it is not. Instead, a lengthy closing phrase follows, in which the imploring, trilling figure is heard lower, then higher, each time followed by an ominous half-step motive that sounds to my ears like a funeral drum. [**Piano demonstration.**]

The studied avoidance of any resolution in this closing passage creates a mood of existential frustration, after which an explosive arpeggiated figure leads to yet another unresolved dissonance followed by yet another pause. [**Piano performance:** Beethoven, Sonata No. 23 in F Minor, op. 57, movement 1.]

Thus far, this movement has asked a lot of questions—with its unresolved dissonances and pauses—but has yet to provide a single answer in the form of a harmonic resolution. And for all of its pounding, no answers are forthcoming during the second half of the theme either, during which the falling/rising F Minor harmony is viciously declaimed by crashing chords. Here's that second half of theme 1: [**Piano performance:** Beethoven, Sonata No. 23 in F Minor, op. 57, movement 1.]

The modulating bridge that follows just starts without any resolution to mark the end of theme 1. It's a brief but agitated passage characterized by repeated E-flats, the dominant pitch of the approaching new key of theme 2, A-flat Major. Here's the modulating bridge. [**Piano performance:** Beethoven, Sonata No. 23 in F Minor, op. 57, movement 1.]

Check it out: We're about to hear the first closed cadence, the first real resolution in the movement, as the repeated E-flats in the bass ease into an A-flat Major chord in preparation for the entrance of theme 2. It sounds like this. [**Piano demonstration.**] Dang that's a relief. Theme 2 follows. Initially, it would seem to be everything theme 1 is not—lyric, graceful, and set in a major key. Theme 2: [**Piano performance:** Beethoven, Sonata No. 23 in F Minor, op. 57, movement 1.]

Stately and regal though theme 2 appears, it is—in reality—theme 1 in lamb's clothing. Let us compare theme 2's arpeggiated shape and rhythmic profile with theme 1. First, theme 1. [**Piano demonstration.**] And now theme two. [**Piano demonstration.**] These themes do not just "resemble" each other; they are, in truth, two different sides of the same musical personality. Despite the fact that Theme Two begins in A-flat Major, it darkens and concludes in A-flat Minor, with a long, falling line that descends into the same cavernous depths from which theme 1 emerged.

The genius of this second theme is that Beethoven has managed to introduce a gentler, more lyric expressive element into the exposition without sacrificing its essentially "tragic" nature. Let's hear theme 2 again. [**Piano**

performance: Beethoven, Sonata No. 23 in F Minor, op. 57, movement 1.] The descent that concludes theme 2 gives way to a furious cadence theme that like Beethoven's own gastric issues, just erupts from the bowels of the piano. The exposition ends, once again, without a resolution, without a defining harmonic event, by simply coming to a pause on two A-flats spaced five octaves apart. Let's hear the cadence material and the conclusion of the exposition. [**Piano performance:** Beethoven, Sonata No. 23 in F Minor, op. 57, movement 1.]

Beethoven does not call for a repeat of the exposition, and instead, the movement plunges headlong into the development section. By definition, a development section will be characterized by harmonic instability. Well, the truth be told, the exposition—with all of its unresolved dissonances—was not a pinnacle of harmonic stability itself. But the harmonic irresolution of the exposition is nothing compared to the onslaught of harmonic instability we hear in the development section.

As the development section nears its conclusion, the rate of modulation— that is, key change—becomes so rapid that our sense of tonality is shredded like the sails of a three-master in a 100-knot wind. Diminished seventh chords—the most dissonant harmony in Beethoven's vocabulary—sweep up and down the piano like gale force winds. It is a passage described by the famed English musicologist Sir Donald Francis Tovey as being, "Inarticulate. Melody disappears and harmony becomes ambiguous. Rhythm itself would disappear but for the fact that, so long as we remain conscious, we cannot get rid of time. The passion is beyond utterance."

Finally, hammering groups of three repeated notes—the funeral drum idea we previously observed—drive the harmony back towards the home key of F Minor for the beginning of the recapitulation. Let's hear this entire, most disturbing passage, starting with the diminished seventh-chord hurricane, through the hammering, funeral-drum episode and ending with the thrumming low Cs that will eventually initiate the recapitulation. [**Piano performance:** Beethoven, Sonata No. 23 in F Minor, op. 57, movement 1.]

The low, throbbing Cs that concluded that excerpt go on for two full measures. We desperately await a resolution to F Minor at the beginning of the Recapitulation. Well, we wait in vain! You see, even as theme 1 begins, the low C continues to thrum away in the bass, robbing us of an unambiguous resolution to F Minor. Here at the beginning of the recapitulation, the harmonic and spiritual frustration fundamental to this movement continues unabated. Let's hear the stormy and drumming end of the development section once again, though this time followed by the first half of theme 1 in the recapitulation. [**Piano performance:** Beethoven, Sonata No. 23 in F Minor, op. 57, movement 1.]

We move forward to the second half of the lengthy and magnificent coda that concludes the movement. The second half of the coda begins with an expansion of the stormy, drumming music that brought the development section to its conclusion. Let's hear this windswept passage, one described by Wilfrid Mellers as "a maelstrom of kaleidoscopic arpeggios [that] induces chaos!" [**Piano performance:** Beethoven, Sonata No. 23 in F Minor, op. 57, movement 1.]

And now, Vesuvius! The final section of the coda, marked *più allegro*, ("faster"), begins with an explosive resolution finally to the home key of F Minor. Theme 2 then begins quietly but soon becomes loud and brutally dissonant. Next, violent, gunshot-like groups of three repeated chords climb up and down the piano. Finally, theme 1 rises and falls one last time, disappearing into the depths, accompanied by a shivering tremolo. The final six measures of the movement consist solely of the three pitches that make up an F Minor chord. And here we go again: instead of an unambiguous statement of harmonic conclusion that might sound like this— [**Piano demonstration.**]—the music just sort of fizzles out. The effect is frustrating, and while we know that the movement is over, we also know that the story is not! Here's the remainder of the coda. [**Piano performance:** Beethoven, Sonata No. 23 in F Minor, op. 57, movement 1.]

We cannot help but ask, what is this dark-toned and harmonically ambiguous music supposed to mean? Lacking an explanation from the B-man himself, we are left to our own metaphoric devices. According to the eminent American Beethoven scholar Lewis Lockwood, the movement is a metaphor for "sexual arousal, postponement of fulfillment, and eventual fulfillment." Ahem. Yeah.

Look, whatever Beethoven intended the movement to mean, no one can deny the power of such music to evoke deep metaphorical meaning. In my opinion, the entire sonata is about questions, questions projected by harmonic ambiguity, questions that are never answered. In the end—as we will discover when we get to the third movement—all that is left is death. It's all very nihilistic, very proto-punk.

Movement II: Theme and Variations Form

The second movement is the eye of the musical hurricane, a desperately needed break between the stormy, hyper-intense outer movements. The theme is a gentle, chorale-like melody structured in two parts, with each part immediately repeated: A-A-B-B. Let's hear the theme. [**Piano performance:** Beethoven, Sonata No. 23 in F Minor, op. 57, movement 2.]

This theme and the three variations that follow are all rooted in the key of D-flat Major and within the predictable confines of classical theme-and-variations form. As such, this second movement stands in the greatest possible contrast with the expressive turmoil, harmonic instability, and formal idiosyncrasy of the outer movements.

We advance to the coda of this second movement. The coda begins with an abbreviated version of the theme presented in a sort of cubist manner, with each phrase of the theme heard in a different register of the piano. The music comes to an open cadence (an unresolved dissonance), and instead of the expected resolution, two diminished seventh chords—those incredibly dissonant harmonies that were used in the opera house to evoke terror—suddenly and unexpectedly appear, the first one pianissimo. [**Piano demonstration.**] And the second one, fortissimo. [**Piano demonstration.**]

As for the expected resolution, well, once again our expectations have been thrown bodily into the Danube. These two diminished sevenths introduce a level of harmonic disruption and expressive darkness equal to that inspired by receiving a registered letter from the IRS. But before we even have a chance to react, a vicious series of diminished seventh chords drill through our crania and obliterate entirely any remaining vestiges of calm that might have still lingered from the second movement. Our ears thus wiped clean, the third movement introduction begins, consisting of a quiet, rippling descending line in F Minor that slowly but steadily gains momentum.

Let's hear it all: the cubist second movement coda; the interrupted cadence; the vicious, brain-drilling series of diminished seventh chords; and the rippling introduction to the third movement. [**Piano performance:** Beethoven, Sonata No. 23 in F Minor, op. 57, movements 2–3.]

Movement III: Sonata Form

We are going to hear the entire exposition straight on through. Theme 1 begins with a rising and falling sixteenth-note line that in the opera house would represent a storm. Slowly, a series of short-long motives is superimposed over the roiling-storm music, which eventually come together to create this droopy little melody. [**Piano demonstration.**] The modulating bridge that follows is dominated by the storm element of theme 1. Theme 2 is a twitching little theme in C Minor, a theme that offers no relief whatsoever from the relentless darkness of the movement to this point. [**Piano demonstration.**] The cadence material the concludes the exposition combines the storm element of theme 1 with explosive, cadential chords, and concludes with a ginormous rising/falling G-flat diminished seventh arpeggio that spans six full octaves, nearly the entire width of Beethoven's 6½-octave piano. The exposition: [**Piano performance:** Beethoven, Sonata No. 23 in F Minor, op. 57, movement 3.]

As per the first movement, there is no exposition repeat here in the third movement. However, and most uncharacteristically, Beethoven does indicate that the development section and the recapitulation be repeated, which guarantees that the unrelentingly dark, stormy and harmonically unstable music of the development section will become the dominant element of the movement.

For us, time demands that we move directly on to the intestine -twisting, heart-stopping coda. The coda is cast in four parts. In part 1, the driving cadential music that concluded the recapitulation is whipped into a frenzy by the indication *sempre più allegro*, which means, roughly, "faster, faster you fool, faster!" [**Piano performance:** Beethoven, Sonata No. 23 in F Minor, op. 57, movement 3.]

The second part of the Coda — marked *presto*, meaning "very fast"— introduces an entirely new theme. Yes, it is rather late in the game to be introducing new themes, but Beethoven wants this ferocious *totentanz*—this "dance of death" in F Minor—to be pretty much the last thing we remember when the sonata concludes. The expressive message is that the only answer in the end is death. [**Piano performance:** Beethoven, Sonata No. 23 in F Minor, op. 57, movement 3.]

From here it's a maniacal, careening sprint to the end of the movement. In part 3 of the coda, the storm element of theme 1 screams past with accents on the second beat of every measure. Finally, in part 4, a cadential phrase in F Minor collapses into the depths of the piano, followed by an explosive series of F Minor chords, which provide the only unambiguous conclusion to a movement in the entire sonata! Let's do it: parts 3 and 4 of the coda, and with them, the conclusion of the *Appassionata*! [**Piano performance:** Beethoven, Sonata No. 23 in F Minor, op. 57, movement 3.]

Beethoven's Piano

The piano Beethoven owned at the time he composed the *Appassionata* was an Erard, built in Paris in 1803. The piano had a range of 6½ octaves and was 222 centimeters (or 7' 3¾") in length. That was as big as pianos came in those days, and the *Appassionata* uses every inch of it.

Beethoven beat the living daylights out of the Erard for seven years, until 1810, at which point it had become, by his own admission, "useless." It's amazing that any contemporary piano could hold up for seven years under Beethoven's heavy paws. For our information: the piano can be seen today at the Upper Austrian State Museum in Linz, Austria.

Thank you.

Beethoven—*Diabelli Variations*, Op. 120
Lecture 6

There is a general consensus that the two greatest works ever written for keyboard are Johann Sebastian Bach's *Goldberg Variations* of 1741 and Ludwig van Beethoven's *Diabelli Variations* of 1823. The *Diabelli Variations* is a work in which Beethoven reveals in Anton Diabelli's nondescript waltz an unforeseen variety of musical possibilities and expressive states. This is, in turn, what Beethoven's mature compositional art had always been about—about finding transformational, developmental, and variational gold in the commonplace, about creating palaces of sound from tiny, nondescript musical bricks, about discovering the world in a grain of sand.

Diabelli's Project

- Beethoven's *Diabelli Variations* was the brainchild of the Vienna-based music publisher, editor, and composer named Anton Diabelli, who was born outside of Salzburg in 1781 and died in Vienna in 1858. He started his music publishing business in 1817 and quickly built a reputation as a savvy businessman by arranging and publishing a wide variety of popular music—dance music, operatic excerpts, and popular theater songs—for amateurs, to be played at home.

- Sometime in the first half of 1819, Diabelli sent a **waltz** of his own composition to 50 composers living in Austria, inviting each composer to write a single variation on the theme. Diabelli's plan was to publish the set as an anthology entitled "Patriotic Artist's Club," with the profits to benefit widows and orphans of the Napoleonic Wars.

- When Ludwig van Beethoven received Diabelli's theme, his initial reaction to the project and the theme was not good. Beethoven dismissed the theme as a *schusterfleck* (a "cobbler's patch"). Diabelli's theme consists of four phrases that can be schematicized as *a–a–b–b*, which is considered binary form. The theme has no charm.

- Beethoven started thinking about the harmonic framework of the theme. It begins with four measures of a **tonic** C-major chord followed by four measures of a G-dominant seventh. The harmonic turnover then begins to accelerate, as first the subdominant and then the dominant are **tonicized**. Finally, the harmonic turnover goes into hyperdrive as the submediant is tonicized followed by a full modulation to the dominant. It is this harmonic compression that caught Beethoven's attention and convinced him to write a set of variations of his very own.

A waltz composed by Anton Diabelli (1781–1858) is what Beethoven's *Diabelli Variations* is based on.

- For Beethoven, it was not Diabelli's thematic melody but, rather, the underlying harmonic structure that became the theme of his variations. The result is a set of variations of unprecedented harmonic nuance and complexity.

- In early 1819, at some point after dismissing Diabelli's theme as a "cobbler's patch," Beethoven decided to accept Diabelli's offer after all. But Beethoven made it clear that his contribution would be a set of variations, the number of which had yet to be determined. Beethoven put aside his work on the *Missa Solemnis* and began work on the variations, and by the summer of 1819, he had completed 23 of them. But then he stopped and put the variations aside for nearly four years in order to complete the *Missa Solemnis* and compose his final three piano sonatas. He finally returned to the variations in February 1823 and finished the set in March or April.

Beethoven and Bach

- No music was more important to Beethoven both early and late in his life than that of Johann Sebastian Bach. While Bach's large-scale vocal and orchestral music fell into obscurity after his death in 1750, his keyboard music did not, and it was used as a pedagogic tool throughout the late 18th and early 19th centuries. Beethoven grew up playing Bach's *The Well-Tempered Clavier* and Bach's organ music.

- Beethoven was almost certainly given a hand-copied edition of Bach's *Goldberg Variation* by one of his Viennese patrons, probably the diplomat named Baron Gottfried van Swieten. In 1817, the *Goldberg Variations* was published in Zurich, two years before Beethoven began the *Diabelli Variations*. The point is that Beethoven knew the *Goldberg Variations*, and it exerted a primary influence on the *Diabelli Variations*.

- Three variations in the *Diabelli Variations* were explicitly inspired by Bach, all of them placed later in the set: numbers 24, 31, and 32. As the *Diabelli Variations* progresses, it grows closer to the spirit of Bach. Variation 24 is a slow, quiet fugue, with the devotional sensibility of an organ prelude.

- Variation 31 was inspired by the 25th variation of the *Goldberg Variations*. Both variations are slow, set in **triple meter** and in minor; both are highly embellished and sublimely expressive. Bach's variation is haunting and tragic; it begins with a series of gentle roulades, each followed by a sighing descent. Beethoven's variation 31 likewise begins with a series of gentle roulades, each followed by a sighing descent.

- The next and second-to-last variation—number 32—reflects, as well, Beethoven's assimilation of the ethos and technique of Johann Sebastian Bach even as it brings the *Diabelli Variations* to its climax. The variation is a fugue of extraordinary power and complexity.

- In a work by Bach, a lengthy and complex fugue (like this one) would symbolize the Utopian achievement of truth, wisdom, balance, and faith. As such, in Bach, a fugue like this one would conclude the work in which it appeared—but not in Beethoven's *Diabelli Variations.*

- About two minutes in, the fugue suddenly breaks off. A rippling diminished seventh arpeggio purges the fugue from our ears and is followed by a mysterious series of harmonies that dissipate the energy and prepare us for what is to follow. The conclusion to the fugue is both strange and wonderful. It transports us to the 33rd and final variation, which dwells in a place of transcendent peace.

Larger Organization
- Beethoven's *Diabelli Variations* consists of 34 discrete sections of music—a theme followed by 33 variations. Given the majesty and momentum of the piece and Beethoven's propensity to build grand musical structures from the smallest of musical ideas, it is virtually impossible to perceive the *Diabelli Variations* as consisting of 34 separate parts related only to the theme itself.

- Beethoven's inspiration for the *Diabelli Variations*—Bach's *Goldberg Variations*—is designed with the precision of a Swiss chronometer: Bach's 30 variations are explicitly organized in 10 groups of three and two larger groups of 15. The variational grouping in the *Diabelli Variations* is not as symmetrical. Rather, Beethoven's groupings have to do with moment-to-moment narrative flow and are not the product—as they are in the *Goldberg Variations*—of a carefully conceived, precompositional blueprint.

- The 33 variations of Beethoven's *Diabelli Variations* are grouped into three parts. Variations 1 through 10 constitute the first part, variations 11 through 20 the second part, and variations 21 through 33 the third part. In order to perceive these divisions, the last variation in each of these groups has to sound somehow like an ending, and the first variation in each group has to sound somehow like a beginning.

- The first large group concludes with variation 10, which is the most brilliant of all the variations—a whirlwind of break-neck speed, filled with trills, tremolos, and staccato octave scales. The gentle, delicate, roulade-filled variation 11 that follows sounds like a new beginning, a blossom opening at dawn.

- This second grouping of variations concludes with variation 20. With its incredible degree of harmonic ambiguity, its placement low in the piano and its rhythmic stasis, variation 20 offers an enigmatic stillness unique to the piece. The fast, loud, trilling, and registrally all-encompassing variation 21 that follows creates a shocking degree of contrast that, once again, sounds like a new beginning.

- Generally, the first group of variations—numbers 1 through 10—is cumulative, with each successive variation growing out of some aspect of the one that preceded it. Generally, the second group of variations—numbers 11 through 20—displays an increasing degree of disassociation and contrast, climaxed by the enigmatic variation 20. Generally, the third group of variations—variations 21 through 33—moves toward Bach, toward the explicit references to Bach that are variations 31 and 32. Variation 33 stands apart from this Bach revival.

Variation 33
- Beethoven labels variation 33 *tempo di menuetto moderato*, meaning "in the moderate tempo of a **minuet**," which is a moderate three-step dance of French origin that became, during the classical era, something of a cliché—a predictable (if elegant) middle movement that evoked the elite, aristocratic ballrooms from which it had emerged. Beethoven had no use for the minuet's aristocratic pretentions, so early in his career he did away with composing them entirely.

- So, at the very end of his last major keyboard work, Beethoven evokes an antique musical genre and expressive sensibility that years before he had personally rendered obsolete. The exquisite nostalgia evoked in the opening of variation 33 looks back to a time before the previous 32 variations, to a time before Diabelli's theme—before Beethoven's deafness and before Napoleon—to an idealized past of order and elegance, youth and beauty.

- Beethoven concluded his 32nd and final piano sonata—the Piano Sonata in C Minor, Op. 111, completed in January of 1822—with the same sort of minuet-inspired nostalgia. That two-movement piano sonata ends with a massive, 18-minute-long theme-and-variations-form movement based on a moderately slow, lightly dancing, triple-meter theme set in C major. Like the Piano Sonata in C Minor of 1822, the *Diabelli Variations* of 1823 concludes in C major on a note of good cheer and peace.

Important Terms

minuet: A dance of the 17th and 18th centuries, graceful and dignified, in moderately slow three-quarter time.

tonic: Home pitch and chord of a piece of tonal music. Think of the term as being derived from "tonal center" (tonic). For example, if a movement is in C, the pitch C is the tonic pitch, and the harmony built on C is the tonic chord.

tonicization: The process of creating a temporary tonic by articulating a dominant-to-tonic progression of a key other than the one currently in use.

triple meter: Metrical pattern having three beats to a measure.

waltz: A dance of Austrian/Viennese origin in triple meter.

Beethoven—*Diabelli Variations*, Op. 120

Lecture 6—Transcript

Welcome back to *The 23 Greatest Solo Piano Works*. This is Lecture 6, and it is entitled Beethoven—*Diabelli Variations*, Op. 120.

There is a general consensus—for whatever it's worth—that the two greatest works ever composed for keyboard are Johann Sebastian Bach's the *Goldberg Variations* of 1741 and Beethoven's *Diabelli Variations* of 1823. According to the venerable English musicologist Sir Donald Francis Tovey, the *Diabelli Variations* is: "the greatest of all variations works." The pianist Alfred Brendel goes a step further when he asserts that the *Diabelli Variations* is "the greatest of all piano works."

Certainly the publisher of the *Diabelli Variations*—Anton Diabelli himself, the man who composed the theme on which Beethoven's variations are based—believed the piece to be among the greatest ever composed for the keyboard, and he was pleased as punch to be its publisher. He announced its publication in June of 1823 with the following notice, which is equal parts salesmanship and truth:

> We present to the world a great and important masterpiece, a work as only Beethoven and no other can produce. The most original structures and ideas, the boldest musical idioms and harmonies are here exhausted; every pianoforte effect based on a solid technique is employed, and this work is the more interesting from the fact that it is elicited from a theme which no one would otherwise have supposed capable of a working-out of that character in which our exalted Master stands alone among his contemporaries. These variations will entitle the work to a place beside Sebastian Bach's famous masterpiece in the same form, [the *Goldberg Variations*].

During the course of his notice, Diabelli also mentions that Beethoven's piece requires a solid technique. That my friends is a major understatement. In fact, the *Diabelli Variations* is one the most technically difficult works in the repertoire to perform, a piece that makes tremendous intellectual demands on performers and listeners alike. Thus a paradox: This arguably greatest of all piano works is rarely performed and generally unknown to the music-loving public.

The "Project"

Beethoven's *Diabelli Variations* was the brainchild of the Vienna-based music publisher, editor, and composer Anton Diabelli. His Italian surname notwithstanding, Diabelli was Austrian: He was born outside of Salzburg in 1781 and died in Vienna in 1858. He started his music-publishing business in 1817, and quickly built a reputation as a savvy businessman by arranging and publishing a wide variety of popular music—dance music, operatic excerpts, and popular theater songs—for amateurs, to be played at home.

But Diabelli was also a man of taste who was willing to take risks in the name of art. For example, he was the first to publish the music of a shy and obscure Viennese composer named Franz Schubert, and Diabelli remained a champion of Schubert's music for 30 years after Schubert's death in 1828.

Sometime in the first half of 1819, Diabelli sent a waltz of his own composition to 50 composers living in Austria, inviting each composer to write a single variation on the theme. Diabelli's plan was to publish the set as an anthology entitled "Patriotic Artists' Club," with the profits to benefit widows and orphans of the Napoleonic Wars. The list of composers who contributed variations reads like both a who is who and a who is no longer who of contemporary Austrian music.

Among the "known" composers who contributed variations were Franz Schubert, Johann Hummel, Ignaz Moscheles, and Carl Czerny. Czerny also arranged for one of his piano students to provide a variation, an 11-year-old wunderkind from Hungary named Franz Liszt. The roster of forgotten composers is long, and is headed by the name Franz Xaver Wolfgang Mozart, Mozart's youngest surviving son; and further includes such non-household names as Ignaz Assmayer, Carl Maria von Bocklet, Leopold Eustachius Czapek, Johann Baptist Gänsbacher, Johann Peter Pixis, and a host of other long-forgotten composers.

The Theme

Ludwig van Beethoven also received Diabelli's theme. His initial reaction to the project and the theme was not good. Writing with excruciating English restraint, Donald Francis Tovey observed that "Beethoven was about to begin the Ninth Symphony, and his first impulse was doubtless to advise Diabelli —with Beethovenish precision—to go elsewhere!" Beethoven dismissed Diabelli's theme as a *schusterfleck*: a cobbler's patch. Let's hear Diabelli's *schusterfleck*, which consists of four phrases which can be schematicized as A-A-B-B, something called binary form. [**Piano performance:** Beethoven, *Diabelli Variations*, op. 120, Diabelli's theme.]

No doubt about it; Diabelli's theme has all the charm of an ingrown nail. But then Beethoven started thinking about the harmonic framework of the theme. It begins with four measures of a tonic C-Major chord followed by four measures of a G-dominant seventh chord. [**Piano demonstration.**] The harmonic turnover then begins to accelerate, as first the sub-dominant and then the dominant are tonicized. [**Piano demonstration.**] Finally, the harmonic turnover goes into hyperdrive as the submediant is tonicized followed by a full modulation to the dominant! [**Piano demonstration.**] It is this harmonic compression that caught Beethoven's attention big-time and convinced him to write a set of variations of his very own. [**Piano demonstration.**] For Beethoven, it was not Diabelli's thematic melody, but rather the underlying harmonic structure that became the theme of his variations. The result is a set of variations of unprecedented harmonic nuance and complexity.

In his book *Structural Functions of Harmony*, the twentieth century composer Arnold Schoenberg—himself no stranger to harmonic complexity—asserts that the *Diabelli Variations* "in respect of its harmony, deserves to be called the most adventurous work by Beethoven." Let's hear Diabelli's theme again. [**Piano performance:** Beethoven, *Diabelli Variations*, op. 120, Diabelli's theme.]

To my ear, Diabelli's theme sounds less like a complete thematic entity than it does an accompaniment to an implied thematic entity. I believe this is how Beethoven heards Diabelli's theme as well: as a plastic object of utter neutrality that could be manipulated any way he chose. As for the tiny little blips and burps that pass for Diabelli's "melodic" ideas—[**Piano demonstration.**]—Beethoven will use them (or not use them) as he sees fit. For example, variation 22 is Beethoven's famous parody variation of Leporello's aria "Night and day I slave away", from Mozart's opera *Don Giovanni*. Beethoven bases this variation on the oscillating perfect fourths in the bass of Diabelli's theme. [**Piano demonstration.**]

Beethoven pulls these oscillating fourths out of the bass, re-rhythmicizes them, and ends up with this variation. [**Piano performance:** Beethoven, *Diabelli Variations*, op. 120, variation 22.] Leporello's aria "Night and day I slave away" from Mozart's *Don Giovanni* begins this way. [**Piano/vocal demonstration.**]

This aria is the stuff of every disgruntled contract worker since the beginning of time, including Beethoven himself. Yes, yes! According to Beethoven's friend and student Carl Czerny, Beethoven created this variation in reply to Anton Diabelli's insistence that Beethoven finish composing his set: "Night and day I slave away." Are we to believe that this is an example of musical humor from the legendary curmudgeon van Beethoven? Yes, humor. Poor Beethoven: He was a physical and emotional mess, but he was not at heart a bad man; he loved a good story and when he laughed, he laughed without shame or restraint.

By every account, Beethoven thoroughly enjoyed composing the variations. According to Carl Czerny, "Beethoven wrote these variations in a merry [mood]." According to Beethoven's assistant Anton Schindler, the composition of the work "amused Beethoven to a rare degree; [it was written] in a rosy mood [and it is] 'bubbling with humor.'" According to Wilhelm Von Lenz, one of Beethoven's earliest biographers and a most perceptive Beethovenian, Beethoven shines through in the *Diabelli Variations* as "the most thoroughly initiated high priest of humor." (I'll bet not a one of us ever thought of Beethoven as the high priest of humor!)

Von Lenz goes on to call Beethoven's *Diabelli Variations* "a satire on their theme." A satire on their theme. I like that. As an example of such satire, we turn to variation 1. Despite its primary position, variation 1 was among the very last to be composed, and by giving it pride-of-place as number 1, Beethoven makes an important statement about we can expect as the set unfolds. Beethoven labels variation 1 *alla marcia maestoso*—"like a majestic march." And a march it is; the triple-meter waltz time of the theme—1-2-3, 1-2-3—is here supplanted by a marching, lead-footed duple meter: hup-2-3-4. Let's hear the first half of variation 1. [**Piano performance:** Beethoven, *Diabelli Variations*, op. 120, variation 1.]

Majestic the march is: full of big, blustery sonorities and pomp-filled short-long rhythms. But with its obsessively repeated rhythms, its lack of any melodic charm or decoration, indeed, by its endemic clunkiness, this march becomes a caricature of a march: music long on brawn but short on brains. Here's the second half of the variation. [**Piano performance:** Beethoven, *Diabelli Variations*, op. 120, variation 1.]

Some commentators assert that this march pays homage to the wartime widows and orphans Diabelli's project was intended to benefit. No; it's too obviously clunky by a mile! It is, rather, Beethoven's way of saying: "You've heard Diabelli's theme; now it's my turn, so listen good and listen tight." On just these lines the pianist Alfred Brendel writes, "The theme [does not] reign over its unruly offspring. Instead of being confirmed, adorned and glorified, [Diabelli's theme] is parodied, ridiculed, disclaimed, transfigured, mourned, stamped out and finally uplifted."

So, back to early 1819. At some point after dismissing Diabelli's theme as a cobbler's patch, Beethoven decided to accept Diabelli's offer after all. But Beethoven made it clear that his contribution would be a set of variations, the number of which had yet to be determined. Beethoven put aside his work on the great mass (the *Missa Solemnis*) and began work on the variations, and by the summer of 1819 he had completed 23 of them. But then he stopped and put the variations aside for nearly four years in order to complete the *Missa* and compose his final three piano sonatas. He finally returned to the variations in February of 1823, and finished the set in March or April.

Why 33 Variations

Thirty-three might seem a strange number for Beethoven to fasten onto, but in fact, Beethoven had a number of good reasons to compose 33 variations on Diabelli's theme. Back in 1806, Beethoven composed for piano a work entitled "32 Variations in C Minor on an Original Theme." Though the piece was published, Beethoven was so unhappy with it that he refused to assign it an opus number. He went so far as to scoff at himself for having composed the thing, writing in a journal: "Oh Beethoven, what an ass you were!"

Well, perhaps Beethoven composed 33 variations on Diabelli's theme in order to do himself one better than his earlier work. There is also speculation that Beethoven's decision to compose 33 variations was an oblique reference to his piano sonatas. Beethoven completed his final piano sonata, No. 32 in C Minor, Op. 111, in 1822. The valedictory character of Op. 111 made it clear that Beethoven had no intention of composing another piano sonata. Having completed his 32nd sonata, Beethoven returned to the *Diabelli Variations* intent, perhaps, on crowning 32 sonatas with 33 variations. It is also very likely that Beethoven wanted to one-up Johann Sebastian Bach's epochal *Goldberg Variations*, which consists of 32 sections of music: two statements of the theme and 30 variations.

Beethoven and Bach

No music was more important to Beethoven both early and late in his life than that of Johann Sebastian Bach.

While Bach's large-scale vocal and orchestral music fell into obscurity after his death in 1750, his keyboard music did not fall into obscurity, and it was used as a pedagogic tool throughout the late 18th and early 19th centuries. Beethoven grew up playing Bach's *The Well-Tempered Clavier* and Bach's organ music. Moreover, a number of the high-end aristocrats Beethoven hung out with in Vienna were Bach freaks: connoisseurs who considered Johann Sebastian to be a deity, the first great coming of German music.

Beethoven was almost certainly given a hand-copied edition of Bach's *Goldberg Variation* by one of his Viennese patrons, probably the diplomat and Bach-o-phile named Baron Gottfried van Swieten. In 1817, the *Goldberg Variations* was published in Zurich, two years before Beethoven began the *Diabelli Variations*. Given Beethoven's adoration of Bach, it is inconceivable that he wasn't among the first to get a copy.

The point: Beethoven knew the *Goldberg Variations*, and it exerted a primary influence on the *Diabelli Variations*. Three variations in the Diabellis were explicitly inspired by Bach, all of them placed later in the set: numbers 24, 31, and 32. We can rightly state that as the *Diabelli Variations* progresses, it grows closer to the spirit of Bach. Variation 24 is a slow, quiet fugue, with the devotional sensibility of an organ prelude. According to Maynard Solomon, this fugue "might have issued from the *Goldberg Variations*." Let's hear it, variation 24: [**Piano performance:** Beethoven, *Diabelli Variations*, op. 120, variation 24.]

Variation 31 of the Diabellis was inspired by the 25th variation of the Goldbergs. Both variations are slow, set in triple meter and in minor; both are highly embellished and sublimely expressive. Bach's variation is haunting and tragic; the harpsichordist Wanda Landowska (who was the first person to record the Goldbergs on harpsichord, in 1931) called this variation "the black pearl" and "the crown of thorns." Bach's variation begins with a series of gentle roulades, each followed by a sighing descent. The Bach: [**Piano performance:** Bach, *Goldberg Variations*, variation 25.]

Beethoven's variation—number 31—likewise begins with a series of gentle roulades, each followed by a sighing descent. Let's hear the first half of this gorgeous variation. [**Piano performance:** Beethoven, *Diabelli Variations*, op. 120, variation 31.] Beethoven biographer Maynard Solomon waxes quite poetic in his description of this variation:

> Beethoven seems to be describing the trembling, ecstatic ascent of a soul as it drifts towards heaven, likening the stirrings of the heart to sequences of shimmering trills and copiously ornamented cadenza. Once again [continues Solomon], the voice is J. S. Bach's, the variation showing a special affinity with the 25th of the *Goldberg Variations*. Bach's tone, sound, and voice have been thoroughly assimilated into Beethoven's own late-style persona.

The next and second-to-last variation, number 32, reflects, as well, Beethoven's assimilation of the ethos and technique of Johann Sebastian Bach even as it brings the *Diabelli Variations* to its climax. The variation is a fugue of extraordinary power and complexity. We hear the first half of variation 32. [**Piano performance:** Beethoven, *Diabelli Variations*, op. 120, variation 32.]

In a work by Bach, a lengthy and complex fugue (like this one) would symbolize the utopian achievement of truth, wisdom, balance, and faith. As such—in Bach—a fugue like this one would conclude the work in which it appeared. But not here, not now, not in Beethoven's *Diabelli Variations*. About two minutes in, the fugue suddenly breaks off. A rippling diminished-seventh arpeggio purges the fugue from our ears and is followed by a mysterious series of harmonies that dissipate the energy and prepare us for what is to follow. [**Piano performance:** Beethoven, *Diabelli Variations*, op. 120, variation 32.] This conclusion to the fugue is both strange and wonderful. It transports us to the 33rd and final variation, which dwells in a place of transcendent peace. We will hear this final variation in a bit, but first an excursion.

Beethoven and the Piano

Beethoven was born in December of 1770 and died in March of 1827. His lifetime corresponded exactly with the development of the piano from a small, portable, wooden-harped instrument spanning five octaves to a big, heavy, metal-harped, seven-plus-octave instrument that is understood to be the proto-modern piano. The evolving technology of the piano profoundly affected the way Beethoven thought about and composed for the piano, though we would acknowledge that the demands he placed on his pianos always seemed to be a step or two ahead of what was actually available at the time.

Beethoven never had the opportunity to play a metal-harped piano, the first of which was built in Philadelphia by John Isaac Hawkins in 1825. Sadly, Beethoven wouldn't have been able to appreciate it even if he had had the opportunity, given that he was deaf by 1818, at the age of 48. The piano Beethoven owned at the time he composed the *Diabelli Variations* was an eight-foot-long, six-octave-wide, mahogany-cased English Broadwood, a gift from the manufacturer in 1818. Much has been written about this Broadwood, serial number 7362, which has become the single most famous piano in history.

Deaf though he was, Beethoven was mighty proud of his Broadwood. The critic Ludwig Rellstab visited Beethoven in 1825 and reported that Beethoven proudly showed off the Broadwood. Rellstab remembered:

> "It is a handsome gift," [Beethoven] continued, stretching his hands towards the keys, yet without ceasing to hold my eyes. He gently struck a chord. [**Piano demonstration.**] Never again will [another chord] penetrate my soul with such a wealth of woe, with so heart-rending an accent! He had struck the C Major chord with his right hand, and [mistakenly] played a B in the bass. His eyes never left mine; and in order that [he] might make the soft tone of the instrument sound at its best, he repeated the "chord" several times … [**Piano demonstration.**] … and the greatest musician on earth did not [hear] its dissonance!"

The fact was that Beethoven couldn't hear didn't keep him from playing his Broadwood. The Broadwood may have been sturdy, but it was not Beethoven's equal, and at the time of his death, the piano's innards were a maze of snapped strings and broken hammers. The piano was later owned by Franz Liszt and today resides in the Budapest National Museum, no doubt in better condition today than when it was moved out of Beethoven's flat in Vienna's Schwarzspanier House after his death.

The *Diabelli Variations*: Larger Organization

Beethoven's *Diabelli Variations* consists of 34 discrete sections of music: a theme followed by 33 variations. Given the majesty and momentum of the piece and Beethoven's propensity to build grand musical structures from the smallest of musical ideas, it is virtually impossible to perceive the Diabellis as consisting of 34 separate parts related only to the theme itself.

Beethoven's inspiration for the *Diabelli Variations*, Bach's *Goldberg Variations*, is itself designed with the precision of a Swiss chronometer: Bach's 30 variations are explicitly organized in ten groups of 3 and two larger groups of 15. The variational grouping in the Diabellis is not as symmetrical. Rather, Beethoven's groupings have to do with moment-to-moment narrative flow and are not the product—as they are in the Goldbergs—of a carefully conceived, pre-compositional blueprint.

To my ear, the 33 variations of Beethoven's *Diabelli Variations* are grouped into three large parts. Variations 1 through 10 constitute the first part, variations 11 through 20 the second part, and variations 21 through 33 the third part. In order to perceive these divisions, the last variation in each of these groups has to sound somehow like an ending, and the first variation in each group has to sound somehow like a beginning.

The first large group concludes with variation 10. Variation 10 is the most brilliant of all the variations, a whirlwind of break-neck speed, filled with trills and tremolos and staccato octave scales. Here it is, variation 10. [**Piano performance:** Beethoven, *Diabelli Variations*, op. 120, variation 10.] The gentle, delicate, roulade-filled variation 11 that follows sounds like a new beginning, a blossom opening at dawn, if you'll pardon me a brief horticultural flight! [**Piano performance:** Beethoven, *Diabelli Variations*, op. 120, variation 11.]

This second grouping of variations concludes with variation 20. With its incredible degree of harmonic ambiguity (like, what key are we in?), its placement low in the piano, and its rhythmic stasis, variation 20 offers up an enigmatic stillness unique to the set. Franz Liszt called it the sphinx. Let's hear it. [**Piano performance:** Beethoven, *Diabelli Variations*, op. 120, variation 20.] The fast, loud, trilling, and registrally all-encompassing variation 21 that follows creates a shocking degree of contrast that, once again, sounds like a new beginning. [**Piano performance:** Beethoven, *Diabelli Variations*, op. 120, variation 21.] And we are back off to the races!

Generally but accurately speaking, the first group of variations, numbers 1 through 10, is cumulative, with each successive variation growing out of some aspect of the one that preceded it. Generally but accurately speaking, the second group of variations—numbers 11 through 20—displays an increasing degree of disassociation and contrast, climaxed by the enigmatic variation 20. Generally but accurately speaking, the third group of variations—variations 21 through 33—moves towards Bach, towards the explicit references to Bach that are variations 31 and 32. Variation 33, the final variation, stands apart from this Bach revival. It's time to talk about it.

At Journey's End: Variation 33

Beethoven labels variation 33 *tempo di menuetto moderato*, meaning "in the moderate tempo of a minuet." A minuet, of all things! A minuet is a moderate three-step dance of French origin that became during the classical era something of a cliché: a predictable (if elegant) middle movement that evoked the elite, aristocratic ballrooms from which it had emerged. Beethoven had about as much use for the minuet's aristocratic pretentions as he did a hairbrush, and so—early in his career—he did away with composing them entirely.

So here, at the very end of his last major keyboard work, Beethoven evokes an antique musical genre and expressive sensibility that years before he had personally rendered obsolete. Let's hear the opening of variation 33. [**Piano performance:** Beethoven, *Diabelli Variations*, op. 120, variation 33.] The exquisite nostalgia evoked here looks back to a time before the previous 32 variations, to a time before Diabelli's theme, before Beethoven's deafness, and before Napoleon, to an idealized past of order and elegance, of youth and beauty.

Beethoven concluded his 32nd and final piano sonata—the Sonata in C Minor, Op. 111, which completed in January of 1822—with the same sort of minuet-inspired nostalgia. That two-movement piano sonata ends with a massive, 18-minute-long theme and variations form movement based on a moderately slow, lightly dancing, triple-meter theme set in C Major. Here is the opening of that theme, from the last movement of Beethoven's last piano sonata, Op. 111. [**Piano demonstration.**]

Like the Piano Sonata Op. 111 of 1822, the *Diabelli Variations* of 1823 concludes in C Major on a note of good cheer and peace. We hear the coda that follows the 33rd variation and which concludes the work. [**Piano performance:** Beethoven, *Diabelli Variations*, op. 120, variation 33.] Of these closing moments Donald Tovey writes:

> It is characteristic of the way in which this work develops and enlarges the principles embodied in the *Goldberg Variations* that it ends quietly. Beethoven, like Bach, rounds off his work by a peaceful return home - a home that seems far removed from the [earlier] stormy experiences through which alone such ethereal calm can be attained.

Transformations

According to Beethoven's instructions, the *Diabelli Variations* was published with the title *33 Veränderungen on a waltz by Diabelli*. That Beethoven chose to use the word *Veränderungen* Rather than the usual Italian-derived word *Variationen* is most significant. You see, in German, the word *Veränderungen* means not only "variations" but also "transformations." While the word "variation" implies the decoration of a theme, the word "transformation" implies metamorphosis: the transmutation of something into a new state of being. That is, of course, precisely what happens in the Diabellis, so if it were up to me, we'd call the piece the *Diabelli Transformations*.

According to the musicologist William Kinderman:

> No other work by [Beethoven] is so rich in allusion, humor, and parody. We might almost regard the Variations as an enormously extended chain of puns; in each transformation, aspects of [Diabelli's] waltz are developed with far more determination than is evident in Diabelli's [theme].

"An extended chain of puns." You know, I do believe that statement cuts to the very heart of the *Diabelli Variations*. And for the record: Beethoven was partial to word games and puns. According to the Beethoven scholar Martin Cooper, "Beethoven's verbal humor was plainly of the kind that friends tolerate, and even come to enjoy, not because it is in fact amusing but because they associate it with the good humor and the happy moods of a man they love and admire."

Contrary to those verbal snobs who, incapable of moving their own vowels, would have us believe that the pun is the lowest form of humor, I would point out that punning is by its nature a transformational process about finding unexpected, perhaps even revelatory meaning in unforeseen places. That is, of course, exactly what the *Diabelli Variations* is all about: a work in which Beethoven reveals in Anton Diabelli's nondescript waltz an unforeseen variety of musical possibilities and expressive states.

This is, in turn, what Beethoven's mature compositional art had always been about: about finding transformational, developmental, and variational gold in the commonplace; about creating palaces of sound from tiny, nondescript musical bricks; about discovering the world in a grain of sand.

Thank you.

Schubert—Piano Sonata No. 21 in B-flat Major
Lecture 7

F ranz Schubert was a competent pianist of the old school. Schubert's "piano music" is not the product of an experimental virtuoso; it does not push the piano to its outer limits (as does so much of the piano music of Beethoven, for example). Nor does Schubert's piano music celebrate virtuosity for its own sake (like the piano music of Liszt, for example). Rather, the great bulk of Schubert's piano music—including his Piano Sonata no. 21—is music first and piano music second.

Movement One: Sonata Form

- The Piano Sonata no. 21 in B-flat Major is pure mature Schubert: expansive and leisurely; filled with lengthy, songlike themes; and characterized by warm, graceful surfaces. The tone and spirit of the music betray not a hint of Schubert's physical condition, which was, at the time of its composition in September of 1828, increasingly dire. (He died just two months later, on November 19, 1828.)

- Sonata form is the classical-era formal construct that evolved to accommodate the presentation, development, and reconciliation of two or more principal themes. The first large section is called the exposition; it is during the exposition that principal themes are "exposed." Typically two in number, these contrasting themes are presented in different keys. This means that a typical sonata form exposition will feature two key areas: the key of the first theme, which is the home (or tonic) key, and the key of the second theme, which is the contrasting key.

- The second large section of a sonata form movement is called the development section. In a typical development section, the music heard during the exposition is fragmented, recombined, overlapped—in a word, "developed."

- The third large section of a sonata form movement is the recapitulation. In the recap, the themes typically appear in the same order as in the exposition. However, in the recapitulation, they will be set in the same key, meaning that theme 2 will appear in the home key of theme 1. In this way, the once harmonically contrasting themes are reconciled to one another, and this reconciliation allows the movement to end in the same key in which it began.

- In any piece of music, it's not the form but the way in which a composer tweaks, bends, and even mutilates the form that creates intrinsic interest. We put aside our expectations of sonata form because Schubert does some pretty atypical things in his first movement, so the challenge is to hear what he does with the ears—with the expectations—of his own contemporaries.

- The exposition of this sprawling, 19-minute-long first movement sonata form features not just two principal themes set in two principal keys, but three themes, each set in its own key. Our examination of this movement will focus on the following two elements of the exposition.
  - We will observe that the themes—three in number—are lengthy, self-standing entities that contain within themselves the sort of harmonic variety and melodic development that other composers reserve for their development sections.

  - We will observe the fact that transitions—such as the modulating bridge that separates themes 1 and 2—are kept to a bare minimum. This movement—this entire sonata, like pretty much all of Schubert's late music—is about its long, songlike themes and not its transitions.

- Theme 1 is cast in three parts, which can be schematicized as A-A^1-A^2. In the first part, the elegant, stately thematic melody in B-flat major is twice punctuated with a gently rumbling trill on a G-flat at the very bottom of the piano. The explanation for the rumbling trill on the pitch G-flat arrives with the beginning of the second part of theme 1, which is set in the key of G-flat major. This varied, almost developmental second part of the theme concludes with a harmonic shift back toward the home key of B-flat major.

The majestic third and final part of theme 1, set back in B-flat major, brings the theme to its conclusion.

Franz Schubert (1797–1828) was a compulsive composer who would no sooner complete one piece than start the next.

- Taken all together, that's an incredibly long theme, about two minutes in performance. And theme 2, which is about to follow, is nearly as long. This sort of thematic scale is a key element of Schubert's mature art, in which his themes are typically self-standing entities that exhibit as part of their substance a full gamut of expressive and developmental writing. For Schubert, much more often than not, the themes are the fully realized personalities that constitute the essential "reason to be" of a given movement.

- After the 43-measure-long theme 1, the four-measure-long modulating bridge flies by so quickly that we might miss it if we weren't paying attention. The harmony transits to the key of F-sharp minor, the second principal key in this three-key exposition. This shockingly abrupt harmonic leap to the key of F-sharp minor has actually been carefully prepared by Schubert. The pitch F-sharp is the **enharmonic** equivalent of G-flat, which means that F-sharp and G-flat are the same pitch.

- We've been hearing G-flats since the beginning of the movement— first in the low, rumbling trills and then as the key area of the second part of theme 1. Thus, the precipitous move to F-sharp minor doesn't sound nearly as shocking as it might. Theme 2 begins in F-sharp minor and concludes with a modulation to F major, which is the third key area in this three-key, three-theme exposition.

- Theme 3, set in F major, is a dancing, arpeggio-dominated melody built from triplet eighth notes that up to now had been heard accompanimentally. Finally, a leisurely, pause-filled, and eventually fragmented cadential passage brings this over five-minute-long exposition to its conclusion.

- Based on this examination of the exposition, we can draw three conclusions—conclusions that apply as well to the entire movement.
  o This music is overwhelmingly thematic in nature. In an exposition that runs 125 measures, there are precisely four measures of purely "transitional" music.

  o Within each of the themes is a degree of harmonic and thematic development that we might ordinarily expect to find in a development section.

  o The thematic melodies themselves are ravishing; they seem to unwind forever, with each new phrase a revelation. They are the sorts of long, effortless, vocally conceived melodies that lie at the heart of Schubert's song-inspired compositional voice.

Movement Two: Andante
- The movement is structured in three parts, which can be schematicized as A–B–A[1]. The beginning of the opening A section in C-sharp minor was addressed earlier in this lecture. This time, we note two observations. First, the harmonies change very slowly, creating a sense of time standing still. Second, the theme itself appears in the middle register of the keyboard, surrounded by ringing notes above and strumming notes below.

- Following the contrasting B section, the timeless C-sharp-minor A section resumes. As before, the music projects a mood of wistful melancholy. But then, roughly one minute into the return, there occurs a small miracle: a sudden and entirely unexpected shift down a half step from C-sharp minor to the key of C major. Gentle and quiet though the moment is, it is, nevertheless, breathtaking in its impact. This is very characteristic of Schubert's harmonic imagination and dramatic timing.

Movement Three: Scherzo

- Schubert labels this three-part, A–B–A–form movement as being *allegro vivace con delicatezza*—meaning "fast, lively, and delicate"—and except for the very brief B section, fast, lively, and delicate it is.

- After the harmonic stasis of the second movement, this third movement would seem to be harmonically all over the map, all the time. The opening **scherzo**—the first "A" section—brilliantly and delicately moves through eight different key areas in its one-minute length.

Movement Four: Rondo

- The large-scale form of this rondo is A–B–A–C–A–B–A (the first A being the rondo theme). This movement is often referred to as being a sonata rondo because the central episode—C—is not a contrasting passage but, rather, a development of the themes gone before it. These themes, in turns, are dancing, lyric, and explosively dramatic—all marked by a harmonic subtlety and variety.

- The dancing rondo theme itself is a harmonic case in point. Though presumably set in the home key of B-flat major, not one of the six large phrases that make up this theme actually begins in B-flat. The theme begins with an octave G, the dominant pitch of C minor. From there, the opening phrase of the rondo theme proceeds in C minor, until it turns on a dime and concludes in B-flat major.

- Then, the opening octave G returns, and the theme resumes in C minor. Like the first phrase, this second phrase concludes in B-flat major before barreling headlong into the third phrase, which begins on an E-flat major chord and concludes in G minor.

- The fourth thematic phrase begins with the same octave Gs and starts up again in C minor. It concludes in B-flat major and then barrels headlong into the fifth phrase, which begins on an E-flat major chord before zipping through a multitude of keys, starting with A-flat major and concluding on a G-major chord, the dominant chord of C minor.

- The sixth and final phrase of the rondo theme begins again with the octave Gs, starts up in C minor, and momentarily touches B-flat major before moving on to F-major in preparation for the first contrasting episode. This sixth phrase contains more harmonic sleight of hand per measure than many entire movements by other composers.

- Within this rondo, the first large contrasting episode—B—consists of two very different thematic elements. The first is gentle and lyric and is underlain with a rippling accompaniment. The second half of the first contrasting episode—B—could not be more different. It consists of an entirely new theme that begins explosively and passionately in F minor.

- These three themes—the rondo theme and the two themes that constitute the first contrasting episode—span a huge expressive gamut, from dancing to lyric to explosively passionate. They provide the grist for the development section that is the second contrasting episode—C—and they will all be heard again before the conclusion of the movement.

- That conclusion, the coda, is a brief but most satisfying curtain closer, and it constitutes the last solo piano music Schubert ever composed.

Important Terms

enharmonic: Pitches that are identical in sound but with different spellings, depending on the key context, e.g., C-sharp and D-flat.

scherzo form: Meaning literally "I'm joking," scherzo is the designation Beethoven gave to his modified use of minuet and trio form.

Schubert—Piano Sonata No. 21 in B-flat Major
Lecture 7—Transcript

Welcome to *The 23 Greatest Solo Piano Works*. This is Lecture 7. It is entitled Schubert—Piano Sonata No. 21 in B-flat Major.

My friends, Franz Schubert was many things. He was a compulsive composer, who would no sooner complete one piece than start the next. He was so severely myopic and so dependent on his glasses that he actually slept with them on. Schubert was, without a doubt, among the worst classroom teachers to ever hoist a piece of chalk. He taught first grade for four years, from the age of 17 to 21. He hated teaching and tried to compose in the classroom when he should have been instructing the kids in his charge. He later confessed, "It is true that they irritated me whenever I tried to create. Naturally I would beat them up."

Naturally. Schubert stood 1.57 meters tall (that's about 5' 1"). He was "cherubic" as a child and plump-bordering-on obese as an adult. (As an adult, his friends called him *schwammerl*, which means "little mushroom.") When he got into his cups, which he did with increasing frequency as he got older, he liked nothing more than to smash tableware and glassware. Schubert's friends were in agreement when they said he was of "two natures." Today we would call him bipolar.

Yes, Franz Schubert was many things. But among the things he was not was a professional-grade concert pianist. Now, this is not to say that Schubert couldn't get around the keyboard; that he could. According to his friend Anselm Hüttenbrenner, "Schubert was not an elegant pianist but he was a safe and fluent one." Another friend, Albert Stadler, described Schubert as having "a beautiful touch, a quiet hand, clear, neat playing, full of insight and feeling. He belonged to the old school of piano players, whose fingers [did] not attack the poor keys like birds of prey."

Allow me, please, to rephrase that last statement to account for what was said between the lines: "Schubert had a light touch and played 'from the hand,' like our esteemed masters Mozart and Clementi and unlike those bangers Beethoven and Liszt, who don't 'play' the piano so much as beat the snot out of it!" The point: Schubert was a competent pianist of the old school. The larger point: Schubert's piano music is not the product of an experimental virtuoso. It does not push the piano to its outer limits, as does so much of the piano music of Beethoven, for example. Neither does Schubert's piano music celebrate virtuosity for its own sake, like the piano music of Liszt, for example.

Rather, the great bulk of Schubert's piano music (including his Piano Sonata no. 21) is music first and piano music second. This is an important distinction, one we will return to in a few minutes. But first, let's hear the gorgeous, expansive opening of the first movement of Schubert's 21st and final piano sonata, the Piano Sonata in B-flat Major of 1828. [**Piano performance:** Schubert, Piano Sonata No. 21 in B-flat Major, movement 1.]

Franz Peter Schubert was born in Vienna on January 31, 1797, and it was in Vienna that he died, on November 19, 1828, two months shy of his 32nd birthday. At the age of nine he began formal music studies with a local organist named Michael Holzer. Of his young student Holzer said, "If I wished to instruct him in anything fresh, he already knew it. Consequently, I eventually stopped giving him lessons [and] merely conversed with him and watched him with silent astonishment."

Schubert's first masterwork was a song for voice and piano entitled "Gretchen at the Spinning Wheel" which he composed on October 19, 1814, when he was 17 years old. My friends, it was songs for voice and piano like "Gretchen at the Spinning Wheel" that brought Schubert to the compositional table. He cut his musical teeth writing songs; his first masterworks were songs. It was by writing songs that Schubert learned to convey literary and expressive meaning with extraordinary subtlety and brevity. And it was by writing songs that Schubert developed his amazing gifts as a melodist, harmonist, and a dramatist.

Schubert wrote a total of 637 songs. But that fact doesn't come close to illustrating the degree to which "song" lay at the heart of Schubert's music because, in fact, the lyricism and dramatic content of song lie at the heart of pretty much everything Schubert ever composed, and that includes his Piano Sonata No. 21 in B-flat Major. Let's hear the brooding, song-like opening of the second movement *Andante*. [**Piano performance:** Schubert, Piano Sonata No. 21 in B-flat Major, movement 2.] We will return to the importance of song to Schubert's Piano Sonata in B-flat major in due time. But first, some necessary biographical info, under the heading of ...

Schubert's Health

Sometime in the late summer of 1822, the 25-year-old Schubert contracted syphilis. The primary symptoms of the disease appeared in January of 1823. If Schubert's case was typical, he suffered from painful lymphatic swelling, pustules, rashes, hair loss, lesions in his mouth and throat, and debilitating muscle aches. For Schubert, depression and despair accompanied the symptoms. On March 31, 1824, a despondent Schubert wrote his friend Leopold Kupelweiser:

> I feel myself to be the most unhappy and wretched creature in the world. Imagine a man whose health will never be right again, a man whose most brilliant hopes have perished, to whom love and friendship have nothing to offer but pain, whose enthusiasm for all things beautiful [is gone], and I ask you, is he not a miserable, unhappy being? Each night, on retiring to bed, I hope I may not wake again, and each morning but recalls yesterday's grief.

This was Schubert's state of mind for a year and a half, as his syphilis ran through its initial stages. But then—from the fall of 1824 until mid-1827 or so—the disease entered its latency and consequently, for nearly three years, Schubert was symptom free and noninfectious. Yes, he still suffered from depression, exacerbated by the fear that his disease would return. And yes, he self-medicated by drinking way too much alcohol, at which time the ordinarily mild-mannered Schubert became vulgar, abusive, and physically destructive. While under the influence, he liked nothing more than to smash glassware and crockery, making him quite understandably a less-than-welcome guest in many homes and hostelries.

Having said that, for the nearly three years of Schubert's latency he was able to lead what passed for him as a normal life. In March of 1825 his friend Johanna Lutz wrote to her fiancé: "Schubert in now very busy and well-behaved, which pleases me very much." A few months later Schubert's friend Anton Ottenwalt was able to write: "Schubert looks so well and strong, is so nice and cheerful and so genially communicative that one cannot fail to be delighted." His bad moments aside, Schubert's latency gave him hope, hope that he might be among those lucky few whose latency was permanent.

Schubert and Beethoven

It was during this period of latency that Schubert's musical god—Ludwig van Beethoven—died in his flat at the Schwarzspanier House, about three-quarters of a mile from where Schubert was living on the Tuchlauben, near St. Stephen's Cathedral. Beethoven's impact on Schubert's mature music was singular. This was not because Schubert imitated Beethoven; no, Beethoven's influence went much deeper than that. For the syphilitic Schubert, Beethoven became the ultimate role model: a fellow composer battling his own demons and physical illness, who managed to give voice to his struggles through music. Beethoven's example liberated Schubert to be all that he—Franz Schubert—could be.

Beethoven died on March 26, 1827. His funeral was held three days later, on March 29th. We know that Schubert attended the service—which was held at the Holy Trinity Church in the Alsergrund parish—and that afterwards he participated as a torch-bearer in the processional to the cemetery.

The Dedication

Among the other torch-bearers at Beethoven's funeral was the pianist and composer Johann Hummel, who was at the time one of the most famous musicians in all of Europe. Oh my goodness. Who would have guessed back then that by the 21st century Hummel would be nearly forgotten while the obscure, roly-poly Franz Schubert would reside in the pantheon of greatest composers? Who would have guessed? Surely not Schubert nor Hummel!

Anyway, Hummel had come to Vienna to do some business with Beethoven, and instead ended up carrying a torch at his funeral. During his stay in Vienna, Hummel was invited to a dinner party at the home of a former opera singer named Katharina Laszny. Madame Laszny also invited Schubert and

Schubert's friend, the baritone Johann Michael Vogl. Hummel, who was 49 years old at the time, knew next to nothing about Schubert and his music. The composer and conductor Ferdinand Hiller was there as well, and after dinner there began what Hiller described as:

> A unique concert. Song after song ensued—the performers [Schubert and Vogl] inexhaustibly generous, the audience inexhaustibly receptive. Schubert had but little technique, Vogl had not much of a voice, but they both had such life and feeling, and were so completely absorbed in their performances, that [Schubert's] wonderful compositions could not have been interpreted with greater clarity and vision. You did not notice the piano playing or the singing. It was as though the music needed no material sound, as though the melodies, like visions, revealed themselves to spiritualized ears.

According to Hiller, "[Hummel] was so deeply moved that tears trickled down his cheeks." For his part, Schubert was so deeply moved by Hummel's reaction that a year later he dedicated his last three piano sonatas to Hummel, sonatas composed in September of 1828. It's a nice story, though in the end the dedication didn't work out. You see, the sonatas were not published until 1839, 11 years after Schubert died, and two years after Hummel's death in 1837. The publisher Artaria decided that there was no commercial benefit to dedicating the set to Hummel, despite the fact that that had been Schubert's wish.

Instead, the sonatas were dedicated to the composer and pianist Robert Schumann, whose efforts in bringing Schubert's music out of obscurity were nothing short of Herculean. (For example, it was Schumann who discovered the long-lost manuscript of Schubert's Symphony No. 9 and arranged for its premiere under the baton of Felix Mendelssohn.) For this reason we can't help but believe that Schubert would have approved of the rededication of the sonatas to Schumann, had he had the chance to do so!

Piano Sonata No. 21 in B-flat Major

The sonata is pure, mature Schubert: expansive and leisurely; filled with lengthy, song-like themes; and characterized by warm, graceful surfaces. The tone and spirit of the music betray not a hint of Schubert's physical condition, which was, at the time of its composition in September of 1828, increasingly dire. (He died just two months later, on November 19, 1828.)

Movement One: Sonata Form

Expressive essence: Calm serenity.

Sonata form is that classical-era formal construct that evolved to accommodate the presentation, development, and reconciliation of two or more principal themes. The first large section is called the exposition; it is during the exposition that principal themes are exposed. Typically two in number, these contrasting themes are presented in different keys. This means that a typical sonata form exposition will feature two key areas: the key of the first theme, which is the home (or tonic) key, and the key of the second theme, which is in what's called the contrasting key.

The second large section of a sonata form movement is called the development section. In a typical development section, the music heard during the exposition is fragmented, re-combined, overlapped, whatever: in a word, developed. The third large section of a sonata form movement is the recapitulation. In the recap, the themes typically appear in the same order as in the exposition. However—and this is the grandmother of all structural howevers—these themes will, here in the recapitulation, be set in the same key, meaning that theme 2 will appear in the home key, the key of theme 1. In this way the once-harmonically-contrasting themes are reconciled to one another and this reconciliation allows the movement to end in the same key in which it began.

OK, that's sonata form orthodoxy, a structural given that Schubert's audience followed with the same ease that we follow a football or baseball game. But form can only provide context. It's not the structure of a ball game that makes it interesting but rather, how the specifics of a particular game play out within the structure. Just so, in any piece of music, it's not the form but the way in which a composer tweaks, bends, and even mutilates the form that creates intrinsic interest.

I've waxed a bit on the "expectations" of sonata form because Schubert is going to do some pretty atypical things here in his first movement, and to the degree we can, I'd like us to hear what he does with the ears—with the expectations—of his own contemporary audience. We cut to the chase: the exposition of this sprawling, 19-minute-long first movement sonata form features not just two principal themes set in two principal keys, but three themes, each set in its own key. Our examination of this movement will focus, then, on the following two elements of the exposition.

One: We will observe that the themes—three in number—are lengthy, self-standing entities that contain within themselves the sort of harmonic variety and melodic development that other composers reserve for their development sections. Two: We will observe the fact that transitions—like the modulating bridge that separates themes 1 and 2—are kept to a bare minimum. This movement—this entire sonata, like pretty much all of Schubert's late music—is about its long, song-like themes and not its transitions.

Theme 1 is cast in three parts, which can be schematicized as A-A¹-A². Let's hear the opening part—part A—and let's be aware that the elegant, stately thematic melody in B-flat major … [**Piano demonstration.**] … is twice punctuated with a gently rumbling trill on a G-flat at the very bottom of the piano. [**Piano demonstration.**] Let's hear it. Theme 1, part 1. [**Piano performance:** Schubert, Piano Sonata No. 21 in B-flat Major, movement 1.]

The explanation for the rumbling trill on the pitch G-flat arrives with the beginning of the second part of theme 1, which is set in the key of G-flat Major! Let's hear this varied, almost developmental second part of the theme, which concludes with a harmonic shift back towards the home key of B-flat Major. Theme 1, part 2. [**Piano performance:** Schubert, Piano Sonata No. 21 in B-flat Major, movement 1.] The majestic third and final part of theme 1—set back in B-flat Major—brings the theme to its conclusion. Theme 1, part 3. [**Piano performance:** Schubert, Piano Sonata No. 21 in B-flat Major, movement 1.]

We'll discuss the rather abrupt nature of theme 1's conclusion in a moment, but first let's observe the obvious: Taken altogether, that's a mighty long theme, about two minutes in performance. And I would tell you that theme 2, which is about to follow, is nearly as long. This sort of thematic scale is a key element of Schubert's mature art in which his themes are typically self-standing entities that exhibit as part of their substance a full gamut of expressive and developmental writing. For Schubert, much more often than not, the themes are the thing: fully realized personalities that constitute the essential reason to be of a given movement.

After the 43-measure-long theme 1, the four-measure-long modulating bridge flies by so quickly that we might miss it if we're not paying attention. OK, let's pay attention. Here it is. [**Piano performance:** Schubert, Piano Sonata No. 21 in B-flat Major, movement 1.] And just like that, the harmony transits to the key of F-sharp Minor, the second principal key in this three-key exposition. This shockingly abrupt harmonic leap to key of F-sharp Minor [**piano demonstration**] has actually been carefully prepared by Schubert. You see, the pitch F-sharp [**piano demonstration**] is the enharmonic equivalent of g-flat [**piano demonstration**], which means that F-sharp and G-flat are actually the same pitch. Well, we've been hearing G-flats since the beginning of the movement, first in the low, rumbling trills [**piano demonstration**], and then as the key area of part 2 of theme 1. [**Piano demonstration.**]

Thus, the precipitous move to F-sharp minor doesn't sound nearly as shocking as it might. Let's hear theme 2 in its entirety, beginning in F-sharp Minor. [**Piano demonstration.**] ... And concluding with a modulation to F Major, which will be the third key area in this three-key, three-theme exposition! Theme 2. [**Piano performance:** Schubert, Piano Sonata No. 21 in B-flat Major, movement 1.]

Theme 3, set in F Major, is a dancing, arpeggio-dominated melody built from triplet eighth-notes that up to now have been heard accompanimentally. Theme 3. [**Piano performance:** Schubert, Piano Sonata No. 21 in B-flat Major, movement 1.] Finally, a leisurely, pause-filled and eventually fragmented cadential passage brings this five-plus-minute-long exposition to its conclusion. [**Piano performance:** Schubert, Piano Sonata No. 21 in B-flat Major, movement 1.]

Based on this examination of the exposition, let's draw three conclusions, conclusions that apply as well to the entire movement. One: This music is overwhelmingly thematic in nature. In an exposition that runs 125 measures, there are precisely four measures of purely transitional music. Two: Within each of the themes is a degree of harmonic and thematic development that we might ordinarily expect to find in a development section. Three: The thematic melodies themselves are ravishing; they seem to unwind forever, with each new phrase a revelation. They are the sorts of long, effortless, vocally conceived melodies that lie at the heart of Schubert's song-inspired compositional voice.

Movement Two: Andante

Expressive essence: Wistful melancholy.

The movement is structured in three parts, which can be schematicized as A-B-A¹. We sampled the beginning of the opening A section in C-sharp Minor earlier in this lecture. Let's hear that opening again, but now informed by two observations. One, the harmonies change very slowly, creating a sense of time standing still. Two, the theme itself appears in the middle register of the keyboard, surrounded by ringing notes above and strumming notes below. [**Piano performance:** Schubert, Piano Sonata No. 21 in B-flat Major, movement 2.]

There's a detail I must share with you, because it is so characteristic of Schubert's harmonic imagination and dramatic timing. Following the contrasting B section, the timeless C-sharp Minor A section resumes. As before, the music projects a mood of wistful melancholy. But then, roughly one minute into the return, there occurs a small miracle: a sudden and entirely unexpected shift down a half step from C-sharp Minor to the key of C Major. Gentle and quiet though the moment is, it is, nevertheless, breathtaking in its impact! Here's the moment of harmonic shift. [**Piano demonstration.**] Let's hear that incredible harmonic shift in context, starting with the reprise of the

A section. [**Piano performance:** Schubert, Piano Sonata No. 21 in B-flat Major, movement 2.]

Movement Three: Scherzo

Expressive essence: Incandescent brilliance.

Schubert labels this three-part, A-B-A form movement as being *allegro vivace con delicatezza*. Except for the very brief B section, "fast, lively, and delicate" it is. After the harmonic stasis of the second movement, this third movement would seem to be harmonically all over the map, all the time. Let's hear the opening scherzo—the first A section. Brilliant and delicate, this music moves, by my count, through eight different key areas in its one-minute length. [**Piano performance:** Schubert, Piano Sonata No. 21 in B-flat Major, movement 3.]

Movement Four: Rondo

Expressive essence: A little of everything!

The large-scale form of this whiz-bang rondo is A (A being the rondo theme) A-B-A-C-A-B-A. This movement is often referred to as being a sonata rondo, because the central episode—C—is not a contrasting passage but rather a development of the themes gone before it. And what themes they are: in turns dancing, lyric, and explosively dramatic, all marked by a harmonic subtlety and variety that makes this music dazzle like a Passion Cut Diamond in bright sunlight!

Harmonic case in point: the dancing rondo theme itself. Though presumably set in the home key of B-flat Major, not one of the six large phrases that make up this theme actually begins in B-flat Major. The theme begins with an octave G, the dominant pitch of C Minor. [**Piano demonstration.**] From there, the opening phrase of the rondo theme proceeds in C Minor, until it turns on a dime and concludes in B-flat Major. [**Piano performance:** Schubert, Piano Sonata No. 21 in B-flat Major, movement 4.]

And then? The opening octave G returns and the theme resumes in C Minor! Like the first phrase, this second phrase concludes in B-flat Major before barreling headlong into the third phrase, which begins on an E-flat Major chord and concludes in G Minor! Phrases two and three: [**Piano performance:** Schubert, Piano Sonata No. 21 in B-flat Major, movement 4.]

The fourth thematic phrase begins—yes!—with the same-octave Gs and starts up again in C Minor. It concludes in B-flat major and then barrels headlong into the fifth phrase, which begins on an E-flat Major chord before zipping through an entire Sears catalog worth of keys, starting with A-flat major and concluding on a G-Major chord, the dominant chord of C Minor! [**Piano performance:** Schubert, Piano Sonata No. 21 in B-flat Major, movement 4.]

The sixth and final phrase of the Rondo Theme begins again with the octave Gs, starts up in C Minor, momentarily touches B-flat Major before moving on to F Major in preparation for the first contrasting episode. Rondo theme, phrase six. [**Piano performance:** Schubert, Piano Sonata No. 21 in B-flat Major, movement 4.] That, my friends, is quite a theme, with more harmonic sleight of hand per measure than many entire movements by other composers.

In order to properly appreciate the thematic and expressive variety of this rondo, let's identify the contrasting thematic elements. The first large contrasting episode, B, consists of two very different thematic elements. The first is gentle and lyric, and is underlain with a rippling accompaniment. Here's how it begins. [**Piano performance:** Schubert, Piano Sonata No. 21 in B-flat Major, movement 4.] The second half of the first contrasting episode, B, could not be more different. It consists of an entirely new theme which begins explosively and passionately in F Minor. [**Piano performance:** Schubert, Piano Sonata No. 21 in B-flat Major, movement 4.]

These three themes (the rondo theme and the two themes that together constitute the first contrasting episode) span a huge expressive gamut, from dancing to lyric to explosively passionate. They provide the grist for the development section that is the second contrasting episode (part C) and they will all be heard again before the conclusion of the movement. That conclusion—the coda—is a brief but most satisfying curtain closer, and constitutes the last solo piano music Schubert ever composed. Here is the coda. [**Piano performance:** Schubert, Piano Sonata No. 21 in B-flat Major, movement 4.]

Conclusion

In mid-October of 1828, just a few weeks after having completed the piano sonata, Schubert's appetite for food fled to points unknown. His brother Ferdinand, with whom Schubert was living at the time, claimed that Franz' terminal illness began two weeks later, on October 31, 1828. Weakened by tertiary syphilis and the toxic, mercury-based medications he was taking for the syphilis, Schubert took to his bed with a high, persistent fever, almost certainly caused by a bacterial typhoid infection.

Schubert died at three o'clock in the afternoon on November 19, 1828. He rests today in Vienna's main cemetery, the *Zentralfriedhof*, in a special area called the Garden of Honor, just a few feet away from Beethoven's grave. They each rest in good company.

Thank you.

Chopin—*Préludes*, Op. 28
Lecture 8

Frédéric Chopin's preludes—like all of his piano music—are true "piano music," music written idiomatically for the piano. No matter how easy or difficult the piece, no matter how idiosyncratic the fingering, Chopin's piano music "fits the hand," meaning that the music was conceived with the physiognomy of the human hand in mind and how the hand lies on a keyboard. Chopin's mature music was conceived for a very different piano than those available to Mozart. Chopin, unlike Mozart—or even Beethoven—was composing for a full metal-harped piano, an instrument capable of much more volume and resonance than the wooden-harped pianos of a generation before.

Rubato

- *Rubato* is Italian for "robbed time." The rubato technique requires a performer to rob time from one note in order to give it to another. By such delicate displacement of the beat, Chopin the pianist could create a degree of rhythmic fluidity and lyric nuance that allowed him to make the piano sing.

- Rubato cannot be notated; the tiny gradations of beat and tempo would be impossible to write down. Like swinging a tune, rubato is something a player learns by ear and by "feel." For Chopin, rubato came naturally; it was an element of traditional Polish music.

- Chopin's Prélude no. 7 in A Major, Op. 28, is an example of rubato. This shortest of all Chopin's preludes demands the sort of rhythmic flexibility and exhibits the sorts of lyricism, harmonic complexity, and expressive nuance that are collectively the hallmarks of Chopin's compositional voice.

- Chopin's notation about the rhythm of the prelude tells us that the piece is set in triple meter, which the accompanimental left hand clunks out with clocklike regularity. The tempo marking—

andantino—is ambiguous, as it can mean either a little slower than **andante** (moderately slow) or a little faster than andante. The melodic material above the accompaniment exhibits a rhythmic pattern that is repeated verbatim eight times over the course of the prelude's 16 measures.

- This rhythmic pattern—a dotted rhythm on the first beat in triple meter—is the characteristic rhythm of the Polish dance called the mazurka. While Chopin doesn't call this prelude a "mazurka," it can be played as one by ever so slightly accenting the second beat of each measure. It was for this reason that the 19th-century pianist and conductor Hans von Bülow nicknamed this prelude "The Polish Dancer."

- On paper, the apparent regularities of this prelude would seem to indicate music of mechanical repetitiousness. But of course, mechanical it is not, because a proper performance will employ a judicious bit of rubato. The dotted eighth-sixteenth note figures on the downbeats should be played as though they were tightly wound springs, releasing with a slight push to the notes that follow. The two quarter notes and half note that follow each of the dotted rhythms is something called a written ritard, in which progressively longer note values indicate a waning of rhythmic momentum.

- The momentum is reestablished when the following pickup kick-starts things, leading to the next dotted eighth-sixteenth note figure, which is followed by another written ritard, and so forth. Thus, in performance, there should be a constant—if subtle—rise and fall of rhythmic momentum, of rhythmic tension and release.

- The harmonic language of the prelude further focuses our attention on the dotted eighth-sixteenth note figures. Every one of those dotted eighth notes falls on a downbeat, the first and most powerfully felt beat in each measure, and every one of those dotted eighth notes is something called an appoggiatura, which is a non-chord tone—a dissonance—that falls on a strong beat, a dissonance that then resolves on a weaker beat. In the case of this prelude, the appoggiaturas resolve upward to the sixteenth note that follows the dotted eighth. For example, the harmony in measure 1 is the dominant chord of the tonic A major, an E-dominant seven chord.

- The C-sharp on the downbeat of measure 1 is a dissonance; it resolves upward to the chord tone D on the sixteenth note that follows. The chords that fall on beats 2 and 3 and the downbeat of measure 2 repeat the harmony and have the effect of settling things down until the next

Frédéric Chopin (1810–1849) composed solo piano works of exquisite subtlety and nuance—works that sound as if only he could have written them.

appoggiatura on the downbeat of measure 3. These appoggiaturas create an exquisite sense of tension and yearning by beginning every other measure with a dissonance.

24 Préludes

- In 1836, Franz Liszt introduced Chopin to a divorcée named Amantine-Aurore-Lucile Dupin, Baroness Dudevant (who lived from 1804 to 1876). The baroness was a novelist, playwright, and feminist who wrote under the pen name of George Sand. At the time they met, Chopin was 26 and Aurore/George was 32. If we are to believe contemporary gossip, Chopin was at first repelled by her, but by 1838, they were living together, and their relationship continued until 1847.

- Their famously disastrous family vacation on the island of Majorca took place during the winter of 1838 to 1839. It rained nonstop, their rental house was damp and moldy, and Chopin's troubled lungs almost gave out.

- Thankfully, Chopin was neither dead nor dying, and despite his health, he worked on his *Préludes*. It was in Majorca that George Sand personally observed Chopin's compositional agonies. It was while in Majorca that Chopin completed the preludes and sent them off to his publisher. And while it is true that he had begun working on the set back in 1836, it was on Majorca that the set took on its final form.

- That final form is based on the 24 preludes—one in each major and minor key—of Johann Sebastian Bach's *The Well-Tempered Clavier*. Of course, the big difference is that Bach's preludes are indeed preludes—short, freeform works that precede fugues. For Chopin's contemporaries, the idea of a self-standing prelude made no sense.

- Each of the 24 preludes represents a single "emotional setting." In his desire to identify the emotion that each prelude represents, the 19th-century pianist and conductor Hans von Bülow went so far as to title each of the preludes. Von Bülow's titles range from "Heartfelt Happiness" (no. 19) to "Suicide" (for no. 18) and from "A Pleasure Boat" (no. 23) to "Funeral March" (no. 20). We will use von Bülow's titles as a guide as we seek to identify the emotion that a selection of preludes represents.

Prélude No. 1 in C Major: "Reunion"
- The "reunion" described by von Bülow is certainly not one with a former spouse. The breathless and ecstatic opening gives way to a tender conclusion. This is joyful music—the perfect way to begin the set.

Prélude No. 4 in E Minor: "Suffocation"
- This prelude was composed in Majorca in November of 1838. Cast in two large phrases—A and A^1—it consists of a slow-moving

melody set over throbbing, falling chords in the accompaniment. The irregular manner in which the accompanying chords change adds a tremendous degree of expressive nuance to this prelude, which is informed with a sense of despair, one that Hans von Bülow characterized as "suffocation."

- Along with the dour Prélude no. 6 in B Minor, this prelude, in E minor, was played at Chopin's funeral, which was held on October 30, 1849. Acceding to Chopin's deathbed request "to play Mozart for me," among the other works performed was Mozart's *Requiem*.

Prélude No. 5 in D Major: "Uncertainty"
- Despite the fact that this prelude does indeed conclude in the advertised key of D major, it spends the bulk of its time flitting about a tremendous number of different key areas during its 40-second life, particularly the key of D minor. The "uncertainty" that is von Bülow's nickname has to do with this harmonic ambiguity, unresolved until the prelude's very last chord.

Prélude No. 15 in D-flat Major: "Raindrop"
- This 15th prelude is the longest in the set; it runs about five minutes in performance. It also comes with more anecdotal baggage than any other prelude, thanks to George Sand, who wrote a description of the circumstances in Majorca under which the prelude was presumably composed.

> "[The prélude] came to him through an evening of dismal rain. Maurice and I had left him to go shopping. The rain came in overflowing torrents. We [returned] in the middle of a flood. We hurried, knowing how our sick one would worry. Indeed he had; weeping, he was playing his wonderful prélude. Seeing us come in, he got up with a cry, then said, 'I was sure that you were dead.' When he recovered his spirits he confessed to me that while waiting he had seen it all in a dream: that he was dead himself [and] heavy drops of icy water fell in a regular rhythm on his breast. When I made him listen to the sound of the drops of water falling in

rhythm on the roof, he denied having heard it, angry that I should interpret [the prélude] in terms of imitative sounds. [So, while] his composition was surely filled with raindrops, they had been transformed in his imagination into tears falling upon his heart from the sky."

- Unfortunately, George Sand never specified precisely which prelude she was referring to, but posterity has decided that it is the D-flat major.

Prélude No. 16 in B-flat Minor: "Hades"
- Von Bülow's nickname is a reference to the fact that this is a hellaciously difficult piece to play. Chopin indicates that the prelude is to be played *presto con fuoco*, meaning "very fast and with fire." The pianist's task is to play the four pages of nonstop sixteenth notes at the indicated tempo, which comes out to a speed of nine sixteenth notes per second. Anything faster and a piano will ignite.

Prélude No. 20 in C Minor: "Funeral March"
- Of all von Bülow's nicknames, "Funeral March" is the most obviously appropriate. This slow, dark prelude plods along in quarter notes, with a new harmony occurring every quarter note. More than any other of Chopin's Op. 28 preludes, it is no. 20 that has taken on a life of its own.

- The Italian composer Ferruccio Busoni composed a theme-and-variations-form work based on this prelude. In 1903, Sergey Rachmaninoff composed his own set of variations based on this prelude, a piece appropriately entitled *Variations on a Theme of Chopin*.

Important Term

andante: Moderately slow.

Chopin—*Préludes*, Op. 28
Lecture 8—Transcript

Welcome back to *The 23 Greatest Solo Piano Works*. This is Lecture 8. It is entitled Chopin—*Préludes*, Op. 28.

For the artistes and intellectuals of the 19th century, instrumental music—ephemeral, non-tactile, and therefore boundless—became the ultimate art form. According to Ernst Theodore Amadeus (or E. T. A.) Hoffmann, who lived from 1776 to 1822 and was the most influential music critic of his time, instrumental music "discloses to man an unknown realm, a world that has nothing in common with the external world; [an unknown realm] in which he leaves behind him all definite feelings to surrender himself to an inexpressible longing."

It was this perception of the mysterious and immeasurable expressive power of instrumental music that led the 19th-century English essayist and critic Walter Pater to suggest that "all art constantly aspires to the condition of music."

My friends, writers are urged to write what they know. The equivalent advice for a cutting-edge 19th-century composer would have been compose what you feel. The post-Beethoven artistic fetish for heightened individual expression saw composers evoke in their music an ever-wider range of emotional states even as they sought to cultivate a personal musical sound. For Frédéric Chopin (1810–1849), this meant composing solo piano works of exquisite subtlety and nuance, works that sound as if only he could have written them.

For a 19th-century musical scene so enamored of the mysterious power of instrumental music and heightened personal expression, the solo piano became the ultimate instrument: a virtual orchestra operated by a single player whose deepest musical thoughts and feelings could be expressed with total freedom, unhindered by any other instrumental parts.

"Romantic Era" Defined

We commonly associate the adjective "romantic" with love and affection. While many of us are quite attached to the art of the 19th century, the love thing has nothing to do with the period designation. The adjective "romantic" comes from the noun "romance." A romance was a medieval story that celebrated heroism and chivalry; a story written in one of the Roman languages: that is, one of the languages descended from Latin. By the 19th century, the word "romantic" had come to identify something remote, mysterious, sublime, boundless, and beyond the everyday; in contemporary surf-speak, "far out."

The intrinsic far-outness of much 19th-century music manifested itself in various ways, but it all boiled down to one basic artistic premise: In the post-Beethoven, increasingly middle-class-oriented, 19th-century Euro-world, composers took for granted that they should somehow express themselves in their music. Hand-in-hand with this self-expressive mindset was the emergence of our modern concept of the composer, based on the idealized model of Beethoven, "of the lonely artist-hero whose suffering produces works of awe-inspiring greatness that give listeners otherwise unavailable access to an experience that transcends all worldly concerns." "His kingdom is not of this world," declared Hoffmann of Beethoven, making explicit reference to the figure regarded by Christians as the world-redeeming Messiah.

The self-expressive urge of the 19th century took many forms. For example, Frédéric Chopin used the intimacy of the solo piano to create nuanced miniature works of kaleidoscopic expressive variety and delicacy. During the first part of his career, Robert Schumann (1810–1856) used the piano to create a series of autobiographical works, which span the expressive gamut from musical portraits of his friends (*Carnaval* of 1835) to his passion for his future wife (*Kreisleriana* of 1838). Franz Liszt (1811–1886) elevated pianism and pianistic virtuosity to an art form unto itself, and created a body of work that served to celebrate the virtuoso (meaning Liszt himself) as hero.

Chopin: The Anti-Romantic Romantic

Chopin's last words were reportedly, "Play Mozart in memory of me." Apocryphal or not, Chopin's request reveals a basic truth about his musical priorities. Despite the fact that his music and pianism were nothing short of revolutionary, Chopin maintained that his music and pianism had evolved from Mozart, and certainly not from that "thumper" Beethoven and absolutely not from the so-called romantics among whom he numbered his friends, colleagues, and lovers.

Chopin's attitude was contradictory. On one hand, the expressive nuance of his music, its lyric spontaneity, and the harmonic and rhythmic syntax he employed to create that nuance and spontaneity was in all ways modern. That Chopin's music was perceived by his contemporaries as being in all ways modern is evidenced by the consistent drubbing it took from conservative critics. For example, in a review of Chopin's *Mazurkas* written in 1833, the well-known German critic Ludwig Rellstab wrote, "in search of ear-rending dissonances, tortuous transitions, repugnant contortions of melody and rhythm, Chopin is altogether tireless. Had he submitted this music to a teacher, the latter, it is hoped, would have torn it up and thrown it at his feet—and this is what we symbolically wish to do."

The fact remains that Chopin's music is utterly romantic by every standard we might choose to employ. His use of the piano was entirely idiosyncratic: brand new, despite his claim that his pianism grew out of Mozart. Chopin's ultra-advanced harmonic language gives his music a color and depth of expressive nuance that, again, is sui generis. Chopin's music sounds like Chopin's music, and no one else's. His cultivation of his own, personal musical voice is the essence of the expressive individuality that stands at the heart of romanticism. As an example of Chopin's signature sound, we hear his brilliant and subtle Prélude No. 19 in E-flat Major, composed between 1836 and 1839. [**Piano performance:** Chopin, Prélude No. 19 in E-flat Major, op. 28.]

So, back to the contradiction. For all of his arch-romantic modernity, Chopin claimed to abhor romantic art and music. While the painter Eugene Delacroix was one of his best friends, Chopin confessed that he neither liked nor understood Delacroix's work. Chopin claimed that the music of Hector Berlioz made him physically ill and that Franz Liszt's music was meaningless. He rarely missed an opportunity to disparage the music of Robert Schumann, ignored almost entirely the works of Felix Mendelssohn and Franz Schubert, and went out of his way to avoid the music of Beethoven, which he claimed was in "poor taste." The only composers he claimed to like were Johann Sebastian Bach, Wolfgang Mozart, and the contemporary composer of Italian opera, Vincenzo Bellini.

Chopin: Biographical Background

Chopin was born on March 1, 1810 in suburban Warsaw. His mother, Justyna, was a native Pole from the lower nobility. His father, Nicolas, was French. Nicholas had come to Poland in 1787 when he was 16 years old and stayed there to avoid being drafted into the French Revolutionary Army. By the time Frédéric was born in 1810, his father, who taught French for a living, had become a die-hard Polish patriot. It was a patriotic spirit he passed on to all four of his children.

Unlike so many artists whose independence of spirit made them lousy students, Chopin was a bright and conscientious pupil. He was also so precocious a musician that the locals in Warsaw began referring to him as "Mozart's successor." Chopin's early celebrity put him in contact with Warsaw's upper crust, in whose homes he performed, whose daughters he taught, and with whose daughters he flirted. By the time he was a teenager he had acquired an attitude and a love for the high life. It was an aristo-attitude that assured him entry into the *haute monde* of Parisian society when, seeking his fame and fortune, he moved to Paris in 1831 at the age of 21. According to Harold Schonberg:

> He was a slight, refined-looking man, not much over a hundred pounds in weight, with a prominent nose, a pale complexion and beautiful hands. He was a snob and a social butterfly, to whom moving in the best circles meant everything. He dressed in the height of fashion, kept a carriage, had a precise mind and precise manners, could be witty, was a fine mimic, and was ultra-conservative in his aesthetic tastes. He made a good deal of money

and spent it lavishly, always complaining that he did not have more. "You think I am making a fortune?" [he wrote a friend.] "Carriages and white gloves cost a lot, and without them one would not be in good taste." Certainly, good taste meant more to him than the romantic movement that was sweeping Europe.

Chopin composed almost exclusively for the piano. Except for two early piano concerti, a few works for piano and orchestra, an early 'cello sonata, and a few songs, Chopin's output consists entirely of works for solo piano. The majority of these are sets of instrumental miniatures: compositions that rarely last more than a few minutes.

Taken together, Chopin's piano works are a pillar of the modern piano repertoire and constitute an encyclopedia of modern pianism. They include 15 *Polonaises*, or "Polish dances," (sixteen, if we include the so-called *Polonaise-Fantaisie*), 21 *Nocturnes*, 20 *Waltzes*, 4 *Scherzos*, 4 *Impromptus*, 58 *Mazurkas* (another type of Polish dance), 27 *Etudes*, and 28 *Préludes*.

Chopin was a great piano virtuoso. However, unlike his on-again, off-again buddy Franz Liszt, virtuosity in Chopin's piano music is the means to an expressive end rather than the end unto itself. In fact, the lyric intimacy and harmonic subtlety of Chopin's music make it almost anti-heroic, despite its often formidable difficulty. As an example of Chopin's craft and voice, we will—in a moment—analyze his jewel-like Prélude No. 7 in A Major. But first, we must talk about the performance technique that lies at the heart and soul of Chopin's style.

Rubato

Rubato is Italian for "robbed time." It's a technique that requires a performer to become a musical Robin Hood, robbing time from one note in order to give it to another. By such delicate displacement of the beat, Chopin the pianist could create a degree of rhythmic fluidity and lyric nuance that allowed him to make the piano sing.

Rubato cannot be notated; the tiny gradations of beat and tempo would be impossible to write down. Like swinging a tune, rubato is something a player learns by ear and by feel. For Chopin, rubato came naturally, as it was an element of traditional Polish music. Chopin's friend, the pianist and conductor Charles Hallé, told this story:

> A remarkable feature of his playing was the entire freedom with which he treated rhythm. It must have been in 1845 or 1846 that I once ventured to observe to him that most of his *mazurkas* - when played by himself - appeared to be written not in ¾ but in 4/4 time, the result of his dwelling so much longer on the first note of the bar. He denied it strenuously, until I made him play one of them and counted audibly four to the bar. Then he laughed and explained that it was the national character of the dance which created the oddity. I understood later how ill-advised I had been to make that observation to him, and how well disposed towards me he must have been to have taken it with such good humor.

As an example of rubato, we turn to Chopin's Prélude No. 7 in A Major, Op. 28. This shortest of all Chopin's préludes demands the sort of rhythmic flexibility and exhibits the sorts of lyricism, harmonic complexity, and expressive nuance that are collectively the hallmarks of Chopin's compositional voice.

Here's what Chopin's notation tells us about the rhythm of the prélude. The piece is set in triple meter, which the accompanimental left hand clunks out with clock-like regularity. [**Piano demonstration.**] The tempo marking, *Andantino*, is ambiguous, as it can mean either a little slower than *andante* (moderately slow) or a little faster than *andante*. The melodic material above the accompaniment exhibits a rhythmic pattern that is repeated verbatim eight times over the course of the prélude's 16 measures. This rhythmic pattern—a dotted rhythm on the first beat in triple meter—is the characteristic rhythm of the Polish dance called the mazurka. While Chopin doesn't call this prélude a mazurka, it can be played as one by ever-so-slightly accenting the second beat of each measure. It was for this reason that the nineteenth century pianist and conductor Hans von Bülow nicknamed this prélude "The Polish Dancer."

On paper, the apparent regularities of this prélude would seem to indicate music of mechanical repetitiousness. [**Piano demonstration.**] But of course, mechanical it is not, because a proper performance will employ a judicious bit of rubato. The dotted eighth-sixteenth note figures on the downbeats should be played as though they were tightly wound springs, releasing with a slight push to the notes that follow. [**Piano demonstration.**] The two quarter notes and half note that follow each of the dotted rhythms is something called a written *ritard*, in which progressively longer note values indicate a waning of rhythmic momentum. [**Piano demonstration.**] The momentum is reestablished when the following pickup kick-starts things, leading to the next dotted eighth-sixteenth note figure, which is followed by another written *ritard*, and so forth. Thus, in performance, there should be a constant, if subtle, rise and fall of rhythmic momentum, of rhythmic tension and release. [**Piano performance:** Chopin, Prélude No. 7 in A Major, op. 28.]

Chopin's Health

Chopin was as physically fragile as a floor lamp from IKEA (don't get me started on that). He was thin, frail, and sickly his entire life, which lasted only a bit over 39 years. Throughout his life he had trouble breathing and constant fevers; he coughed continuously; experienced frequent lung infections; and suffered from depression, hallucinations, and migraine headaches.

Various diagnoses have been proposed to explain Chopin's health problems, from pulmonary tuberculosis to temporal lobe epilepsy. We need not settle on any particular diagnosis; let's just say that Chopin was not a healthy man. Our interest in Chopin's health is not merely anecdotal, because Chopin completed the Op. 24 préludes during a particularly bad bout of ill health during one of the worst vacations of all time. Here's the story.

Aurore, Majorca, and 24 Préludes

In 1836, Franz Liszt introduced Chopin to a divorcee named Amantine-Aurore-Lucile Dupin, Baroness Dudevant (who lived from 1804–1876). The Baroness was a novelist, playwright, and a feminist, given to smoking cigars and pipes in public and wearing men's clothing (which, the Baroness pointed out, were less expensive and much more durable than the outfits noble women were expected to wear). Baroness Dudevant wrote under the penname of "George Sand." At the time they met, Chopin was 26 and

Aurore/George was 32. If we are to believe contemporary gossip, Chopin was at first repelled by the short, dumpy, tobacco-breathed Ms. Sand. But by 1838 they were living together, and their relationship continued until 1847.

Their famously disastrous family vacation on the island of Majorca took place during the winter of 1838–1839. It rained nonstop, their rental house was damp and moldy, and Chopin's troubled lungs almost gave out. Chopin wrote a friend: "The three most celebrated doctors on the island have seen me. One sniffed at what I spat, the second tapped where I spat, the third listened as I spat. The first said I was dead, the second that I am dying, the third that I'm going to die."

Thankfully, Chopin was neither dead nor dying, and despite his health, he worked on his préludes. It was in Majorca that George Sand observed Chopin's compositional agonies up-close and personal. She wrote:

> His creation was spontaneous and miraculous. He found it without seeking it, without foreseeing it, complete, sublime. But then began the most heart-rending labor I ever saw. It was a series of efforts to seize certain details he had heard [in his mind's ear]; and his regret at not finding them again threw him into despair. He shut himself up for whole days, weeping, walking, breaking his pens, repeating and altering a bar a hundred times, writing and erasing it, and recommencing the next day with desperate perseverance. He spent six weeks over a single page to write it at last as he had noted it down at the very first.

It was while in Majorca that Chopin completed the préludes and sent them off to his publisher. And while it is true that he had begun working on the set back in 1836, it was on Majorca that the set took on its final form. That final form is based on the 24 préludes—one in each major and minor key—of Johann Sebastian Bach's *The Well-Tempered Clavier*. Of course, the big difference is that Bach's préludes are indeed PRE-ludes—short, free-form works that PRE-cede fugues. For Chopin's contemporaries, the idea of a "self-standing prélude" made about as much sense as "deep fried ice cream." The French author André Gide wrote:

I admit that I do not understand the title that Chopin [gave] to these short pieces: Préludes. Préludes to what? Each of Bach's préludes is followed by its fugue. But I find it [impossible] to imagine any one of these Préludes of Chopin followed by any other piece in the same key. Each one of them is a prélude to a meditation; nowhere has Chopin revealed himself more intimately. Each of them creates a particular atmosphere, establishes an emotional setting, then fades out. Some are charming, others terrifying. None are indifferent.

Gide's assertion that each of the 24 préludes represents a single emotional setting is absolutely correct. In his desire to identify that whiff of emotion each prélude represents, the 19th-century pianist and conductor Hans Von Bülow went so far as to entitle each of the préludes. Von Bülow's titles range from "Heartfelt Happiness" (for No. 19) to "suicide" (for No. 18); from "A Pleasure Boat" (No. 23) to "Funeral March" (No. 20). We are going to use von Bülow's titles as our guide as we seek to identify that whiff of emotion that a selection of préludes represents.

Prélude No. 1 in C Major: "Reunion"

The "reunion" described by von Bülow is certainly not one with a former spouse. The breathless and ecstatic opening gives way to a tender conclusion. This is joyful music, and to my ear, the perfect way to begin the set. [**Piano performance:** Chopin, Prélude No. 1 in C Major, op. 28.]

Prélude No. 4 in E Minor: "Suffocation"

This prélude was composed in Majorca in November of 1838. Cast in two large phrases—A and A^1—it consists of a slow-moving melody set over throbbing, falling chords in the accompaniment. The irregular manner in which the accompanying chords change adds a tremendous degree of expressive nuance to this prélude, which is informed with a sense of despair, one that Hans von Bülow characterized as "suffocation." [**Piano performance:** Chopin, Prélude No. 4 in E Minor, op. 28.]

Along with the dour Prélude No. 6 in B Minor, this prélude in E Minor was played at Chopin's funeral, which was held at Paris's Church of the Madeline on October 30, 1849. Acceding to Chopin's deathbed request "to play Mozart for me," among the other works performed was Mozart's *Requiem*. An additional factoid, offered without editorial comment: This prélude was used in the soundtrack of the 1982 motion picture *Death Wish II*, one of a series of urban vigilante movies starring the granite-faced Charles Bronson.

Prélude No. 5 in D Major: "Uncertainty"

Despite the fact that this prélude does indeed conclude in the advertised key of D Major, it spends the bulk of its time flitting about a tremendous number of different key areas during its 40-second life, particularly the key of D Minor. The uncertainty that is von Bülow's nickname has to do with this harmonic ambiguity, unresolved until the prélude's very last chord. [**Piano performance:** Chopin, Prélude No. 5 in D Major, op. 28.]

Prélude No. 15 in D-flat Major: "Raindrop"

This 15th prélude is the longest in the set: It runs about five minutes in performance. It also comes with more anecdotal baggage than any other prélude, thanks to George Sand, who wrote a description of the circumstances—in Majorca—under which the prélude was presumably composed. We read Madame's description:

> [The prélude] came to him through an evening of dismal rain. Maurice and I had left him to go shopping. The rain came in overflowing torrents. We [returned] in the middle of a flood. We hurried, knowing how our sick one would worry. Indeed he had; weeping, he was playing his wonderful prélude. Seeing us come in, he got up with a cry, then said, "I was sure that you were dead." When he recovered his spirits he confessed to me that while waiting he had seen it all in a dream: that he was dead himself [and] heavy drops of icy water fell in a regular rhythm on his breast. When I made him listen to the sound of the drops of water falling in rhythm on the roof, he denied having heard it, angry that I should interpret [the prélude] in terms of imitative sounds. [So, while] his composition was surely filled with raindrops, they had been transformed in his imagination into tears falling upon his heart from the sky.

It's a great story. Unfortunately, George Sand never specified precisely which prélude she was referring to! Posterity has decided that it is the D-flat Major, and right or wrong, we will go along with that. Here it is. [**Piano performance:** Chopin, Prélude No. 15 in D-flat Major, op. 28.]

Prélude No. 16 in B-flat Minor: "Hades"

To my mind von Bülow's nickname is a direct reference to the fact that this is a hellaciously difficult piece to play. Chopin indicates that the prélude is to be played *presto con fuoco*, meaning "very fast and with fire." Fire is right, given the pianist's task, which is to play the four pages of nonstop sixteenth notes at the indicated tempo, which comes out to a speed of nine sixteenth notes per second. Anything faster and a piano will ignite. Let's hear it. [**Piano performance:** Chopin, Prélude no. 16 in B-flat Minor, op. 28.]

The concert pianist Vladimir De Pachmann, who lived from 1848–1933 and whose reputation was built on his performances of Chopin, said of this prélude: "The sixteenth is my great favorite! It is the greatest *tour de force* in Chopin. It is the most difficult of all the préludes technically, excepting possibly the nineteenth. In this case, *presto* is not [fast] enough! It should be played *prestissimo*." A suggestion for maestro De Pachmann: Top off your piano's radiator with some industrial-grade coolant, 'cause at that speed, you risk ignition!

Prélude No. 20 in C Minor: "Funeral March"

Of all von Bülow's nicknames, "Funeral March" is the most obviously appropriate. This slow, dark, prélude plods along in quarter notes, with a new harmony occurring every quarter note. [**Piano performance:** Chopin, Prélude no. 20 in C Minor, op. 28.] More than any other of Chopin's Op. 28 préludes, it is this one—No. 20—that has taken on a life of its own. The Italian composer Ferruccio Busoni composed a theme and variations form work based on this prélude. In 1903, Sergei Rachmaninoff composed his own set of variations based on this prélude, a piece appropriately entitled *Variations on a Theme of Chopin.*

On a rather more prosaic note, Barry Manilow based his song "Could It Be Magic" on this prélude. Manilow's ditty reached number 6 on the US pop charts in 1975. To add further insult to Chopin's injury, Manilow's song was recorded by the disco queen Donna Summer and the English vocal group Take That. Poor Chopin. "Take That" is right!

Chopin and the Piano

Chopin's préludes—like all of Chopin's piano music—are true piano music: music written idiomatically for the piano. No matter how easy or difficult the piece, no matter how idiosyncratic the fingering, Chopin's piano music fits the hand, meaning that the music was conceived with the physiognomy of the human hand in mind and how the hand lies on a keyboard.

Chopin's mature music was conceived for a very different piano than those available to his fave-rave, Wolfgang Mozart. You see, Chopin, unlike Mozart—or even Beethoven—was composing for a full metal-harped piano, an instrument capable of an order of magnitude more volume, resonance, and punch than the wooden-harped pianos of a generation before. Let's hear one more prélude, No. 22 in G Minor, and let's be aware of the octaves in the bass that make this music roar like Niagara Falls! (Slowly I turn.) This is new music being written for what was, in the 1830s, a very new instrument. [**Piano performance:** Chopin, Prélude No. 22 in G Minor, op. 28.]

Thank you.

Chopin—Ballade in G Minor, Op. 23
Lecture 9

I t is a waste of time trying to distinguish between Chopin the composer and Chopin the pianist. They were, in fact, the same. Chopin composed at the piano. He required the feel of the keys beneath his fingers and the actual sound of the piano in his ears to write his music, music of stunning originality. Chopin's very special way of playing the piano, in which different fingers were associated with different sorts of melody lines, grew out of his very special way of hearing music. Or did Chopin's music grow out of the way he played the piano? It's a chicken-or-egg question that does not need to be answered. Chopin the composer and Chopin the pianist coevolved.

Chopin at the Piano

- The 21-year-old Chopin arrived in Paris in late September of 1831 seeking fame and fortune. He found both, very quickly, which comes as no surprise, given that at 21 he was already a fully formed composer and, along with Franz Liszt, the greatest pianist on the planet. He arrived with a passel of new works in hand; among them were his two piano concerti and 11 of the 12 Études for Piano, Op. 10.

- Among the friends Chopin made early on in Paris was Camille Pleyel, who was—along with Sébastian Erard—France's most important piano manufacturer. Chopin adored Pleyel's pianos and used them whenever he could. Camille Pleyel was likewise thrilled with his new Polish friend, and it was under Pleyel's marquee that Chopin made his Paris public debut, at the Salle Pleyel, on February 26, 1932. It was a most auspicious debut; among the many important attendees were Franz Liszt, Felix Mendelssohn, Ferdinand Hiller, and Luigi Cherubini.

- What the attendees heard at the Salle Pleyel was a sort of music and a sort of piano playing they had never heard before. Chopin employed a technique called rubato. They heard a pianist with a remarkably flexible approach to rhythm, what Franz Liszt called "a tempo swaying and balancing." They heard a pianist whose legato, meaning Chopin's ability to string adjacent notes together, "could make the piano sing as vividly as any vocalist."

- They heard a pianist with an exquisitely shaded approach to dynamics. Chopin's loudest notes rarely got above forte, but the subtle degrees of quietness with which he played made those not-really-very-loud moments sound like thunder. Finally and most importantly, what the audience at the Salle Pleyel heard in Chopin was a pianist and composer who created an entirely new sort of piano music for what was an entirely new sort of piano.

Chopin's Ballades: New Music for a New Piano

- Between 1835 and 1842, Chopin composed four works he entitled "Ballade." They are among the longest solo piano works he ever composed, ranging in length from between 7 and 11 minutes. They remain among the most challenging works to play in the standard repertoire.

- The word "ballad"—or, in French, *ballade*—is one of those generic terms that has meant different things at different times. For Chopin, a "ballade" was a lengthy poem that told a narrative story replete with different characters and even dialogue. By entitling these four musical works as "ballades," Chopin ascribed to them a dramatic/narrative character, although it is an emotional narrative that they describe rather than a literary one.

- Chopin's Ballades are often described as being cast in sonata form, and they do indeed feature multiple contrasting themes that are—to some degree—developed and recapitulated, but it would be best to think of the Ballades as having been informed by, but not rooted in, sonata form.

- Harmonically, formally, and expressively, these pieces go far beyond the rituals of sonata form, particularly in their apotheosis-like character, meaning that the first, third, and fourth ballades are

With the exception of two early piano concerti, a few miscellaneous works for piano and orchestra, an early 'cello sonata, and a few songs, Frédéric Chopin's output consists entirely of works for solo piano.

all dramatically back weighted—in that their rate of change and dramatic intensity accelerates until their final, glorious, apotheosis-like conclusions.

Ballade in G Minor

- The Ballade in G Minor begins with a slow introduction consisting of a meandering melody written in octaves. The introduction concludes with an open cadence: a harmonic dissonance that anticipates a resolution to the home (or tonic) key of G minor.

- In particular, you should be aware of the following two things while listening to the introduction: Its meandering, unaccompanied melody has a genuinely voice-like quality, and the fact that this introductory melody is set in octaves gives it tremendous pianistic resonance and weight.

- The introduction subtly prepares the ear for the climactic octaves that conclude the ballade. In the explosive concluding apotheosis of the ballade, upward-rippling scales lead to a cataclysmic inward collapse in octaves, a collapse that spans the entire seven-octave range of Chopin's piano.

- Chopin indicates that this closing collapse—in which both of the pianist's hands are playing octaves—be performed fortississimo, or "very, very loud." Chopin could not have conceived such a passage had he been writing for a six-octave, wooden-harped piano, which would have splintered into toothpicks under such an assault. But he was composing for a 7'5"-long metal-harped Pleyel, an instrument with thunder to spare, and Chopin spared it not.

- However, Chopin's Pleyel was also capable of an extraordinary degree of quiet nuance, which is put into high relief during the first theme that follows the introduction. Despite being notated in compound duple meter, theme 1 has a vaguely waltz-like sensibility about it. It is a long, intensely lyric theme that starts with a whisper, builds to a magnificent bravura (meaning "virtuosic") climax, and then fades away.

- The theme begins with dissonant, tightly wound melodic figures that find resolution and release in the longer notes that follow. The theme is "through-composed," meaning that its constituent phrases grow and develop continuously until a climax is reached followed by a brief refractory period and the conclusion of the theme.

- In order to perform this theme with the lyric flexibility and sonority it demands, a pianist—aside from playing all the right notes—is going to have to do three things. First, in order to achieve the rhythmic flexibility that the theme demands, a pianist will have to employ rubato—that is, a judiciously lengthening and shortening of the rhythms. It will not do to play this theme in strict time. In the words of Franz Liszt, the tempo must "sway and balance."

- The second thing that a pianist must do to perform this theme properly is play the thematic melody legato, meaning "tied together." For a pianist, this means not releasing one melody note until the next one has been played, with the result being a smooth, unbroken melodic continuity.

- Finally, a pianist must use the sustain pedal in a most artful manner, in order to draw ever-varied sonorities from the piano and, by doing so, allow the music to breathe. On a modern piano, the right-hand pedal is called the "sustain" or "damper" pedal. When it is depressed, all the dampers are lifted away from all the strings, allowing the strings to vibrate freely until the pedal is released.

- The sustain pedal has rightly been called "the soul of the piano." It allows pianists to smoothly connect widely spaced notes that could not be connected through fingering. The sustain pedal allows the sonority of a piano to blossom like a flower or explode like a bomb. When carefully employed, the sustain pedal allows a piano to breathe. However, when overused by a lead-footed barbarian, the sustain pedal will occlude the music under performance.

- In traditional sonata form, theme 1 is followed by a passage called the modulating bridge, a passage tasked with transitioning to the second theme and to the new key area in which the second theme will be heard. Chopin's modulating bridge is something much more than that; it is a piece within a piece—a fantasia—an improvisation of melodic ideas first presented in the introduction.

- Chopin's fabulous second theme in E-flat major would have been instantly recognizable to his contemporaries as a barcarole, a theme composed in the style of a folk song sung by Venetian gondoliers. The exposition concludes with a gentle cadence theme that grows directly out of the boatman's song of theme 2.

- The literature refers to what follows as the development section, but by referring to a passage of music as a sonata-form development section, we bunch it together with a vast number of other development sections that all do more or less the same thing—that is, systematically fragment material presented in the exposition in an essentially unstable, meaning modulatory, harmonic environment. That is most certainly not what Chopin does.

- In reality, Chopin's erstwhile "development section" is a massive variation or extension of the exposition. It begins with theme 1, heard in the key of A minor, which is followed immediately by a huge and heroic version of theme 2, heard initially in the key of E major. When listening to this, be aware that this is modern piano music from top to bottom—music that moves from hushed intimacy to thunderous passion at the drop of a note.

- The remainder of this so-called development section consists of a vastly expanded version of the so-called modulating bridge followed by a passionate version of theme 2 followed by the cadence theme. We heard these same events—in the same order—in the exposition, though now they are presented in an evermore-dramatic context.

- The recapitulation begins with theme 1 stated back in the tonic key of G minor, which is standard sonata-form operating procedure. From that point on, however, nothing is "standard" about the recapitulation. Following theme 1, Chopin dispenses entirely with the modulating bridge and theme 2 and the cadence theme and, instead, powers directly into the ripsnorting coda that brings this ballade to its concluding apotheosis.

Chopin—Ballade in G Minor, Op. 23
Lecture 9—Transcript

Welcome back to *The 23 Greatest Solo Piano Works*. This is Lecture 9, and it is entitled Chopin—Ballade in G Minor, Op. 23.

Chopin composed almost exclusively for the piano. With the exception of two early piano concerti, a few miscellaneous works for piano and orchestra, an early 'cello sonata, and a few songs, Chopin's output consists entirely of works for solo piano. The majority of these are sets of instrumental miniatures: compositions that rarely last more than just a few minutes.

Chopin's music is true piano music. No matter how easy or difficult the piece, no matter how idiosyncratic the fingering or impossibly fast the chord changes, the music was conceived with the actual physiognomy of the human hand in mind, and how the hand falls on a keyboard. Chopin's mature music was also conceived for what was, at the time, a brand new technology: the metal-harped piano.

The piano was invented around the year 1700 by a Paduan-born, Florence-based harpsichord builder named Bartolomeo Cristofori (who lived from 1655–1731). Cristofori's initial intention had been to build a harpsichord—that is, a mechanical harp—that was capable of getting progressively louder and softer. To that end, he created what was a revolutionary new action, one that used hammers to strike the strings rather than picks to pluck them. He called his instrument a *Gravicembalo* (that is, a big harpsichord) *col pian e forte*—a big harpsichord with soft and loud: pian e forte, a pianoforte, a soft-loud. Of course, what Cristofori had actually done was create an entirely new instrument. He spent the rest of his life tinkering with and improving his revolutionary action. To this day, pianos employ an action based on Cristofori's design.

It took awhile for the piano to make inroads against the harpsichord; my friends, people didn't immediately give up their horses when Karl Benz built his first practical automobile with a gasoline engine in 1885. There is always a degree of resistance to a new technology and besides, it takes time to work the kinks and bugs from any new technology. And when it came to early pianos, kinks and bugs there were.

Leadership in piano construction passed to German builders in the 1730s and 40s, thanks in particular to an organ, harpsichord, and piano builder named Gottfried Silbermann. Silbermann's many apprentices fanned out across Europe, and by the turn of the 19th century they were building pianos in Vienna, London, and Paris.

Along with their Cristofori-inspired actions, what all these early-19th-century pianos had in common was that they were built with wooden-framed harps. As long as piano frames continued to be built from wood, there was a limit to the number and thickness of its strings and therefore, a limit to its loudness and resonance; my friends, there's just so much tension you can put on wooden frame before it fails. Which brings us to the 1820s, which saw, according to piano historian Edwin Goode, "the most astonishing outburst of innovation in the history of the piano."

Of all these many astonishing innovations in piano construction, we would single out the two that revolutionized the instrument. Innovation number one: In 1821, the Paris-based piano builder Sébastian Erard patented his double-escapement action, also-known as the repetition action. This allowed a note to be repeated even if its key had not yet risen all the way back up to its full height—that is, back even with the other keys. This allowed rapid playing of repeated notes, a pianistic technique that was exploited to the nines by Franz Liszt, who for a time performed exclusively on these Erards.

A little background. Erard pianos with this action went into production in the early 1820s, at exactly the same time the 12-year-old Franz Liszt arrived in Paris. The Liszt family had been on a concert tour through Germany. By pure coincidence, when they arrived in Paris they checked into the *Hotel d'Angleterre* at No. 10 Rue du Mail, which was directly across the street from the Erard showroom and workshop. Young Franz wandered across the street, played the Erards on display, and was hooked. His father Adam wrote to Carl Czerny, back in Vienna: "I believe this man [Sébastian Erard] merits an important place in the field of piano manufacturers. So far there are three [of his new] pianos ready, and a fourth one is now being built for my son. The Erard piano reaches such a high level of perfection that it looks forward to the next century. It is impossible to describe it; one must see it, hear it, play it." In this Adam Liszt was entirely correct. Sébastian Erard's double-escapement action eventually became the industry standard, which it remains today.

OK, we were talking about the two astonishing innovations of the 1820s that revolutionized the piano. Innovation number two: In 1825, the Boston-based piano builder Alpheus Babcock patented his single-piece cast-iron harp frame, which culminated half a decade's worth of experimentation with metal framing on both sides of the Atlantic. The breakthrough was made, and within two years the Paris-based firm of Pleyel (which would soon enough become Chopin's piano of choice) was building metal-harped pianos. In 1827, the following letter from a Paris-based correspondent appeared in Philadelphia's *Franklin Journal*:

> Here, in Paris, we have lately got pianos, the frame-work of which is formed of cast iron. These instruments have been brought to such perfection by Monsieur Pleyel and Company that [they] surpass the best English instruments. The solidity of the frame-work is so great that they seldom get out of tune. The tone of these instruments is wonderful, both in power and mellowness.

Sounds good to me, though we should be aware that the introduction of iron forever changed the artisanal craft of piano building. The woodworkers and cabinet makers who had dedicated their lives to building pianos by hand were appalled; to their minds, wood lived and breathed, but iron—cold, gray, and dead—had no place in a musical instrument, or so they believed. But the writing had been on the wall for decades, as pianists—Beethoven principal among them—had been begging builders for larger, more resonant, more durable instruments.

By the 1820s, larger performance venues and the ever growing expressive resources employed by composers added to the demand for ever larger, more powerful, and more resonant instruments. Remember, too, that the 1820s were the salad days of the industrial revolution, and it was natural that advances in metallurgical fabrication and mass production would be applied to piano building as well. The metal harp frame changed the piano and the music written for the piano forever.

If Frédéric Chopin and Franz Liszt had not existed, we would have had to invent them: two great keyboard virtuosi of opposite artistic temperaments, who arrived in Paris just as the proto-modern piano was taking shape, there to create the software—that is, write the music—that would define what the new pianos were capable of doing.

Chopin: One of a Kind

Frédéric Chopin was born in what was the Duchy of Warsaw on March 1, 1810, and grew up in the city. His mother Justyna was a native Pole from the lower nobility, what we'd call the upper-middle class. His father, Nicolas, was from Lorraine—in France—and was a teacher of French by profession.

Chopin's formal piano lessons began when he was six. Love them or hate them (I personally drift towards the latter), Chopin was a crazy-amazing musical prodigy. Within a year—at the age of seven—he was giving concerts in the drawing rooms of Warsaw's aristocracy and being compared to Mozart. At the same time, he began to compose: two polonaises—"Polish dances"—one of which became his first publication. An article in the newspaper *Review of Warsaw* read:

> The composer of this Polish dance is only eight years of age. He is the son of Nicolas Chopin, teacher of French and literature at the Warsaw Lyceum. Not only does [young Frédéric] perform at the piano with remarkable ease and taste, but he has composed several dances and variations that fill music-lovers and critics with wonder. Had he been born in Germany or France, he would doubtless be famous in every contry in the world. May this article remind the reader that our country, too, can bring forth geniuses.

Darn straight. Chopin became a local sensation, the pride of Warsaw (which he remains to this day). Chopin's "refinement of ear" was nothing short of miraculous. As a child, aside from his native languages of Polish and French, he learned to speak and read Greek, Latin, German, English, and Italian.

His summers, spent in the countryside outside of Warsaw, exposed him to a wide variety of Slavonic folk music and songs, which he internalized with the same ease as languages: polonaises, mazurkas, krakowiaks, kujawiaks, obereks (are you getting these dances down?), as well as Jewish popular and Cantorial music.

Despite the efforts of many Eastern European writers and composers to categorize Chopin the composer as an explicitly Slavic nationalist, he was nothing of the sort. He was a universalist who created a sound and syntax utterly his own. Writing in *The Cambridge Companion to Chopin*, editor Jim Sampson correctly points out that "[Chopin's] music would prove a useful case study in a history of taste-creating."

Chopin's music doesn't fit into any category; rather, it created its own category, the only single relevant identifying factor of which is that it all sounds like it was composed by Frédéric Chopin. A key element of the Chopin sound is his idiosyncratic approach to traditional harmony. What that means is that Chopin's music often employs a degree of dissonance—of chromaticism—that left his contemporaries holding their hands over their ears and complaining of the ear-splitting dissonance.

For example, Chopin's Prélude in A Minor, Op. 28, No. 2. While the pianist and conductor Hans von Bülow called this prelude "presentiment of death," I would simply call it disturbance because of the incredibly disturbing dissonance that darkens its already dank A-Minor surface.

The prélude consists of a dismal, drooping theme supported by an undulating accompaniment. Here's the opening of the theme. [**Piano demonstration.**] The undulating accompaniment beneath this melody consists of two melodic parts, a bass line that does this: [**Piano demonstration.**] And a tenor line that does this: [**Piano demonstration.**]

So, what's the big deal? The big deal occurs when we hear those two accompanimental parts—the bass part and the tenor—together. When we hear them harmonically, it sounds like this. [**Piano demonstration.**]

Oh. Let's hear the prelude in its entirety, and let us be supremely aware that it is this harmonic dissonance—even more than the dismal, drooping melody line—that creates the sense of foreboding that is the expressive point of this piece. [**Piano performance:** Chopin, Prélude No. 2 in A Minor, op. 28.] My friends, there was no one on this planet who was writing music like that in 1839 except Frédéric Chopin. No one else.

Chopin at the Piano

The 21-year-old Chopin arrived in Paris in late September of 1831 seeking fame and fortune. He found both, very quickly, which comes as no surprise given that at 21 he was already a fully formed composer and, along with Franz Liszt, the greatest pianist on Earth. He arrived with a passel of new works in hand, his "cards of introduction," as they were. Among them were his two piano concerti and 11 of the 12 Etudes for Piano, Op. 10.

It is a waste of time trying to distinguish between Chopin the composer and Chopin the pianist. They were, in fact, one and the same. Chopin composed at the piano. He required the feel of the keys beneath his fingers and the actual sound of the piano in his ears to write his music, music of stunning originality. Chopin's very special way of playing the piano, in which different fingers were associated with different sorts of melody lines, grew out of his very special way of hearing music. Or was it the other way around? Did Chopin's music grow out of the way he played the piano? It's a chicken-or-egg question that needn't be answered. Chopin the composer and Chopin the pianist co-evolved.

Among the friends Chopin made early on in Paris was Camille Pleyel, who was—along with Sébastian Erard—France's foremost piano manufacturer. Chopin adored Pleyel's pianos and used them whenever he could. Camille Pleyel was likewise thrilled with his new Polish amigo, and it was under Pleyel's marquee that Chopin made his Paris public debut, at the Salle Pleyel, on February 26 of 1932. It was a most auspicious debut; among the many important attendees were Franz Liszt, Felix Mendelssohn, Ferdinand Hiller, and Luigi Cherubini. A potentially tough crowd, indeed.

You know what? Chopin blew them all away. Ferdinand Hiller wrote with astonishment that "Mendelssohn applauded triumphantly!" The Polish violinist Antoni Orlowski wrote in a letter home that "our dear Frédéric gave a concert that brought him great reputation. All Paris was stupefied!" Orlowski was not exaggerating. Franz Liszt, who was already an important figure on the Paris scene, wrote that, "the most vigorous applause seemed not sufficient to our enthusiasm of this talented musician, who revealed [to us] a new phase of poetic sentiment in [his] art." François-Joseph Fétis, the influential editor of the journal *Revue Musicale*, wrote in his review, "here is a young man who, taking nothing as a model, has found something that has long been sought in vain: namely, an abundance of original ideas that are not to be heard anywhere else."

What the attendees heard at the Salle Pleyel was a sort of music and a sort of piano playing they had never heard before. Employing a technique called *rubato*, they heard a pianist with a remarkably flexible approach to rhythm, what Franz Liszt called "a tempo swaying and balancing." They heard a pianist whose *legato*, meaning Chopin's ability to string adjacent notes together, "could make the piano sing as vividly as any vocalist." They saw a small, slight man with apparently small, slim hands; hands that, according to Ferdinand Hiller, "[would] suddenly expand and cover a third of the keyboard. It was like the opening of the mouth of a serpent about to swallow a rabbit whole!"

They heard a pianist with an exquisitely shaded approach to dynamics. Chopin's loudest louds rarely got above *forte*, but the subtle degrees of quietness with which he played made those not-really-very-loud moments sound like thunder. Later in his life, with his body ravaged by tuberculosis, Chopin's playing rarely got above a whisper. There is a story about the pianist Sigismond Thalberg leaving a Chopin recital and shouting at the top of his lungs all the way home. He explained: "I need some noise because I've heard nothing but pianissimo all evening!"

Finally and most importantly, what the audience at the Salle Pleyel heard in Chopin was a pianist and composer who created an entirely new sort of piano music for what was an entirely new sort of piano. Chopin's student, Karol Mikuli, described Chopin's piano playing this way:

The tone he could draw from the instrument, especially in *cantabiles* [that is, in "singing" passages], was always immense. He gave a noble, manly energy to appropriate passages with overwhelming effect—energy without roughness—just as, on the other hand, he could captivate the listener through the delicacy of his soulful rendering—delicacy without affectation. For all the warmth of Chopin's temperament, his playing was always measured, chaste, distinguished and at times, even restrained.

Chopin's Ballades: New Music for a New Piano

Between 1835 and 1842, Chopin composed four works he entitled "Ballade." They are among the longest solo piano works he ever composed, ranging in length from between seven and eleven minutes. They remain among the most challenging works to play in the standard repertoire.

The word "ballad"—or, in French, "ballade"—is one of those generic terms that has meant different things at different times. For Chopin, a "ballade" was a lengthy poem that told a narrative story replete with different characters and even dialogue. By entitling these four musical works as being ballades, Chopin ascribed to them a dramatic/narrative character, although it is an emotional narrative that they describe rather than a literary one.

Chopin's Ballades are often described as being cast in sonata form. And yes, they do indeed feature multiple, contrasting themes that are to some degree developed and recapitulated. But it would be best to think of the Ballades as having been informed by, and not rooted in, sonata form. Harmonically, formally, and expressively these pieces go far beyond the rituals of sonata form, particularly in their "apotheosis-like character." What that means is that the first, third, and fourth ballades are all dramatically back-weighted, in that their rate of change and dramatic intensity accelerates until their final, glorious, apotheosis-like conclusions.

Ballade in G Minor, 1835

The G Minor begins with a slow introduction consisting of a meandering melody written in octaves. The introduction concludes with an open cadence:

a harmonic dissonance that here anticipates a resolution to the home (or tonic) key of G Minor. Let us be particularly aware of the following two things while listening to the introduction. One: Its meandering, unaccompanied melody has a genuinely voice-like quality. Two: The fact that this introductory melody is set in octaves gives it tremendous pianistic resonance and weight. [**Piano performance:** Chopin, Ballade in G Minor, Op. 23.]

That introduction subtly prepares the ear for the climatic octaves that conclude the Ballade. I know it's a bit like telling the punch line before the joke, but let's hear the explosive concluding apotheosis of the Ballade, as upwards rippling scales lead to a cataclysmic inward collapse in octaves, a collapse that spans the entire seven-octave range of Chopin's piano. [**Piano performance:** Chopin, Ballade in G Minor, Op. 23.]

Whoa. Chopin indicates that this closing collapse—in which both of the pianist's hands are playing octaves—be performed *fortississimo*: very, very loud. My friends, Chopin could not have conceived such a passage had he been writing for a six-octave, wooden harped piano, which would have splintered into toothpicks under such an assault. But he was composing for a 7'5"-long metal harped Pleyel, an instrument with thunder to spare, and Chopin spared it not.

However, Chopin's Pleyel was also capable of an extraordinary degree of quiet nuance, which is put into high relief during the first theme that follows the introduction. Despite being notated in compound duple meter, in 6/8, theme 1 has a vaguely waltz-like sensibility about it. It is a long, intensely lyric theme that starts with a whisper, builds to a magnificent *bravura* (meaning "virtuosic") climax, and then fades away. The theme begins with dissonant, tightly wound melodic figures that find resolution and release in the notes that follow. [**Piano demonstration.**]

The theme is through-composed, meaning that its constituent phrases grow and development continuously until a climax is reached followed by a brief refractory period and the conclusion of the theme. In order to perform this theme with the lyric flexibility and sonority it demands, a pianist—aside from playing all the right notes—is going to have to do three things.

One: in order to achieve the rhythmic flexibility the theme demands, a pianist will have to employ *rubato*; that is, a judiciously lengthening and shortening of the rhythms. It will not do to play this theme in strict time. [**Piano demonstration.**] No, no, no. This music must sing, not dance! In the words of Franz Liszt, the tempo must "sway and balance." [**Piano demonstration.**]

The second thing a pianist must do to perform this theme properly is play the thematic melody legato. *Legato* means "tied together." For a pianist, this means not releasing one melody note until the next one has been played, with the result being a smooth, unbroken melodic continuity. [**Piano demonstration.**]

Finally, a pianist must use the sustain pedal in a most artful manner, in order to draw ever varied sonorities from piano and, by doing so, allow the music to breathe. Explanation: On a modern piano the right-hand pedal is called the sustain or damper pedal. When it is depressed, all the dampers are lifted away from all the strings, allowing the strings to vibrate freely until the pedal is released. [**Piano demonstration.**] The sustain pedal has rightly been called "the soul of the piano." It allows pianists to smoothly connect widely spaced notes that could not be connected through fingering. [**Piano demonstration.**] The sustain pedal allows the sonority of a piano to blossom like a flower or explode like a daisy-cutter bomb. [**Piano demonstration.**]

When carefully employed, the sustain pedal allows a piano to breathe. However, when over-used by a lead-footed barbarian, the sustain pedal will smear and occlude the music that's being performed like peanut butter smeared on your windshield. [**Piano demonstration.**] Yuck. We're ready. Let's hear the lengthy, rubato, legato, through-composed first theme of Chopin's Ballade in G Minor. [**Piano performance:** Chopin, Ballade in G Minor, Op. 23.]

Chopin, Liszt and their Pianos of Choice

Never were the personalities of two different composers and pianists better reflected than in Chopin's and Liszt's choice of pianos. Chopin preferred Pleyels because he found them capable of creating more detail, refinement, and nuance than the pianos built by Erard. Liszt, on the other hand, preferred the more robust Erards because he found them more sonorous and less restrained than the Pleyels.

Aside from being the two greatest pianists of their time, Chopin and Liszt were also exact contemporaries, neighbors in Paris, opposites in term of their physical and emotional constitutions, fierce competitors, and on-again-and-off-again friends. Truth be told, Chopin envied Liszt his energy and vitality, and dearly wished he had some of Liszt's pianistic mojo. In a letter to Ferdinand Hiller Chopin wrote: "I write not knowing what my pen is scribbling because at this very moment Liszt is playing my etudes, and [he] transports me beyond the limit of rational thought. I would like to steal from him his way of performing my own creations!"

Ballade in G Minor, 1835

In traditional sonata form, theme 1 is followed by a passage called the modulating bridge, a passage tasked with transitioning to the second theme and to the new key area in which the second theme will be heard. Chopin's modulating bridge is something much more than that; it is a piece-within-a-piece: a fantasia, an improvisation (or "impromptu"), of melodic ideas first presented in the introduction. Check it out. Here's how the introduction begins. [**Piano demonstration.**] Let's isolate that last bit. [**Piano demonstration.**] Let's further isolate those first four notes. [**Piano demonstration.**] Again. [**Piano demonstration.**]

The fantasy-impromptu that is Chopin's modulating bridge starts with this melodic idea, drawn directly, as just demonstrated, from the introduction. [**Piano demonstration.**] Let's hear Chopin's modulating bridge. [**Piano performance:** Chopin, Ballade in G Minor, Op. 23.] Chopin's fabulous second theme in E-flat Major would have been instantly recognizable to his contemporaries as a barcarolle: a theme composed in the style of a folk song sung by Venetian gondoliers. Theme 2: [**Piano performance:** Chopin, Ballade in G Minor, Op. 23.] The exposition concludes with a gentle cadence theme that grows directly out of the "boatman's song" that was theme 2. Let's hear it, closing material. [**Piano performance:** Chopin, Ballade in G Minor, Op. 23.]

The literature refers to what follows as the development section. I wouldn't call it that. By referring to a passage of music as a "sonata form development section," we bunch it together with a vast number of other development sections that all do more or less the same thing; that is, systematically fragment material presented in the exposition in an essentially unstable— meaning modulatory—harmonic environment. That is most certainly not what Chopin does. In reality, Chopin's erstwhile development section is a massive variation/extension of the exposition. It begins with theme 1, heard now in the key of A Minor which is followed immediately by a huge and heroic version of theme 2 initially heard in the key of E Major.

Let's listen that far, and let us be supremely aware that this is modern piano music from top-to-bottom, bottom-to-top, coast-to-coast; music that moves from hushed intimacy to thunderous passion at the drop of a note! **[Piano performance:** Chopin, Ballade in G Minor, Op. 23.] The remainder of this so-called development section consists of a vastly expanded version of the so-called modulating bridge, followed by a passionate version of theme 2, followed by the cadence theme. We heard these same events—in the same order—in the exposition, though now they are presented in an ever more dramatic context.

We advance directly to the recapitulation, which begins with theme 1 stated back in the tonic key of G Minor, which is standard sonata form operating procedure From that point on, however, nothing is standard about the recapitulation. Following theme 1, Chopin dispenses entirely with the modulating bridge and theme 2 and the cadence theme and instead, powers directly into the fire-snorting coda that brings this ballade to its concluding apotheosis. Let's hear that conclusion: the recapitulation of theme 1, followed by the apotheosis; the ferocious, climactic coda; and the collapse in octaves that brings the piece to its conclusion. **[Piano performance:** Chopin, Ballade in G Minor, Op. 23.] That is new music for a new piano.

Thank you.

Schumann—*Kreisleriana*
Lecture 10

Romanticism meant the emergence of a new sort of European literature during the 19th century. The cutting-edge composers of the 19th century believed that the future of music was tied to merging music with literature in order to create a composite art form greater than either music or literature alone. For such composers, this meant instrumental music that would somehow depict emotions, paint pictures, and tell stories in purely instrumental terms. No 19th-century composer believed more completely in the necessity of combining music and literature with intimate self-confession than did Robert Schumann, who was born in 1810 and died in 1856.

Romantic-Era Melody and Harmony

- The self-expressive urge intrinsic to romanticism demanded that composers create ever-new musical means to describe the ever-new expressive content of their music. Speaking generally but accurately, thematic melodies became longer, more complex, and less prone to follow a strict phrase structure.

- Likewise, harmonic practice became more complex as composers sought to create evermore original, evermore evocative musical environments. For example, the aching melancholy we hear so often in the music of Frédéric Chopin is typically a result of harmonic resolutions delayed or avoided entirely or by exquisitely subtle modulations to new keys.

- The startling juxtapositions of contrasting moods and broad splashes of color we hear in the music of Robert Schumann are more often than not the result of bold and unexpected harmonic pivots, meaning sudden harmonic shifts between distantly related keys.

- While the harmonic language of composers like Chopin and Schumann was still rooted in traditional tonality, their harmonic vocabulary became increasingly complex and varied. It was a harmonic vocabulary capable of evoking tremendous metaphoric meaning to anyone whose ears were attuned to its subtleties.

Robert Schumann (1810–1856) composed many of his best-known piano works for his wife, a pianist by the name of Clara Schumann.

A Love Story

- Clara Wieck, Schumann's piano teacher's daughter, turned 16 on September 13, 1835. She was a rare young woman: talented, intelligent, playful, and strikingly beautiful—at ease among adults and increasingly aware of her power over men. The 25-year-old Robert Schumann was at her 16th birthday party, and it was on that day that, by his own admission, he fell in love with her.

- When Clara's father, Friedrich Wieck, found out about Robert and Clara, he went absolutely haywire. He threatened to kill Schumann and categorically forbade the two to ever see each other again. Wieck hauled Clara away on an extended concert tour, intent on keeping her far away from Leipzig and Robert Schumann.

- For the next four years, Clara's father used every weapon in his arsenal to get rid of Schumann, including threats, slander, and even physical assault. In the end, Robert and Clara had to take Wieck to court and sue for the right to be married. After a long and brutal legal battle, the court found in favor of Robert and Clara. They were married, finally, on September 12th of 1840.

- Nothing occupied and affected Schumann more in the years between 1836 and 1840 than his desperate passion for Clara, which was the inspiration for the great majority of the music he composed during that period.

Kreisleriana, Op. 16

- Clara turned 18 on September 13, 1838. In honor of his daughter's 18th birthday, Friedrich Wieck conceded two points to Schumann: Robert and Clara would be allowed to see one another, providing that it were in a public place, and to write to each other when she was on tour. Schumann, who was a grown man of 27, found these provisos humiliating and was convinced—rightly, as it turns out—that they were nothing but a temporary concession to Clara's desires.

- Over the next year, Schumann's spirits rose to manic heights and fell to depressive depths, depending on his perception of his relationship with Clara. It was during one of his manic jags in 1838 that Schumann composed a set of eight pieces for piano in five days and called it *Kreisleriana*. When Friedrich Wieck got word that Schumann intended to dedicate the piece to Clara, he freaked out. At Clara's behest (and to her great relief), Robert withdrew the dedication and rededicated the piece to Frédéric Chopin, who had just dedicated his own Ballade no. 2 to Schumann.

- The title *Kreisleriana* refers to a fictional musician created by E. T. A. Hoffman by the name of Kapellmeister Johannes Kreisler. Hoffmann himself led a Jekyll-and-Hyde existence, working as a respected judge for the Prussian civil courts during the day only to become a carousing, story-telling man-about-town at night. The good Kapellmeister Kreisler, a certifiable schizophrenic, was Hoffmann's alter ego, someone who, like Hoffmann himself, moved back and forth between a conservative establishment he loathed and his devotion to free thought and art.

- Kapellmeister Kreisler appears in three novels by Hoffmann. The first of these novels was written in 1813 and is entitled *Kreisleriana*. Schumann had been enthralled by the character of Kreisler since he was a child, and as an adult, he had come to personally identify with Kreisler as a musician and as a man driven half mad by his passion for Clara.

- Schumann's *Kreisleriana* consists of eight short movements. Like Kapellmeister Kreisler and Robert Schumann himself, *Kreisleriana* is bipolar, exhibiting violent mood swings not just between the movements but within them as well.

- As an example of this musical bipolarity, we turn to movement 1. This opening piece is cast in three large parts that can be schematicized as A–B–A. Schumann indicates that the A sections be performed in a manner "extremely animated." Set in the key of D minor and characterized by unremitting rhythmic drive, these A sections feature roiling, rising, incessant triplets in the right hand, supported and punctuated by a syncopated left hand that obsessively gooses the music forward. The effect of the opening phrase is nothing less than a twitching yelp of passion, rising from the middle of the keyboard to the very top.

- The central B section of the movement is so different from the outer sections that it almost seems a non sequitur. The B section consists of a quiet, tender melody in B-flat major accompanied by harp-like arpeggios. The extreme degree of contrast between the A and B sections of this movement must be interpreted metaphorically, because there's no purely musical reason to explain it.

- The obsessive angst of the A sections and the delicate, dreamlike quality of the B section are two sides of the same expressive coin. The A sections describe the anxiety—even terror—that Schumann felt when contemplating the situation with Clara, while the B section describes the dreamlike bliss Schumann felt when actually thinking about Clara herself. *Kreisleriana*, for Schumann, is nothing less than an analyst's couch; it is music that gives voice to his innermost feelings and fears.

- The second movement is structured as a rondo: A–B–A–C–A¹ with a brief coda. The rondo theme is one of the most gorgeous melodies ever written. It has the rise and fall of a gentle sigh and is said to represent Schumann's feelings of tenderness and passion for Clara. The rondo theme is set in B-flat major and is labeled "very inwardly and not too quickly."

- The energized and passionate first contrasting episode is set in B-flat major while the somewhat gentler second contrasting episode is set in G minor. The final restatement of the rondo theme—A¹—begins with a passage filled with an amazing degree of chromaticism. As this passage progresses, it loses almost entirely any sense of key area, of harmonic grounding. It is a metaphor for Schumann's own loss of center, of emotional grounding.

- Next occurs a harmonic event of such beauty and expressive power that it leaves us breathless as Schumann himself. The harmonic motion congeals in the key of F-sharp major, and the rondo theme begins anew.

- The phrase set in F-sharp major is immediately (and enharmonically) repeated in G-flat major. The G-flat harmony is then reinterpreted as something called an **augmented** sixth chord, which then resolves to a B-flat 6/4 chord. The moment of resolution from G-flat to B-flat is so sublimely satisfying that it can only be called orgasmic. This passage displays just the sort of extended harmonic practice that was used to depict the extended expressive imagery characteristic of so much 19th-century music.

- Movement 3—marked "very agitated"—is understood to represent Schumann's restless and mercurial nature. Movement 4 is understood to represent Schumann's depth of feeling. Movement 5—marked "very lively" and set in G minor—is understood to represent Schumann's moodiness and rapid changes of heart.

- Movement 6—which is marked "very slowly" and set in B-flat major—is understood to represent Schumann's steadfastness of character. In contrast to the slow and gorgeously lyric movement set in B-flat major, the next one—movement 7—is fast, agitated, and set initially in C minor. The first part of this movement is understood to represent Schumann's impetuousness and wildness.

- This manic, rapid-fire music suddenly comes to a screaming halt, as a measured, chorale-like passage in E-flat major brings the movement to its conclusion. That's quite a contrast between the beginning and the end of this movement. Schumann would seem to be saying that beneath his wildness and impetuousness, there is strength and calm.

- Finally, movement 8—marked "fast and playful" and set in G minor—is understood to represent Schumann's nobility of character and spryness of spirit. This closing number is alternately furtive and heroic.

- *Kreisleriana* paints a portrait of Schumann's state of mind in 1838—a state of mind overwhelmingly affected by his feelings for Clara Wieck. The piece is nothing less than a spiritual diary, as each movement represents some fragment or fragments of Schumann's personality and desires, of his conscious and unconscious life.

The Tragic End
- Robert and Clara's love story had a tragic end. In 1831, at the age of 21, Schumann contracted syphilis from a prostitute, and for the next 23 years, he suffered from a series of increasingly severe neurological illnesses until, in February of 1854, he went mad. On February 27, 1854, Schumann—tormented by hallucinations—attempted suicide by jumping off a bridge in Düsseldorf into the Rhine River.

- He was rescued, but his mind was gone. He was placed in an asylum near Bonn, about 50 miles south of Düsseldorf. It was there that he spent the final few years of his life, muttering and babbling and wasting away. He died on July 29, 1856. Clara, who had been at his side for two days, had gone to the train station to pick up a friend. She returned to the hospital only to be told that Robert had died.

Important Term

augmentation: The process of systematically extending the note values of a given melodic line.

Schumann—*Kreisleriana*
Lecture 10—Transcript

We return to *The 23 Greatest Solo Piano Works*. This is Lecture 10. It is entitled Schumann: *Kreisleriana*.

The 19th century saw the emergence of a new sort of European literature. The cutting-edge writers of the time were consumed by a number of particular themes: the glorification of extreme emotion, particularly love; nostalgia for a distant, mystical, legendary past; and a passionate enthusiasm for nature wild and free, unspoiled by humanity and its bourgeois values.

Soon enough, visual artists and composers embraced these themes as well. For many such 19th-century writers, poets, artists and composers, over-the-top expressive content, nostalgia for the past and the depiction of nature wild and free were the vehicles for achieving what their art was at its essence, and that was spontaneous emotion and emotional expression.

The adjective "romantic" first came to be used to describe the literature of such early 19th-century English writers as William Wordsworth, Samuel Taylor Coleridge, Percy Shelley, John Keats, and Lord George Gordon Byron. What we today call romanticism—the 19th-century art movement that celebrates spontaneous emotion and emotional expression—remained, at its heart, a literary movement.

Just so, the cutting-edge composers of the 19th century believed that the future of music was tied to merging music with literature in order to create a composite art form greater than either music or literature alone. For such composers, this meant writing instrumental music that would somehow depict emotions, paint pictures, and tell stories in purely instrumental terms. No 19th-century composer believed more completely in the necessity of combining music and literature with intimate self-confession than did Robert Schumann, who was born in 1810 and died in 1856.

Early Life

Robert Schumann was born in the central German town of Zwickau on June 8, 1810. He was the fifth and last child of August Schumann and Joanna Christiana Schumann, whose maiden name was Schnabel. While he was still a teenager, Schumann's father August—who was born in 1773—was completely swept away by the *Sturm und Drang* movement, that pre-romantic German literary movement that celebrated passion and freedom of expression above all else. According to August Schumann's friend C. E. Richter, the liberating "spirit" of the *Sturm und Drang* movement drove the bookish and sensitive August "close to insanity." Oh, close to insanity. That's an unfortunate choice of words given that his son Robert, his mind reduced to barbecue drippings by syphilis, died in an insane asylum.

We are told that if we do what we love, we'll never work a day in our lives. Certainly that applied to August Schumann, whose parlayed his love of books and literature into a career as an author, translator, and publisher. August Schumann passed on his love of self-cultivation, the spirit of *Sturm und Drang*, and his passion for literature to his youngest and favorite child, Robert.

An avid reader from the very first, Robert began writing poetry around the age of 10. By 13, he was filling notebooks with poems, lyrics for songs, bits and pieces of dramas, and fictitious letters. At the same time, he was developing as a musician. At the age of seven he began taking piano lessons with a local church organist named Johann Kuntsch. Schumann's progress was rapid, and within a year—at the age of eight—he had written his first composition, a set of dances for the piano.

His early compositions aside, it was Schumann's gift for improvisation that appears to have given him his greatest musical pleasure, a gift that he used to entertain his family and friends as well. Schumann biographer Peter Ostwald writes, "Almost every biography of the composer mentions his uncanny ability to produce musical portraits that captured people's mannerisms, movement, speech patterns, and physical appearance in sound. Schumann was 'a portraitist who painted people, their likeness, their physiognomy, mentality and passions.'"

Schumann's youthful skill at creating such musical portraits became the stuff of his mature compositions as well. For example, his solo piano work entitled *Carnaval*—which Schumann composed in 1835, at the age of 25—consists of 21 short movements, many of which are just the sort of musical portraits that Schumann took such pleasure in improvising as a child. At the time he composed *Carnaval*, Schumann was engaged to a young lady named Ernestine von Fricken. (Oh, how I love saying that name. Ernestine von Fricken.) His musical portrait of Ernestine—a movement entitled "Estrella," which was her nickname—is proud and punchy. Schumann tells us that it should be played *con affetto*, "with feeling." Here she is. [**Piano performance:** Schumann, *Carnaval*, no. 13, "Estrella."]

Now, I would tell you that at the time Schumann composed *Carnaval*, he had a big-time crush on his piano teacher's daughter, an incredibly talented, 16-year-old sugarplum named Clara Wieck. Two movements before "Estrella"—which we just heard—is a movement entitled "Chiarina," which was Schumann's pet name for Clara. Schumann indicates that the movement should be played passionately, and its music does indeed betray a passion, a fire, and a delicacy that describes the young Clara as well as Schumann's still-secret feelings for her. "Chiarina." [**Piano performance:** Schumann, *Carnaval*, no. 11, "Chiarina."] By comparing these two portraits, it should be pretty obvious whom Schumann really had the hots for. And yes: five years after Schumann composed *Carnaval*, he and Clara were married. As for Ernestine, well, Schumann dropped her like a moldy piroshky, and she disappeared from sight forever.

Back—briefly—to Schumann's childhood. Typical of so many creative people, Schumann was not a particularly good student; he was given to daydreaming, and later admitted, "I wasn't always diligent, though I was by no means lacking in [intelligence]." No, he wasn't lacking in intelligence or creativity or verbal skills or ambition; not at all. The fact is, Schumann—like many of us—did not respond well to rigidity and orthodoxy, two things in large supply in the German educational system of his time. So instead, Schumann saved the best of his energies for his music, his writing, and for his improvised theater productions, for which he became something of a neighborhood celebrity.

Schumann's father August died in 1826, when Robert was 16. According to the terms of his father's will, Schumann was left a generous trust from which he was to receive a stipend, but there was a catch: Before he got a pfennig, he had to complete a three-year university course of study. Schumann's mother, who considered her son's artistic pretensions to be a case of self-indulgent adolescent folly, insisted that Robert study law. To that end, Schumann was enrolled in the legal program at the University of Leipzig in March, 1828, just short of his 18th birthday.

So, did Schumann honor his mother's wishes and dedicate himself to the law? My friends, do vegans eat *foie gras*? Schumann did what young people have done from the beginning of time: He went off to school, and thus far away from prying eyes he did exactly what he pleased. He later admitted, "At 18 I went to Leipzig, in accordance with my mother's wishes, to study law, but in accordance with my own still vaguely formed intent, [I intended instead] to devote myself entirely to the study of music."

That devotion to music took the form of composing and taking piano lessons from a local pedant named Friedrich Wieck. Wieck was a hard and charmless man. But he had created what he claimed was a foolproof pedagogic method for creating great pianists. The proof of Wieck's method was his own daughter Clara, who was a budding, nine-year-old virtuoso at the time she met the 18-year-old Robert Schumann. Wieck promised Schumann that within five years, he—Friedrich Wieck—would make Robert Schumann one of the greatest pianists in all of Europe!

Well, Friedrich Wieck was full of crap. Schumann studied with Wieck for four years, long enough to seriously damage the ring finger on his right hand by practicing his assigned exercises for up to eight hours at a time. Schumann then made a bad thing much worse by attempting to cure himself by using a finger-strengthening machine called a chiroplast, a miniature weightlifting device invented by a sadist named Johann Logier. By 1832— four years after he left home and moved to Leipzig—Schumann's finger was permanently lamed.

Friedrich Wieck was horrified. Oh, not because he gave a rat's rump for Robert Schumann; oh no, it was his reputation he feared for. He was terrified that he might become known as a piano teacher who crippled promising young pianists through overwork. Thus, after four years of almost daily contact, Wieck threw Schumann under the bus and ceased all contact with him. Schumann was doubly wounded: Not only did he see his career as a pianist crash and burn, but he was rejected by the man who had both promised him that career and had caused him his injury!

The laming of his hand might have been bad news for Robert Schumann, but it was good news for the rest of us. Schumann executed a course correction, and in doing so dedicated himself to composition. The result was nothing short of stunning. The 1830s saw Schumann compose a series of astonishingly original works for solo piano (indeed, his first 23 works were for solo piano). They include some of the most personal and cutting-edge romantic works in the repertoire, works like *Papillons* (of 1831), *Carnaval* (1835), *Fantasiestücke* (of 1837), *Davidsbündlertänze* (of 1837), *Novelletten* (of 1838), *Fantasie* (of 1838), and *Kreisleriana* (of 1838), works in which music, literature, and autobiography are inseparably bound up together.

Clara

Clara Wieck turned 16 on September 13, 1835. She was a rare young woman: talented, intelligent, playful, and strikingly beautiful; at ease among adults and increasingly aware of her power over men. The 25-year-old Robert Schumann was at her 16th birthday party, and it was on that day that by his own admission he fell in love with her. A few months later, he wrote in his diary: "Clara's birthday on September 13…The first kiss in November …. Lovely hours in her arms in the evenings in the Wieck house. Christmas 1835—New Year's Day 1836—the break with Wieck."

Yes, "break with Wieck." When Friedrich Wieck found out about Robert and Clara, he went absolutely haywire. He threatened to kill Schumann and categorically forbade the two to ever see each other again. Wieck hauled Clara away on an extended concert tour, intent on keeping her far away from Leipzig and that washed up, nine-fingered loser Robert Schumann. On March 1, 1836, Schumann wrote his friend August Kahlert, "Wieck is carrying on like a madman and forbids Clara and me to have any contact under pain of death."

You know what? It was nothing personal. There was simply no way that Friedrich Wieck was going to let anyone get between himself and his greatest creation, meaning his daughter Clara. For the next four years he used every weapon in his arsenal to get rid of Schumann, including threats, slander, and even physical assault (he would actually spit at Schumann when he saw him in the street).

In the end, Robert and Clara had to take Wieck to court and sue for the right to be married. After a long and brutal legal battle, the court found in favor of Robert and Clara. They were married, finally, on September 12 of 1840, a date purposely chosen to rub salt, sand, and Draino crystals in Wieck's open, suppurating wound. You see, September 12, 1840—the day they were married—was the day before Clara's 21st birthday. Once she turned 21—the next day, September 13—Clara would have been legally free to marry anyone she wanted to marry. By marrying on the 12th the couple was celebrating their victory over Wieck as well as making sure that Wieck knew that he had been beaten.

Feeling is Believing

All of this is germane to Schumann's music, in particular the music he composed between 1836 and 1840 during what passed for his courtship of Clara. In a letter to Clara, Robert proved himself to be a prototypical romantic when he confessed:

> I am affected by everything that goes on in the world—politics, literature, people—I think it over in my own way, and then I long to express my feelings in music. That is why my compositions are sometimes difficult to understand, because they are connected with distant interests; and sometimes unorthodox, because anything that happens impresses me and compels me to express it in music.

Nothing occupied and affected Schumann's more in the years between 1836 and 1840 than his desperate passion for Clara, which was the inspiration for the great majority of the music he composed during that period. This is not speculation, as a letter Schumann wrote to his old teacher Heinrich Dorn on September 5, 1839 bears out: "Certainly much in my music embodies, and indeed, can only be understood against the background of the battles that Clara has cost me. She was practically the sole inspiration for the *Concerto* [*without Orchestra* Op. 14], the Sonata [Op. 11], the *Davidsbündlertänze*, *Kreisleriana*, and the *Novelletten*."

Kreisleriana, Op. 16, of 1838

Clara turned 18 on September 13, 1838. In honor of his daughter's 18th birthday, Friedrich Wieck conceded two points to that worthless scallywag Schumann: Robert and Clara would be allowed to see one another providing it were in a public place and write to each other when she was away on tour. Schumann, who was a grown man of 27, found these *provisos* humiliating, and was convinced—rightly, as it turns out—that they were nothing but a temporary concession to Clara's desires. Over the next year, Schumann's spirits rose to manic heights and fell to depressive depths depending upon his perception of his relationship with Clara.

It was during one of his manic jags in 1838 that Schumann composed a set of eight pieces for piano in just five days, and called it *Kreisleriana*. To Clara, away on tour, Schumann wrote, "Ah, Clara! How full of music I am now, and such lovely melodies all the time! Just think: since my last letter I have finished an entire piece! I am going to call it *Kreisleriana*, and I want to dedicate it to you—yes, to you and no one else!" When Friedrich Wieck got word that Schumann intended to dedicate the piece to Clara, he freaked out. At Clara's behest (and to her great relief), Robert withdrew the dedication and rededicated the piece to Frédéric Chopin, who had just dedicated his own Ballade No. 2 to Schumann.

The title *Kreisleriana* refers to a fictional musician created by E.T.A. Hoffman by the name of Kapellmeister Johannes Kreisler. Hoffmann himself led a Jekyll-and-Hyde existence, working as a respected judge for the Prussian civil courts during the day only to become a carousing, storytelling man-about-town at night. The good Kapellmeister Kreisler—a certifiable schizophrenic crazy person—was Hoffmann's alter ego, someone who, like Hoffmann himself, moved back and forth between a conservative, Philistine establishment he loathed and his devotion to free thought and art.

Kapellmeister Kreisler appears in three novels by Hoffmann. The first of these novels was written in 1813 and is entitled *Kreisleriana*. Schumann had been enthralled by the character of Kreisler since he was a child, and as an adult, he had come to personally identify with Kreisler as a musician and as a man, driven, as he was, half mad by his passion for Clara.

Schumann's *Kreisleriana* consists of eight short movements. Like Kapellmeister Kreisler and Robert Schumann himself, *Kreisleriana* is bipolar, exhibiting violent mood swings not just between the movements but within them as well. As an example of this musical bipolarity, we turn to movement no. 1. This opening piece is cast in three large parts that can be schematicized as A-B-A. Schumann indicates that the A sections be performed in a manner "extremely animated." And animated they are: Set in the key of D Minor and characterized by unremitting rhythmic drive, these A sections feature roiling, rising, incessant triplets in the right hand, supported and punctuated by a syncopated left hand that obsessively gooses the music forward. The effect of the opening phrase is nothing less than a twitching yelp of passion, rising from the middle of the keyboard to the very top. [**Piano performance:** Schumann, *Kreisleriana*, op. 16, movement 1.] Let's hear the entire opening A section: music of obsessive turmoil and high anxiety. [**Piano performance:** Schumann, *Kreisleriana*, op. 16, movement 1.]

The central, B section of the movement is so different from the outer sections as to almost seem a non sequitur. The B section consists of a quiet, tender melody in B-flat Major accompanied by harp-like arpeggios. [**Piano performance:** Schumann, *Kreisleriana*, op. 16, movement 1.] The extreme degree of contrast between the A and B sections of this movement must be interpreted metaphorically, because there's no purely musical reason to explain it.

I would suggest that the obsessive angst of the A sections and the delicate, dreamlike quality of the B sections are two sides of the same expressive coin. The A sections describe the anxiety—even terror—Schumann felt when contemplating the situation with Clara, while the B section describes the dreamlike bliss Schumann felt when actually thinking about Clara herself.

Now, are we reading too much into this movement and, by extension, the entire piece? No, we're not. Just a few days after he finished *Kreisleriana*, Schumann described it in a letter to Clara: "You and the thought of you play the dominant role. You will smile when you recognize yourself." In another letter, Robert wrote, "Play my *Kreisleriana*. You will find a wild, unbridled love, together with your life and mine." *Kreisleriana* , for Schumann, is nothing less than an analyst's couch: It is music that gives voice to his innermost feelings and fears.

The second movement is structured as a rondo: A-B-A-C-A¹ with a brief coda. The rondo theme is one of the most gorgeous melodies ever written by anybody. It has the rise and fall of a gentle sigh, and is said to represent Schumann's feelings of tenderness and passion for Clara. Let's hear the rondo theme, set in B-flat Major and labeled "very inwardly and not too quickly." [**Piano performance:** Schumann, *Kreisleriana*, op. 16, movement 2.]

The energized and passionate first contrasting episode is set in B-flat Major; here is its opening. [**Piano performance:** Schumann, *Kreisleriana*, op. 16, movement 2.] The somewhat gentler second contrasting episode is set in G Minor; here's its opening phrase. [**Piano performance:** Schumann, *Kreisleriana*, op. 16, movement 2.] The final restatement of the rondo theme—A¹—begins with a passage filled with an amazing degree of chromaticism. As this passage progresses, it loses almost entirely any sense of key area, of harmonic grounding. It is a metaphor for Schumann's own loss of center, of emotional grounding. Let's hear this thoroughly modern-sounding passage. [**Piano performance:** Schumann, *Kreisleriana*, op. 16, movement 2.]

Now occurs a harmonic event of such beauty and expressive power that it leaves us breathless as Schumann himself. The harmonic motion congeals in the key of F-sharp Major, and the rondo theme begins anew. [**Piano demonstration.**] That phrase set in F-sharp Major is immediately (and enharmonically) repeated in G-flat Major. [**Piano demonstration.**] The G-flat harmony is then reinterpreted as something called an augmented sixth chord (specifically, a German sixth; does that help?) which then resolves to a B-flat 6/4 chord. All right, technical jargon aside, the moment of resolution from G-flat to B-flat is so sublimely satisfying that it can only be called orgasmic. Here it is. [**Piano demonstration.**] Exquisite.

Let's hear this entire passage, from the moment the harmony congeals to F-sharp Major through this magical resolution to B-flat Major. [**Piano performance:** Schumann, *Kreisleriana*, op. 16, movement 2.] This passage displays just the sort of extended harmonic practice that was used to depict the "extended expressive imagery" characteristic of so much 19th-century music. A brief but most important sidebar …

Romantic Era Melody and Harmony

The self-expressive urge intrinsic to romanticism demanded that composers create ever new musical means to describe the ever new expressive content of their music. Speaking generally but accurately, thematic melodies became longer, more complex, and less prone to follow a strict phrase structure. Likewise, harmonic practice became more complex as composers sought to create ever more original, ever more evocative musical environments. For example, the aching melancholy we hear so often in the music of Frédéric Chopin is typically a result of harmonic resolutions delayed or avoided entirely or by exquisitely subtle modulations to new keys. The startling juxtapositions of contrasting moods and broad splashes of color we hear in the music of Robert Schumann are more often than not the result of bold and unexpected harmonic pivots, meaning sudden harmonic shifts between distantly related keys.

The point: While the harmonic language of composers like Chopin and Schumann was still rooted in traditional tonality, their harmonic vocabulary became increasingly complex and varied. It was a harmonic vocabulary capable of evoking tremendous metaphoric meaning to anyone whose ears were attuned to its subtleties. Richard Taruskin observes that:

> Never had so many routes of harmonic navigation been open to composers, so many ways of making connections, so many methods of creating and controlling fluctuations of harmonic tension. And to the extent that these fluctuations were understood as metaphors [for] nuances of feeling, never had there been such a supple means

of "graphing" the subjective self. Never had [instrumental music] been so articulately expressive of the verbally inexpressible.

Back to *Kreisleriana*

Movement 3—marked "very agitated"—is understood to represent Schumann's restless and mercurial nature. [**Piano performance:** Schumann, *Kreisleriana*, op. 16, movement 3.] Number 4 is understood to represent Schumann's depth of feeling. [**Piano performance:** Schumann, *Kreisleriana*, op. 16, movement 4.] Number 5—marked "very lively" and set in G Minor—is understood to represent Schumann's moodiness and rapid changes of heart. [**Piano performance:** Schumann, *Kreisleriana*, op. 16, movement 5.]

Number 6—which is marked "very slowly" and set in B-flat Major—is understood to represent Schumann's steadfastness of character. [**Piano performance:** Schumann, *Kreisleriana*, op. 16, movement 6.] In contrast to that slow and gorgeously lyric movement set in B-flat Major, the next one—No. 7—is fast, agitated, and set initially in C Minor. The first part of this movement is understood to represent Schumann's impetuousness and wildness. [**Piano performance:** Schumann, *Kreisleriana*, op. 16, movement 7.] This manic, rapid-fire music suddenly comes to a screaming halt, as a measured, chorale-like passage in E-flat Major brings the movement to its conclusion. [**Piano performance:** Schumann, *Kreisleriana*, op. 16, movement 7.] That's quite a contrast between the beginning and the end of this movement! Schumann would seem to be saying that beneath his wildness and impetuousness there is strength and calm. We will take him at his word.

Finally, movement no. 8—marked "fast and playful" and set in G Minor—is understood to represent Schumann's nobility of character and spryness of spirit. Let's hear this alternately furtive and heroic closing number in its entirety. [**Piano performance:** Schumann, *Kreisleriana*, op. 16, movement 8.]

A Spiritual Diary

Kreisleriana paints a portrait of Schumann's state of mind in 1838, a state of mind overwhelmingly affected by his feelings for Clara Wieck. The piece is nothing less than a "spiritual diary," as each movement represents some fragment or fragments of Schumann's personality and desires, of his conscious and unconscious life. Now, our understanding of Schumann's *Kreisleriana* is based on over 170 years of experience with the piece. It is a perspective that Clara didn't have when she first saw it, and her reaction to it was typical for the time: "[Robert], sometimes your music actually frightens me, and I wonder: is it really true that the creator of such things is going to be my husband?" On April 4, 1839, Clara wrote a letter to Robert from Paris. Referring directly to *Kreisleriana*, Clara—ever the pragmatist—wrote:

> Listen, Robert, won't you for once compose something easy to understand, something that is complete and coherent without special titles, not too long and not too short? I would so much like to have something of yours to play in public, something written for an audience. I know this is degrading to a "genius", but once in a while it would be the politic thing to do.

Nice try, Clara, but no can do. Schumann's expressive language was a product of his time, his place, his personality and his artistic temperament. Asking him to compose with a more populist voice would have stripped his music of just those things that made it interesting in the first place!

Conclusion

Robert and Clara's love story had a tragic end. In 1831, at the age of 21, Schumann contracted syphilis from a prostitute known to us only as Christel. For the 23 years he suffered from a series of increasingly severe neurological illnesses until, in February of 1854, he went mad. On February 27, 1854, Schumann—tormented by hallucinations—attempted suicide by jumping off a bridge in Düsseldorf into the Rhine River.

He was rescued, but him mind was gone. He was placed in an asylum near Bonn, about 50 miles south of Düsseldorf. It was there that he spent the final two and a half years of his life, muttering and babbling and wasting away. He died on July 29, 1856. Clara, who'd been at his side for two days, had gone to the train station to pick up a friend. She returned to the hospital only to be told that Robert had died. She wrote in her diary: "I saw him only half an hour later. I stood by his corpse, my ardently beloved husband, and was quiet; all my thoughts went up to God with thanks that he was finally free. As I knelt at his bed, it seemed as if a magnificent spirit was hovering over me. If only he had taken me along."

Thank you.

Liszt—*Years of Pilgrimage*
Lecture 11

T he primary goal of this lecture is to explore Franz Liszt's phenomenally innovative approach to the piano—his full-contact pianism. The musical examples for this exploration will be drawn from the first two volumes of a three-volume set of works called *Années de pèlerinage*, or *Years of Pilgrimage*. This lecture will selectively mine the two volumes, entitled "First Year: Switzerland" and "Second Year: Italy," for examples of Liszt's pianistic innovations. However, that should not preclude you from listening to these masterworks in their entirety.

Franz Liszt: A Showman Like None Other
- Franz Liszt (1811–1886) was the first "modern" pianist: the first pianist and composer to completely appreciate (and exploit) the fact that the new metal-harped piano was not just a new sort of piano but an entirely new instrument altogether. Liszt's great pianistic contemporaries—Frédéric Chopin, Johann Hummel, and Ignaz Moscheles—still considered the piano (even the metal-harped piano) to be a chamber instrument, meant to be played in a small room or salon before a select audience. But not Liszt. He made his fame and fortune by democratizing the piano: by touring throughout Europe and performing in big public concert halls.

- Liszt was the greatest virtuoso of the 19th century and very possibly the greatest pianist of all time. The great bulk of Liszt's music is for solo piano. His solo piano music is about three things: It's about the metal-harped piano that came into existence at exactly the time he was entering his musical maturity; about a degree of virtuosity that becomes an artistic end unto itself; and about Liszt himself—an overt celebration of the composer as hero, the virtuoso as God.

- The three sets of pieces entitled *Years of Pilgrimage* were inspired by Liszt's travels across Europe. The first volume was published in 1855 and is entitled "First Year: Switzerland." The second volume, entitled "Second Year: Italy," was published in two parts: the first in 1858 and the second in 1861. The third volume was published in 1883. Taken together, these three volumes put pretty much every aspect of Liszt's groundbreaking pianism on display.

- On April 20, 1832, Niccolò Paganini—perhaps the most technically accomplished violinist of all time—gave a concert at the Paris Opera House. In the audience was a not-quite 21-year-old Hungarian-born pianist named Franz Liszt.

- Liszt was transfixed, and he had an epiphany that changed his life: He realized that Paganini did not just play the violin better than anyone else but that Paganini played the violin as well as it could be played. He also realized that the "Paganini of the piano" had yet to materialize. There and then, Liszt decided that his mission in life was to become the "Paganini of the piano."

- At the time he heard Paganini play, Liszt was already a first-rate pianist with some high-end credentials. Over the following 6 years, Liszt practiced almost nonstop, discovering and then solving almost every conceivable challenge associated with playing the piano.

- In this, Franz Liszt was very much the right man at the right place at the right time, because at exactly the time he figuratively threw himself into the piano—the 1830s—the proto-modern piano, with a full-metal harp and a modern mechanism, was emerging from the Paris workshops of the companies Pleyel and Erard.

- Unlike Paganini, whose instrument had been perfected 200 years before, Liszt was defining what was possible on an instrument that was just coming into existence. The music Liszt composed to exploit the new metal-harped piano amounted to cutting-edge software created for a brand-new technology.

- Liszt was more than just the greatest pianist of his time. He parlayed his pianism into a performing persona the likes of which Europe had never before seen. He became the most recognized performing artist of the 19th century. He came to be considered a living god, and he created something approaching madness wherever he performed.

- However, many of Liszt's contemporaries were disgusted with his "act": They found it not just tasteless but detrimental to the art of music as they understood it. Liszt's most outspoken critics were his fellow pianists, who were most likely envious of his success. The fact is that Liszt's pianism was of a different order, a level of pianism that was capable of driving audiences to ecstasy.

- Liszt's concert tours took him to every corner of Europe, during which hundreds of thousands of people had the opportunity to hear and see him perform. In 1839, the 28-year-old Liszt—refusing to share the stage with anyone—invented the solo recital. He called them "soliloquies." When Liszt announced that such a soliloquy would take place in

Franz Liszt (1811–1886), together with Frédéric Chopin, defined what was possible to do on the new metal-harped pianos of the 1830s.

the Assembly Hall of the People in St. Petersburg before an audience of 3,000, the local critics initially considered it a joke. They changed their tune after they heard the concert.

Liszt's Pianos of Choice
- Liszt's pianos of choice were those built by Sébastian Erard in Paris. By the 1830s, these Erard pianos could boast of having three technologies/characteristics that had not existed 15 years before.

- First, the Erards featured a mechanism called a double escapement, which allowed a note to be repeated even if the piano key had not risen all the way back to its full height. This allowed notes to be repeated very rapidly, a capability that Liszt exploited audaciously. There is no way Liszt could have conceived of the music found in *"Tarantella"* from "Second Year" of *Years of Pilgrimage*—with its incredibly fast repeated notes—had he not had access to an instrument capable of playing them.

- Second, the Erards Liszt played had cast-iron harp frames. The metal frame was invented in the 1820s, and it changed the piano forever. Never again would pianos be the relatively light, portable, wooden instruments they had been since their invention in 1700. A metal-harp frame supported more and thicker strings—steel strings—and offered increased rigidity to larger soundboards. Such pianos were heavy as a horse and significantly louder and more resonant than their wooden ancestors.

- The over-the-top virtuosic passage that is "After Reading Dante," found in "Second Year" of *Years of Pilgrimage*, simply could not have been conceived or played on a wooden-harped piano, which has neither the requisite number of keys nor the physical strength to hold up under the megatonnage of the music's assault.

- Third, the Erards were particularly known for their sonority and volume, admittedly achieved at the expense of quiet nuance. It should come as no surprise that the small and sickly Frédéric Chopin chose to play a Pleyel, an instrument known for its nuance rather than its big sound—an instrument Liszt dismissed as a *pianino*, a "little piano."

Liszt at the Piano: Freedom for the Fingers
- Liszt's revolutionary approach to the piano involved breaking through the wall of traditional pianism—the traditional view of what was physically possible at a piano. By and large, contemporary pedants and piano teachers hated Liszt, whom they accused of "destroying the true art of piano playing." Great innovators always disturb the status quo and, by doing so, raise the hackles of those who represent the status quo.

- Franz Liszt knew that he was the piano's indispensible man: a uniquely gifted, uniquely dedicated pianist whose development as a pianist corresponded exactly with the emergence of the proto-modern piano. In his effort to define the outer limits of what was possible, Liszt made it his life's mission to see just how far he could push his own body and the new piano.

- Admittedly, on occasion, his musical imagination was not equal to his technical accomplishments, but the bottom line is that Liszt's technical accomplishments of the 1830s and 1840s laid the groundwork for all subsequent schools of pianism, and thus, it has been argued that Franz Liszt "was the first modern pianist."

- At the heart of Liszt's pianistic revolution was his concept of absolute digital independence. For example, Liszt practiced every scale with the fingering of every other scale. What he was looking for—and what he achieved—was a degree of finger dexterity and independence completely new to piano playing.

- A sample passage from the "Gondolier's Song" from "Second Year: Italy" begins with a rippling, high-velocity, two-handed descent. The "Gondolier's melody" follows, played by the third, fourth, and fifth fingers of the right hand, while the thumb and second finger of the right hand play a trill. At the same time, the left hand supplies a gentle, watery accompaniment. From there, ripple and trill upon ripple and trill curl and seethe around the melody in a miraculously delicate and miraculously difficult interplay. It is digital dexterity raised to the level of high art.

- Liszt's dexterity was such that any one of his fingers was interchangeable with any other; his dexterity went far beyond the old-school doctrine of finger equalization. Liszt did not conceive of his digital equipment as consisting of two hands with five fingers each but, rather, as a single unit consisting of 10 independent fingers. By interlocking and overlapping his hands, Liszt could make it appear as if he were everywhere at once on the keyboard.

Liszt—*Years of Pilgrimage*
Lecture 11—Transcript

We return to *The 23 Greatest Solo Piano Works*. This is Lecture 11. It is entitled Liszt—*Years of Pilgrimage*.

As men, Franz Liszt and Frédéric Chopin were the odd couple of romantic-era music. Where Chopin (who was born in 1810) was a small, sickly, private man who limited his performances to small gatherings at the most exclusive salons, Liszt (who was born in 1811) was a natural-born showman, an extrovert with movie-star looks and the stamina of a tri-athlete, someone who performed everywhere on the European continent.

Yet for all their differences, it was Chopin and Liszt who together defined what it was possible on the new, metal-harped pianos of the 1830s. Chopin's music taught Liszt that the piano was capable of creating a level of delicacy, intimacy, nuance, and lyricism that Liszt had never imagined, which Liszt gratefully acknowledged. Liszt showed Chopin that the piano could be played with a verve and a power that rendered it a veritable one-person orchestra. For example, this passage from Liszt's piano work "After Reading Dante," from the second volume of his *Years of Pilgrimage*. [**Piano performance:** Liszt, *Years of Pilgrimage*, Year Two, "After Reading Dante."] A one-person orchestra, indeed.

The primary goal of this lecture is to explore Liszt's phenomenally innovative approach to the piano—his "full-contact pianism," as it were. The musical examples for this exploration will be drawn from the first two volumes of a three-volume set of works called *Années de pèlerinage*, or *Years of Pilgrimage*. The three sets of pieces thus entitled were inspired by Liszt's travels across Europe. Liszt described the nature of his inspiration this way: "Having recently travelled to many new countries, through different settings and places consecrated by history and poetry, I have tried to portray in music a few of my strongest sensations and most lively impressions."

The first volume of *Years of Pilgrimage* was published in 1855 and is entitled "First Year: Switzerland." The second volume, entitled "Second Year: Italy" was published in two parts, the first in 1858 and the second in 1861.

The third volume was published in 1883. Taken together, these three volumes put pretty much every aspect of Liszt groundbreaking pianism on display. We are going to selectively mine these works for examples of Liszt's pianistic innovations. However, that should not preclude you—my friends—from listening to these masterworks in their entirety.

Putting the "V" in Virtuosity

Franz Liszt (1811–1886) was the greatest virtuoso of the 19th century and very possibly the greatest pianist of all time. The great bulk of Liszt's music is for solo piano. This solo piano music is "about" three things. First, it is about the metal-harped piano that came into existence at exactly the time Liszt was entering his musical maturity. Second, it is about a degree of virtuosity that becomes an artistic end unto itself. Third, Liszt's piano music is about Liszt himself: an overt celebration of the composer as hero, the virtuoso as God.

Of People and Heroes

Back in the 18th century, Enlightenment philosophy put an idealized "everyperson" at the forefront of society, an individual reveling in his individuality. It was a philosophical ideal that reflected current events, as the growing middle class was in the process of changing the social and economic priorities of European society.

With the advent of the American and French Revolutions, which spanned the years 1775 to 1795, the Enlightenment departed the talk-the-talk stage and entered the walk-the-walk stage. In particular, the destruction of the French monarchy and the subsequent rise of Napoleon put an end to the notion that European monarchies were indestructible or even necessary for national life.

Napoleon Bonaparte (1769–1821), like his exact contemporary Ludwig van Beethoven (1770–1827), was a man of his time, a man whose ascent would have been unthinkable without the social, cultural, and political environment created by the Enlightenment. Napoleon became the prototype for the new, post-Enlightenment "secular hero": a person who achieved greatness not by the luck of his birth, but through talent, intelligence, audacity, and hard work: the meritocracy in action.

By the 1830s, such secular heroes had become an established feature of the European scene. By "secular heroes" we're referring to the selective deification of members of the middle class, a sort of deification that in pre-Enlightenment Europe had been reserved for royalty, warriors, popes and saints.

Nowhere was the impact of the 19th-century secular hero-trip more powerfully felt than in music, with the rise of the virtuoso performer. Granted, virtuosic instrumental music had been composed since at least the early 18th century. My friends, there is nothing even remotely easy about Vivaldi's violin concerti or Sebastian Bach's *Goldberg Variations*. But in these and countless other baroque-era instrumental works, technique is employed in the service of the music and not merely to glorify the performer.

That all changed in the increasingly middle-class-dominated musical world of the 1830s, a musical world that perceived instrumental music as the ultimate art form and the instrumental virtuoso as the high priest of the new music. The first of these high priests of virtuosity was a violinist named Niccolò Paganini (1782–1840).

Paganini cut quite a figure:

> He dressed from head to foot in black. He glided rather than walked across the stage—like a vulture floating into position to consume its prey. His eyes had receded deep into their sockets, and this, together with his waxen complexion, gave him a spectral appearance which was enhanced by the dark-blue glasses he wore. The mercury prescribed for his syphilis had rotted his jawbone, causing his teeth to fall out and his mouth to disappear into his chin. When Paganini played, the impression was that of a bleached skull with a violin tucked under its chin. Even his name—Paganini [which means "little pagan"] reinforced the satanic aura which surrounded his personality.

Niccolò Paganini was a one-man heavy-metal band. He was born in 1782, in the northern Italian seaport city of genoa. He was a brilliant child prodigy who claimed to have practiced upwards of 12 hours a day. Building on and then extending violin technique as it existed to the time, Paganini became—perhaps—the most technically accomplished violinist of all time. Among the things that made Paganini different from the violin technicians of the past was that he combined technical wizardry with artistry by incorporating his technical innovations into genuinely musical compositions. By doing so, he made his technical innovations part of the musical mainstream.

In 1809—at the age of 27—Paganini began touring in Italy as a violinist. Given the spirit of the time, he came to be known not as a sideshow oddity, but as a hero, the personification of middle-class self-ennoblement. He dazzled his audiences wherever he went, and by 1813—at the age of 31—he had become a legend on the Italian peninsula. However, it was not until 1828 that Paganini—in his 48th year—made his debut on the other side of the Alps by playing 14 concerts in Vienna. So, how did the tough, prickly, hyper-critical Viennese react to this violinist from Italy? They went nuts. According to Alan Walker:

> Paganini was the supreme artist who could do anything. His virtuosity was such that in order to account for it, people supposed him to be in league with the devil. Rumor had it that his fourth string [the highest, the E string], from which he could draw ravishing sounds, was made from the intestine of his mistress, who he had murdered with his own hands. It was whispered that he had languished in jail for twenty years as a punishment for his crime, with a violin as his sole companion, and, being uniquely isolated from the outside world, had thus wrested from the instrument its innermost secrets.

From Vienna, Paganini travelled across Europe, blowing away audiences wherever he went. Everyone who saw Paganini's music said it was unplayable, until he showed up and played it. He managed to do things that even his fellow professionals thought impossible. If he broke a string, he would continue playing on three. If another string broke, well, he'd continue playing on two. One of his favorite tricks was to play an entire piece on just one string, something that drove audiences absolutely wild.

On April 20, 1832, Paganini gave a concert at the Paris Opera House. In the audience was a not-quite-21-year-old Hungarian-born pianist named Franz Liszt. Liszt was transfixed, and he had an epiphany at that concert that changed his life: He realized that Paganini did not just play the violin better than anyone else but that Paganini played the violin as well as it could be played. At the same time he realized that the "Paganini of the piano" had yet to materialize. There and then, Liszt decided that his mission in life was to become the Paganini of the piano.

At the time he heard Paganini play, Liszt was already a first-rate pianist with some high-end credentials. As a child living in Vienna, he had studied piano with Beethoven's student Carl Czerny and composition with ubiquitous Antonio Salieri (the one and only). In 1822, at the age of 11, Liszt began his concert career, and at the age of 12 Liszt and family moved to Paris, which became his base of operations. By the age of 20 he was already a 10-year veteran of the concert stage and was getting dangerously close to burnout.

Well, not after he "epiphed" at Paganini's concert! Liszt spent the next six years practicing almost nonstop, discovering and then solving almost every conceivable challenge associated with playing the piano. In this, Franz Liszt was very much the right man at the right place at the right time, because at exactly the time he figuratively threw himself into the piano—the 1830s—the proto-modern piano, with a full metal harp and a modern mechanism, was emerging from the Paris workshops of the companies Pleyel and Erard. Unlike Paganini, whose instrument had been perfected 200 years before, Liszt was defining what was possible on an instrument that was just coming into existence. The music Liszt composed to exploit the new, metal-harped piano amounted to cutting-edge software created for a brand-new technology.

A Showman Like No Other

Liszt was more than just the greatest pianist of his time. He parlayed his pianism into a performing persona the likes of which Europe had never before seen. He became the most recognized performing artist of the 19th century. Like other performers who need only one name to identify them, Liszt was Sinatra, Elvis, Sting, Brando, and Bono all rolled up into one amazing package. He came to be considered a living god, and he created something approaching madness wherever he performed. Harold Schonberg tells us:

> When Liszt played the piano, ladies flung their jewels on the stage instead of bouquets. They shrieked in ecstasy and sometimes fainted. Those who remained mobile made a mad rush to the stage to gaze upon the features of the divine man. They fought over the green gloves he purposely left on the piano. They [saved] the stubs of cigars Liszt had smoked, [and the] broken strings from the pianos he had played. These cigar butts and broken strings were mounted in frames and lockets and worshipped. Liszt did not give mere concerts; they were saturnalia.

"Saturnalia" they were: happenings, riots, orgies. The poet Heinrich Heine called it Lisztomania. Not everyone got so carried away. Many of Liszt's contemporaries were disgusted with his act: they found the whole Lisztomania-trip not just tasteless but detrimental to the art of music as they understood it. Liszt's most outspoken critics were, as we might guess, his fellow pianists, whose distaste—I would respectfully suggest—was also a product of white-hot envy. The fact is Liszt's pianism was of a different order, a level of pianism that was capable of driving audiences to ecstasy. In 1840, the Danish writer Hans Christian Andersen heard Liszt perform in Hamburg. Anderson recalled the event in religious terms:

> As Liszt sat before the piano, the first impression of his personality was derived from the passions in his face, so that he seemed to me a demon nailed fast to the instrument whence the tones streamed forth—they came from his blood, from his thoughts; a demon who would liberate his soul from thraldom! He was on the rack; his blood flowed and nerves trembled. [Then] I saw that face assume a brighter expression: the divine soul shone from his every feature; he becomes as beauteous as only spirit can make their worshippers.

Oh boy. As an example of the sort of music and pianism that inspired Hans Christian Andersen to write that, let's hear the final two minutes of "Tarantella" from Year Two: Italy of Liszt's *Years of Pilgrimage*. [**Piano performance**: Liszt, *Years of Pilgrimage*, Year Two: Italy, "Tarantella."] Liszt's concert tours took him to every corner of Europe, during which hundreds of thousands of people had the opportunity to hear and see him perform. Robert Schumann heard Liszt in Leipzig, where he reviewed the concert for the *Neue Zeitschrif fur Musik*. It is most telling that, like Hans Christian Anderson, Schumann referred to Liszt as a demon:

> The demon began to flex his muscles. He first played along with [the audience], as if to feel them out, and then gave them a taste of something more substantial until, with his magic, he had ensnared each and every one and could move them this way or that as he chose.

> It is unlikely that any other artist, excepting Paganini, has the power to lift, carry, and deposit an audience to such a high degree. In listening to Liszt we are overwhelmed by an onslaught of sounds and sensations; in a matter of seconds we have been exposed to tenderness, daring, fragrance, and madness. The instrument glows and sparkles under the hands of its master. This has all been described a hundred times, [but] it has to be heard and seen to be believed."

In 1839, the 28-year-old Liszt—refusing to share the stage with anyone—invented the solo recital. He called these solo recitals soliloquies, and described them to his friend, the Princess Belgiojoso, as "these tiresome musical soliloquies. Imagine that: I have ventured to give a series of concerts all by myself, affecting the Louis XIV style and saying cavalierly to the public, "*Le Concert c'est Moi.*" When Liszt announced that such a soliloquy would take place in the Assembly Hall of the Nobles in St. Petersburg before an audience of 3,000, the local critics initially considered it a joke. They changed their tune after they heard the concert. The critic Vladimir Stasov wrote in his memoirs:

Liszt was wearing a white cravat and various orders [and medals] jangled from the lapels of his coat. I strongly disliked this mania for decorations and had as little liking for the saccharine, courtly manner Liszt affected with everyone he met. But most startling of all was his enormous mane of hair. In those days no one in Russia would have dared [to] wear his hair that way; it was strictly forbidden.

Instead of using the steps [onto the stage], he leaped onto the platform. He tore off his white kid gloves and tossed them on the floor, under the piano. Then, after bowing low in all directions to a tumult of applause such as had [never] been heard in St. Petersburg, he seated himself at the piano.

He played...and our misgivings shrank to meaningless insignificance. We had never in our lives heard anything like this; we had never been in the presence of such a brilliant, passionate, demonic temperament, at one moment rushing like a whirlwind, at another pouring forth cascades of tender beauty and grace. Liszt's playing was absolutely overwhelming.

Liszt's Piano

Liszt's pianos of choice were those built by Sébastian Erard in Paris. By the 1830s, these Erard pianos could boast of having three technologies/characteristics that had not existed 15 years before. One, the Erards featured a mechanism called a double escapement, which allowed a note to be repeated even if the piano key had not risen all the way back to its full height. This allowed notes to be repeated very rapidly, a capability that Liszt exploited audaciously. My friends, there is no way Liszt could have conceived of the following music—with its incredibly fast repeated notes—had he not had access to an instrument capable of playing them. We return to the "Tarantella" from Year Two of the *Years of Pilgrimage*. [**Piano performance**: Liszt, *Years of Pilgrimage*, Year Two: Italy, "Tarantella."]

Technology/characteristic two: The Erards Liszt played had cast-iron harp frames. The metal frame was invented in the 1820s, and it changed the piano forever. Never again would pianos be the relatively light, portable, wooden instruments they had been since their invention in 1700. A metal harp frame supported more and thicker strings—steel strings—and offered increased rigidity to larger soundboards. Such pianos were—literally—heavy as a horse and significantly louder and more resonant than their wooden ancestors.

Just so, the following over-the-top virtuosic passage simply could not have been conceived or played on a wooden-harped piano, which has neither the requisite number of keys nor the physical strength to hold up under the megatonnage of the music's assault. We hear Liszt's incredible evocation of the inferno, from "After Reading Dante" found in Year Two of *Years of Pilgrimage*. [**Piano performance**: Liszt, *Years of Pilgrimage*, Year Two: Italy, "After Reading Dante."]

Technology/characteristic three: The Erards were particularly known for their sonority and volume, achieved, admittedly, at the expense of quiet nuance. It should come as no surprise that the small and sickly Frédéric Chopin chose to play a Pleyel, an instrument known for its nuance rather than its big sound, an instrument Liszt dismissed as a *pianino*, a "little piano." According to Chopin's student Emilie von Gretsch:

> Things that come out perfectly well on my robust Erard become abrupt and ugly on Chopin's [Pleyel]. [Chopin] found it dangerous to work on an instrument with a beautiful, ready-made sound like the Erard. He said those instruments spoil one's touch: [according to Chopin] "You can thump and bash it, it makes no difference: the sound is always beautiful and the ear doesn't ask for anything more, since it hears a full, resonant tone."

This idea of a robust Erard does not mean that that these relatively robust Erard pianos could stand up to a full-out assault by Liszt. In his prime Liszt was a slim man with narrow hands who had—when he chose—a touch as light as a feather. Nevertheless, he had thunderous power and endless stamina, the product of his ten-to-twelve hour-a-day practice regimen. Liszt's power was such that even Erards quivered at his approach. In 1844, the German poet and music critic Heinrich Heine visited Paris, where he heard Liszt play. Heine left us with this account: "He is here, the Attila, the scourge of God for all Erard's pianos, which trembled at the news of his coming and now writhe, bleed and wail under his hands."

The fifth movement of Year One: Switzerland is entitled "Storm." Storm it does, as thunderous octaves race up and down the keyboard amid explosive clusters of chords. Yes indeed my friends, properly played this will make any piano beg for mercy. [**Piano performance**: Liszt, *Years of Pilgrimage*, Year One: Switzerland, "Storm."] Ka-boom. It's passages like that one that forced concert producers to line up two or even three pianos on stage for Liszt, so that when one piano became unplayable he could glide over to the next and pick up where he left off.

Liszt at the Piano

Among the maxims created by the Roman rhetorician Marcus Fabius Quintilianus (who lived from roughly the year 35 to 100) is this little gem: *Si non datur porta, per murum erumpendum.* "If there is no doorway, one must break out through the wall." Never will we read a better description of Liszt's revolutionary approach to the piano: "If there is no doorway, one must break out through the wall." The wall Liszt broke through was that of traditional pianism: the traditional view of what was physically possible at a piano.

It pretty much goes without saying that by and large, contemporary pedants and piano teachers hated Liszt, whom they accused of "destroying the true art of piano playing." Antoine Francois Marmontel, the Professor of Keyboard at the Paris Conservatoire, accused Liszt of "striving too much after eccentric effects!" We doubt Marmontel's accusation cost Liszt much sleep. Great innovators always disturb the status quo and by doing so raise the hackles of those who represent the status quo.

Besides, professor Marmontel could not have been more wrong. Franz Liszt was not striving for "eccentric pianistic effects." Rather, he knew—with the certitude of a prophet—that he was the piano's indispensible man: a uniquely gifted, uniquely dedicated pianist whose development as a pianist corresponded exactly with the emergence of the proto-modern piano. In his effort to define the outer limits of what was possible, Liszt made it his life's mission to see just how far he could push his own body and the new piano.

Yes, I will be the first to admit that on occasion Liszt's musical imagination was not equal to his technical accomplishments, but so what? The bottom line is that Liszt's technical accomplishments of the 1830s and 1840s laid the groundwork for all subsequent schools of pianism, and thus it has been argued, correctly, I think, that Franz Liszt was the first modern pianist. In his superb, three-volume biography of Liszt, Alan Walker writes:

> Liszt's influence had to do with his unique ability to solve technical problems. Liszt is to the piano what Euclid is to geometry. Pianists turn to his music in order to discover the natural laws governing the keyboard. It is impossible for a modern pianist to keep Liszt out of his playing, since modern piano playing spells Liszt.

I offer this story to back up those words. In 1896—at the age of 30—the phenomenal Italian pianist Ferruccio Busoni decided to start his training as a pianist from scratch in order to address what he believed were flaws in his technique. To whom do you turn for such instruction when you're already one of the greatest pianists in the world? Busoni turned to the piano music of Franz Liszt, from which he rebuilt his technique. Busoni later wrote, "Gratitude and admiration made Liszt my master and my friend."

Freedom for the Fingers!

At the heart of Liszt's pianistic revolution was his concept of absolute digital independence. For example, Liszt practiced every scale with the fingering of every other scale. What he was looking for—and what he achieved—was a degree of finger dexterity and independence completely new to piano playing. Let's hear a passage from the "Gondolier's Song" from Year Two: Italy. Our excerpt will begin with a rippling, high-velocity, two-handed descent. The gondolier's melody follows, played by the third, fourth and fifth fingers of the right hand, while the thumb and second finger of the right hand play a trill. At the same time, the left hand supplies a gentle, watery accompaniment. From there, ripple-and-trill upon ripple-and-trill curl and seethe around the gondolier melody in a miraculously delicate and miraculously difficult interplay. This is digital dexterity raised to the level of high art. [**Piano performance**: Liszt, *Years of Pilgrimage*, Year Two: Italy, "Gondolier's Song."]

Liszt's dexterity was such that any one of his fingers was interchangeable with any other. Oh the stories. The violinist Joseph Joachim loved to tell the story of how Liszt accompanied him in the finale of Mendelssohn's Violin Concerto, all the time holding a lit cigar between the index and middle fingers of his right hand. Here's another: Just before a performance of Beethoven's Fifth Piano Concerto in Vienna in 1877, Liszt badly cut the index finger of his left hand. Did he cancel the concert? No, of course not. He simply played the concerto without the injured finger by redistributing the notes to his other fingers. No one in the audience had even an inkling that he had been injured.

Liszt's dexterity went far beyond the old-school doctrine of finger equalization. You see, Liszt did not conceive of his digital equipment as consisting of two hands with five fingers each, but rather, as a single unit consisting of ten independent fingers. By interlocking and overlapping his hands, Liszt could make it appear as if he were everywhere at once on the keyboard. For example, the fourth movement of Year One: Switzerland is entitled "Beside a Spring." The gently gurgling effect of this music belies its virtuosity; music in which the constant hand-crossing and huge, dangerous leaps make it sound as if it is being played by four hands, not just two.

Let's listen to the central portion of the piece, and let's be aware that the 10 fingers of the pianist seem to be everywhere at once. [**Piano performance**: Liszt, *Years of Pilgrimage*, Year One: Switzerland, "Beside a Spring."] It's passages like that one that led contemporary cartoonists to depict Liszt as having six and eight hands, his countless fingers flying across the keyboard.

The First Modern Pianist

Liszt was the first modern pianist: the first pianist and composer to completely appreciate (and exploit) the fact that the new metal-harped piano was not just a new sort of piano but an entirely new instrument altogether. Liszt's great pianistic contemporaries—Frédéric Chopin, Johann Hummel, and Ignaz Moscheles—still considered the piano, even the metal-harped piano, to be a chamber instrument, meant to be played in a small room or salon before a select audience.

But not Liszt. He made his fame and fortune by democratizing the piano, by touring throughout Europe and performing in big, public concert halls. In 1837, at the age of 26, he did something of typical Lisztian audacity, something unthinkable up to that time: He gave a recital in Milan's La Scala opera house before an audience of 3,000 and brought the house down. He played an Erard, and on the morning after the concert he wrote to Sebastian Erard's successor, Pierre Erard, to let him know how things had gone:

> Let them not tell me any more that the piano is not a suitable instrument for a big hall, that the sounds are lost in it, that the nuances disappear, etc. I bring as witness the three thousand who filled the immense Scala theater yesterday evening, from the pit to the seventh balcony, all of whom heard and admired, down to the smallest details, your beautiful instrument. This is not flattery; you have known me too long to think me capable of the least deception. But it is a fact—publicly recognized here—that never before has a piano created such an effect.

To which we would add, "and never had a pianist and his piano music created such an effect!"

Thank you.

Liszt—Sonata in B Minor
Lecture 12

E arly in his career, Liszt was encouraged by his friends to "branch out" into orchestral music. The young Liszt responded to his friends by describing the importance of the piano to his body, mind, and soul. In his Sonata in B Minor, Liszt fulfills entirely his desire to turn the seven octaves of the piano not just into an orchestra, but into a vehicle for the heroic and the sublime. This lecture will focus on perceiving the large-scale sonata-form structure of Liszt's Sonata in B Minor.

Liszt in Weimar

- In 1848, Franz Liszt settled in the central German city of Weimar, where he accepted the position of Kapellmeister—music director—for the court and city. He was tired, and after 10 years of incessant touring, he knew he had to rest. He also had artistic ambitions that he could not pursue on the road: He wanted to branch out and compose orchestral music; he wanted to learn to conduct; and he wanted to teach and to proselytize for the new romantic music.

- Despite the fact that Bach, Schiller, and Goethe had all lived and worked in Weimar, at the time Liszt moved there in 1848, it was a dusty backwater. That an international star like Liszt would move to Weimar to take over what was an extremely modest musical establishment came as a shock to many of his contemporaries.

- But Liszt was smart and sly and knew exactly what he was doing, and within just a few years, he had turned Weimar into "the Mecca of the avant-garde movement in Germany." He gathered about him a veritable court of students, writers, propagandists, spokespersons, rich hobbyists, and sycophants that came to be known collectively as the New German School or the Futurists. With Liszt in the lead, the Futurists dedicated themselves to creating a new art in which music and literature would be inextricably merged, in which feeling was given free reign.

Sonata as Genre versus Musical Form

- Liszt lived and worked in Weimar for 13 years, from 1848 to 1861. Despite the fact that most of the music he composed during those years was for orchestra, the crowning glory of Liszt's Weimar years is for solo piano: the Sonata in B Minor.

- Liszt began the sonata late in 1852 and inscribed it as being completed on February 2, 1853. It is a huge, magisterial, virtuosic, and remarkably modern work—over 30 minutes long and set in a single movement.

- This raises the question as to why Liszt saddled the piece with what was, by 1853, the quaintly old-fashioned designation "sonata"? Liszt would have understood the word "sonata" to mean two different things: one of them an instrumental genre and the other a musical form. As an instrumental genre, a "sonata" is a multimovement composition for solo piano or solo piano plus one other instrument.

- "Sonata form" refers to a specific musical form, one that features two (or more) principal, contrasting themes. The melodically and harmonically contrasting themes are presented in a section called the exposition; the materials presented in the exposition are then in some way "argued" in a section called the development; the themes then return in their original order but in the same key in a section called the recapitulation; and finally, a coda typically brings such a movement to its conclusion.

- Given the title Sonata in B Minor, our first impulse might be to think that it is a piano sonata and thus expect it to adhere to the time-honored traditions of a piano sonata, with its multiple movements and such. However, Liszt didn't call the piece "Piano Sonata in B Minor"; he called it, simply, "Sonata in B Minor." In reality, the piece is a single, sprawling, sonata-form movement. Had Liszt been of a mind, he might have more accurately (but much less poetically) named his piece the "B Minor Sonata Form."

Franz Liszt was the first performer to play entire programs from memory.

The Sonata's Introduction

- The sonata begins with a diabolic introduction in five parts, during which Liszt lays out the thematic grist for the entire piece. The first part of the introduction takes place in the deep, cavernous spaces of the bottom of the piano, as repeated octave Gs are followed by ominous descending figures.

- The second part of the introduction expands on and intensifies the first part. In the second part, the repeated octaves of part 1 leap upward in short-long rhythms. In part 2 of the introduction, the formerly ominous descending figures become violent and precipitous.

- With the almost fanfare-like second part as a setup, part 3 introduces a new melodic idea: a devilish, Mephistophelian cackle heard deep in the bass.

- In part 4 of the introduction, hell begins to break loose, as rising two-chord units in the treble strain against falling lines in the bass, falling lines intent on dragging the harmonies down to wherever.

- The climactic fifth and final part of the introduction combines the violent and precipitous music of part 2 with the Mephistophelian cackles of part 3.

A Work Based on Goethe's *Faust*

- Among Liszt's many inventions was the term "program music," which is instrumental music that seeks, in some way, to evoke specific moods and emotions, or to depict specific imagery, or even to tell a literary story. The opposite of program music is absolute music, which is music that presumably can be understood in purely musical terms without resorting to extramusical explanation—Mozart's **symphonies**, for example.

- Of course, any absolute distinction between absolute music and program music is impossible, because musical inflection—like spoken language—will inevitably evoke an associative response of some sort in the ears, hearts, and minds of its listeners. Our textbooks might tell us that Mozart's symphonies are absolute music, although it is impossible not to feel profound gloom during the fourth movement of the G Minor Symphony, K. 550, and euphoria during the fourth movement of the "Jupiter" Symphony.

- The real issue is one of compositional intent. Mozart did not set out to explicitly evoke any literary stories or visual imagery in his symphonies. Franz Liszt, however, who more often than not gave his compositions literary titles, did indeed set out to explicitly evoke literary stories and/or visual imagery in his instrumental music.

- While the title Sonata in B Minor invokes sonata form, it does not describe any programmatic content. Nevertheless, the music itself—with its extremes of contrast—invokes all sorts of metaphors that in turn evoke a narrative story. Various narratives have been attributed to the sonata: It has been described as an autobiographical document; as an allegory based on Milton's *Paradise Lost*; and as a work based on Goethe's *Faust*.

- The Faustian interpretation is by far the most compelling. We will identify and explore the themes using a Goethe's *Faust*-derived vocabulary: Theme 1 will represent Mephistopheles (a demon in the employ of Satan himself; theme 2 will represent the flawed but heroic Faust; and theme 3 will represent the young, virginal, self-sacrificial Gretchen.

Exposition

- The exposition introduces the three thematic protagonists— Mephistopheles, Faust, and Gretchen—as themes 1, 2, and 3. Rippling, crazed, and virtuosic, theme 1 is built from parts 3 and 4 of the introduction: the Mephistophelian cackle of part 3 and the rising two-chord units of part 4.

- A furious modulating bridge follows, one that expands on elements of the introduction. The majestic and heroic theme 2 is set in D major, the personification of Faust. This lush and passionate theme grows out of the first notes of the introduction. Part 1 of the introduction began with two repeated Gs. Theme 2 develops this idea, consisting as it does of a series of repeated two-note units, units that rise toward heavenly redemption over the course of the opening of the theme.

- Theme 3 represents Gretchen, the sweet-as-maple-syrup nubile whose goodness and purity will redeem Faust. And despite the fact that her gentle, lyric music would seem to be light-years removed from that of the heroic (if flawed) Faust, Gretchen's theme is based on the same repeated notes as Faust's theme. There can be no doubt that the close relationship between themes 2 and 3 is intended to be a metaphor for the spiritual and emotional relationship between Faust and Gretchen.

- Over the course of the movement, these three themes are presented in a dazzling and virtuosic array of permutations; they alternate with each other, overlap with each, and are transformed constantly by their interactions, as Liszt follows—in his imagination—the dramatic interactions and developments of the Faust story. The miracle is that the sonata works perfectly well as a piece of abstract music; that is, it makes sense as pure music—its "program" aside.

Development Section

- The development section begins roughly 12 minutes into the movement. The beginning of the development section—marked "slowly and sustained"—offers one of the rare moments of tranquility in the sonata. Things do not stay this peaceful for very long.

- The tender parts of the music are drawn from Gretchen's theme. In a moment of high drama, Faust's theme—theme 2—attempts to climb ever higher and struggles with vicious downward lines in the bass, an explicit evocation of Mephistopheles's attempts to drag Faust down to hell.

Recapitulation

- The recapitulation begins in the depths of the piano with part 1 of the introduction. A fantastic hunk of music follows, as Liszt transforms what had been parts 2 and 3 of the introduction into a fugue based on devilish Mephistophelian melodic ideas.

- The bristling fugue that follows is nothing less than a *totentanz*, or "dance of death." The pianist Alfred Brendel writes: "I do not know what to admire most: the introduction of the fugue at this point; how the three-part writing gradually grows back into [a] 'symphonic **texture**'; the Mozartean effortlessness of its polyphony; [or] the originality that sets this fugue apart from baroque stereotypes."

Coda

- The first one-and-a-half minutes of the five-minute-long coda is an oxygen-depleting, muscle-tearing, phalanges-snapping exercise in virtuosity, a passage that begins with an evermore fervent, evermore thunderous evocation of Gretchen (that is, theme 3) and concludes with a final, teeth-rattling, ecstatically heroic statement of Faust's theme—theme 2.

- From this point, the sonata ends quietly and magically. That was not Liszt's original intention. In his original manuscript, the sonata concluded with a 25-measure apotheosis, to be played fortississimo—as loudly as possible. Liszt then crossed out those last 25 measures and put in their place a 32-measure passage that gradually fades away to pianississimo—as quietly as possible. Liszt's second impulse was brilliant. The last moments of the sonata are cast not in B minor but, rather, in B major.

Important Terms

symphony: A multimovement work composed for an orchestra.

texture: Number of melodies present and the relationship between those melodies in a given segment of music; they include monophony, polyphony (counterpoint), heterophony, and homophony.

Liszt—Sonata in B Minor
Lecture 12—Transcript

Welcome back to *The 23 Greatest Solo Piano Works*. This is Lecture 12. It is entitled Liszt—Sonata in B Minor.

More than anyone before him—including the composer Ludwig van Beethoven, the poet Lord George Gordon Byron, or the violin virtuoso Niccolò Paganini—it was Franz Liszt who best embodied the romantic-era archetype of the artist who walks with God and brings down fire from heaven in order to kindle the hearts of mankind. Yes, Liszt was a egomaniac. But his egomania was born in the knowledge that he attained what he had through his own devices and hard work. Liszt considered himself the equal of anyone, saying (and believing) as he did that "to become noble is much more than to be born noble."

Liszt suffered no one gladly, and that included monarchs. While giving a recital in St. Petersburg, Tsar Nicholas I arrived late and then, while Liszt was playing, began talking. Liszt stopped, put his hands in his lap, and bowed his head over the keyboard. The Tsar asked Liszt why he had stopped and Liszt replied, "Music herself should be silent when Nicholas speaks." There was no more talking during the recital.

Humble Beginnings

Talk about the meritocracy in action: Franz Liszt—composer, virtuoso, friend to kings and emperors, hero, god—grew from the humblest of beginnings. His paternal great-grandparents were German-speaking migrant workers who wandered into Hungary sometime in the mid-1700s. (For our information: the family name was spelled L-i-s-t, List. It was Franz' father Adam who "Hungarianized" the name by adding the "Z" and thus rendering its Hungarian pronunciation "Lischt".)

Hungary was good to the Liszts. Through good genetics and hard work, certain members of the family climbed out of poverty, received an education, and became important members of their community. Among these upwardly mobile Liszts was Franz's father Adam, who was born in 1776. He was a talented pianist and 'cellist, who as a teenager played 'cello in the Esterhaza summer orchestra under the direction of none other than Joseph Haydn. (Later in life, Adam loved to talk about how he played cards with Haydn during their breaks.) Adam Liszt became an administrator and bookkeeper for the Esterhazy family, the same family of Hungarian nobles that had employed Haydn for 29 years.

The 35-year-old Adam Liszt married a 23-year-old chambermaid named Anna Lager on January 11, 1811. Adam and Anna's one and only child—a boy—was born 10 months later, on October 22, 1811. The boy's baptismal certificate gives his first name as Franciscus: Franz in German, Ferenc in Hungarian, Francois in French, and Frank in English. As a child he was nicknamed "Franzi."

"Franzi's" phenomenal musical talent made itself apparent early on, and Adam Liszt took it upon himself to begin the child's musical training. Thank goodness: There's no paternal horror story here. Adam Liszt was a wise and sympathetic teacher. He allowed his son to develop at his own pace and then stepped aside when the time was right. Franz Liszt adored his father for all the right reasons, and was heartbroken when he died on August 28, 1827, at the age of 51. Adam Liszt was Franz's single greatest influence, and there can be little doubt that his confidence in and love for his son allowed Franz to be both confident and loving as an adult. To the end of his life, when faced with difficult decisions, Franz Liszt would admit to asking himself, W.W.D.D.? "What would dad do?"

By the age of 11, Franz had begun to make critics drool. On December 1, 1822, he made his Vienna debut. The review in the *Allgemeine Zeitung* read, in part, "A young virtuoso has, as it were, fallen from the clouds, and compels us to the highest admiration. The performance of this boy, for his age, borders on the incredible, and one is tempted to doubt any physical impossibility when one hears the young giant."

Paris

Nine months later—on September 20, 1823—the Liszt family left Vienna, intent on recreating the child Mozart's coming-out tour, which had taken place 60 years before. In each town and city where young Liszt performed, stunned and amazed nobles provided letters of introduction for the next town or city. The Liszts arrived in Paris on December 11, 1823.

By sheer coincidence, they checked into the Hotel d'Angleterre at No. 10 Rue du Mail. The hotel was directly across the street from La Maison Erard—the showroom and workshop of the piano manufacturer Sébastian Erard. My friends, it happened just like in the movies. The 12-year-old Liszt walks across the street, sits down at a piano, and plays. Everyone and everything just stops. Jaws hang open. Eyes glaze over.

The Liszt and Erard families bonded, and for the rest of his life, Liszt refered to the Erards as his adopted family. They became business partners as well. Sébastian Erard opened doors across Paris for Liszt, and in return, Liszt played Erard pianos exclusively for the next few years. Erard's pianos—with their metal harps and double-escapement mechanisms—were at the very cutting edge of the new piano technology, a technology that shaped Liszt's vision of the piano and his music for the piano.

> The Parisians were entranced by "*Le Petit Litz*" as they called him. As an example of the sort of review Liszt received after arriving in Paris we read one published in *Le Drapeau Blanc*, on March 9, 1824. "I cannot help it: since yesterday evening I am a believer: I am convinced that the soul and spirit of Mozart have passed into the body of young Liszt, and never has an identity revealed itself by plainer signs. His little arms can scarcely stretch to both ends of the keyboard, his little feet scarcely reach the pedals, and yet this child is beyond compare; he is the first pianist in Europe."

And so it went, for a while, at least. Liszt continued to tour, concertize, and give lessons in ever increasing number. But by early 1832, the now 20-year-old Liszt was no longer a prodigy. His father was gone and he was close to burnout. Then, in April of 1832 he heard the violinist Niccolò Paganini perform at the Paris Opera House. It was for Liszt a revelation: Here was someone who not only played the violin better than anyone else, but someone who played the violin as well as it could possibly be played. Liszt decided, there and then, to become the Paganini of the piano.

I'll admit, he went a little crazy. Practicing up to twelve hours a day, Liszt created and then solved technical problems that no one had ever known existed. During the mid and late-1830s he began writing piano works that incorporated his technical discoveries into music of genuine artistic worth, works like his *Six Grand Études After Paganini* and the *Transcendental Études* of 1838.

The Legend is Made

The Franz Liszt that went back out on the road as a concert performer in 1839 was an entirely different pianist than the one who had heard Paganini seven years before. The new Liszt appeared with a pianistic technique the likes of which no one had ever imagined and a large batch of new compositions with which to show off that technique. He was a consummate showman who changed forever the image of the performing musician. Liszt's list of firsts show him to be not just the first modern pianist but the first modern performing artist.

In 1839, when he went back out on the road, Liszt refused to share the stage with anyone, and in doing so invented the solo recital. At first he called such performances soliloquies" but soon enough he started using the term "solo recital," applying it for the first time to a concert in London on June 9, 1840. The term "solo recital" inspired some amusement among the English. One critic wrote, "What does he mean? How can one recite upon the piano?"

Liszt was the first pianist to place the piano keyboard at a right angle to the front of the stage, so that the piano's open lid would project its sound directly to the audience. Liszt liked to say that when performing one did not "play the piano" but, rather, one "played the room." Liszt was the first pianist to perform—as it then existed—the entire keyboard repertoire, from the music of Johann Sebastian Bach to that of Frédéric Chopin. Liszt was the first performer to play entire programs from memory. In both Milan and St. Petersburg Liszt played before audiences of over 3,000 people, the first pianist to ever perform before such huge crowds.

Between 1839 and 1847, Liszt toured incessantly, and in doing so created his legend. Writing in the periodical *Der Humorist*, M. G. Saphir wrote of the 28 year-old Liszt, "Liszt knows no rules, no form, no dogma; he creates everything for himself." In 1841, the Russian Alexis Verstovsky wrote, "Liszt has created a madness. He plays everywhere and for everyone." Even those fellow professionals who were appalled by Liszt's shtick were nevertheless blown away by his pianism. Clara Schumann, who was disgusted by what she considered Liszt's "degradation of the art of music," wrote after hearing him play, "I sobbed out loud, [his playing] overcame me so."

Liszt had the stamina of a super-marathoner. Nevertheless, over time, the tremendous strain of his touring began to show. Alan Walker writes, "No one could have withstood the constant round of concerts, speeches, balls, and banquets by day, often followed by [bone-jarring] travel to the next town by night—year after unremitting year—without suffering injury to his health, and Liszt's was often near the breaking point."

Under the circumstances, Liszt did what many of us do: He self-medicated. He took opium, quinine, and all sorts of homeopathic medications in his effort—in his own words—to "keep the machine running." But no substances were more important to Liszt's "survival" than alcohol and tobacco. Cigars and cognac were his drugs of choice, and he often indulged them to excess. For example, in the spring of 1846, the French composer Hector Berlioz met up with Liszt in Prague. There was to be a banquet in Berlioz's honor and Berlioz asked Liszt to speak. Berlioz later remembered, "Unhappily, if he spoke well, he drank likewise. [That evening], such tides of champagne flowed through Liszt's cup that his eloquence was shipwrecked in it!"

At two in the morning Berlioz had to bodily pull Liszt away from a Bohemian with whom he wanted to fight a duel and then half-carry him back to his hotel. Liszt was scheduled to give a concert the next day—at noon—but was still asleep at 11:30. The hotel staff managed to get him out of bed and into a waiting carriage. Berlioz picks up the story from there: "[Liszt] arrived at the hall, entered to a triple-barreled broadside of applause, sat down and played as I do not believe he has ever played in his life. Truly: there IS a god—for pianists!"

Liszt Takes a Job

In 1848, Franz Liszt settled in the central German city of Weimar, where he accepted the position of Kapellmeister—music director—for the court and city. He was tired, and after 10 years of incessant touring he knew he had to rest. He also had artistic ambitions he could not pursue on the road: He wanted to branch out and compose orchestral music; he wanted to learn to conduct; and he wanted to teach and to proselytize for the new romantic music.

Despite the fact that Bach, Schiller, and Goethe had all lived and worked in Weimar, at the time Liszt moved there in 1848 it was a dusty backwater. That an international star like Liszt would move to Weimar to take over what was an extremely modest musical establishment came as a shock to many of his contemporaries. But Liszt was smart and sly and knew exactly what he was doing, and within just a few years had turned Weimar into "the Mecca of the avant-garde movement in Germany."

He gathered about him a veritable court of students, writers, propagandists, spokespersons, rich hobbyists and sycophants that came to be known collectively as the "New German School" or just the "Futurists." With Liszt in the lead, the Futurists dedicated themselves to creating a new art in which music and literature would be inextricably merged, in which feeling was given free reign, and in which, according to Liszt's chief propagandist Franz Brendel, "content creates its own form."

Sonata in B Minor

Liszt lived and worked in Weimar for 13 years, from 1848 to 1861. Despite the fact that most of the music he composed during those years was for orchestra, the crowning glory of Liszt's Weimar years is for solo piano: the Sonata in B Minor. Liszt began the sonata late in 1852, and inscribed it as being completed on February 2, 1853. It is a huge, magisterial, virtuosic, and remarkably modern work: 30-plus minutes long and set in a single movement. Which raises the question as to why Liszt saddled the piece with what was, by 1853, the quaintly old-fashioned designation "sonata"?

Liszt would have understood the word "sonata" to mean two different things, one of them an instrumental genre and the other a musical form. As an instrumental genre, a sonata is a multi-movement composition for solo piano or solo piano plus one other instrument. "Sonata form" refers to a specific musical form, one that features two (or more) principal, contrasting themes. The melodically and harmonically contrasting themes are presented in a section called the exposition. The materials presented in the exposition are then in some way argued in a section called the development. The themes then return in their original order but in the same key in a section called the recapitulation. Finally, a coda typically brings such a movement to its conclusion.

Back to Liszt's Sonata in B Minor. Given its title, our first impulse might be to think that it is a piano sonata and thus expect it to adhere to the time-honored traditions of a piano sonata, with its multiple movements and such. However, Liszt didn't call the piece "Piano Sonata in B Minor"; he called it, simply, "Sonata in B Minor." In reality, the piece is a single, sprawling, sonata form movement. Had Liszt been of a mind, he might have more accurately (but rather less poetically) named his piece the "B Minor Sonata Form." Our examination will focus on perceiving the large-scale sonata form structure of the B Minor Sonata.

Introduction

The Sonata begins with a diabolic introduction in five parts, during which Liszt lays out the thematic grist for the entire piece. The first part of the introduction takes place in the deep, cavernous spaces of the bottom of the piano, as repeated octave Gs are followed by ominous descending figures. [**Piano performance:** Liszt, Sonata in B Minor, introduction.] The second part of the introduction expands on and intensifies the first part. In the second part, the repeated octaves of part 1—[**piano demonstration**]—leap upwards in short-long rhythms. [**Piano demonstration.**]

In part 2 of the introduction, the formerly ominous descending figures become violent and precipitous. [**Piano demonstration.**] Introduction, part 2. [**Piano performance:** Liszt, Sonata in B Minor, introduction.] With that almost fanfare-ish second part as a setup, part 3 introduces a new melodic idea: a devilish, Mephistophelian cackle heard deep in the bass.

[**Piano demonstration.**] Introduction, part 3. [**Piano performance:** Liszt, Sonata in B Minor, introduction.]

In part four of the introduction, hell literally begins to break loose, as rising two-chord units in the treble—[**piano demonstration**]—strain against falling lines in the bass, falling lines intent on dragging the harmonies down to wherever! Part 4 of the introduction. [**Piano performance:** Liszt, Sonata in B Minor, introduction.] The climactic fifth and final part of the introduction combines the violent and precipitous music of part 2 with the Mephistophelian cackles of part 3! Part 5: [**Piano performance:** Liszt, Sonata in B Minor, introduction.] From the top, the introduction in its entirety: [**Piano performance:** Liszt, Sonata in B Minor, introduction.]

What Is the Sonata in B Minor "About"?

Among Liszt's many inventions was the term "program music." Program music is instrumental music that seeks, in some way, to evoke specific moods and emotions; or depict specific imagery; or even to tell a literary story. The opposite of program music is absolute music, music that presumably can be understood in purely musical terms without resorting to extra-musical explanation; Mozart's symphonies, for example.

Of course, any absolute distinction between absolute music and program music is impossible, because musical inflection—like spoken language—will inevitably evoke an associative response of some sort in the ears, hearts, and minds of its listeners. Our textbooks might tell us that Mozart's symphonies are absolute music, although, to my mind, it is impossible not to feel profound gloom during the fourth movement of Mozart's G Minor Symphony, K. 550 and euphoria during the fourth movement of Mozart's Jupiter Symphony.

I would suggest, then, that the real issue here is one of compositional intent. I would suggest that Mozart did not set out to explicitly evoke any literary stories or visual imagery in his symphonies. Franz Liszt, however, who more often than not gave his compositions literary titles, did indeed set out to explicitly evoke literary stories and/or visual imagery in his instrumental music.

Back, then, to Liszt's Sonata in B Minor. While its title invokes sonata form, it does not identify or describe any programmatic content. Nevertheless, the music itself—with its extremes of contrast—invokes all sorts of metaphors which in turn evoke a narrative story. Various narratives have been attributed to the sonata: It has been described as an autobiographical document, as an allegory based on Milton's *Paradise Lost*, and as a work based on Goethe's *Faust*.

The Faustian interpretation is by far the most compelling, and it even has some anecdotal evidence to back it up. The great Chilean-American pianist Claudio Arrau (1903–1991) studied with Liszt's pupil Martin Krause. In an interview, Arrau was asked this question: "To what extent do you apply a Faustian scenario [to] your interpretation [of the Sonata in B Minor]? Do you think in terms of Faust, Gretchen, and Mephistopheles?" Arrau replied, "Definitely. This was something that was taken for granted among Liszt's pupils." From Arrau's lips to our ears: We will identify and explore the themes using a Goethe's *Faust*–derived vocabulary: Theme 1 will represent Mephistopheles (a demon in the employ of Satan himself); theme 2 will represent the flawed but heroic Faust; and theme 3 will represent the young, virginal, self-sacrificial Gretchen.

Exposition

The exposition introduces the three thematic protagonists—Mephistopheles, Faust, and Gretchen—as themes 1, 2 and 3. Theme 1: Rippling, crazed, and virtuosic, theme 1 is built from parts 3 and 4 of the introduction—the Mephistophelian cackle of part 3 and the rising two-chord units of part 4. Here we go—exposition, theme 1: Mephistopheles. [**Piano performance:** Liszt, Sonata in B Minor, exposition, theme 1.]

A furious modulating bridge follows, one that expands on elements of the introduction. We move directly to the majestic and heroic theme 2, set in D Major, the personification of Faust. [**Piano performance:** Liszt, Sonata in B Minor, exposition, theme 2.] We are honor-bound to observe that this lush and passionate theme grows out of the first notes of the introduction. Part 1 of the introduction began with two repeated Gs. [**Piano demonstration.**] Theme 2 develops this idea, consisting—as it does—of as series of repeated two-note units, units that rise towards heavenly redemption over the course of the opening of the theme. [**Piano demonstration.**]

Theme 3 represents Gretchen, the sweet-as-maple-syrup nubile whose goodness and purity will redeem Faust. And despite the fact that her gentle, lyric music would seem to be light-years removed from that of the heroic (if flawed) Faust, Gretchen's theme is based on the same repeated notes as Faust's theme. Check it out: Here's the opening of Faust's theme. [**Piano demonstration.**] And here's the opening of Gretchen's theme. [**Piano demonstration.**] There can be no doubt that the close relationship between themes 2 and 3 is intended a metaphor for the spiritual and emotional relationship between Faust and Gretchen.

Here is the first part of theme 3, the personification of Gretchen. [**Piano performance:** Liszt, Sonata in B Minor, exposition, theme 3.] Over the course of the movement, these three themes are presented in a dazzling and virtuosic array of various permutations; they alternate with each other, overlap with each, and are transformed constantly by their interactions, as Liszt follows—in his imagination—the dramatic interactions and developments of the Faust story. The miracle is that the sonata works perfectly well as a piece of absolute music; that is, it makes sense as pure music, its program aside.

Development Section

The development section begins roughly 12 minutes into the piece. The beginning of the development section—marked "slowly and sustained"— offers one of the rare moments of tranquility in the sonata. Here's how the development section begins. [**Piano performance:** Liszt, Sonata in B Minor, development opening.] Things do not stay this peaceful for very long. The pianist and musicologist Michael Davidson correctly points out that the development section "is the spiritual heart of the sonata, where the most extreme emotions, ranging from extreme tenderness to extreme anger vie with each other in a tremendous psychodrama."

We just heard some of the tenderness Davidson refers to, music drawn from Gretchen's theme. Let's hear a moment of high drama, during which Faust's theme—theme 2—attempting to climb ever higher, struggles with vicious downwards lines in the bass, an explicit evocation of Mephistopheles's attempts to drag Faust down to hell. [**Piano performance:** Liszt, Sonata in B Minor, development.]

Recapitulation

The recapitulation begins in the depths of the piano with part 1 of the introduction: [**Piano performance:** Liszt, Sonata in B Minor, recapitulation.] A fantastic hunk of music now follows, as Liszt transforms what had been parts 2 and 3 of the introduction into a fugue based on Mephistophelian melodic ideas! Check it out: Here are parts 2 and 3 of the introduction as they appeared at the beginning of the sonata. [**Piano performance:** Liszt, Sonata in B Minor, introduction.] Here are parts two and three of the introduction as they appear in the recapitulation, now transformed into a devilish fugue subject. [**Piano performance:** Liszt, Sonata in B Minor, recapitulation.]

The bristling fugue that follows is nothing less than a *totentanz*: a "dance of death." The pianist Alfred Brendel writes: "I do not know what to admire most: the introduction of the fugue at this point; how the three-part writing gradually grows back into [a] 'symphonic texture'; the Mozartean effortlessness of its polyphony; [or] the originality that sets this fugue apart from baroque stereotypes." Let's hear the fugue—this devilish *totentanz*—and the passage during which the music congeals back into what Brendel calls symphonic texture. [**Piano performance:** Liszt, Sonata in B Minor, recapitulation.]

Coda

The first one and a half minutes of the five-minute-long coda is an oxygen-depleting, muscle-tearing, phalanges-snapping exercise in virtuosity, a passage that begins with an ever more fervent, ever more thunderous evocation of Gretchen (that is, theme 3) and concludes with a final, teeth-rattling, ecstatically heroic statement of Faust's theme, theme 2. Let's hear that. [**Piano performance:** Liszt, Sonata in B Minor, coda.]

From this point, the sonata ends quietly and magically. That was not Liszt's original intention. In his original manuscript, the sonata concluded with a

25-measure apotheosis, to be played *fortississimo*: as loudly as possible. Liszt then crossed out those last 25 measures and put in their place a 32-measure passage that gradually fades away to *pianississimo*: as quietly as possible. Liszt's second impulse was brilliant. The quiet conclusion creates what Charles Rosen calls "an effect of religious absolution and a brief glimpse of heaven." Here are the last moments of the sonata, cast not in B Minor but rather now in B Major: [**Piano performance:** Liszt, Sonata in B Minor, closing.]

Early in his career, Liszt was encouraged by his friends to branch out into orchestral music. The young Liszt responded to his friends by describing the importance of the piano to his body, mind, and soul. Liszt wrote:

> My piano is to me what his vessel is to the sailor, his horse to the Arab, nay even more; [it] is myself, my speech, my life. It is the repository of all that stirred my nature in the passionate days of my youth. I confided to it all my desires, my dreams, my joys, and my sorrows. Its strings vibrated to my emotions, and its keys obeyed my every caprice. Would you have me abandon it and strive for the more brilliant triumphs of the orchestra? Oh, no! Even if I were competent for music of that kind, [I] would not abandon the study and development of piano playing until I had accomplished whatever is practical, whatever it is possible to attain.
>
> I consider the piano to be of great consequence. In my estimation it holds the first place in the hierarchy of instruments. In the compass of its seven octaves it includes the entire scope of the orchestra, and the ten fingers suffice for the harmony which is produced by an ensemble of a hundred players!

In his Sonata in B Minor, Liszt fulfills entirely his desire to turn the seven octaves of the piano not just into an orchestra, but into a vehicle for the heroic and the sublime.

Thank you.

Brahms—*Handel Variations*, Op. 24
Lecture 13

The full name of the piano work that is the subject of this lecture is "Variations and Fugue on a Theme by G. F. Handel" (1861). In modern times, this title raises not an eyebrow. It sounds like various other "concert music" titles—generic, passionless, and lacking any indication of the expressive content of the piece. At a time when most other composers were doing their best to come up with titles that reflected the expressive spirit and substance of their works, the 28-year-old Johannes Brahms remained intent on employing the blandest titles possible.

Brahms's Influences

- There is a graceful, if archaic, formality to the theme on which Brahms builds his magnificent *Handel Variations*—a theme written by Georg Frederic Handel in the 1730s. It has the measured pace of a processional, a simple and regular harmonic rhythm, and is cast in that most ubiquitous and predictable of all baroque-era structural templates, binary dance form: A–A–B–B.

- Brahms appropriated the theme from the third movement of Handel's Harpsichord Suite in B-flat Major, a movement entitled "Air with Variations." The Harpsichord Suite was published in London in 1733, and Brahms—who was a serious collector of music manuscripts—owned a first edition of the piece. Typical of harpsichord music, Handel's thematic melody is filled with embellishments.

- Such embellishments are characteristic of harpsichord music. Unlike a piano, a harpsichord can neither accent notes nor sustain them for any period of time. The only way to emphasize or sustain notes on a harpsichord is to embellish them.

- The first thing Brahms's title, *Handel Variations*, tells us is that the movement is cast in theme and variations form, a form in which a theme is stated and then varied in the sections that follow.

Theme and variations form is a classical-era (that is, 18th-century) construct, one that demands strict adherence to a preexisting formal template.

- Theme and variations form is precisely the sort of old-style, presumably rigid musical form that romantics like Berlioz, Liszt, and Wagner, for example, rejected out of hand, claiming that it constrained feeling and put form before expression.

Johannes Brahms (1833–1897) predominantly focused on composing chamber music, choral music, and music for solo piano.

- Brahms's fugue occupies the work's final four-and-a-half minutes. It is worth discussing the fact that Brahms composed this set of variations capped with a fugue. It was one thing to include fugue-style music within a larger work—even Liszt did that in his Sonata in B Minor— but by including "Fugue" in his title, Brahms links his piece incontrovertibly with works composed during the baroque era 140 years before.

- By entitling his work "Variations and Fugue," Brahms was not just indicating that the work contains a fugue but was also staking out his claim to the past—to his spiritual link to Bach and Handel (a link made abundantly clear by basing the work on a theme by Handel).

- In addition, by composing a theme-and-variations-form movement capped by a fugue based on a theme by Handel and then saying so in his title, Brahms was purposely rubbing bad-smelling stuff in the noses of arch-romantics like Liszt and Wagner, whose musical politics he hated and who, for their part, despised Brahms for his "apparent" conservatism.

- In reality, Brahms's so-called conservatism is a red herring. In terms of his melodic and harmonic usage and the expressive zap his music delivers, Brahms is every inch a feeling-is-believing romantic-era composer. However, he never lost his affection for certain time-honored musical processes and forms, and he believed that fancy titles and over-the-top expressive blather were no substitute for old-fashioned musical craft.

- Unlike such self-professed "futurists" as Liszt and Wagner, Brahms did not believe that a composer had to sacrifice traditional formal discipline in order to be "modern." In fact, his music is a brilliant synthesis of the best of the old combined with the best of the new.

- Brahms's two great influences for his *Handel Variations* are Johann Sebastian Bach's *Goldberg Variations* of 1741 and Beethoven's *Diabelli Variations* of 1823. Beethoven's *Diabelli Variations* were also inspired by Bach's *Goldberg Variations*, so this is a case where all three of these composers wrote works that follow the same approximate outline.

- All three works are for solo keyboard. All three works feature a splendiferous multitude of variations: Bach's contains 30 variations, Beethoven's contains 33 variations, and Brahms's contains 25 variations plus the closing fugue. In all three works, the composers group the variations together in such a way as to create a larger musical structure.

- Most significantly, all three works are what was called during the baroque era a ground bass (or a passacaglia or a chaconne—these designations are basically interchangeable). A ground bass is a variations-type procedure in which the theme is not the melody heard at the beginning of the piece but, rather, the bass line and harmonies beneath that melody. The challenge in such a piece is not to embellish and transform the melody during the variations but, rather, to create ever-new melodic material above the bass line.

Variational Groupings

- The 25 variations of the *Handel Variations* clump together into six large groups of variations. We perceive these grouping as a series of waves: Generally speaking, they start out quietly and build to a climax; the next group begins quietly and then, once again, builds to a climax, and so forth.

Variations Group 1: Variations 1–4

- Variation 1, with its unadorned harmony and occasional embellishment, acts as a temporal bridge, one that transports the music from the early 18th to the mid-19th century.

- Variation 2 sees the upper voice set in slithery, chromatic triplets, and just like that, we have arrived at the musical world of the mid-19th century.

- Variation 3—marked *dolce*, meaning "sweetly"—is most Schumann-esque, as the hands alternate back and forth in a manner typical of Robert Schumann's piano music.

- Variation 4, in which the full resources of the romantic piano are fully unleashed, brings the first large part of the piece to its climax.

Variations Group 2: Variations 5–10

- The six variations of group 2 are cast as three pairs. Variations 5 and 6 are both quiet and set in B-flat minor.

- Variation 5 has the flowing, melancholy sensibility of Chopin's music. Variation 6—still in B-flat minor—is a ghostly canon in octaves.

- Variations 7 and 8 are paired as well. Set back in B-flat major, they are both vigorous bits of riding music, based on a rhythmic pattern of eighth-sixteenth-sixteenth.

○ The concluding variations of group 2 are both royal in mood and employ triplets. Variation 9 is filled with all sorts of chromatic elaboration. The jackhammer-like variation 10 covers the entire keyboard, top to bottom, and brings this second group of variations to its climax and conclusion.

Variations Group 3: Variations 11–13
○ Variations 11 and 12 are both quiet and lyric. Variation 13 brings this third group of variations to its conclusion. It is nothing less than a soulful Hungarian Gypsy rhapsody, set in B-flat minor and replete with a thrumming, cimbalom-like accompaniment. (A "cimbalom" is a Hungarian hammered dulcimer.)

Variations Group 4: Variations 14–18
○ The five variations of group 4 are conceived as a single, continuous passage. The first of these variations—variation 14—explodes out of the gate with parallel sixths in the right hand set against a walking bass in the left. The last of these variations—variation 18—brings this fourth group to a relatively quiet conclusion.

Variations Group 5: Variations 19–22
○ The fifth group of variations features a series of character pieces. For example, variation 19 is cast as a *siciliana*—an elegant, moderately paced baroque-era dance in **compound meter**. Group 5 concludes with the music box–like variation 22.

Variations Group 6: Variations 23–25
○ The three variations of this sixth and final batch constitute a continuous buildup toward the climactic fugue that will conclude the piece. Listen to variations 23, 24, and 25 straight on through; this excerpt should have you hyperventilating by its conclusion.

Fugue
• The fugue is both a development section and a coda, and it gives Brahms the opportunity to do all sorts of things that he could not have done earlier during the more strictly controlled variations.

In his description of the fugue's conclusion, Brahms's biographer Malcolm Macdonald notes: "The immense cumulative power of this Fugue, gathered up in a chiming dominant **pedal**, issues in a coda of granitic splendor, the vertical and horizontal demands of theme and harmony equally fulfilled in a majestic convergence of descending chords and ascending fugue-motifs."

Brahms and Clara Schumann

- In February 1854, four-and-a-half months after Brahms met Robert and Clara Schumann, Robert attempted suicide by jumping off a bridge in Düsseldorf into the Rhine River. He was rescued, but his mind—ravaged by syphilis—had snapped entirely. He was committed to an insane asylum, where he died two-and-a-half years later.

- At the time of Robert's suicide attempt, Clara Schumann was 34 years old. She was the mother of six children and was pregnant with number seven. She was distraught and entirely overwhelmed. When the not-yet 21-year-old Brahms heard what had happened, he rushed to Clara's side and pledged to stay with her until the baby was born and Schumann had recovered. Visitors came and went, but it was Brahms who stayed. He helped take care of the kids, took on some piano students, and—of course—they fell in love.

- Robert Schumann died on July 29, 1856, and was buried two days later. Properly chaperoned, the now 23-year-old Brahms and the almost 37-year-old Clara took a vacation together to Switzerland. We do not know what they said to each other, but Brahms had already decided—despite all that they had gone through during the previous two-and-a-half years (perhaps because of it)—that he could not marry Clara.

- Clara Schumann was the great love of Brahms's life, and they remained friends for the rest of their lives. As a pianist, Clara championed Brahms's music to her dying day. Brahms completed the *Handel Variations* in early September of 1861. It was a birthday gift for Clara, whose 42nd birthday fell on September 13. In lieu of a dedication, Brahms's manuscript is headed "Variations for a beloved friend." Clara gave the premiere performance of the work in Brahms's hometown of Hamburg on December 7, 1861.

compound meter: Any meter that features a triple subdivision within each beat.

pedal: A single pitch or harmony sustained or repeated for a period of time.

Brahms—*Handel Variations*, Op. 24
Lecture 13—Transcript

Welcome back to *The 23 Greatest Solo Piano Works*. This is Lecture 13. It is entitled Brahms—*Handel Variations*, Op. 24.

The full name of the piano work that is the subject of this lecture is *Variations and Fugue on a Theme by Handel*. *Variations and Fugue on a Theme by Handel*. For us, today, this title raises not an eyebrow. It sounds like a thousand-and-one other "oncert music titles: generic, passionless, and lacking any indication of the expressive content of the piece. Had the 28-year-old Johannes Brahms been wise enough to consult with yours truly on this subject of title, I would have suggested, among others: *Handel with Care*. Or perhaps, *Musty Old Wine, Funky New Bottle*. Or how about *By Various Means* (actually, I've already used that one, but I'd be happy to share it with Mr. B). Or how about, simply, *Fugue It*. Yeah!

In truth, the 28-year-old Johannes Brahms—around five feet tall, blonde, blue-eyed, still fairly slim, and with nary a whisker on his baby face—would have squashed my suggestions like a banana slug under a car tire. At a time when most other composers were doing their darnedest to come up with titles that reflected the expressive spirit and substance of their works, Brahms remained intent on employing the blandest, most flaccid titles possible. We'll discuss Brahms's titular politics in a moment, but first, let's hear the theme on which Brahms builds this magnificent work, a theme written by Georg Frederic Handel way back in the 1730s. [**Piano performance:** Brahms, *Handel Variations*, Op. 24, theme.]

There is a graceful, if archaic, formality to that theme. It has the measured pace of a processional, a simple and regular harmonic rhythm, and is cast in that most ubiquitous and predictable of all baroque era structural templates, binary dance form: A-A-B-B. Brahms appropriated the theme from third movement of Handel's Harpsichord Suite in B-flat Major, a movement entitled "Air with Variations." The harpsichord suite was published in London in 1733, and Brahms—who was a serious collector of music manuscripts—owned a first edition of the piece. Typical of harpsichord music, Handel's thematic melody is filled with embellishments.

[**Piano demonstration.**] Such embellishments are characteristic of harpsichord music. Unlike a piano, a harpsichord can neither accent notes nor sustain them for any period of time. The only way to emphasize or sustain notes on a harpsichord is to embellish them. [**Piano demonstration.**]

Back, please, to the meaning of Brahms's title and the musical politics behind it. The first thing the title tells us is that the movement is cast in theme and variations form, a form in which a theme is stated and then varied in the sections that follow. Theme and variations form is a classical-era (that is, 18th century) construct, one that demands strict adherence to a preexisting formal template. Theme and variations is precisely the sort of old-style, presumably rigid musical form that romantics like Berlioz, Liszt, and Wagner (for example) rejected out of hand, claiming that it constrained feeling and put form before expression. A theme and variations form movement, in 1861? Cows in Berkeley? Moo. (Bay Area joke, that.)

And then to compose a set of variations capped with a fugue. A fugue? OK, it was one thing to include a fugue or fugue-styled music within a larger work; heck, even Liszt did that in his Sonata in B Minor. But by indicating "fugue" in his title, Brahms links his piece incontrovertibly with works composed during the baroque era 140 years before, works with titles like *Prelude and Fugue*, and *Toccata and Fugue*, and *Fantasy and Fugue*. Here is the beginning of Brahms's fugue, a fugue that occupies the work's final four-and-a-half minutes! [**Piano performance:** Brahms, *Handel Variations*, Op. 24, fugue.]

I can assure you that by entitling his work *Variations and Fugue*, Brahms was not just indicating that the work contains a fugue but staking out his claim to the past as well—to his spiritual link to Bach and Handel (a link made abundantly clear by basing the work on a theme by Handel). And there's more! You see, by composing a theme and variations form movement capped by a fugue based on a theme by Handel and then saying so in his title, Brahms was purposely rubbing smelly bad stuff in the noses of arch-romantics like Liszt and Wagner, whose musical politics he so hated, and who, for their part, despised Brahms for his "apparent" conservatism.

That's "apparent" with quotation marks around it, 'cause in reality, Brahms's so-called conservatism is a red herring. You see, in terms of his melodic and harmonic usage and the expressive zap his music delivers, Brahms is every inch a feeling-is-believing, romantic-era composer. However, he never lost his affection for certain time-honored musical processes and forms, and he believed that fancy titles and over-the-top expressive blather were no substitute for good old-fashioned musical craft. Unlike such self-professed futurists as Liszt and Wagner, Brahms did not believe that a composer had to sacrifice traditional formal discipline in order to be modern. In fact, his music is a brilliant synthesis of the best of the old combined with the best of the new.

An anecdote. On February 6, 1864, the not quite 31-year-old Brahms met the not quite 51-year-old Richard Wagner for the first and only time. They met at Wagner's villa in suburban Vienna, where Wagner received Brahms with what we are told was "grace and charm." Brahms played the *Handel Variations* for Wagner, and Wagner stated for the record that "It shows what still can be done with the old forms by somebody who knows how to handle them." What a hypocritical gasbag. Wagner spent the remaining 19 years of his life trashing Brahms in both print and conversation, whereas Brahms, his reservations aside, "continued to admire Wagner's single-minded vision and immense creative energy."

Brahms: The Making of a Composer

Johannes Brahms was born on May 7, 1833 in a run-down apartment house in Hamburg's red light district. His father Johann Jakob was an ambitious if only marginally talented musician. His mother Johanna Henrike Christiane Nissen was a small and sickly spinster who—at 41—was 17 years older than Jakob Brahms when they were married. Her age and health aside, Jakob chose well: Christiane was intelligent, articulate, and an excellent seamstress and cook.

She was also as fertile as the Tennessee Valley: From the age of 42 to 46, she managed to pop out three kids who survived into adulthood: Elisabeth, Johannes, and Friedrich. By the time he was eight, it was clear that Johannes—or Hannes, as he was called—was a musical prodigy of extraordinary promise. When he was 11, Brahms's piano teacher—a highly regarded local named Eduard Marxen—began giving the boy composition and theory lessons along with piano lessons. It soon became clear that Brahms's potential as a composer was even greater than his potential as a pianist. Marxsen recalled:

> When I started teaching him composition, he exhibited a rare acuteness of mind which enchanted me, and I was bound to recognize in [his earliest works] an intelligence that convinced me that an exceptional, great, and peculiarly profound talent was dormant in him. I therefore shrank from no effort or work in order to awaken and form it, that I might one day rear a priest of art, who should preach what was sublime, true, and eternally incorruptible.

Fancy words. But Marxen walked the walk and insisted on teaching Brahms for free. Brahms later recalled: "I'll never forget how he refused to accept the moneybag my father had saved up for the lessons; he wouldn't take it, yet I was to come [for lessons] four times a week." Marxsen's training grounded Brahms in the discipline and repertoire of the German/Austrian tradition, meaning the music of Bach, Handel, Haydn, Mozart, Beethoven, and Schubert. These composers were Brahms's heroes, his gods, and they remained so for the rest of his life.

The Hungarian Connection

In 1848, revolutions broke out across Europe. By 1849 they had been crushed, each and every one of them. Hamburg—as a major port city—saw a huge influx of refugees in 1848 and 1849. Among these refugees were urban hungarians who brought with them their Hungarian gypsy music: a soulful, exotic, rhythmically unrestrained music that hit the 15-year-old Johannes Brahms like one of those cartoon safes dropped from a 10th-story window. Brahms's subsequent love affair with Hungarian gypsy music would last for the rest of his life.

It was Brahms's "Hungarophilia" that triggered a series of events when Brahms was 20 that shaped virtually every aspect of his future! Here's what happened. In August of 1850, the 17-year-old Brahms began performing with a 21-year-old Hungarian violinist named Eduard Hoffman. In an effort to trumpet his Hungarian nationalist bona fides, Hoffman had renamed himself Eduard Reményi, and it was as Reményi that Brahms came to know him.

In the spring of 1853, Brahms and this Reményi decided to do a concert tour of Germany. About six weeks into the tour—in late May, 1853—the boys stopped in Hanover and dropped in on a classmate of Reményi's from the Vienna Conservatory, a violinist and fellow Hungarian named Joseph Joachim. Joachim was famous. Though not quite 22 years old, he had been a regular on the Euro concert scene for over ten years. Joachim had been appointed Professor of Violin at the Leipzig Conservatory at 17; concertmaster of the Weimar Court Orchestra at 19; and at 20, he joined the Hanover Court Orchestra as its concertmaster and violin soloist. Mad credentials, my friends. Mad credentials.

So. Joachim asked Reményi's accompanist ("Your name is Brahms?") to play something he had composed. Brahms did so and Joachim's jaw hit the floor. Fifty years later he recalled, "Never in the course of my artist's life had I been more completely overwhelmed." What Joachim heard was music with the expressive power of Beethoven, the discipline of Bach and the melodic grace of Mozart; serious, beautifully crafted music that didn't sound like anything he'd ever heard. It was, for Joachim, a revelation. Within two days Brahms and Joachim had forged a friendship that would last for the rest of their lives.

Before they left Hanover, Joachim presented Brahms and Reményi with a gift: a letter of introduction to the "duce" of the avant-garde, the Hungarian-born Franz Liszt, who was living and working in the German city of Weimar. Privately, Joachim told Brahms that should things not work out with Reményi, Brahms was always welcome to come on back and hang. Well, things didn't work out in Weimar or with Reményi. Brahms was appalled by the whole "Liszt trip": his god-like manner and attitude; the obsequious acolytes and fawning women; and the zealotry that claimed Liszt's particular brand of music was the one and only path for the music of the future. Brahms got surly, Liszt got annoyed, and Reményi—convinced that Brahms was about to ruin his fledgling career—upped and walked, leaving Brahms in Weimar with hardly a penny to his name. Brahms wrote to Joachim:

Dear Herr Joachim,

If I were not an optimist I should now have well-found reasons to curse my art and to retire as a clerk into an office. I cannot return to Hamburg without anything to show. I must at least see two or three of my compositions in print, so that I can look my parents in the face. May I visit you? Perhaps I am presumptuous, but my position and my dejection force me to it.

Brahms did re-visit Joachim. He stayed for roughly two months, during which time Brahms composed, practiced, and concertized with Joachim, with whom he bonded completely. Brahms decided to use his share of the profits from their concerts to finance a hiking tour of the Rhine. Gracious, when Brahms's mother found out that her little boy was going to hike on the Rhine, she was *verklempt*! She wrote to her son (no joke; this is a real letter): "Such steep rocks! How easily you could fall! Nestler's daughter died of a hemorrhage after such a hikE! Malwine Erk was killed in Heligoland by lightning! For today, enough of these terrors: buy a winter coat, write if you need money."

On August 26, 1853—roughly four months after he left Hamburg—Brahms and Joachim parted, but not before Joachim arranged the meeting that would change Brahms's life. On parting, Joachim suggested that while Brahms was in the Rhineland, he should stop in Düsseldorf and introduce himself to the composer Robert Schumann and his wife, the legendary pianist Clara Wieck Schumann.

The Curse

On the morning of October 1, 1853, the 20 year-old Johannes Brahms, knocked on the door of Robert and Clara Schumann's house in Düsseldorf. Robert Schumann answered the door. Brahms introduced himself; Schumann led Brahms to a piano. Brahms sat down and began to play his Piano Sonata No. 1 in C Major. Brahms biographer Jan Swafford describes what happened next:

Brahms felt Schumann's touch on his shoulder. "Please wait a moment. I must call my wife." Schumann rushed from the room as Brahms sat staring at the keyboard, his heart pounding. He may never have heard Clara Schumann play piano, but he knew all about her: [she was] spoken of with awe. Clara greeted him with a smile. "Here, dear Clara," Schumann said, "you shall hear music as you have never heard before. Now begin your sonata again, young man."

Brahms proceeded to play for the better part of two hours. That evening Clara wrote in her journal, "Here is one who comes as if sent from god!" That same evening Robert wrote in his diary, "Visit from Brahms. A genius." Brahms stayed with the Schumanns for a month. It was, Brahms later said, the best time of his life. Clara wrote in her journal, "Robert says there is nothing to wish [for] except that heaven may preserve Brahms's health." Robert Schumann did more than just wish. He contacted his publisher and arranged for the publication of a number of works by Brahms. And Schumann didn't stop there. As a music critic of great renown, he wrote "the article," his Rhapsody on Brahms. It appeared on October 28, 1853 in the prestigious *Neue Zeitschrift für Musik*. We quote it in briefest part:

I have [often] thought that someone would appear, destined to give ideal presentation to the highest expression of the time, who would bring us his mastership springing forth like Minerva from the head of Jove. And he is come, a young blood by whose cradle graces and heroes kept watch. He is called Johannes Brahms. His companions greet him on his first course through the world, where, perhaps, wounds may await him, but laurels and palms as well.

Twenty years old and a virtual nobody, Johannes Brahms was declared by Robert Schumann to be the messiah of German music. Brahms must have swallowed really hard when he read that. No one had to tell Brahms that the messiah was greeted with laurels and palms and then he was crucified. The article—so well intended—was, for Brahms, a disaster. Schumann's article—I prefer to call it the curse—brought Brahms much too much attention much too soon. One immediate result was that Brahms decided not to compose—or at least, not to release to the public—music that would bring him into direct comparison with Beethoven—meaning, specifically, symphonies and string quartets. Instead—for the next 23 years—Brahms focused on chamber music, choral music, and music for solo piano. Among those works for solo piano is the *Handel Variations*, composed in 1861, when Brahms was 28 years old, eight years into the curse.

Brahms's two great influences for his *Handel Variations* are Johann Sebastian Bach's *Goldberg Variations* of 1741 and Beethoven's *Diabelli Variations* of 1823. Beethoven's *Diabelli Variations* were also inspired by Bach's Goldbergs, and so here's a case where all three of the Three Bs—the "Killer Bs": Bach, Beethoven, and Brahms—wrote works that follow the same approximate outline. All three works are for solo keyboard. All three works feature a splendiferous multitude of variations: Bach's Goldbergs, 30 variations; Beethoven's Diabellis, 33 variations; and Brahms's *Handel Variations*, 25 variations plus the closing fugue. In all three works, the composers group the variations together in such a way as to create a larger musical structure.

Most significantly, all three works are what was called during the baroque era a ground bass (or a passacaglia or a chaconne; these designations are basically interchangeable). A ground bass is a variations-type procedure in which the theme is not the melody heard at the beginning of the piece but rather, the bass line and harmonies beneath that melody. The challenge in such a piece is not to embellish and transform the melody during the variations, but rather create ever new melodic material above the bass line. Brahms said exactly as much in a letter, stating that, "In a theme for a [set of] variations, it is only the bass that has any meaning for me. [The bass] is sacred to me: it is the foundation on which I build my stories. What I do with a melody is only playing around."

Variational "Groupings"

The 25 variations of the *Handel Variations* clump together into six large groups of variations. We perceive these grouping as a series of waves: generally speaking, they start out quietly and build to a climax; the next group begins quietly and then, once again, builds to a climax, and so forth.

In our effort to perceive these groupings as well as their cumulative dramatic impact, we are going to sample roughly three-quarters of the variations.

Variations Group 1: Variations 1–4

Variation 1, with its unadorned harmony and occasional embellishment acts as a temporal bridge, one that transports the music from the early 18th to the mid-19th century. [**Piano performance:** Brahms, *Handel Variations*, Op. 24, variation 1.] Variation 2 sees the upper voice set in slithery, chromatic triplets; and just like that, we have arrived to the musical world of the mid-19th century! [**Piano performance:** Brahms, *Handel Variations*, Op. 24, variation 2.]

Variation 3—marked *dolce*, meaning "sweetly," is most "Schumannesque," as the hands alternate back and forth in a manner typical of Robert Schumann's piano music. [**Piano performance:** Brahms, *Handel Variations*, Op. 24, variation 3.] Variation 4—in which the full resources of the romantic piano are fully unleashed—brings the first large part of the piece to its climax. We hear this variation in its entirety: [**Piano performance:** Brahms, *Handel Variations*, Op. 24, variation 4.]

Variations Group 2: Variations 5–10

The six variations of group two are cast as three pairs. Variations 5 and 6 are both quiet and set in B-flat Minor. Variation 5 has the flowing, melancholy sensibility of Chopin's music. [**Piano performance:** Brahms, *Handel Variations*, Op. 24, variation 5.] Variation 6—still in B-flat minor—is a ghostly canon in octaves. [**Piano performance:** Brahms, *Handel Variations*, Op. 24, variation 6.]

Variations 7 and 8 are paired as well: Set back in B-flat major, they are both vigorous bits of riding music, based on a rhythmic pattern of eighth-sixteenth-sixteenth note. Variation 7: [**Piano performance:** Brahms, *Handel Variations*, Op. 24, variation 7.] And variation 8: [**Piano performance:** Brahms, *Handel Variations*, Op. 24, variation 8.]

The concluding variations of group 2 are both royal in mood and employ triplets. Variation 9 is filled with all sorts of chromatic elaboration. [**Piano performance:** Brahms, *Handel Variations*, Op. 24, variation 9.] The jackhammer-like variation 10 covers the entire keyboard, top to bottom, and brings this second group of variations to its climax and conclusion. We hear it in its entirety. [**Piano performance:** Brahms, *Handel Variations*, Op. 24, variation 10.]

Variations Group 3: Variations 11–13

Variations 11 and 12 are both quiet and lyric. Variation 11 begins this way. [**Piano performance:** Brahms, *Handel Variations*, Op. 24, variation 11.] And variation 12 begins this way. [**Piano performance:** Brahms, *Handel Variations*, Op. 24, variation 12.] Variation 13 brings this third group of variations to its conclusion. This variation is nothing less than a soulful Hungarian gypsy rhapsody, set in B-flat Minor and replete with a thrumming, cimbalom-like accompaniment! (For our information, a cimbalom is a Hungarian hammered dulcimer.) We hear variation 13 in its entirety. [**Piano performance:** Brahms, *Handel Variations*, Op. 24, variation 13.]

Variations Group 4: Variations 14–18

The five variations of group 4 are conceived as a single, continuous passage. We will sample the first of these variations—number 14—and the last, number 18. Variation 14 explodes out of the gate with parallel sixths in the right hand set against a walking bass in the left. [**Piano performance:** Brahms, *Handel Variations*, Op. 24, variation 14.] Variation 18 brings this fourth group to a relatively quiet conclusion. [**Piano performance:** Brahms, *Handel Variations*, Op. 24, variation 18.]

Variations Group 5: Variations 19–22

This fifth group of variations features a series of character pieces. For example, variation 19 is cast as a siciliana: an elegant, moderately paced baroque-era dance in compound meter. Here's how it begins. [**Piano performance:** Brahms, *Handel Variations*, Op. 24, variation

19.] Group 5 concludes with the music box–like variation 22.
[**Piano performance:** Brahms, *Handel Variations*, Op. 24, variation 22.]

Variations Group Six: Variations 23–25

The three variations of this sixth and final batch constitute a continuous buildup towards the climactic fugue that will conclude the piece. Because we must, we will hear variations 23, 24, and 25 straight on through. I will indicate the beginning of each variation. If this excerpt doesn't have us hyperventilating by its conclusion, we'll need to turn up our oxygen tanks!
[**Piano performance:** Brahms, *Handel Variations*, Op. 24, variations 23–25.]

Fugue

The fugue is both a development section and a coda, and it gives Brahms the opportunity to do all sorts of things that he could not have done earlier during the more strictly controlled variations. We have already heard the opening of the fugue; let us now hear its magnificent conclusion. But first, a description of this conclusion in prose so purple that it must be shared, written by Brahms's biographer Malcolm MacDonald:

> The immense cumulative power of this Fugue, gathered up in a chiming dominant pedal, issues in a coda of granitic splendor, the vertical and horizontal demands of theme and harmony equally fulfilled in a majestic convergence of descending chords and ascending fugue-motifs.

All right! Fugue, conclusion. [**Piano performance:** Brahms, *Handel Variations*, Op. 24, fugue.]

Conclusion

In February 1854, four-and-a-half months after Brahms met Robert and Clara Schumann, Robert attempted suicide by jumping off a bridge in Düsseldorf into the Rhine River. He was rescued, but his mind—ravaged by syphilis—had snapped entirely. He was committed to an insane asylum where he died two-and-a-half years later, a shrunken husk of what he once was.

At the time of Robert's suicide attempt, Clara Schumann was 34 years old. She was the mother of six children and was pregnant with number seven. She was distraught and entirely overwhelmed. When the not yet 21-year-old Brahms heard what had happened, he rushed to Clara's side and pledged to stay with her until the baby was born and Schumann had recovered. Visitors came and went, but it was Brahms who stayed. He helped take care of the kids, took on some piano students and, of course, he fell in love with Clara, and Clara fell in love with him.

Robert Schumann died on July 29, 1856 and was buried two days later. For the now 23-year-old Brahms and the almost 37 year-old Clara it was crunch time. Properly chaperoned, they took a vacation together to Switzerland. We do not know what they said to each other, but Brahms had already decided— despite all that they had gone through during the previous two-and-a-half years (or perhaps because of it!)—that he could not marry Clara. Brahms had decided to accept for himself his friend Joachim's personal motto: *Frei aber einsam*—"lonely but free."

Clara Schumann was the great love of Brahms's life, and they remained friends for the rest of their lives. As a pianist, Clara championed Brahms's music to her dying day. Brahms completed the *Handel Variations* in early September of 1861. It was a birthday gift for Clara, whose 42nd birthday fell on September 13. In lieu of a dedication, Brahms's manuscript is headed "Variations for a beloved friend." Clara gave the premiere performance of the work in Brahms's hometown of Hamburg on December 7, 1861.

Thank you.

Brahms—Six Pieces for Piano, Op. 118
Lecture 14

Brahms found his mature compositional voice as a young man, in his late 20s. Brahms structured his works along the formal lines of the 18th century. These formal procedures—and the craft and intellectual discipline they represent—are the objective aspect of his compositional style. However, Brahms's melodic and harmonic language and expressive content were fully contemporary, fully romantic. The heart of Brahms's musical language is the intuitive, inspiration-driven, subjective aspect of his style. In essence, Brahms was an objective subjectivist.

Brahms and the Piano

- Brahms started his musical life as a piano prodigy. At the age of 12, his pianistic studies began to share equal time with composition lessons. Soon enough, Brahms became a composer for the piano. Sadly, we cannot know what Brahms's early compositions sounded like, because he destroyed each and every one of them.

- The earliest of his works to survive is his Scherzo in E-flat Minor for Piano, which was composed in 1851, when he was 18 years old, and published—thanks to Robert Schumann—in 1853 as Op. 4. The other "earliest" of his works to survive—three grand piano sonatas and three sets of songs for piano and voice—all date to 1853. The preeminent role of the piano in all of these pieces is logical; they are works Brahms composed to play himself.

- As Brahms matured and his career as a composer developed, the primacy of piano in his compositions gave way, as he established himself as a composer of chamber music, choral music, and—finally—orchestral music.

- Brahms composed his last orchestral work—the Double Concerto in A Minor for Violin and 'Cello—in 1887. Four years later, in

1891, the 58-year-old Brahms finally returned to the instrumental genre that had brought him to the dance 40 years before: solo piano.

- Brahms composed four sets of solo piano works between 1891 and 1893: the Seven Fantasias, Op. 116; the Three Intermezzi, Op. 117; the Six Pieces of Op. 118; and the Four Pieces of Op. 119. These are all relatively short works, by and large intimate in tone. They represent a withdrawal from the public world of the orchestra to a very private, introspective, and personal place.

- It is a place both nostalgic and progressive, because even as Brahms was getting back in touch with his roots as a composer of solo piano music, the music itself is some of the most thematically, rhythmically, and harmonically modern music written of that time, music that pushes the traditional tonal language to its breaking point—and sometimes beyond.

- Brahms completed the Six Pieces for Piano in 1893. They are dedicated to Clara Schumann, who was the first person "not named Brahms" to see them in manuscript.

No. 1: Intermezzo in A Minor

- Brahms's use of the title "Intermezzo" is extremely idiosynchratic. "Intermezzo" means "in the middle"; an **intermezzo** is an interlude, a musical number of generally limited compositional content and expressive character that occurs in between two more "significant" chunks of music.

- Like Chopin's preludes—works that stand by themselves and are, in reality, a prelude to nothing—Brahms's intermezzi are self-standing works that stand in between nothing.

- We could interpret Brahms's use of the word "intermezzo" poetically; we could claim that he used the designation to indicate interludes of sublime loveliness in our otherwise beauty-starved, workaday lives, but Brahms himself would likely tell us that we were being ridiculous for even suggesting such a thing. In truth, a Brahmsian "intermezzo" is simply a relatively short piece, typically gentle and meditative character.

- This opening intermezzo, marked "not too fast, but very passionately," has the character of a dramatic overture and is thus a most appropriate piece to begin the set.

Johannes Brahms was born on May 7, 1833, in a run-down apartment house in Hamburg's red-light district.

No. 2: Intermezzo in A Major

- The Intermezzo in A Major is a wistful, exquisitely beautiful piece that is fairly easy to play and, thus, the most frequently performed of the Op. 118 set. Nevertheless, it is filled with compositional virtuosity: with all sorts of contrapuntal techniques, rhythmic and harmonic ambiguities, and motivic development, all of which are so beautifully incorporated into the substance of the work that they are de facto invisible—a brilliant example of the art of concealing art.

- The Intermezzo is cast in three-part, A–B–A form. The thematic melody on which the entire piece is based is heard in the upper voice at the very beginning of the piece. This thematic melody consists of three particular elements, all of which will be developed: two melodic motives and a rhythmic/harmonic idea.

- Melodic motive 1 consists of just three notes; when first heard, those notes are C-sharp, B, D. That motive is heard twice at the beginning of the thematic melody, the second version being an expansion of the first.

- The second motive follows immediately. It consists of a leaping, dotted-rhythm (meaning long-short) ascent followed by an essentially stepwise descent.

- The third notable element of this thematic melody is a very subtle but very important rhythmic/harmonic idea.

- The intermezzo is set in triple meter—that is, in three. The intermezzo is not a waltz, with the rhythmic emphasis on the first and strongest beat of each measure; in reality, the emphasis is on beat 3, which adds a tremendous degree of rhythmic fluidity and unpredictability to the music.

- The harmony reinforces the emphasis on beat 3. For example, the opening harmony—on beat 3—is a **consonance**, whereas the harmony that falls on the following beat 1 is a dissonance, something called a 6/4 chord. In this way, Brahms destabilized many of the first beats—the down beats—and in doing so, shifts harmonic primacy to beat 3.

- About 45 seconds into the piece, a transitional passage sees the emphasis shift from beat 3 to beat 1 and then back to beat 3 again, creating a wonderfully subtle bit of cross-rhythm. This opening A section of the movement reaches its climax with this music.

- The sighing, descending melody of the first part of that climactic music is an extension of the descending thematic motive heard at the beginning of the piece. Meanwhile, in the bass, the opening thematic motive subtly but powerfully pushes the climax forward.

- The melancholy middle, or B, section of the movement is initially set in F-sharp minor. But, of course, in reality, the B section is a further development of melodic material first heard at the very beginning of the intermezzo.

- Even though this analysis has only skimmed the surface of this intermezzo, the larger point is that this is music of incredible craft and compositional integrity as well as music of unearthly beauty.

No. 3: Ballade in G Minor

- At its most generic, a musical "ballade" is a one-movement work with both dramatic and lyric qualities. It is to this most generic definition of "ballade" that Brahms refers in his title for this work.

- Like most of the pieces of Op. 118, this ballade is cast in three-part, A–B–A form. The outer A sections are most dramatic; they feature bristling, swaggering music heard in chords that alternate between the pianist's hands.

- The lyric music follows in the B section—a gorgeous, rolling, vaguely Hungarian-sounding passage that stands in polar contrast with the galumphing A section.

No. 4: Intermezzo in F Minor

- The earthy, delicate, sentimental, lyric, loving, profoundly human Brahms comes out in his music. An example of this is the passionate conclusion of his Intermezzo in F Minor. This is wonderful music.

No. 5: Romance in F Major

- Cast in A–B–A form, the opening (and closing) A sections have the natural radiance of folk song, albeit a very sophisticated folk song. The opening A section of the romance in F Major might best be described as a song without words.

- The folklike flavor of this romance becomes even more pronounced in the B section, during which a simple, gracious, ever-further embellished tune is heard over a thrumming pedal D.

No. 6: Intermezzo in E-flat Minor

- Brahms indicates that this intermezzo be played "moderate to slowly and sadly." This intermezzo is one of the most forward-looking works Brahms ever composed. Its harmonic ambiguity pushes it past traditional tonality, and its continuously developed thematic material and motivic saturation have became a textbook model for 20th- and 21st-century composers.

- If this work had been by Franz Liszt, with his fondness for programmatic titles, he probably would have entitled it something along the lines of "Obsession." The intermezzo is a work based on the "obsessive" repetitions, variations, and reharmonizations of a single motive. That germinal motive is presented all by itself at the start of the piece. The resemblance of this sinuous, melancholy motive to the Catholic prayer for the dead—the famed 13th-century *Dies Irae*—is obvious.

- Heard beneath Brahms's deathly thematic motive is a dissonant, diminished seventh-chord arpeggio. It is a dissonant arpeggio that effectively destroys any sense of tonal center. Indeed, across the opening A section of this piece—cast in A–B–A form—there is only the slightest hint of tonal centricity beneath the murmuring repetitions of the thematic motive.

- The middle B section of the intermezzo is defiant and increasingly violent in tone and spirit. Set in the key of D-flat major, it would seem to represent "the good fight" against the darkness and despair projected by the opening A section. Alas, it is a good fight that cannot be won, and at its climactic moment, the *Dies Irae*-inspired thematic melody returns, at which point, in the words of Brahms's biographer Malcolm MacDonald, "This inspired work subsides into its former tragic monologue, dying out eventually in exquisite but bleak despair."

- Brief though it is, Brahms's Intermezzo in E-flat Minor is a first-order masterwork and one of the most important single pieces Brahms ever composed.

Important Terms

consonance: A musical entity or state that can be perceived as a point of rest.

intermezzo: An instrumental interlude between the acts of a performance.

Brahms—Six Pieces for Piano, Op. 118
Lecture 14—Transcript

We return to *The 23 Greatest Solo Piano Works*. This is Lecture 14. It is entitled Brahms—Six Pieces for Piano, Op. 118.

Images. It is a remarkable thing, the degree to which the physical image of a composer can condition our response to his music For example, the most familiar image of Johann Sebastian Bach is a painting by Elias Gottlob Hausmann, painted in 1746 when Bach was 61 years old.

His is a serious, jowly face. He is wearing a wig, a black coat, and holding a piece of music paper bearing a theme given to him by none other than Frederick the Great, a theme that became the basis for Bach's work *The Musical Offering*. The grim set of Bach's mouth, the steely intensity of his star,e and the downward turn of his eyebrows combine to create the image of a high school math teacher from hell, about to hand back an assignment bleeding in red pencil and bearing a huge, Fraktur "F" across the top. The image does nothing to transmit Bach's passion, his exuberance and joy; his love for his family and for his god; his humor and his superhuman energy. All it does is reinforce the tired cliché that he was a serious man who created serious music.

While we're talking about composers whose names start with the letter B, we would observe that pretty much all of the extant images of Beethoven's can be boiled down to a single word: "glower," a glower the likes of which we usually only see on the face of someone in the throes of serious gastric distress (which Beethoven, admittedly, suffered from). Did anyone ever think to depict Beethoven when he smiled or threw his head back and guffawed, as he was prone to do when he was with his friends? Never. With the glower in our mind's eye it's easy to forget that Beethoven's music is filled with sweetness, gentleness, and humor as well as struggle and grandiosity.

And then there's Johannes Brahms, the third of our three Bs. Our enduring image of Brahms is that of an aged patriarch, every inch the pedantic German professor, a visual image that reinforces the idea of Brahms as a composer of conservative Teutonic music. If Beethoven's look can be summarized by the word "glower", then Brahms's can be summed by the word "beard," his beard. And thus we might think, when we hear—for example—the apparently learned fugue that brings Brahms's *Handel Variations* to its conclusion that it is just another example of the sort of stuffy, learned pedantry that the beard would seem to represent. [**Piano performance:** Brahms, *Handel Variations*, Op. 24, fugue.]

I have some news for us. When Brahms composed that fugue, he was 28 years old and had not a whisker on his face. He had not a whisker on his face because at 28, his beard hadn't grown in yet: His face was still as smooth as a child's. He was exceedingly short, around five feet tall by most accounts. He had blue eyes, blonde-darkening-to-sandy colored hair, and a rather high voice.

Between his height, his lack of facial hair, and his voice, Brahms's machismo took quite a beating; he did serious damage to his vocal chords by forcing himself to speak in a low, gravely manner. But to the point: Brahms spent the bulk of his adulthood without a beard. He composed much of his greatest music, from the *Handel Variations* to the *German Requiem* to his Symphonies Nos. 1 and 2, to both his first piano concerti and his violin concerto before he grew the beard. Of Brahms's 122 opus-numbered works, the first 77 of them were composed when he was a clean-faced young man.

So much for the image of Brahms as a patriarchal German pedant. He was, in fact, nothing of the sort. In fact, he found his mature compositional voice as a young man, in his late 20s. For the rest of his life (he lived to be 63) Brahms's music remained a synthesis of head and heart. Brahms structured his works along the formal lines of the 18th century. These formal procedures, and the craft and intellectual discipline they represent, are the "head," the objective aspect of his compositional style. However, Brahms's melodic and harmonic language and expressive content were fully contemporary, fully romantic. That's the "heart" of Brahms's musical language: the intuitive, inspiration-driven, subjective aspect of his style. Brahms was an "objective subjectivist" if that's not too gnarly a phrase.

Brahms was also easily irritated, and nothing irritated him more than the claims of the so-called New German School—chaired by Franz Liszt and

Liszt's son-in-law, Richard Wagner—that the one and only future of music lay in merging it with other arts in order to create a composite art that Liszt dubbed "program music." Brahms had zero tolerance for what he called the windbags and swindlers with their theories of art, which he saw as nothing more than sorry attempts to justify bad music. And he categorically rejected program music—where form is determined by the extramusical content of the story being told—as sloppy and haphazard, the refuge of the compositional scoundrel.

Brahms believed that a musical composition—its expressive content notwithstanding—should have a level of abstract, structural logic that enabled it to make sense in purely musical terms. While this ideal is the essence of classicism, it doesn't make Brahms a conservative composer. In reality it makes him a pioneering synthesist. In 1862, when Brahms was just 29 years old, the critic Adolf Schubring wrote the following in the *Neue Zeitschrift fur Musik*:

> Brahms may well have felt that the path he had trodden up to now was a remote dead-end of romanticism [Schubring is referring to Brahms's early piano music and the Piano Concerto in D Minor]; he turned his work back to the eternally clear forms of the classics. He understands how to be classic and romantic, ideal and real – and after all, I believe he is appointed to blend both these eternal oppositions in art.

Bingo. In November of 1862, Johannes Brahms, 29 years old, formerly of Hamburg, moved permanently to Vienna. His first room was in a residence hotel at 55 *Novaragasse*, today called the *Praterstrasse*. He wrote his friend Julius Grimm: "Well, this is it! I have established myself here within ten paces of the Prater and can drink my wine where Beethoven drank his!"

What a revealing statement! Brahms was at home in Vienna just because he could drink his wine where Beethoven drank his! Of Brahms's five great musical heroes, four of them, Haydn, Mozart, Beethoven and Schubert, had lived and worked in Vienna; only Johann Sebastian Bach had not. Brahms, that synthesis of subjective and objective, of classicism and romanticism, felt completely at home in a city that was, itself, a synthesis: a city of Germans and Slavs, of Christians and Jews; the home of the classical style; a place filled with irrepressible energy and romantic Sturm und Drang. Brahms and Vienna were made for each other.

The Beard: Before and After

In late 1878, the 45-year-old Brahms grew the beard. His friend Clara Schumann was horrified, but no amount of screeching or cajoling from Clara (or anybody else for that matter) could induce him to shave it off. Brahms's response to his critics was that "with a shaved chin, people take you for either an actor or a priest." To his infinite amusement, Brahms discovered that the beard rendered him unrecognizable to anyone who hadn't seen him while it was growing. During his brief period of anonymity Brahms would introduce himself as "Kapellmeister Muller from Braunschweig" and then he'd wait to see how long it took people to recognize him. In the case of Brahms's old friend, the pianist, teacher and composer Gustav Nottebohm, it was an entire evening: Nottebohm reported having spent an entire evening in polite conversation with one Kapellmeister Muller.

Growing the beard was, for Brahms, a statement of machismo, not a sign of encroaching age or conservatism. His post-beard music continued to be as beautifully crafted, expressively powerful, and gorgeously lyric as his pre-beard music. As an example of that post-beard lyricism, let's hear the opening of Brahms's Intermezzo in A Major, Op. 118, No. 2 of 1893 [**Piano performance:** Brahms, Op. 118, No. 2.]

Bad Habits

Johannes Brahms had some very bad habits. From the age of 18 or so— when he was still a beardless, blonde-haired cherub—he took up smoking cigars. He smoked them by the case; later in life, when he could afford them, he smoked Havanas, exclusively. Never was his beard (once he grew it) free of cigar ash, and never were his clothes (which were shabby to begin with) without smears of ash.

Brahms's clothes. My goodness, he tended to dress more like a peasant farmer than one of the great composers of his time. The hats he wore made him look like a hick from the boonies. He absolutely insisted on cutting his trouser legs about four inches above his ankles, which was as extremely uncool then as it is now. He preferred to wear flannel shirts and would only wear a tie under the most extreme duress.

Bad habits. Of all of Brahms's bad habits, not one was worse than his pathological self-criticism Brahms's attitude towards his own music is well reflected in this compositional advice he gave to his friend, George Henschel:

> Let it rest, let it rest, and keep going back to it and working at it, over and over again, until it is a complete, finished work of art, until there is not a note too many or too few, not a bar you could improve on. Whether it is beautiful also is an entirely different matter, but perfect it must be.

On exactly these lines, Brahms once famously remarked: "It's not hard to compose, but it's wonderfully hard to let the extra notes fall under the table." To that end Brahms—by his own admission—allowed over 20 string quartets to fall under the table before finally going public with his first quartets, consigning those fallen quartets to the furnace along with countless other works, from songs to symphonies, manuscripts, sketches, and his juvenile compositions, as well as his personal papers, letters, receipts, jottings, doodles: He burned everything.

Brahms's pyromania was a symptom of his existential fear. He was terrified by the thought of posterity and believed that only his very best work should survive him. As a result, he protected his musical legacy with a ferocity that bordered on the pathological. He rarely revealed much of himself to anyone. He kept no journal or diary. He gave few interviews and wrote no reminiscences. He was a very hard man to know and, as an adult, a very difficult man to get along with. His friend Louise Japha said that Brahms was, "*sehr herbe im wesen*": very harsh, bitter, acrid in nature. Brahms's great friend, the Hungarian-born violinist and conductor Joseph Joachim, for whom Johannes Brahms composed his one and only violin concerto, famously said that, "Sitting next to Brahms is like sitting next to a barrel of gunpowder!"

Of course, the real Brahms—the earthy, delicate, sentimental, lyric, loving, profoundly human Brahms—comes out in his music. As an example of just what I'm talking about, let's hear the passionate conclusion of Brahms's Intermezzo in F Minor, Op. 118, No. 4: [**Piano performance:** Brahms, Op. 118, No. 4.] This is wonderful music, and having heard it, we are prepared to forgive Brahms all of his bad habits with one exception, and that would be the destruction of so many of his own creations, for whatever flaws he believed them to possess.

Brahms and the Piano

Brahms started his musical life as a piano prodigy. At the age of 12, his pianistic studies began to share equal time with composition lessons. Soon enough, Brahms became a composer for the piano. Sadly, we cannot know what Brahms's early compositions sounded like, because he destroyed each and every one of them.

The earliest of his works to survive is his Scherzo in E-flat Minor for Piano, which was composed in 1851 when he was 18 years old and published— thanks to Robert Schumann—in 1853 as Op. 4. The other earliest of his works to survive—three in-all-ways "grand" piano sonatas and three sets of songs for piano and voice—all date to 1853. The preeminent role of the piano in all of these early pieces is logical: They are works Brahms composed to play himself.

As Brahms matured and his career as a composer developed, the primacy of piano in his compositions gave way, as he established himself as a composer of chamber music, choral music, and, finally, orchestral music. Brahms composed his last orchestral work—the Double Concerto in A Minor for Violin and 'Cello—in 1887. Four years later, in 1891, the 58-year-old Brahms finally returned to the instrumental genre that had brought him to the dance 40 years before: solo piano.

Brahms composed four sets of solo piano works between 1891 and 1893: the seven fantasias, Op. 116; the three intermezzi, Op. 117; the six pieces of Op. 118, and the four pieces of Op. 119. These are all relatively short works, by and large intimate in tone. They represent a withdrawal from the public world of the orchestra to a very private, introspective and personal place. It is a place both nostalgic and progressive, because even as Brahms was getting back in touch with his roots as a composer of solo piano music, the music itself is some of the most thematically, rhythmically, and harmonically modern music written to that time, music that pushes the traditional tonal language to its breaking point, and sometimes beyond.

Six Pieces for Piano, Op. 118

Brahms completed the six pieces in 1893. They are dedicated to Clara Schumann, who was the first person not named Brahms to see them in manuscript.

No. 1: Intermezzo in A Minor

Brahms's use of the title "Intermezzo" is extremely idiosyncratic. "Intermezzo" means, literally, "in the middle"; an intermezzo is an interlude, a musical number of generally limited compositional content and expressive character that occurs in between two more significant chunks of music. Well, like Chopin's préludes—works that stand by themselves and are, in reality, a prelude to nothing—Brahms's intermezzi are self-standing works that stand in between nothing. Yes, we could interpret Brahms's use of the word "intermezzo" poetically; we could claim that he used the designation to indicate interludes of sublime loveliness in our otherwise beauty-starved, workaday lives, but Brahms himself would likely tell us we were being jackasses for even suggesting such a thing. In truth, a Brahmsian intermezzo is simply a relatively short piece, typically gentle and meditative character. This opening intermezzo, marked "not too fast, but very passionately," has the character of a dramatic overture, and is thus a most appropriate piece to begin the set. Let's hear its opening. [**Piano performance:** Brahms, Op. 118, No. 1.]

No. 2: Intermezzo in A Major

We sampled the Intermezzo in A Major earlier in this lecture. It is a wistful, exquisitely beautiful piece, fairly easy to play and thus the most frequently performed of the Op. 118 set. Nevertheless, it is filled with compositional virtuosity, with all sorts of contrapuntal techniques, rhythmic and harmonic ambiguities, and motivic development, all of which are so beautifully incorporated into the substance of the work that they are de facto invisible: a brilliant example of the art of concealing art. A few examples of what I'm referring to will suffice.

The intermezzo is cast in three-part, A-B-A form. The thematic melody on which the entire piece is based is heard in the upper voice at the very beginning of the piece. It goes like this. **[Piano demonstration.]** Again. **[Piano demonstration.]** This thematic melody consists of three particular elements, all of which will be developed: two melodic motives and a rhythmic-slash-harmonic idea. Melodic motive one consists of just three notes; when first heard, those notes are a C-sharp, a B, and a D. **[Piano demonstration.]**

That motive is heard twice at the beginning of the thematic melody, the second version being an expansion of the first. Here are both versions at the beginning of the thematic melody. **[Piano demonstration.]** The second motive follows immediately. It consists of a leaping, dotted rhythm (meaning long-short) ascent followed by an essentially stepwise descent. **[Piano demonstration.]** Again. **[Piano demonstration.]**

The third notable element of this thematic melody is a very subtle but very important rhythmic/harmonic idea. The intermezzo is set in triple meter, that is, in three. Here's how it begins; I will count the beats. **[Piano demonstration.]** I trust you noticed that the intermezzo is not a waltz, with the rhythmic emphasis on the first and strongest beat of each measure. If it had been a waltz, it would have sounded like this. **[Piano demonstration.]** No, in reality, the emphasis is not on beat one; it's on beat three, which adds a tremendous degree of rhythmic fluidity and unpredictability to the music. **[Piano demonstration.]**

The harmony reinforces the emphasis on beat three. For example, the opening harmony—on beat three—is a consonance. **[Piano demonstration.]** Whereas the harmony that falls on the following beat one is a dissonance, something called a 6-4 chord. **[Piano demonstration.]** In just this way,

Brahms destabilizes many of the first beats—the downbeats—and in doing so, shifts harmonic primacy to beat three.

Some more rhythmic manipulation: About 45 seconds into the piece the following transitional passage sees the emphasis shift from beat three to beat one and then back to beat three again, creating an wonderfully subtle bit of cross-rhythm. I'll count. [**Piano demonstration.**] This opening A section of the movement reaches its climax with this music. [**Piano demonstration.**] The sighing, descending melody of the first part of that climactic excerpt sounds like this. [**Piano demonstration.**] This is an extension of the descending thematic motive heard at the beginning of the piece. [**Piano demonstration.**] Meanwhile, in the bass, the opening thematic motive, [**piano demonstration**], subtly but powerfully pushes the climactic passage forward. I'll exaggerate that because it's in the bass. Here we go. [**Piano demonstration.**]

The melancholy middle or B section of the movement, initially set in F-sharp Minor, begins this way. [**Piano performance:** Brahms, Op. 118, No 2.] But, of course, there's nothing new under the sun, and in reality, the B section is a further development of melodic material first heard at the very beginning of the intermezzo. Listen, here is the opening thematic melody. [**Piano demonstration.**] Here is the second, rising-and-then-descending motive of that thematic melody. [**Piano demonstration.**] Here is the sighing, descending climax of part A. [**Piano demonstration.**] Finally, here's the sighing, descending line on which the B section is based. [**Piano demonstration.**] Even though our little analysis has only skimmed the surface of this intermezzo, I trust the larger point is clear, that music is music of incredible craft and compositional integrity as well as music of unearthly beauty.

No. 3: Ballade in G Minor

At its most generic, a musical ballade is a one-movement work with both dramatic and lyric qualities. It is to this, most generic definition of "ballade" that Brahms refers. Like most of the pieces of Op. 118, this ballade is cast in three-part, A-B-A form. The outer A sections are most dramatic; they feature bristling, swaggering music heard in chords that alternate between the pianist's hands. Here's the opening A section. [**Piano performance:** Brahms,

Op. 118, No 3.] The lyric music follows in the B section: a gorgeous, rolling, vaguely Hungarian-sounding passage that stands in polar contrast with the galumphing A section. The B section. [**Piano performance:** Brahms, Op. 118, No 3.]

No. 4: Intermezzo in F Minor

We heard the passionate conclusion to the Intermezzo in F Minor earlier in this lecture; time demands that we move forward to:

No. 5: Romance in F Major

My friends, if a piece of music can actually glow, then we should be able to read by the light of this romance! Cast in A-B-A form, the opening (and closing) A sections have the natural radiance of a folk song, albeit a very sophisticated folk song! Let's hear the opening of what might best be described as a song without words: the opening A section of the Romance in F Major. [**Piano performance:** Brahms, Op. 118, No 5.] The folk-like flavor of this romance becomes even more pronounced in the B section, during which a simple, gracious, ever-further-embellished tune is heard over a thrumming pedal D. [**Piano performance:** Brahms, Op. 118, No 5.]

No. 6: Intermezzo in E-flat Minor

Brahms indicates that this intermezzo be played "moderate-to-slowly and sadly." This intermezzo is one of the most forward-looking works Brahms ever composed. Its harmonic ambiguity pushes it past traditional tonality, and its continuously developed thematic material and motivic saturation have became a textbook model for 20th- and 21st- century composers.

If this work had been composed by Franz Liszt, with his fondness for programmatic titles, I would suggest Liszt would have entitled it something on the lines of "obsession." The intermezzo is a work based on the obsessive repetitions, variations, and re-harmonizations of single motive. That germinal motive is presented all by itself at the start of the piece. [**Piano demonstration.**]

The resemblance of this sinuous, melancholy motive to the Catholic prayer for the dead—the famed 13th-century *Dies Irae*—is obvious. (Again, it's just the sort of relationship that, should someone have been foolish enough to point out to Brahms, would have evoked a response on the lines of, "Any jackass can see that!") Anyway, once again, here's Brahms's thematic motive. [**Piano demonstration.**] And now the opening of the *Dies Irae*. [**Piano demonstration.**] Heard beneath Brahms's "deathly thematic motive" is a dissonant, diminished seventh chord arpeggio. [**Piano demonstration.**] It is a dissonant arpeggio that effectively destroys any sense of tonal center. Indeed, across the opening A section of this A-B-A form piece there is only the slightest hint of tonal centricity beneath the murmuring repetitions of the thematic motive. Let's hear the first large part of the piece in its entirety. [**Piano performance:** Brahms, Op. 118, No 6.]

The middle, B section of the intermezzo is defiant and increasingly violent in tone and spirit. Set in the key of D-flat Major, it would seem to represent "the good fight" against the darkness and despair projected by the opening A section. Alas; it is a good fight that cannot be won; and at its climactic moment the *Dies Irae*–inspired thematic melody returns, at which point, in the words of Brahms biographer Malcolm Macdonald, "This inspired work subsides into its former tragic monologue, dying out eventually in exquisite but bleak despair." Let's hear the remainder of the intermezzo, beginning with the defiant B section. [**Piano performance:** Brahms, Op. 118, No 6.] Brief though it may be, Op. 118, No. 6 is a first-order masterwork, and one of the most important single pieces Brahms ever composed.

Conclusion

The Austrian musicologist and writer Richard Specht was a close friend of Brahms during Brahms's last decade. Specht had the opportunity to hear Brahms play his late piano works, as he wrote: "fresh from the manuscript, in the intimacy of his room." Specht described Brahms's playing this way:

Each time – and each time in a different way – he made an indelible impression on me. He had by then given up all concert giving and therefore all regular practice. His technique was equal to any difficulty encountered in his own works, but it was not dazzling; he would often play as if to himself and was then capable of muttering the choicest things into his beard. His touch was sometimes hard when he played loudly, but in delicate passages magically fragrant, songful and rich in light and shade. It is certain that I have never heard anyone else play Brahms's piano music as the creator played it himself: the whole man was in the performance.

Just as the whole man is in the music as well.

Thank you.

Mussorgsky—*Pictures at an Exhibition*
Lecture 15

Pictures at an Exhibition is a suite, or collection, of character pieces inspired by an exhibition of Russian art and design by Modest Mussorgsky's friend, the artist and architect Viktor Alexandrovich Hartmann, who lived from 1834 to 1873. Recurring periodically across the span of piece is a movement entitled "Promenade," which depicts Mussorgsky himself as he strolls through the exhibition. This movement is pure 19th-century Russian national music—music characterized by a decidedly non-Western European approach to rhythm and harmony. Mussorgsky's studied avoidance of the sorts of harmonic, contrapuntal, developmental, and formal procedures associated with German music guaranteed that *Pictures at an Exhibition* would have a sound utterly its own.

Mussorgsky and Hartmann

- Mussorgsky met the artist and architect Viktor Hartmann in 1870, when he was 31 years old and Hartmann was 36. They became fast friends, in no small part due to their shared devotion to the "cause" of Russian art.

- Hartmann died from an aneurism in August of 1873 at the age of 39. In his memory, the Academy of Fine Arts in St. Petersburg staged a Hartmann retrospective in February and March of 1874; the exhibition featured over 400 of Hartmann's paintings and designs, a number of which were on loan from Mussorgsky himself. (Sadly, most of those 400 works have disappeared. Either they remain undiscovered or they have been lost due to neglect. Mussorgsky, for one, would be heartbroken to know this.)

- Mussorgsky attended the exhibition and was inspired—in his own words—to "draw in music" what he considered Hartmann's best pieces. In doing so, he created *Pictures at an Exhibition*. The binding compositional element of the piece is a movement entitled

"Promenade," which by Mussorgsky's own admission describes his "stroll" through the exhibition.

- The "Promenade" is heard in various guises a total of five times, interspersed among 10 programmatic movements, each a musical depiction of one of Hartmann's paintings, drawings, or designs.

- The "Promenade" is pure 19th-century Russian national music. Mussorgsky indicates that the opening promenade be played "moderately fast, and in Russian style." By "Russian style," Mussorgsky refers to the asymmetrical rhythm of the promenade, a rhythmic asymmetry characteristic of the Russian language and Russian folk music.

© Majorly/Wikimedia Commons/Public Domain.

Modest Mussorgsky (1839–1881) began piano lessons at the age of 6, and by the age of 10, he was able to perform various works by Franz Liszt.

- The promenade begins with four metric units of 11 beats each, with each 11-beat unit subdivided into a group of 5 plus 6. We will look long, hard, and in vain to find any such rhythmic asymmetry in Western European music composed in the 1870s.

- In the fifth and final appearance of the promenade, the rhythmic asymmetry goes into hyperdrive. This final promenade, like the first one, begins with four units of 11, with each set of 11 being subdivided as 5 plus 6. Following that are two units of 6, followed by another 11, a 6, another 11, two 6s, then two 7s, then a 3, another 11, and finally a 13. Here's how it all adds up: $11 + 11 + 11 + 11 + \| 6 + 6 + \| 11 + 6 + \| 11 + 6 + 6 + \| 7 + 7 + 3 + \| 11 + 13 \|$.

Mussorgsky's Choice of Pictures

- Some of the "pictures" Mussorgsky chose to depict are downright bizarre. And if Mussorgsky wants to musically depict a visually bizarre image, he's going to need to come up with music that is as bizarre as the visual image he wants to depict. That means composing music that goes outside the box—music that breaks the rules, music that fits no preexisting context, music that some listeners will find crude and ugly.

- For example, the first "picture" following the opening promenade is called "Gnomus," which is Latin for "the gnome." This is not referencing one of those red-hatted lawn gnomes but, rather, a sketch by Hartmann depicting a nutcracker in the shape of a twisted, deformed dwarf with huge teeth.

- Mussorgsky's music lurches back and forth, as might the poor, dentally challenged gnome on his bandy legs. Presumably cast in the key of E-flat, there is, in reality, little sense of traditional tonal centricity in this music. If it sounds creepy to us today, with all the horror movie scores we've heard, just think how weird this would have sounded to audiences in 1874.

- According to the Russian musicologist Emilia Fried, Mussorgsky's "Gnomus" is also an intensely humanist statement: "Mussorgsky's piece is grotesque, with a touch of tragedy, a convincing example of the humanization of a ridiculous prototype. In the music portraying the dwarf's awkward leaps and bizarre grimaces are heard cries of suffering, moans and entreaties [for mercy]."

- Another of the stranger images Mussorgsky set to music is one entitled "Ballet of the Unhatched Chicks." The piece is based on Hartmann's drawing of costumes for a projected ballet, depicting children wearing egg-shaped outfits and birds' head masks. Mussorgsky's wonderfully comic music snaps and crackles with whimsy and a birdlike lightness.

- The strangest and most pianistically progressive movement in all of *Pictures at an Exhibition* is "The Hut on Hen's Legs: Baba Yaga." Baba Yaga was a storybook witch who terrified generations of Russian children at bedtime. Her hut, hidden deep in the forest, was perched on chicken legs so that it could turn to face anyone who was unfortunate enough to stumble upon it. She rode cackling through the woods on a huge wooden mortar propelled by an equally formidable pestle, which she used to grind the bones of the naughty children on whom she dined.

- Mussorgsky's portrait of Baba Yaga is spectacular, particularly in his use of the piano, which becomes a percussion instrument.

- One of the less fantastic and more realistic of Mussorgsky's Hartmann-inspired images is "Bydło," which depicts a huge, lumbering Polish oxcart. Like many of Mussorgsky's musical images in *Pictures at an Exhibition*, "Bydło" has been subject to various interpretations over the years. Western listeners tend to hear it simply as a stereotypically heavy bit of Slavic peasant music, a sort of terrestrial "Song of the Volga Boatmen." For Soviet musical authorities, it depicted nothing less than "the nobility and suffering of the peasant [class] and the hardships [borne by] that patient and perseverant toiler."

- The movement entitled "Tuileries"—with its rapid movements and generally high range—depicts children playing and arguing in Paris's Tuileries Garden.

- The most controversial "picture" in *Pictures at an Exhibition* is entitled "'Samuel' Goldenberg and 'Schmuÿle.'" The movement was said to be based on two pictures: one of them depicting a wealthy Jew (Samuel Goldenberg) and the other a poor Jew (Schmuÿle, whose lack of material resources extends to having no last name).

- Mussorgsky's proclivity for writing music based on the contours of speech is put in high relief in this movement. Samuel Goldenberg, the wealthy Jew, speaks first. He speaks in a deep, "rich" voice and with a measured pace, with a melody line just "oriental" enough to identify him as a Jew.

- Schmuÿle then speaks. He is presumably begging Goldenberg for money; his voice is high, wheedling, and whining, and his vocal line is filled with rapid repeated notes that are understood to represent either his chattering teeth or shivering body.

- In the end, Goldenberg blows Schmuÿle off. According to Mussorgsky scholar Michael Russ: "Goldenberg—a nasty, wily and mean character—gives nothing to Schmuÿle, simply sending him off with a flea in his ear."

- The controversy regarding this movement has to do with Mussorgsky's own virulent anti-Semitism. Russian aristocrats of his era were expected to be anti-Semitic, but Mussorgsky went over the line; in particular, his letters to wannabe composer Mily Alekseyevich Balakirev—who was himself a terrible anti-Semite—are really awful.

- Modern research has revealed that the portraits of the Jews on which Mussorgsky based this piece were never part of the Hartmann exhibit in the first place. It was Mussorgsky himself who "named" the Jews in the pictures and Mussorgsky himself who, most revealingly, put quotations around the names "Samuel" and "Schmuÿle" in the title of his piece.

The Grand Finale: "The Great Gate of Kiev"

- Hartmann's picture depicts his design for the city gates of Kiev, which he designed in the "ancient Russian 'massive' style" and capped with a huge cupola shaped like a Slavic war helmet. Hartmann designed the gate to commemorate Tsar Alexander II's narrow escape from assassination in St. Petersburg on April 4, 1866. Hartmann's design, which he considered the best work he had ever done, won a national competition, although the gate itself was never built.

- Mussorgsky's "picture" features two thematic entities. The first is a majestic processional, music that grows out of the "Promenade." The second thematic element is a solemn **hymn** based on a Russian Orthodox chant. There's a textural element that we should be aware of as well, and that is chiming, bell-like scales heard initially over the majestic processional music.

- The two thematic elements and the bell-ringing music together build up to a magnificent coda based on the majestic processional. Given Mussorgsky's nationalist leanings, this music is about much more than just a city gate in Kiev; it is about nothing less than the magnificence and might of mother Russia herself.

Important Term

hymn: A religious song.

Mussorgsky—*Pictures at an Exhibition*
Lecture 15—Transcript

We return to *The 23 Greatest Solo Piano Works*. This is Lecture 15. It is entitled Mussorgsky—*Pictures at an Exhibition*.

Pictures at an Exhibition is a suite—or collection—of character pieces inspired by an exhibition of Russian art and design by Mussorgsky's friend, the artist and architect Viktor Alexandrovich Hartmann, who lived from 1834–1873. Recurring periodically across the span of piece is a movement entitled "Promenade," which depicts Mussorgsky himself as he strolls through the exhibition.

The Promenade—which we will discuss in due time—is pure, 19th-century Russian national music, music characterized by a decidedly non–Western European approach to rhythm and harmony. Let's hear the promenade as it appears at the beginning of *Pictures*. [**Piano performance:** Mussorgsky, *Pictures at an Exhibition*, Promenade.]

The Birth of Russian Concert Music

The defeat of Napoleon in 1812 made Russia a great power, which it remained until the fall of the Soviet Union in 1991. Background: By 1810, Napoleon Bonaparte and his Continental System, based in Paris, had come to dominate the European continent. England, however, remained free. According to historians Robert Palmer and Joel Colton:

> Napoleon could be overthrown only by the destruction of his army, … which neither British wealth nor British sea power, nor the European nationalists, nor the Prussian nor the Austrian armed forces [could do]. All eyes turned to Russia. An international clientele of émigrés and anti-Bonapartists congregated in St. Petersburg, where they poured into the Tsar's ears the welcome message that Europe looked to him for its salvation.

On December 31, 1810, Russia withdrew from Napoleon's Continental System and immediately resumed trade with England. Napoleon decided to teach the Tsar a lesson he'd never forget. In June of 1812, Napoleon's Grand Armée of roughly 600,000 troops entered Russia. Five months later—in late November—fewer than 40,000 survived their retreat from Moscow. That was a serious spanking.

The Russian campaign proved that Napoleon was not invincible. Napoleon's end was indeed in sight, for which Europe had Russia to thank. Russian national pride and prestige grew Tremendously after Napoleon's defeat, and Russian artists of all stripes began to consider how they might express that pride and prestige in purely Russian terms, by creating homegrown Russian national art, art that grew out of the spirit, traditions, and language of Russia and not from Western European models and traditions.

The work credited for initiating the Russian concert music tradition is the opera *A Life for the Tsar*, composed between 1834 and 1835 by Mikhail Glinka (who lived from 1804–1857). For all its debt to contemporary Italian and French opera, what made *A Life for the Tsar* special was that it was a full-blown grand opera by a Russian-born composer, set in the Russian language, based on a tale of Russian heroism in the face of foreign peril, and shaped musically by the idiosyncrasies of Russian folk music and the Russian language to which it is set.

For Glinka's contemporaries, *A Life for the Tsar* breathed *národnost*: Russian national authenticity. It was a Russian language opera that deployed its "Russianisms" intrinsically and not just decoratively. Overnight and forever after, Mikhail Glinka came to be considered the godfather of Russian concert music. When Glinka died in 1857, he was canonized as the patron saint of Russian music. Among those who worshiped at the shrine of Glinka was a 20-year-old pianist and wannabe composer by the name of Mily Alekseyevich Balakirev.

The Russian "Five"

Male-model material Balakirev was not. According to one description, he was: "Short, squat, [and] Asiatic-looking." According to his friend, the violinist Peter Baboriken, Balakirev never owned a single book on music theory, harmony, or orchestration. A competent pianist, the 18-year-old

Balakirev met and played for Glinka. Glinka liked what he heard and he encouraged Balakirev to make music his career. Balakirev, inspired to the tips of his toes, did just that, and put out his shingle in St. Petersburg as both a music teacher and critic.

That he could do so was a case of "only in Russia," where the musical vacuum was so great that given the requisite moxie (which Balakirev had in endless supply), even a amateur like himself could pass himself off as a professional. Even more amazing is that Balakirev came to be accepted as Glinka's successor. But most amazing of all is that during the 1860s, Balakirev gathered around him a group of young amateur composers— hobbyists—who eventually changed the face of not just Russian music, but Western music as well. The composers who came to make up Balakirev's circle were Cesar Cui, a career army officer and fortifications expert; Modest Mussorgsky, an ensign in the Russian Army; Nicolai Rimsky-Korsakov, a naval officer; and Alexander Borodin, a doctor and chemist.

They came to be called the *Moguchaya Kuchka*, which might be translated variously as the "Mighty Heap," the "Magnificent Few," the "Mighty Handful," or simply, "The Five." The members of The Five were rigidly nationalist in their outlook; they believed that constant vigilance was necessary against the insidious influence of German music. At the heart of The Five's compositional xenophobia was their loathing of what they called Germanic development: the tendency by German composers to rehash, rework, and reinterpret their musical materials. The members of The Five believed with the fervor of biblical zealots that that sort of developmental process grew out of a Germanic predisposition for intellectualization, analysis, and logical argument, a predisposition that they believed was completely foreign to the Russian creative impulse. On August 15, 1868, Mussorgsky wrote a letter to Nikolai Rimsky-Korsakov in which he expressed exactly these sentiments:

> And another thing about "development": In short, development in the technical sense is just like German philosophy—all worked out and systematized. When a German thinks, he reasons his way to a conclusion. Our Russian brother, on the other hand, starts with the conclusion and then might amuse himself with reasoning.

The artist is a law unto himself. When an artist revises, it means he is dissatisfied. When he adds to what already satisfies, he is Germanizing, chewing over what has [already] been said. We [Russians] are not cud-chewers, [we are] omnivores.

In his letter, Mussorgsky expressed a truism about not just his music, but most Russian nationalist music of his time. That truism is that that music is essentially expository music, music that is about its themes and not about developing those themes. Mussorgsky believed that this predisposition towards expository music was intrinsic to the Russian national musical character—and that to employ German compositional techniques and models was to embrace the actions and aesthetic of the evil musical empire.

Modest Petrovich Mussorgsky (1839–1881)

Mussorgsky was born into a wealthy, land-owning family in the Imperial Russian town of Toropets, about 250 miles south of St. Petersburg. He began piano lessons at the age of six, and by the age of ten he was able to perform a concerto by the English composer John Field and various works by Franz Liszt. At the age of 12, Mussorgsky's family moved to St. Petersburg so that he and his brother could attend an elite military academy called the Cadet School of the Guards. Mussorgsky graduated at 17—in 1856—and received his commission, as was the Mussorgsky family tradition, in the Preobrazhensky Regiment, the most prestigious regiment of the Russian Imperial Guards. According to Harold Schonberg, Mussorgsky "had been taught what every good regimental officer of the Preobrazhensky had to know: how to drink, how to wench, how to wear clothes, how to gamble, how to flog a serf, how to sit on a horse. Of this set of accomplishments, Mussorgsky found drinking the most congenial." In October of 1856, the 17-year-old Mussorgsky met the 22-year-old Alexander Borodin. Years later Borodin remembered:

I had just been appointed an army doctor and Mussorgsky was a newly hatched officer. Being on hospital duty, we met and found one another congenial. Mussorgsky was at that time a very callow, most elegant, perfectly contrived little officer: brand-new, close-fitting uniform, toes well turned out, hair well oiled and carefully smoothed out, hands well cared for. He spoke through his teeth and his carefully chosen words were interspersed with French phrases. He showed, in fact, pretentiousness; but also perfect breeding. [At a party at the army doctor's house] he sat down at the piano and, coquettishly raising his hands, started playing delicately and gracefully, with the circle around him rapturously murmuring "Charming! Delicious!"

At the age of 18 Mussorgsky began studying composition with Balakirev, and just like that—poof!—he bid goodbye to his career in the army in order to devote himself to his music. (I'll bet that went over real big with Mom and Dad Mussorgsky!) When Mussorgsky was 26, Tsar Alexander II put forward the Emancipation Reform of 1861, which gave more than 23 million serfs their freedom. The Mussorgsky family went from "haves" to "have-nots" almost overnight, which necessitated that the prodigal Modest take the first of a number of jobs with the Russian Civil Service, jobs he took about as seriously as his military career.

What he did take seriously was music, and his desire to compose music that faithfully reproduced the contour, rhythm, and expressive spirit of Russian speech. He wrote, "I should like to make my characters 'speak' on the stage exactly as people do in real life, without exaggeration or distortion, and yet write music that will be thoroughly artistic. What I foretell is the melody of life, not of classicism." Along with Mussorgsky's obsessive desire to create this "sung speech" was an equally obsessive desire to compose unmistakably "Russian" music. To this end Mussorgsky was prepared to reject almost the entire canon of Western European music and to break pretty much every so-called rule and compositional convention.

Mussorgsky's great masterwork—the opera *Boris Godunov*—was composed between 1868 and 1872 and premiered in 1874. The premiere should have represented a highpoint in his career, but, unfortunately, by 1874 Mussorgsky's compulsive drinking (what was then called dipsomania) had started to take a real toll. While he managed to compose a number of works that year—including *Pictures at an Exhibition*—his alcohol-fueled decline was in full swing. Mussorgsky's friend, the artist Ilya Repin, described his disintegration:

It was really incredible how that well-bred Guards officer, with his beautiful and polished manners, that witty conversationalist, that inexhaustible punster quickly sank, sold his belongings—even his elegant clothes—and before long descended to cheap saloons were he personified the familiar type of "has been" [where], with his red potato-shaped nose, [he] was already unrecognizable. Was it really he? The once impeccably-dressed, heel-clicking society man, scented, dainty, fastidious, [now a denizen] of basement dives, nearly in rags, swollen with alcohol.

Just days before Mussorgsky died, this same Ilya Repin painted the portrait for which Mussorgsky is best known, in which a bleary eyed, red-nosed, tousle-haired Mussorgsky—dressed in peasant clothing—stares out blankly, seemingly oblivious to everything. He died on March 16, 1881, a week after his 42nd birthday. Mussorgsky's fame rests on a small number of works: his operas *Boris Godunov* and *Khovanshchina*, a series of superb songs, and the instrumental works *St. John's Night on Bare Mountain* and *Pictures at an Exhibition*.

Pictures at an Exhibition (1874)

Mussorgsky met the artist and architect Viktor Hartmann in 1870, when he was 31 years old and Hartmann was 36. They became fast friends, in no small part due to their shared devotion to the cause of Russian art. Hartmann died from an aneurism in August of 1873 at the age of 39. In his memory, the Academy of Fine Arts in St. Petersburg staged a Hartmann retrospective in February and March of 1874; the exhibition featured over 400 of Hartmann's paintings and designs (a number of which were on loan from Mussorgsky himself). Sadly, most of those 400 works have disappeared. Either they remain undiscovered or they have been lost due to neglect. Mussorgsky, for one, would be heartbroken to know this. It would probably cause him to drink.

Mussorgsky attended the exhibition, and was inspired—in his own words—to "draw in music" what he considered Hartmann's best pieces. In doing so he created *Pictures at an Exhibition*. The binding compositional element of the piece is the Promenade we heard earlier in the lecture, music that by

Mussorgsky's own admission describes his stroll through the exhibition. The Promenade is heard in various guises a total of five times, interspersed among 10 programmatic movements, each a musical depiction of one of Hartmann's paintings, drawings, or designs.

When we first heard it, we observed that the promenade"is pure, 19th-century Russian national music. It's time to demonstrate just what that means. Mussorgsky indicates that the opening promenade be played "moderately fast, and in Russian style." By "Russian style", Mussorgsky refers to the promenade's asymmetrical rhythm, a rhythmic asymmetry characteristic of the Russian language and Russian folk music.

The "Promenade" begins with four metric units of 11 beats each, with each eleven beat unit subdivided into a group of five plus six. Let's listen to this opening, and let's count to 11 four times! [**Piano performance:** Mussorgsky, *Pictures at an Exhibition*, "Promenade."] We will look long, hard, and in vain to find any such rhythmic asymmetry in Western European music composed in the 1870s!

In the fifth and final appearance of the promenade, the rhythmic asymmetry goes into hyper drive. This final promenade, like the first one, begins with four units of eleven, with each set of eleven being subdivided as five plus a six. Following that are two units of 6, followed by another 11, a 6, another 11, two 6s, then two 7s, then a 3, another 11, and finally, a 13! Here's how it all adds up: 11 + 11 + 11 + 11 + || 6 + 6 + || 11 + 6 + || 11 + 6 + 6 + || 7 + 7 + 3 + || 11 + 13 ||. I'll count it while we listen. [**Piano performance:** Mussorgsky, *Pictures at an Exhibition*, "Promenade."]

Some of the pictures Mussorgsky chose to depict are downright bizarre. Well, you know what? "Bizarre is as bizarre does," which means that if Mussorgsky wants to musically depict a visually bizarre image, he's going to need to come up with music that is as bizarre as the visual image he wants to depict. That means composing music that goes outside the box: music that breaks the rules, music that fits no preexisting context, music that some listeners will find crude and ugly.

For example, the first picture following the opening promenade is called "Gnomus" which is Latin for "the gnome". We're not talking about one of those cute, red-hatted lawn gnomes here, but rather, a sketch by Hartmann depicting a nutcracker in the shape of a twisted, deformed dwarf with huge teeth.

Mussorgsky's music lurches back and forth, as might the poor, dentally challenged gnome on his bandy legs. Presumably cast in the key of E-flat, there is, in reality, little sense of traditional tonal centricity in this music. If it sounds creepy to us, today, what with all the horror movie scores we've heard, just think how weird this would have sounded to audiences in 1874! Here's the first half of "Gnomus." [**Piano performance:** Mussorgsky, *Pictures at an Exhibition*, "Gnomus."]

According to the Russian musicologist Emilia Fried, Mussorgsky's "Gnomus" is also an intensely humanist statement: "Mussorgsky's piece is grotesque, with a touch of tragedy, a convincing example of the humanization of a ridiculous prototype. In the music portraying the dwarf's awkward leaps and bizarre grimaces are heard cries of suffering, moans and entreaties [for mercy]."

Another of the stranger images Mussorgsky set to music is one entitled "Ballet of the Unhatched Chicks." The piece is based on Hartmann's drawing of costumes for a projected ballet, depicting children wearing egg-shaped outfits and bird's-head masks. Mussorgsky's wonderfully comic music snaps and crackles with whimsy and a bird-like lightness. Let's hear it: "Ballet of the Unhatched Chicks." [**Piano performance:** Mussorgsky, *Pictures at an Exhibition*, "Ballet of the Unhatched Chicks."]

The strangest and most pianistically progressive movement in all of *Pictures at an Exhibition* is "The Hut on Hen's Legs: Baba Yaga." Baba Yaga was a storybook witch, who terrified generations of Russian children at bedtime. Her hut, hidden deep in the forest, was perched on chicken legs so that it could turn to face anyone who was unfortunate enough to stumble upon it. She rode cackling through the woods on a huge wooden mortar propelled by an equally formidable pestle, which she used to grind the bones of the naughty children on whom she dined, hahahah! Mussorgsky's portrait of Baba Yaga is spectacular, particularly in his use of the piano, which becomes—here—a big ol' percussion instrument. Let's hear the opening third of the piece. [**Piano performance:** Mussorgsky, *Pictures at an Exhibition*, "Baba Yaga."]

Let's sample a few of the less fantastic and more realistic of Mussorgsky's Hartmann-inspired images.

"Bydło" depicts a huge, lumbering, Polish oxcart. [**Piano performance:** Mussorgsky, *Pictures at an Exhibition*, "Bydło."] Like many of Mussorgsky's musical images in *Pictures*, this "Bydło" has been subject to various interpretations over the years. Western listeners tend to hear it simply as a stereotypically heavy bit of Slavic peasant music, a sort of terrestrial "Song of the Volga Boatmen." For Soviet musical authorities, it depicted nothing less than "the nobility and suffering of the peasant [class] and the hardships [borne by] that patient and perseverant toiler."

The movement entitled "Tuileries"—with its rapid movements and generally high range—depicts children playing and arguing in Paris's Tuileries Garden. [**Piano performance:** Mussorgsky, *Pictures at an Exhibition*, "Tuileries."]

The most controversial picture in *Pictures* is entitled "'Samuel' Goldenberg and 'Schmuÿle.'" The movement was said to be based on two pictures: one of them depicting a wealthy Jew ("Samuel Goldenberg") and the other a poor Jew (that would be "Schmuÿle," whose lack of material resources extends to having no last name!). Mussorgsky's proclivity for writing music based on the contours of speech is put in high relief in this movement. Samuel Goldenberg—Mr. "Gold Mountain," the wealthy Jew—speaks first. He speaks in a deep, "rich" voice and with a measured pace, with a melody line just "oriental" enough to identify him as a Jew. [**Piano performance:** Mussorgsky, *Pictures at an Exhibition*, "'Samuel' Goldenberg and 'Schmuÿle.'"]

Schmuÿle now speaks. He is presumably begging Goldenberg for money; his voice is high, wheedling and whining, and his vocal line is filled with rapid repeated notes which are understood to represent either his chattering teeth or shivering body. Schmuÿle. [**Piano performance:** Mussorgsky, *Pictures at an Exhibition*, "'Samuel' Goldenberg and 'Schmuÿle.'"] In the end, Goldenberg blows Schmuÿle off. According to Mussorgsky scholar Michael

Russ, "Goldenberg—a nasty, wily and mean character—gives nothing to Schmuÿle, simply sending him off with a flea in his ear."

The controversy regarding this movement has to do with Mussorgsky's own virulent anti-Semitism. Yes, Russian aristocrats of his era were expected to be anti-Semitic, but Mussorgsky went way over the line; in particular his letters to Balakirev—who was himself a terrible anti-Semite—are truly awful. And here's a fact: Modern research has revealed that the portraits of the Jews on which Mussorgsky based this piece were never part of the Hartmann exhibit in the first place. It was Mussorgsky himself who named the Jews in the pictures and Mussorgsky himself who, most revealingly, put quotations around the names "Samuel" and "Schmuÿle" in the title of his piece. I would explain: Samuel and Schmuÿle are the same name, Schmuÿle being the Hebraic/Yiddish version of Samuel. Richard Taruskin, the preeminent Russian music scholar of his generation, writes:

> The use of quotation marks points up the fact that the two *Zhidy* [meaning Yids; Mussorgsky's word, not Taruskin's] The two *zhidy* have the same first name: one Germanicized, the other in Yiddish. They are in fact one *zhid*, not two. The portrayal is a brazen insult: [Mussorgsky is claiming that] no matter how dignified or sophisticated or Europeanized a *Zhid's* exterior, on the inside he's a jabbering, pestering little "Schmuÿle."

The Grand Finale: "The Great Gate of Kiev"

Hartmann's picture depicts his design for the city gates of Kiev, which he designed in the "ancient Russian 'massive' style" and capped with a huge cupola shaped like a Slavic war helmet. Hartmann designed the gate to commemorate Tsar Alexander II's narrow escape from assassination in St. Petersburg on April 4, 1866. Hartmann's design—which he considered the best work he had ever done—won a national competition, although the gate itself was unfortunately never built.

Mussorgsky's picture features two thematic entities. The first is a majestic processional, music that grows out of the promenade. [**Piano performance:** Mussorgsky, *Pictures at an Exhibition*, "The Great Gate of Kiev."] The second thematic element is a solemn hymn based on a Russian Orthodox chant. [**Piano performance:** Mussorgsky, *Pictures at an Exhibition*, "The Great Gate of Kiev."] There's a textural element we should be aware of as well, and that is chiming, bell-like scales heard initially over the majestic processional music. [**Piano performance:** Mussorgsky, *Pictures at an Exhibition*, "The Great Gate of Kiev."] The two thematic elements and the bell-ringing music together build up to a magnificent coda based on the majestic processional. Here is that coda which brings *Pictures* to its conclusion. [**Piano performance:** Mussorgsky, *Pictures at an Exhibition*, "The Great Gate of Kiev."] Given Mussorgsky's nationalist leanings, this music is about much more than just a city gate in Kiev. My friends, it is about nothing less than the magnificence and might of Mother Russia herself.

Mussorgsky's *Pictures* is the single instrumental work that best embodies the views and tenets of the *kuchka*. Musicologist Michael Russ writes: "There is no other instrumental work like this one, with its social messages from nineteenth century Russia, its saturation in folk music and culture, and its innovative harmonic language all wrapped up in an alluringly colorful exterior."

Colorful it is, and to Mussorgsky's mind, completely Russian. Mussorgsky's studied avoidance of the sorts of harmonic, contrapuntal, developmental, and formal procedures associated with German music guaranteed that *Pictures* would have a sound utterly its own.

Harsh Criticism and a Legacy Rewritten

Unfortunately, many of Mussorgsky's contemporaries considered his unwillingness to use German compositional techniques "in a grammatically correct way" as a sign not of originality, but rather of ignorance and poor training. In the 1905 edition of The Oxford History of Music, Edward Dannreuther wrote: "Mussorgsky appears willfully eccentric. His style impresses the Western ear as barbarously ugly." In a letter to his patroness, Nadezhda von Meck, Peter Tchaikovsky wrote:

Mussorgsky [is] a hopeless case. In talent he is perhaps superior to all the [other members of The Five], but his nature is narrow-minded, devoid of any urge towards self-perfection, blindly believing in the ridiculous theories of his circle. In addition, he has a certain base side to his nature which likes coarseness, uncouthness, roughness. He flaunts his illiteracy, takes pride in his ignorance, [and] mucks along, blindly believing in the infallibility of his genius.

Mussorgsky's music might very well have fallen into oblivion if not for the efforts of his friend and fellow Fiver, Nikolai Rimsky-Korsakov. Among The Five, Mussorgsky and Rimsky-Korsakov were especially close. Rimsky-Korsakov was devastated when Mussorgsky died at the age of 42, and he took upon himself the Herculean task of sorting through, completing, orchestrating, and preparing for performance and publication Mussorgsky's scattered, disorganized manuscripts. It was a colossal labor of love that took years. For example, Mussorgsky's five-act opera *Khovanshchina* was left incomplete and unorchestrated when he died. Rimsky-Korsakov revised, completed, and orchestrated the opera, after which he supervised its premiere in February of 1886. The orchestral work known today as *Night on Bare* (as in "barren") *Mountain* is actually an arrangement of themes by Mussorgsky assembled and orchestrated by Rimsky-Korsakov. (I'd take this moment to observe that the amazingly popular orchestral version of *Pictures at an Exhibition* is the work of the French composer Maurice Ravel, who orchestrated Mussorgsky's piano version in 1922.)

There can be no doubt that Rimsky-Korsakov rescued and revivified Mussorgsky's music. But at a certain price to the music, because many observers today believe that in his attempt to clean up Mussorgsky's works, Rimsky-Korsakov glossed over their purposeful roughness. In his memoires, Rimsky-Korsakov was frankly defensive about what he found in Mussorgsky's manuscripts:

All were in exceedingly imperfect order; there occurred absurd, incoherent harmonies, ugly part-writing, strikingly illogical modulation [or a] depressing absence of any at all, ill-chosen instrumentation, in general an audacious self-conceited dilettantism; at times moments of technical dexterity and skill but more often of utter technical impotence. However, these compositions showed so much talent, so much originality, [and] offered so much that was new and alive, that their publication was a positive obligation. But publication without a skillful hand to put them in order would have [made] no sense. There was need of an edition for performances, for making his colossal talent known, and not for the mere study of his artistic sins.

Whether Rimsky-Korsakov liked it or not (and the answer is "not"), Mussorgsky was a compositional primitive. That primitivism—and with it, the fantastic power and directness that are the hallmarks of his music—that primitivism is intrinsic to his musical language. His compositional roughness is what gives his music its black-earthed muscle, its "Russian-ness."

According to the American composer and author Eric Salzman, "Mussorgsky's so-called crudities were in reality departures from the accepted western [European compositional] norms." If Salzman is correct—and I believe that he is—then we must accept that as a composer, Mussorgsky chose not to be limited by what he perceived as the arbitrary rules of Western tradition. Thus relieved of having to follow the rules, he was free to create a melodic and harmonic style based primarily on the idiosyncrasies of Russian speech.

All of this takes on great importance beyond the Russian musical politics of Mussorgsky's time, because 20 years after his death, at the turn of the 20th century, his music became an influential cause célèbre in Paris. The Parisians adored what they perceived as the brilliant, exotic, anti-Victorian music of Russia, and no one's music better fit that bill than Mussorgsky's, at least until Igor Stravinsky came along. Mussorgsky's music was embraced by the spectacularly original and influential modernist French composer Claude Debussy (1860–1918). Debussy wrote of Mussorgsky: "He is unique and will remain so because his art is spontaneous and free from arid formula. Never has a more refined sensibility been conveyed by such simple means."

Thank you.

Debussy—"The Sunken Cathedral"
Lecture 16

Claude Debussy wrote two books of preludes for piano. Debussy's preludes owe a clear debt to Johann Sebastian Bach and Frédéric Chopin. Like Chopin, Debussy composed a total of 24 preludes. Like Chopin, Debussy's preludes are self-standing works. Like Chopin, Debussy's preludes constitute a virtual catalog of his pianistic and compositional innovations. Unlike Chopin (and Bach), Debussy's preludes do not feature all 24 major and minor keys, one prelude per key. This issue of "key area" was, for Debussy, increasingly immaterial, as his music ventured beyond the tonal harmonic system.

Préludes, Book One, No. 10: *La Cathédrale engloutie* ("The Sunken Cathedral")

- A prelude called "The Sunken Cathedral" is an example of Debussy's pianistic and compositional innovations. This prelude, composed in 1910, is based on the legend of the mythical city of Ys, built in the Douarnenez Bay in Brittany.

- According to legend, the city was swallowed by the waters of the bay due to the extremely naughty behavior of its princess, named Dahut, whose hobby was staging orgies and then killing her lovers at daybreak. According to the legend, on certain mornings, the Cathedral of Ys rises from the sea to warn of approaching storms, its bells tolling and its priests praying, only to sink back below the surface.

- This is the story Debussy suggests in his prelude. The musical means with which he creates atmosphere, evokes events, and moves from one event to the next are stunningly original.

- The prelude begins with a lengthy passage of rising octaves, fifths, and fourths—which are meant to evoke a type of 10th-century church music called parallel organum. Played pianissimo—meaning "very quietly"—this music suggests an ancient, religious, predawn environment, as the slowly rising motion of this parallel organum depicts as well the slow, upward motion of the still-submerged cathedral.

- The mysterious sense of weightlessness we hear in this opening can be attributed to the fact that not a single one of its harmonic units contains an interval of a third. There are no complete **triads**—just rising octaves, fifths, and fourths. Instead of using complete triads, he composed open intervals. The effect is one of harmonic suspension.

- We don't know what key we are in or whether the mode is major or minor. The bass line does not move in such a way as to create any sense of tendency, of tension and rest; instead, it simply descends by step, from G to F to E.

- Buried within these rising gestures is a tiny melodic idea—called a motive—that in some form or another will underpin the entire prelude. It consists of a rising major second followed by a rising perfect fifth, and we will call it the "bell motive."

- Following the rising organum, a series of octave Es quietly rings out. Then, a thematic melody slowly emerges. The melody has the character of a plainchant, and it is meant to evoke the quiet, muffled praying of the priests. This plainchant-like melody is heard against repeated, bell-like Es high on the piano keyboard.

- The repeated Es that accompany the plainchant-like melody do not mean that we are now in the key of E major or E minor. In fact, the pitch collection employed by the plainchant-like melody is a C-sharp Dorian mode, an ancient modal construct that lacks entirely the sort of harmonic "tendency" (meaning tension and release) inherent to the more modern (and familiar) major and minor modes.

- At the conclusion of the plainchant-like melody, the bass line slips downward from the E to a D to a C, and finally to a B, at which point a rolling, wavelike left hand and harmonized bell motives in the right would indicate the glistening cathedral rising from the depths and into the brilliant light of day. Note the occasional bell-like harmonies that punctuate this passage, built as they are from clusters of notes that are, in fact, the notes of the bell motive heard simultaneously.

Motives and Motivic Development

- This first one-third of the prelude tells us much of what we need to know about Debussy's revolutionary compositional style. Debussy was a superb compositional technician. Nowhere is this more apparent than in his use of motivic development, which provides the steel-mesh framework for his glowing, atmospheric musical surfaces.

- For example, the bell motive is heard melodically, or as a bass line, or as a chord, in almost every one of the prelude's 89 measures. Generally and accurately speaking, Debussy's music displays a degree of motivic unity and integration that would have made Beethoven proud—a fact that would have irked Debussy to no end had he considered it.

Thematic Melodies and Pitch Collections

- More often than not, Debussy builds his thematic melodies from pitch collections other than major and minor. For example, the plainchant melody is modal, built as it is on Dorian mode.

- Much has been made—and rightly so—of Debussy's exposure to a Javanese gamelan (that is, a Javanese percussion orchestra) he heard at Paris's *Exposition Universelle* in 1889. And while Debussy never explicitly employed gamelan melodies in his music, the five-pitch pentatonic scale employed by the gamelan was a regular feature in his music.

- At other times, he used an eight-pitch collection called an octatonic scale and a six-pitch collection called a whole-tone scale—anything to avoid the familiar sounds of major and minor and the traditional tonal harmonic expectations that go along with them.

Rhythm

- While Debussy could write powerfully pulsed music, his primary rhythmic impulse was toward the "atmospheric." More often than not, his rhythmic profiles have the character of a slowly unfolding continuum, in which metric regularity—the so-called tyranny of the **bar line**—is rarely in evidence. This French language–like rhythmic fluidity is a key to the expressive impact of Debussy's music.

- Debussy's rhythmic suppleness creates a floating, magical, otherworldly sensibility. It also creates a distinctly non-Western effect, as time in Debussy's music is often perceived not as linear but as existential, meaning that the "goal" of a phrase or section is less important than the sensual beauty of the moment.

Harmonic Structures

- Debussy employs familiar harmonic constructs: chords built primarily out of octaves, fifths, fourths, and thirds. This is the primary reason that his music sounds so "consonant," especially when compared to the music of other early-20th-century modernists like Arnold Schoenberg and Igor Stravinsky.

- But we should not be fooled by the relative consonance of Debussy's harmonic usage, because while he might employ familiar-sounding harmonic structures, he does not deploy them in familiar ways.

- For example, the prelude reaches its climax with a clangorous passage that depicts the cathedral, its bells ringing, fully emerged from the sea in the bright light of day. This celebratory event is evoked with a melody based on the bell motive heard over a repeated C deep in the bass. Unlike the mysterious opening of the prelude, each of the harmonies in this passage is a complete triad.

- Despite its triadic structures and the pervasively consonant sound of this passage, it is not functionally tonal: The harmony never changes; there are no cadences or resolutions; there is no differentiation made between consonance and dissonance; there is no harmonic progression. In fact, the chords—which simply move in lockstep with the melody—play no "functional" role whatsoever; they are there to fill out the texture and create color and sonority.

Along with Frédéric Chopin and Franz Liszt, Claude Debussy (1862–1918) is one of history's most original composers of piano music.

- The melody itself, which is a development of the organum-like opening, is set in neither major nor minor but, instead, in Mixolydian mode, another ancient scalar construct. The fact that the bass is totally immobile helps ensure that this passage will remain harmonically static. Thus, the triads heard throughout the passage are familiar harmonic structures deployed in an unfamiliar manner.

- This passage is also about the resonance of the piano and the fantastic bell-like accumulation of overtones that results from holding down the sustain pedal while playing these huge, sonorous chords and the deep thrumming pedal C heard beneath them.

- Following that bell-ringing climax, a brief transition leads to a last version of the plainchant theme. And now, the cathedral slips back beneath the surface of the water and disappears from sight with a deep, gurgling trill. Debussy depicts the cathedral's submergence with a descending string of dissonant chords.

- Each of these chords is a dissonance—a dominant seventh chord that wants to resolve. For example, the first harmony in the descent is a D-sharp dominant seventh chord. According to tonal practice, this dissonance should resolve to a G-sharp chord and thus to a state of rest.

- But Debussy's D-sharp dominant seventh chord does not resolve; it just slips down to a C-sharp dominant seventh chord that does not resolve either. Instead, it slides down to a B dominant seventh chord (which does not resolve), which slips down to an A dominant seventh chord (which does not resolve), which bounces back up to a C-sharp dominant seventh chord (which does not resolve), and which falls down into a G-sharp dominant seventh chord (which will not resolve either). These chords play no traditional harmonic role whatsoever. Debussy uses them in descending parallel motion because they evoke "the sinking cathedral" and because he likes the way they sound.

Bass Lines

- In traditional, "functional" tonality, the bass line has two mutually reinforcing jobs: to underpin the harmonic progressions it supports and to do its harmonic duty melodically, meaning that the bass line should be a line—a melody of some sort, thus rendering the foundation of the musical edifice melodically active in its own right.

- Debussy was not interested in traditional chord progressions. Rather, he was interested in creating stretches of static music during which thematic development could occur and **timbre**—or tone color—could be enjoyed as a sensual pleasure.

- In lieu of harmonically functional bass lines, Debussy employed three different sorts of bass structures. The simplest were pedals, or drones—sustained or repeated pitches used to underpin fairly long stretches of music. The low C that was repeated under the bell-ringing climax was just such a pedal tone.

- The second sort of bass structure Debussy employed were **ostinatos**, brief melodic ideas repeated over and over again. For example, at the conclusion of the prelude, a muffled version of the bell-ringing climax rumbles out from the very bottom of the piano, a quiet memory of what it once was. The muffled, bell-ringing music is accompanied by a murmuring ostinato set at the very bottom of the piano. Layered above the ostinato is the bell-ringing music.

- For all of its rhythmic activity, the passage is harmonically static; the harmonic underpinning never changes. There is no progression from rest to tension, and therefore, there is nothing to resolve. The passage is neither coming nor going. It simply exists, reveling in itself and the moment.

- The third of Debussy's bass line strategies are those passages in which the bass line does move, when transiting between passages underlain by pedals or ostinatos. Such bass lines will typically move by ascending or descending step or by what are called symmetrical intervals (meaning a string of major or minor thirds). The primacy of the perfect fifth that had ruled the harmonic syntax of Western music since the 15th century is nowhere in evidence in such stepwise and symmetrical bass lines.

Timbre

- More than anything else—more than its programmatic story, its themes, its harmonic structures and stasis—"The Sunken Cathedral" is about the piano. It is not about the piano in the technical sense of Chopin and Liszt; rather, it is about the sonority and the timbre (tone color) of the piano—the piano's resonance and overtones; its bell-like upper register and rumbling, almost organ-like lower register; and its ability to create a halo of sustained sound around an unfolding idea as demonstrated at both the beginning and end of the prelude, during which the music appears from and disappears into what Debussy calls "a gently sonorous haze."

bar lines: Notational device: two vertical lines that enclose a measure and are equivalent to one metric unit.

ostinato: A brief melodic idea that is repeated over and over again.

timbre: Tone color.

triad: A chord consisting of three different pitches built from some combination of major and/or minor thirds.

Debussy—"The Sunken Cathedral"
Lecture 16—Transcript

We return to *The 23 Greatest Solo Piano Works*. This is Lecture 16. It is entitled Debussy—"The Sunken Cathedral."

Let us begin with three factual statements about the French composer Claude Debussy. Fact number one: Claude Debussy is one of a handful of the most original composers who ever lived. (I would include among that handful Claudio Monteverdi, Ludwig van Beethoven, Richard Wagner and Igor Stravinsky. Impressive company.) Fact number two: Along with Igor Stravinsky and Arnold Schoenberg, Debussy is the most influential composer of the last 100 years. Fact number three: Along with Frédéric Chopin and Franz Liszt, Debussy is the most original composer of piano music who has yet to live.

To paraphrase the late, great Rodney Dangerfield, when it comes to countries with a Germanic-language heritage—and that includes the U.S. and the U.K.—"the French don't get no respect." If Debussy had been German or Austrian and his name had begun with the letter B, you can bet your bootie that he'd be ackowledged today as one of the "four Bs." As it is, Debussy and his music stand on the periphery of the German-dominated concert repertoire, except in France, of course, where he is treated like the compositional god he is, and where his gob appeared on pre-Euro currency. By comparison, how many composers have appeared on American coins and currency? Correct: zero.

Oh and please, no gratuitous, freedom-fry, French-bashing here. Really, if Americans are put off by the hauteur, sophistication, and perceived arrogance of the French, just think how the French see us, with our shameless a-historic simplifications, the craven manner in which we insist on evaluating virtually every aspect of human activity based on its monetary value, and the creativity-stifling degree to which we indulge in what the writer Norman Manea calls "the tyranny of pragmatism."

The fact is that along with Italy, France has given us civilization, and for that we should be mighty grateful. So, while Claude-Achille Debussy might have had the double whammy of being both French and a rather challenging human being, we are going to love and respect this bad boy, not least because his music is stunningly new, original and beautiful.

A Formative Event

The terrible injuries inflicted on France by Germany in World Wars I and II have tended to obscure the impact of the conflict that helped lead to both world wars, and that was the Franco-Prussian War of 1870 and 1871. Here's what happened.

In 1868, Queen Isabella II of Spain was deposed in what was called the Glorious Revolution, which led to a dispute between France and Prussia as to who should assume the Spanish throne. This dispute was but a pretext for confrontation, as bad feelings had been growing for years between France and Prussia, Prussia being the largest and most powerful of all the various German states. The French emperor, Napoleon III (nephew of the big cahuna himself, Napoleon Bonaparte), had designs on the Rhineland, Belgium, Netherlands, and Luxembourg, and he saw the ever expanding power of Prussia as a direct threat to his imperial ambitions. Thinking he was the Little Big Man reincarnate, Napoleon III decided to use the Spanish succession thing as an opportunity to squash the Prussians good. At the same time, the Prussian prime minister Otto von Bismarck understood that a confrontation with France was a heaven-sent opportunity to unite the German states under Prussia's leadership. Bismarck played Napoleon III for the fool he was, and France declared war on Prussia on July 19, 1870. As Bismarck had calculated, the other German states quickly fell in line behind Prussia.

My friends, it has been observed that where most countries have armies, Prussia was an army with a country. The French were entirely outmatched, and were whupped at every step, culminating in the Battle of Sedan (which occurred on September 1 and 2, 1870), which ended when Napoleon III surrendered and was taken prisoner along with 104,000 of his men. The German army marched on Paris, which was put under siege on September 19, 1870. Having consumed as much dog au vin, ratatouille, and cat bourguignon as they could stomach, the Parisians surrendered on January 28, 1871. Ten days before, on January 18, a united German empire had been proclaimed at the Palace of Versailles, purposely rubbing *fleur de sel* in France's wound. On February 17, the Prussian army marched through Paris. France ceded much of its eastern regions of Alsace and Lorraine to Germany, and agreed to pay a 5 billion franc war indemnity. This was followed by a brief but brutal uprising in Paris between March and May of 1871, known as the Paris Commune. When the smoke finally cleared, tens of thousands more French were dead and the French Third Republic was declared. The Third Republic remained in power until July 10, 1940, when it was swept aside by Nazi Germany following its invasion and defeat of France.

The loathing the French felt towards things German in the years after 1871 was off the charts. Among the many upshots of this Germanophobia was the founding of the National Society Of Music by a group of prominent composers that included Camille Saint-Saëns and Gabriel Fauré. The mission of the society was to stop the influence of German music on French music by cultivating a distinctly French musical art inspired by the French language itself.

All of the just-described events were witnessed and experienced by a pre-teen named Claude Debussy, who would grow up to identify himself simply as *musicien Français*: "French musician." He was born in the Parisian suburb of Saint-Germain-en-Laye on August 22, 1862 and moved to Paris proper in 1867. His mother managed to spirit him out Paris for the more hospitable environs of Cannes in 1870, although he was powerfully affected by the events of the time, as his father spent a year in prison for alleged revolutionary activities associated with the Paris Commune.

Debussy began his piano lessons in Cannes. His talent was obvious from the start, and on his return to Paris in 1872 he was admitted to the *Conservatoire,* at the age of ten. He remained there for 12 years, until 1884. As a student of piano, Debussy showed moments of brilliance, but lacked the discipline required of a concert performer. As a student of composition, he was another thing altogether: a brilliant rebel, the sort of wise-guy student that drives teachers to drink.

Debussy's rebellious streak and his fondness for the sheer sensuality of strange harmonies and harmonic progressions put him on a constant collision course with his teachers. One such pedant was a harmony instructor named Émile Durand. Debussy's fellow student, Antoine Banès, described a typical lesson:

> At the end of the lesson, when [Durand] had examined all our exercises with scrupulous care, he would linger over young Claude's work with almost epicurean enjoyment. Severe criticisms and angry pencil marks rained upon the pupil's head and music paper. However, as soon as the teacher's natural prejudice was overcome, he would reread in silent concentration the pages he had so Cruelly Mutilated, murmuring with an enigmatic smile: "Of course, it is all utterly unorthodox, but still, it is very ingenious!"

In 1884—at the age of 22—Debussy won the *Prix de Rome* and was shipped off to Rome for two years, living in what he complained was "foreign exile." Poor boy. So that the authorities in Paris might keep abreast of his progress, he was required to periodically send back some of the music he'd been composing. The first piece he submitted—part of a work entitled *Zuleïma*—solicited this response from the professors back at the Conservatory: "At present, M. Debussy seems to be afflicted with a desire to write music that is bizarre, incomprehensible, and impossible to execute." We suppose we can't blame the old boys for not understanding what Debussy was doing; academic pedants are among the last to admit that rules were made to be broken and that textbooks that they themselves wrote must periodically be revised and rewritten.

The fact is, as an early 20-something composer, Claude Debussy was in the process of rewriting the textbook by creating a musical language based on the sound, nuance, and color of the French language. Just as so-called French Impressionist art celebrated subtlety of color, blurred edges, open composition, shifting light, and visual fluidity, so Debussy's entirely French music was the French language in musical action. For Debussy, the quality of sound itself was as important as the melodies, harmonies, and rhythms articulated by those sounds. Debussy was most aware of how new was his music. It was around 1910 that he famously said that: "The century of aeroplanes deserves its own music. As there are no precedents, I must create anew."

Claude Debussy, Préludes for Piano

Debussy wrote two books of préludes for piano. Each book contains 12 préludes. The first book was completed in 1910, and the second in 1913. Debussy's préludes owe a clear debt to both Johann Sebastian Bach and Frédéric Chopin. Bach's *Well-Tempered Clavier* consists of two books, each containing 24 pairs of préludes and fugues, each pair set in a different one of the 24 major and minor keys. Chopin's 24 préludes, published in 1839 as Op. 28, are likewise set in each of the 24 major and minor keys, one prélude per key. Like Bach's préludes, Chopin's are cast in no particular musical form. Unlike Bach's préludes, Chopin's préludes do not introduce fugues, but rather are self-standing works.

Just as Chopin's préludes took a step beyond Bach's, so Debussy's préludes take a step (or two) beyond Chopin's. Like Chopin, Debussy composed a total of 24 préludes. Like Chopin, Debussy's préludes are self-standing works that constitute a virtual catalogue of his pianistic and compositional innovations. Unlike Chopin and Bach, Debussy's préludes do not feature all 24 major and minor keys, one prélude per key. As we will observe, this issue of key area was, for Debussy, increasingly immaterial, as his music ventured ever beyond the tonal harmonic system. As an example of Debussy's pianistic and compositional innovations, we turn to a prélude entitled "The Sunken Cathedral" of 1910

Debussy's prélude is based on the legend of the mythical city of Ys, built in the Douarnenez Bay in Brittany. According to legend, the city was swallowed by the waters of the bay due to the naughty behavior of its Princess, a lady named Dahut, whose hobby was staging orgies and then killing her lovers at daybreak. According to the legend, on certain mornings the Cathedral of Ys rises from the sea to warn of approaching storms, its bells tolling and its priests praying, only to sink back below the surface.

This is the story Debussy suggests in his prélude. The musical means with which he creates atmosphere, evokes events, and moves from one event to the next are stunningly original. The prélude begins with a lengthy passage of rising octaves, fifths and fourths. [**Piano demonstration.**]

These rising octaves, fifths, and fourths are meant to evoke a type of 10th-century Church music called parallel organum. Played pianissimo—very quietly—this music suggests an ancient, religious, pre-dawn environment, while its slowly rising motion depicts the cathedral as it begins to rise from the depths. [**Piano performance:** Debussy, *Préludes* for Piano, Book One, No. 10, "The Sunken Cathedral."]

The mysterious sense of weightlessness we hear in this opening can be attributed to the fact that not a single one of its harmonic units contains an interval of a third: There are no complete triads here, just rising octaves, fifths, and fourths. Check it out. This is what the opening would have sounded like had Debussy used complete triads. [**Piano demonstration.**] But Debussy doesn't do that; rather, he employs these open intervals instead: [**Piano demonstration.**] The effect is one of harmonic suspension. Just so, Debussy's instructions tell us to play the opening "in a sonorous haze." What key are we in? We don't know. Is the mode major or minor? We can't tell. Does the bass line move in such a way as to create any sense of tendency, of tension or rest? No, it does not; it simply descends by step, from G to F to E. Here's what happens in the bass. [**Piano demonstration.**]

Buried within these rising gestures is a motive—a brief melodic idea—that in some form or another will underpin the entire prélude. It consists of a rising major second followed by a rising perfect fifth; we will call it the bell motive. [**Piano demonstration.**] Following the rising organum, a series of octave Es quietly ring out. [**Piano demonstration.**] And now a thematic melody slowly emerges. The melody has the character of a plainchant and it is meant to evoke the quiet, muffled praying of the priests. [**Piano demonstration.**] This plainchant-like melody is heard against repeated, bell-like Es high on the piano keyboard. Let's hear this plainchant melody. [**Piano performance:** Debussy, *Préludes* for Piano, Book One, No. 10, "The Sunken Cathedral."]

Do the quietly repeated Es that accompany the plainchant-like melody mean that we are now in the key of E Major or E Minor? No, it does not. In fact, the plainchant-like melody is not set in major or minor, but rather in something called C-sharp Dorian mode, an ancient scalar construct that lacks entirely the sort of harmonic tendency (meaning tension and release) inherent to the more modern (and familiar) major and minor modes. At the conclusion of the plainchant-like melody, the bass line slips downwards from the E to a D to a C and finally to a B, at which point a rolling, wave-like left hand and harmonized bell motives in the right hand depict the glistening cathedral rising from the depths and into the light of day. Note, while we listen, the occasional bell-like harmonies that punctuate the passage, built as they are from clusters of notes which are, in fact, the notes of the bell motive heard simultaneously. [**Piano performance:** Debussy, *Préludes* for Piano, Book One, No. 10, "The Sunken Cathedral."] This first one-third of the prélude tells us much of what we need to know about Debussy's revolutionary compositional style.

Debussy's compositional style, part one: Motives and motivic development. My friends, Debussy was a superb compositional technician. Nowhere is this more apparent than in his use of motivic development, which provides the steel-mesh framework for his glowing, atmospheric musical surfaces. For example, the bell motive. [**Piano demonstration.**] That bell motive appears in some form or another—as a melody: [**Piano demonstration.**] As a bass line: [**Piano demonstration.**] Or as a simultaneity: [**Piano demonstration.**] The bell motive is heard melodically, or as a bass line, or as a chord in almost every one of the prélude's 89 measures. Generally and accurately speaking, Debussy's music displays a degree of motivic unity and integration that would have made any German composer proud, a fact that would have irked Debussy no end had he thought about it.

Debussy's compositional style, part two: Thematic melodies and pitch collections. More often than not, Debussy builds his thematic melodies from pitch collections other than traditional major and minor. For example, the plainchant melody is modal, set as it is on Dorian mode. [**Piano demonstration.**]

Much, by the way, has been made of Debussy's exposure to a Javanese gamelan (that is, a Javanese percussion orchestra) he heard at Paris's *Exposition Universalle* in 1889. And while Debussy never explicitly employed gamelan melodies in his music, the five-pitch pentatonic scale employed by the gamelan was a regular feature in his music. At other times, he used an eight-pitch collection called an octatonic scale and a six-pitch collection called a whole-tone scale: Anything to avoid the familiar sounds of major and minor and the traditional harmonic expectations that go along with them.

Debussy's compositional style, part three: Rhythm. While Debussy could write powerfully pulsed music, his primary rhythmic impulse was towards the atmospheric. More often than not, his rhythmic profiles have the character of a slowly unfolding continuum, in which metric regularity—the so-called tyranny of the bar line—is rarely in evidence. This French language–like rhythmic fluidity is a key to the expressive impact of Debussy's music. The man himself described his rhythmic intent this way: "The music I desire must be supple enough to adapt itself to the lyrical effusions of the soul and the fantasy of dreams." Debussy's rhythmic suppleness creates a floating, magical, otherworldly sensibility. It also creates a distinctly non-Western effect as well, as time in Debussy's music is often perceived not as linear but as existential, meaning that the goal of a phrase or section is less important than the sensual beauty of the moment.

Debussy's compositional style, part four: Harmonic structures. Debussy employs familiar harmonic structures: chords built primarily out of octaves, fifths, fourths, and thirds. This is the primary reason his music sounds so consonant, especially when compared to the music of other early 20th-century modernists like Arnold Schoenberg and Igor Stravinsky. But we should not be fooled by the relative consonance of Debussy's harmonic usage, because while he might employ familiar-sounding harmonic structures, he does not deploy them in familiar ways.

For example, the prélude reaches its climax with a clangorous passage that depicts the cathedral, its bells ringing, fully emerged from the sea in the bright light of day. This celebratory event is evoked with a melody based on the bell motive heard over a repeated C deep in the bass. Unlike the mysterious opening of the prélude, each of the harmonies in this passage is a complete a triad. Let's hear this climactic passage. [**Piano performance:** Debussy, *Préludes* for Piano, Book One, No. 10, "The Sunken Cathedral."]

Despite its triadic structures and the pervasively consonant sound of this passage, it is not functionally tonal: The harmony never changes. There are no cadences or resolutions. [**Piano demonstration.**] There is no differentiation made between consonance and dissonance. [**Piano demonstration.**] There are no harmonic progressions. [**Piano demonstration.**] In fact, the chords— which simply move in lockstep with the melody—play no functional harmonic role whatsoever; they are there to fill out the texture and create color and sonority. The bell-ringing melody itself is set in neither major nor minor, but instead in what's called Mixolydian mode, another ancient scalar construct. The fact that the bass is totally immobile in this section of music assures that this passage will remain harmonically static. Thus, the triads heard throughout the passage are familiar harmonic structures deployed in an unfamiliar manner.

Along with the emerged cathedral, this passage is about the resonance of the piano, and the fantastic, bell-like accumulation of overtones that results from holding down the sustain pedal while playing these huge, sonorous chords and the low pedal C beneath them. [**Piano demonstration.**] Following the bell-ringing climax, a brief transition leads to a last version of the plainchant theme. [**Piano performance:** Debussy, *Préludes* for Piano, Book One, No. 10, "The Sunken Cathedral."] And now the cathedral slips back beneath the surface of the water and disappears from sight with a deep, gurgling trill. [**Piano performance:** Debussy, *Préludes* for Piano, Book One, No. 10, "The Sunken Cathedral."]

Debussy depicts the cathedral's submergence with a descending string of dissonant harmonies. [**Piano demonstration.**] Each of these chords is a dissonance : a big, fat dominant seventh chord that wants to resolve. For example, the first harmony in the descending string is a D-sharp dominant seventh chord. According to tonal practice, this dissonance should resolve to a G-sharp chord and thus to a state of rest. Listen. [**Piano demonstration.**] And here's the resolution. [**Piano demonstration.**] But Debussy's D-sharp dominant seventh chord does not resolve; it just slips down to a C-sharp dominant seventh chord which does not resolve either. Instead, it slides down to a B dominant seventh chord (which does not resolve), which slips down to an A dominant seventh chord (which does not resolve), which bounces back up to a C-sharp dominant seventh chord (which does not resolve), and which falls down into a G-sharp dominant seventh chord (which will not resolve either). These chords play no traditional harmonic role whatsoever.

Debussy uses them in descending parallel motion because they evoke the sinking cathedral and because he likes the way they sound.

Debussy's compositional style, part five: Bass lines. In traditional functional tonality, the bass line has two mutually reinforcing jobs: (1) to support the harmonic progressions above while (2) creating a melodic profile of its own. A bass line, after all, is a line—a melodic structure in its own right. Well, Debussy was no more interested in traditional bass lines and their chord progressions than he was in *bratwurst und schnapps*. Rather, he was interested in creating stretches of static music during which thematic development could occur and timbre—tone color—could be enjoyed as a sensual pleasure.

In lieu of harmonically functional bass lines, Debussy employs three different sorts of bass structures. The simplest are pedals or drones: sustained or repeated pitches used to underpin fairly long stretches of music. The low C heard repeated under the bell-ringing climax was just such a pedal tone.

The second sort of bass structure Debussy employs are ostinatos—brief melodic ideas repeated over and over again. For example, at the conclusion of the prélude, a muffled version of the bell-ringing climax rumbles out from the very bottom of the piano, a quiet memory of what it once was. This muffled, bell-ringing music is accompanied by a murmuring ostinato set at the very bottom of the piano. Here's the ostinato. [**Piano demonstration.**] Layered above the ostinato is the bell-ringing music. [**Piano demonstration.**]

For all of its rhythmic activity, this passage is harmonically static: The harmonic underpinning never changes. There is no progression from rest to tension, and therefore there is nothing to resolve. The passage is neither coming nor going. It simply exists, reveling in the moment.

The third of Debussy's bass line strategies are those passages in which the bass line transits between passages underlain by pedals or ostinatos. Such bass lines will typically move by ascending or descending steps, or by what are called symmetrical intervals (meaning a string of major or minor thirds). The primacy of the perfect fifth that had ruled the harmonic syntax of

Western music since the 15th century is nowhere in evidence in such stepwise and symmetrical bass lines.

Debussy's compositional style, part six: Timbre. More than its programmatic story, more than its themes, more than its harmonic structures and stasis, "The Sunken Cathedral" is about the piano. The sonority and the timbre—the tone color—of the piano; its resonance and overtones; its bell-like upper register and rumbling lower register; its ability to create a halo of sustained sound around an unfolding idea as demonstrated at both the beginning and end of the prélude, during which the music appears from and disappears into what Debussy calls "a gently sonorous haze."

My friends, from the top: Let's hear Debussy's "The Sunken Cathedral" in its entirety. [**Piano performance:** Debussy, *Préludes* for Piano, Book One, No. 10, "The Sunken Cathedral."] Again, despite its consonance and sheer beauty, this is music of astonishing modernity. Compositionally and pianistically, it is entirely original.

Merci, M. Debussy.

Debussy—*Préludes*, Book One
Lecture 17

D ebussy composed a total of 24 preludes for piano, which were published in two books of 12 preludes each—the first in 1910 and the second in 1913. In this lecture, you will examine five preludes from Book One of Debussy's *Préludes* with two goals in mind. The first goal is to focus on the programmatic content of the prelude under study and the manner in which Debussy evokes that content. Second, with each of the preludes you will examine, you will focus on one of Debussy's compositional innovations and, in doing so, create a cumulative sense of Debussy's mind-blowing compositional originality and pianism.

Prélude No. 1: "Dancers of Delphi"

- This prelude was inspired by an ancient sculpture in the Louvre, depicting three maenads, or bacchantes, as in "female followers of Bacchus." Despite their reputation for crazed sex and cannibalism, Debussy's prelude (like the piece of sculpture on which it is based) depicts a dignified dance set initially in triple meter.

- Debussy's innovation is his harmonic usage. About three-quarters of the way through the prelude, Debussy articulates a simple little melodic idea. Debussy does not harmonize this bit of melody in anything approaching a traditional tonal manner; instead, he harmonizes it in an entirely new manner.

- Each of the chords in Debussy's harmonization is a major triad, a traditional construct that can be traced back to the 14th century. Nevertheless, Debussy employs these triads in a manner entirely new. In traditional tonal harmony, such triads (or chords) progress one to the next, with each chord playing a role relative to what came before it and what follows.

- For example, the role (or function) of some chords is to create a sense of rest, meaning consonance. The function of other chords is to create dissonance—that is, harmonic tension. The function of still other chords is to transit between consonance and dissonance, between rest and tension.

- Not one of the chords in Debussy's chord progression bears any harmonic relation to the next. There is no sense whatsoever of a traditional, **functional harmonic** progression. Rather, the effect is pure color—a smear of harmonic sound used for its own sake.

- Debussy's innovation is his use of traditional harmonic structures in idiosyncratic, nontraditional ways. The reason that Debussy's music does not sound overtly dissonant is his predilection for using traditional harmonic constructs, such as major triads. But we should never think that the generally consonant surface of Debussy's music indicates a lack of modernity; in fact, his music is shockingly modern, as demonstrated by the brief bit of harmonic usage just examined.

Prélude No. 2: "Voiles"
- "Voiles" means two things, either of which might have been Debussy's inspiration for this prelude. It can mean "veils" (as in coverings) or "sails" (as in canvas wind catchers). Debussy biographer Leon Vallas opts for the latter, claiming that the piece is full of "floating effects that suggest sailing boats anchored to a fixed point." It can also be argued that the piece is about veils: specifically, the manner in which Debussy veils—that is, obscures—any sense of tonal centricity during the majority of the piece.

- The overwhelming bulk of the prelude is built from a six-pitch collection called a whole-tone scale. Unlike traditional major and minor collections, which contain seven different pitches and feature a mixture of whole steps and half steps between adjacent pitches, a six-pitch **whole-tone collection** features only whole steps—whole tones—between its adjacent pitches.

- A whole-tone collection is called a symmetrical collection, meaning that no matter where it starts, the same order of intervals will be heard between adjacent pitches—in this case, whole tones. What this means is that a whole-tone collection has no intervallic hierarchy and, therefore, no harmonic tendency; because no single tone stands out, a whole-tone collection creates neither tension nor rest.

- Debussy's use of a whole-tone collection in this prelude creates the sort of blurred effect that is the essence of the word "veil." In its 64 measures, there is only a single six-measure passage that does not employ a whole-tone collection, and that six-measure passage constitutes the climax of the movement. It is set using a pentatonic collection, which is a five-pitch collection. The dramatic, pentatonic climax is followed by a quiet, rippling return to the whole-tone music.

- Debussy's innovation here is actually twofold. First, it has to do with using nontraditional pitch collections—in this case, a whole-tone collection and a pentatonic collection—in place of the traditional major and minor collections. Second, Debussy creates contrast in this prelude not through contrasting themes or key areas but, rather, by employing entirely different sorts of pitch collections.

Prélude No. 3: "The Wind in the Plain"
- Debussy evokes the "wind in the plain" using an ostinato anchored by a pedal tone. An ostinato is a brief bit of melody that is repeated over and over again. A pedal tone is a single pitch that is sustained or repeated, usually in the bass. In order to depict his titular "wind in the plain," Debussy employs an ostinato (played by the pianist's right hand) over a pedal tone (played by the pianist's left hand).

- Debussy then inserts a skippy-twitchy little theme between the ostinato and pedal. To play this entire passage effectively, the ostinato and pedal must recede into the background while the twitchy melody must be projected into the foreground.

- Debussy's innovations in this piece are of huge import. In lieu of traditional harmonic progressions and a moving bass line, he

After having graduated from the Paris Conservatoire, Claude Debussy spent two years in Rome, where he met Franz Liszt.

employs ostinatos and pedals to underpin and accompany his thematic material. The result is harmonic stasis: The harmony does not move or transport; it simply exits. These sorts of ostinatos and pedal tones are of decidedly non-Western inspiration. Generally but accurately speaking, traditional Western tonal music is narrative music. Traditional tonal harmonic progressions, which move from rest to tension and then back to rest, create a sense of progressive movement through time in Western tonal music. However, in much world music, accompanimental underpinnings are static: They do not change, and therefore, they do not progress.

- In such music—North Indian raga and Indonesian gamelan, for example—time is not perceived as being linear but, rather, as being cyclical. In such music, listeners are free, like wanderers in a garden, to experience the beauties around them without being hurried along by harmonic progressions intent on moving them to the next location.

- Such ideas and issues regarding non-Western music preoccupied Debussy's mind and ear. He might very well have heard a Javanese gamelan (that is, a percussion orchestra from the Indonesian island of Java) as early as 1887, when the Dutch government gave one to the Paris Conservatoire. He most definitely heard a gamelan in 1889 at the *Exposition Universelle* in Paris (the world's fair that saw the construction of the Eiffel Tower) and then again in 1900 at Paris's next world's fair. For Debussy, gamelan music was a revelation.

Prélude No. 6: "Footprints in the Snow"

- The "footprints" to which Debussy's title refers is an ostinato that appears in almost every measure of this 36-measure prelude. In reference to this ostinato figure, Debussy's performance instructions read: "This should have the sonorous value of a melancholy, ice-bound landscape."

- Soon enough, a dour, meandering melody is superimposed above the ostinato. However, the ostinato soon rises out of the accompaniment, at which point it becomes apparent that the ostinato is not merely an accompanimental figure but the principal theme of the prelude as well. In the first third of the prelude, be particularly aware of the bleak, monochromatic environment created by the obsessive repetitions of the ostinato—this accompaniment that becomes a theme.

- The sort of motivic saturation Debussy achieves in this prelude is reminiscent of Beethoven's Fifth Symphony, in which, likewise, hardly a measure goes by without the real or implied presence of Beethoven's all-too-famous "fate motive."

- The comparison of Debussy to Beethoven is apt, despite whatever annoyance Debussy would feign had he heard it. The fact remains that Debussy was a superb technician who, like Beethoven, built his works from the simplest of thematic materials.

- Like Beethoven, Debussy was a master harmonist who could constantly cast his thematic ideas in new light through subtle harmonic shading. Like Beethoven, Debussy's thematic ideas undergo almost constant variation; indeed, it is the art of continuous variation that lies at the heart of both Debussy's and Beethoven's music.

Prélude No. 12: "Minstrels"

- We conclude with this 12th and final prelude, which, using appropriate showbiz lingo, is a "light-hearted romp through the varied and loony antics of a minstrel show." The "minstrel show" was a type of variety show born in America in the 1830s, a show that featured comedy skits, dog-and-pony acts, juggling, parodies of popular plays, dancing, and music. Before the Civil War, such shows were performed by white people in "blackface"—that is, in black makeup—and after the war, they were as often as not performed by African Americans in blackface.

- The racial stereotyping inherent to minstrelsy was, of course, repulsive—symptomatic of a time that has passed. Nevertheless, it is interesting to note that minstrel shows were decried from both the left and the right: Abolitionists assailed them for their inherent racism and for falsely depicting "happy slaves" while, at the same time, proponents of slavery attacked them for portraying runaway slaves sympathetically and slave owners as being cruel and pompous.

- Debussy's prelude sidesteps the racial issues entirely. Instead, it projects the humor, energy, variety, and turn-on-a-dime musical hodgepodge that occurred over the course of a minstrel show, which were all the rage in Paris at the turn of the 20th century.

- Over its 2-minute course, Debussy's "Minstrels" shifts musical gears constantly, from its laconic beginning to a jittery and humorous cakewalk to a dance hall cancan to a drum tattoo.

- This is delightfully humorous music, music that reflects an aspect of Debussy that his friends knew well: his scalpel-sharp sense of humor. It is also cinematic music, music that shifts and crosscuts and snaps in and out of focus. In this, it is pure 20th-century music, and one could well argue that Debussy was the first major composer to be influenced by the then-brand-new art of cinema.

Important Terms

functional harmony: Harmonic usage that was standardized and codified into a fully coherent system during the baroque period. This method is still used by modern arrangers and orchestrators. The basic concept used in functional harmony is the fact that all harmonic sounds used in music may be classified into three large groups. These groups derive their names from the three important roots of the traditional harmonic system: the tonic, the dominant, and the subdominant.

whole-tone collection: Divides the octave into six equal segments; a whole-tone scale ascends and descends by major seconds, or whole tones.

Debussy—*Préludes*, Book One
Lecture 17—Transcript

Welcome back to *The 23 Greatest Solo Piano Works*. This is Lecture 17. It is entitled Debussy—*Préludes*, Book One.

The sound of Debussy's music was inspired by his native French language, with its long vowels and longer diphthongs; its emphasis on nuance and color; and its lack of sharp articulations. However, the often ethereal, perfumed and otherworldly expressive content of Debussy's music is a function of his own vision and personality, a personality that—by his own admission—was not particularly of this world. In a letter written on July 8, 1910—just a few months after the 48-year-old Debussy had completed the first book of his *Préludes for Piano*—he confessed to his publisher:

> Those around me simply don't understand that I've never been able to live in a world of real things and real people. That's why I have this insurmountable need to escape from myself in adventures which seem inexplicable because they reveal a man that no one knows; and perhaps he represents the best side of me! Besides, an artist is by definition a man accustomed to dreams and living among apparitions. I live in a world of memory and regret: they are my two gloomy companions! But at least they are faithful ones, more so than pleasure and happiness.

Debussy was a complex, contradictory, and often difficult man. According to his great friend, Paul Dukas (who achieved his bit of immortality by composing *The Sorcerer's Apprentice*), some people found Debussy to be "heartless, an egoist, a trifler with the feelings of others. You have to have known him in his adolescence to really understand him and, indeed, really to love him." The composer Alfredo Casella—who was more an acquaintance than a close friend—has left us with this most perceptive appraisal of Debussy. Casella described Debussy as being:

> Extraordinarily nervous, impulsive and impressionable, and he was easily irritated. The oddity of his appearance [with his bulging forehead], his unprepossessing voice, a strong dose of gaucherie,

and finally an almost incredible shyness which he disguised under a show of paradox and often sarcastic and unkind irony, all made for a certain awkwardness in one's first relations with him. But then he was capable of deep and loyal friendship, and his affection for a few friends was boundless. He was generous, and he delighted to aid the needy—[usually] anonymously and with exquisite delicacy.

Casella's concluding words describing the nature of Debussy's philanthropy are telling: with "exquisite delicacy." There are no better words to describe Debussy's spectacularly original, stunningly influential music than "exquisite delicacy." As an example, let's hear the eighth of the twelve préludes from Book One. It is one of Debussy's most famous works, entitled "The Girl with the Flaxen Hair." The piece takes its title from a poem by Leconte De Lisle, who lived from 1818 to 1894. De Lisle's poem begins this way:

Who sits upon the blooming lucerne,
Singing from the earliest morn?
It is the girl with the flaxen hair,
The beauty with cherry-red lips.

Debussy had set the poem to music back in 1882, and had dedicated that song to a married, 30-something redheaded beauty named Marie-Blanche Vasnier, with whom the 20 year-old Debussy was having an affair. Thus, Debussy's prélude is meant to evoke—with exquisite delicacy—the purity and innocence of a young girl's song as well as his youthful passion for the flaxen-haired Madame Vasnier. [**Piano performance:** Debussy, Prélude No. VIII, "The Girl with the Flaxen Hair."]

Debussy's Influences

Debussy admitted to having very few musical models or heroes. One reason for this was Debussy's Parisian orneriness: He disliked most German/Austrian composers out of sheer Gallic chauvinism, and looked down at most of his fellow French composers as sellouts and/or writers of pabulum. There were, however, four composers that Debussy did acknowledge as influences: Johann Sebastian Bach, Modest Mussorgsky, Frédéric Chopin, and Franz Liszt.

For Debussy, Bach was the be-all and end-all, that single composer whose technical skill and expressive spirit were of the highest measure. Of Mussorgsky, Debussy wrote: "No one has given utterance to the best within us with tones more gentle or profound; he is unique, and will remain so, because his art is spontaneous and free from arid formulas. Never has a more refined sensibility been conveyed by such simple means." The influence of Mussorgsky on Debussy's music, particularly his harmonic practice, must be acknowledged. Like Mussorgsky, Debussy refused to follow what he considered the "arid formulas" of traditional tonal harmony. Like Mussorgsky, Debussy used pedals and ostinatos to underpin long passages of music. Like Mussorgsky, Debussy was repelled by sonata form, with its presentation, development, and restatement of themes, a construct that Debussy called "a legacy of clumsy, falsely interposed traditions." Like Mussorgsky, Debussy was particularly put off by the mechanics of Germanic musical development. As he famously whispered to a friend at a concert: "Let's go—he's beginning to develop!"

However, unlike Mussorgsky, Debussy was a highly trained composer who, if he wanted to, could have written sonata form movements with academically correct development sections 'til the *vaches* came home. Debussy's idiosyncratic harmonic practice and the degree to which he cultivated pedals and ostinatos went further than anything Mussorgsky did in his music. Finally, Debussy's ear for timbre and coloristic nuance put his music far beyond (not above, not below, just beyond) anything anyone had composed to his time.

For Debussy, the piano was a string instrument, and most certainly not a percussion instrument. This led Debussy to dismiss Beethoven's piano music out of hand, writing in 1909 that "I [am] finally and completely convinced that Beethoven definitely wrote badly for the piano." For Debussy, it was Chopin—whose variety of touch and use of the sustain pedal (which Debussy called the breathing pedal)—who showed how to make the piano sing. Debussy's friend Marguerite Long recalled his statement that as a composer for the piano, "Chopin is the greatest of all. For [through] the piano alone he discovered everything."

Debussy's other great pianistic influence was Franz Liszt, whose pianism and harmonic audacity Debussy took powerfully to heart. Debussy spent two years in Rome after having graduated from the Paris *Conservatoire*. It was there in Rome that the early-20-something Debussy met Franz Liszt, who was then in his 70s and nearing the end of his life. Debussy had the opportunity to hear Liszt play, and he never forgot what he heard; Debussy recalled how Liszt "used the pedal as a kind of breathing."

In the end, building on the piano music of both Chopin and Liszt, Debussy created an entirely new sort of piano music, one with a new approach to sonority, balance, the use of space, fingering and pedaling. One great early influence on Debussy who turned out not to be an influence at all was Richard Wagner. Debussy—like pretty much all the young composers of his generation—was obsessed with Wagner. However, unlike many of his contemporaries, Debussy's obsession passed fairly quickly, and he came to be disgusted with what he considered the inflated grandiosity and megalomaniacal gigantism of Wagner's unapologetically German art. Later in life, reflecting on Wagner's massive, four-evening *Ring Cycle*, Debussy wrote: "The idea of spreading one drama over four evenings! Is this admissible, especially when in these four evenings you always hear the same thing? My god, how unbearable these people in skins and helmets become by the fourth night!"

Finally, Debussy's other great influence was not musical but poetic: 19th-century French symbolist poetry. We refer here to such poets as Stéphane Mallarmé, Paul Verlaine, and Arthur Rimbaud, whose poetry exploited the fluidity and subtlety of the French language and employed metaphor and symbolic imagery to evoke rather than describe the state of the poet's soul. The manner in which Debussy entitles his préludes was inspired by these symbolist poets and their ideals. The préludes are program music: Each one tells a distinct story, or paints a picture, or depicts some fragment of poetry, or describes some aspect of Debussy's own imagination. Each one of the préludes bears a descriptive title, some of them quite specific, like "The Girl with the Flaxen Hair" and "The Sunken Cathedral"; and some quite generic, like "Veils" and "Mists." Specific or generic, these programmatic titles are not placed at the beginning of their respective pieces but rather they are placed at the end, where they are encased in parentheses. The message is clear: These programmatic titles are meant to be taken as afterthoughts, as impressions, fleeting and ambiguous.

Game Plan

Debussy composed a total of 24 préludes for piano which were published in two books of 12 préludes each, the first in 1910 and the second in 1913. For the remainder of this lecture we will examine five préludes from Book One with two goals in mind. Goal one will focus on the programmatic content of the prélude under study and the manner in which Debussy evokes that content. Our second goal has to do with the actual brass tacks of Debussy's compositional language. Here's an important statement: Never kiss anyone whose saliva isn't clear.

OK, here's another important statement: Claude Debussy was one of the most original and influential composers in the history of Western music. He created a post-romantic musical language in which the melodic and harmonic structures of traditional tonality—which to his mind had become moribund after centuries of use—were replaced with a stunningly innovative approach to melody and harmony. In addition, Debussy's musical language elevated timbre—that is, instrumental tone color—to a place equal to melody and harmony. Debussy's music—with its gorgeous colors, often languid rhythms, its nuance and detail—is the French language in musical action, although we would note that the impact of Debussy's music was not been limited to French composers. Oh, no. For example, the Russian-born Igor Stravinsky and the Hungarian-born Béla Bartók both considered Debussy's music to be the key influence in the development of their mature musical styles. So, goal number two: in each of the préludes we examine, we will focus on one of Debussy's compositional innovations, and in doing so create, over the course of our examinations, a cumulative sense of Debussy's mind-blowing compositional originality and pianism.

Prélude No. I: "Dancers of Delphi"

The program: This prélude was inspired by an ancient sculpture in the Louvre, depicting three Maenads or "Bacchantes," as in female followers of Bacchus as in ancient party girls gone wild. Despite their reputation for crazed sex and cannibalism (we trust indulged separately and not simultaneously), Debussy's prélude (like the piece of sculpture on which it is based) depicts a dignified dance set initially in triple meter. Here is how the prélude begins. [**Piano performance:** Debussy, Prélude No. I, "Dancers of Delphi."]

Debussy's innovation: Harmonic usage. About three-quarters of the way through the prélude Debussy articulates this simple little melodic idea. [**Piano demonstration.**] Had Debussy harmonized that bit of melody in anything approaching a traditional tonal manner, he might have done so this way. [**Piano demonstration.**] But of course, Debussy does not harmonize his bit of melody in a traditional manner. Instead, he harmonizes it this way. [**Piano demonstration.**] Now, each of the chords in Debussy's harmonization is a major triad, a traditional construct that can be traced back to the 14th century. [**Piano demonstration.**]

Nevertheless, Debussy employs these triads in a manner entirely new. You see, in traditional tonal harmony, such triads (or chords) progress one to the next, with each chord playing a role relative to what came before it and what follows. For example, the role (or function) of some chords is to create a sense of rest, meaning consonance. [**Piano demonstration.**] The function of other chords is to create dissonance, that is, harmonic tension. [**Piano demonstration.**] The function of still other chords is to transit between consonance and dissonance, between rest and tension. [**Piano demonstration.**] OK, here's Debussy's chord progression one more time. [**Piano demonstration.**]

My friends, not one of these chords bears any harmonic relation to the next. There is no sense here whatsoever of a traditional, functional harmonic progression. Rather, the effect is pure color, a smear of harmonic sound used for its own sake. Debussy's innovation is his use of traditional harmonic structures in idiosyncratic, nontraditional ways. The reason Debussy's music does not sound overtly dissonant is his predilection for using traditional harmonic constructs, like major triads. But we should never think that the generally consonant surface of Debussy's music indicates a lack of modernity; oh no: His music is shockingly modern, as demonstrated by the brief bit of harmonic usage we just examined. Let's hear the conclusion of the prélude, starting with the measures we've just discussed. [**Piano performance:** Debussy, Prélude No. I, "Dancers of Delphi."]

Prélude No. II: "Voiles"

The program: "Voiles" means two things, either of which might have been Debussy's inspiration for this prelude. It can mean "veils" (as in coverings) or "sails" (as in canvas wind-catchers). Debussy biographer Leon Vallas opts for the latter, claiming that the piece is full of "floating effects that suggest sailing boats anchored to a fixed point." To my mind, the piece is about veils; specifically, the manner in which Debussy veils—that is, obscures—any sense of tonal centricity during the majority of the piece.

The overwhelming bulk of the prélude is built from a six-pitch collection called a whole-tone scale. [**Piano performance:** Debussy, Prélude No. II, "Voiles."] Unlike traditional major and minor collections, which contain seven different pitches and features a mixture of whole steps and half steps between adjacent pitches, a six-pitch whole tone collection features only whole steps—whole tones—between its adjacent pitches. [**Piano demonstration.**] A whole tone collection is something called a symmetrical collection, meaning that no matter where it starts, the same order of intervals will be heard between adjacent pitches, in this case, whole tones. What this means is that a whole tone collection has no intervallic hierarchy and therefore, no harmonic tendency: Since no single tone stands out, a whole tone collection creates neither tension nor rest. [**Piano demonstration.**]

Debussy's use of a whole tone collection in this prélude creates the sort of blurred effect which is the essence of the word "veil." In its 64 measures, there is only a single, 6-measure passage that does not employ a whole tone collection, and that 6-measure passage constitutes the climax of the movement. It is set using a pentatonic collection: a five-pitch collection. [**Piano demonstration.**] Here's the dramatic, pentatonic climax followed by a quiet, rippling return to the whole tone music. [**Piano performance:** Debussy, Prélude No. II, "Voiles."]

Debussy's innovation here is actually twofold. First, it has to do with using nontraditional pitch collections—in this case a whole tone collection and a pentatonic collection—in place of the traditional major and minor collections. Second, Debussy creates contrast in this prélude not through contrasting themes or contrasting key areas, but rather by employing entirely different sorts of pitch collections!

Prélude No. III: "The Wind in the Plain"

Debussy evokes the wind in the plain (not to be mistaken for the rain in Spain) using an ostinato anchored by a pedal tone. I explain: An ostinato is a brief bit of melody that is repeated over and over again. A pedal tone is a single pitch that is sustained or repeated, usually in the bass. In order to depict his titular wind in the plain, Debussy employs an ostinato (played by the pianist's right hand) over a pedal tone (played by the pianist's left hand). Super-slowed down, this combination ostinato-pedal sounds like this. **[Piano demonstration.]** Debussy then inserts a skippy-twitchy little theme between the ostinato and pedal that sounds like this: **[Piano demonstration.]** To play this entire passage effectively, the ostinato and pedal must recede into the background, while the twitchy melody must be projected into the foreground. Let's hear this opening. **[Piano performance:** Debussy, Prélude No. III, "The Wind in the Plain."]

Debussy's innovations in this piece are of huge import. In lieu of traditional harmonic progressions and a moving bass line, he employs ostinatos and pedals to underpin and accompany his thematic material. The result is harmonic stasis: The harmony does not move; it does not transport; it simply is. These sorts of ostinatos and pedal tones are of decidedly non-Western inspiration. Generally but accurately speaking, traditional Western tonal music is narrative music. Traditional tonal harmonic progressions—which move from rest to tension and then back to rest—create a sense of progressive movement through time, from point a to point b and so forth. However, in much world music, accompanimental underpinnings are static: They do not change, and therefore, they do not progress.

In such music—North Indian raga and Indonesian gamelan, for example—time is not perceived as being linear, but rather as being cyclical. In such music, listeners are free—like wanderers in a garden—to experience the beauties around them without being hurried along by harmonic progressions intent on moving them to the next location. Such ideas and issues regarding non-Western music preoccupied Debussy's mind and ear. He might very well have heard a Javanese gamelan (that is, a percussion orchestra from the Indonesian island of Java) as early as 1887, when the Dutch government gave one to the Paris *Conservatoire*. He most definitely heard a gamelan in 1889 at the *Exposition Universelle* in Paris (that was the world's fair that gave saw the construction of the Eiffel Tower), and then again in 1900 at Paris's next world fair.

For Debussy, gamelan music was a revelation. In 1895 he wrote to his friend Pierre Louÿs, "My friend! Do you remember the Javanese music, able to express every shade of meaning, even unmentionable shades, which make our tonic and dominant [chords] seem like ghosts, for use by naughty little children?" In an article written in 1913, Debussy wrote:

> There used to be—indeed, there still are—some wonderful peoples who learn music as easily as one learns to breathe. Their "school" consists of the eternal rhythm of the sea, the wind in the leaves, and a thousand other tiny noises, which they listen to with great care, without ever having to consult any dubious treatises. Their traditions are preserved in ancient songs, sometimes involving dance, to which each individual adds his own contribution. Thus Javanese music obeys laws of counterpoint which make Palestrina seem like child's play. And if one listens to it without being prejudiced by one's European ears, one will find a charm that forces one to admit that our own music is not much more than a barbarous noise more fit for a traveling circus.

Prélude No. VI: "Footprints in the Snow"

The program: The footprints to which Debussy's title refers is an ostinato that appears in almost every measure of this 36-measure prélude. The ostinato sounds like this. [**Piano demonstration.**] In reference to this ostinato figure Debussy's performance instructions read, "This should have the sonorous value of a melancholy, ice-bound landscape." Soon enough, a dour, meandering melody is superimposed above the ostinato. [**Piano demonstration.**] However, the ostinato soon rises out of the accompaniment, at which point it becomes apparent that the ostinato is not merely an accompanimental figure but the principal theme of the prélude as well. Let's hear the first third of the prélude, and let's be particularly aware of the bleak, monochromatic environment created by the obsessive repetitions of the ostinato, this accompaniment that becomes a theme. [**Piano performance:** Debussy, Prélude No. VI, "Footprints in the Snow."]

The sort of motivic saturation Debussy achieves in this prélude is reminiscent of Beethoven's Fifth Symphony in which, likewise, hardly a measure goes by without the real or implied presence of Beethoven's all-too-famous fate motive. [**Piano demonstration.**] The comparison of Debussy to Beethoven is apt, despite whatever annoyance Debussy would feign had he heard it. The fact remains that Debussy was a superb technician who, like Beethoven, built his works from the simplest of thematic materials. Like Beethoven, Debussy was a master harmonist who could constantly cast his thematic ideas in new light through subtle harmonic shading. Like Beethoven, Debussy's thematic ideas undergo almost constant variation; indeed, it is the art of continuous variation that lies at the heart of both Debussy's and Beethoven's music.

Prélude No. XII: "Minstrels"

We conclude with this 12th and final prélude of Book One which, using appropriate showbiz lingo, is a "light-hearted romp through the varied and loony antics of a minstrel show." The minstrel show was a type of variety show born in America in the 1830s, shows that featured comedy skits, dog-and-pony acts, juggling, parodies of popular plays, dancing, and music. Before the Civil War, such shows were performed by white people in blackface—that is, in black makeup—and after the war, they were as often as not performed by African Americans, also in makeup—in blackface.

The racial stereotyping inherent to minstrelsy was, of course, repulsive, symptomatic of a time that has passed. Nevertheless, it is interesting to note that minstrel shows were decried from both the left and the right: Abolitionists assailed them for their inherent racism and for falsely depicting happy slaves, while at the same time proponents of slavery attacked them for portraying runaway slaves sympathetically and slave owners as being cruel and pompous blowhards.

Debussy's prélude sidesteps the racial issues entirely. Instead, it projects the humor, energy, variety, and turn-on-a-dime musical hodgepodge that occurred over the course of a minstrel show, which—by the way—were all the rage in Paris at the turn of the 20th century! Over its two-minute course, Debussy's "Minstrels" shifts musical gears constantly, from its laconic beginning. [**Piano performance:** Debussy, Prélude No. XII, "Minstrels."] To a jittery, humorous cakewalk: [**Piano performance:** Debussy, Prélude No. XII, "Minstrels."] To a dance hall can-can: [**Piano performance:** Debussy, Prélude No. XII, "Minstrels."] To a drum tattoo! [**Piano performance:** Debussy, Prélude No. XII, "Minstrels."] Let's hear Debussy's "Minstrels" in its entirety. [**Piano performance:** Debussy, Prélude No. XII, "Minstrels."]

This is delightfully humorous music, music that reflects an aspect of Debussy that his friends knew well: his scalpel-sharp sense of humor. It is also cinematic music, music that shifts and cross-cuts and snaps in and out of focus. In this, it is pure 20th century music, and one could well argue that Debussy was the first major composer to be influenced by the then brand-new art of cinema. Here a wonderful story, told by Paul Roberts, that illustrates Debussy's love of comedy as well as the motion pictures of his time:

> Debussy delighted in talking with the clowns of the Medrano Circus, and even planned a collaboration with the American vaudeville artist known as "General Lavine". He also met Charlie Chaplain, greeting him backstage at the Folies-Bergère with the words, 'Monsieur, you are instinctively a musician and dancer!' Chaplain, on being told that he had just been speaking to the famous Claude Debussy, retorted that he had never heard of him.

Debussy at the Piano

According to those who heard him, Debussy's manner of playing his piano music was as original as the music itself. The Italian composer Alfred Casella considered Debussy's playing to be a revelation:

> No words can describe his playing of the *Préludes*. He did not have the virtuosity of the specialist, but his touch was extremely sensitive. One had the impression that he was actually playing on

the strings of the instrument, without the mechanical aid of keys and hammers. He used the pedals as nobody else ever did. The result was pure poetry.

So, how did debussy's music play in peoria? In his own day, not particularly well. Yes, the students at the Conservatory loved Debussy, but for many of the older generation, Debussy's was hardly music at all. The same innovations that made Debussy among the most original and influential composers in the history of Western music were considered by his more conservative colleagues to be heretical and supremely unmusical, as even a cursory examination of contemporary criticism bears out. For example, in the May 4, 1902 edition the Parisian journal *Le Ménestrel,* the critic Arthur Pougin wrote this regarding Debussy's recently premiered opera, *Pelléas et* **Mélisande**:

> Rhythm, melody, tonality: these are three things unknown to Monsieur Debussy and deliberately disdained by him. His music is vague, floating, without color and without shape, without movement and without life. What adorable progressions of triads in parallel motion! What a collection of dissonances, sevenths, and ninths, ascending with energy! No, decidedly, I will never agree with the anarchists of music!

Not to be outdone, Camille Bellaigue, writing in the Parisian journal *Revue des Deux Mondes* on May 15, 1902 opined:

> Not the least original trait of M. Debussy is to write an entire score without a phrase, without even a measure of melody. Rhythm is no less abhorrent to him. No one is better qualified than the composer of *Pelléas et* **Mélisande** to preside over the decomposition of our art. The music of M. Debussy contains germs not of life and progress, but of decadence and death.

In 1907, two years after the premiere of his opera *Salome*, Richard Strauss attended a performance of Debussy's opera *Pelléas et* **Mélisande**. His reaction to Debussy's music is reminiscent of Gertrude Stein's evaluation of my hometown of Oakland, California, namely, "there is no there there".) (Stein was a native of Oakland, which made her comment that much more hurtful.) Anyway, after the first act of Debussy's *Pelleas*, a perplexed Strauss turned to his host, the writer Romain Rolland and asked, "Is it like this all the way through?" Rolland said yes. Strauss, undoubtedly feeling that he had better things to do than sit through the next four acts of the five-act opera, responded, "But there's nothing in it. No music. It has nothing consecutive. No musical phrases, no development."

Spoken like a true German. Strauss wanted movement (harmonic progressions and development) and instead Debussy gave him the moment (meaning stasis and timbre). Such music was as foreign to Strauss as a meal of *grenouille a la provencal*: It was intrinsically and intolerably French, and he simply could not fathom it. Strauss's reaction reminds us of Roger Ebert's wonderful comment about an over-artful horror film: For Strauss, Debussy's opera had foreboding and after-boding, but no actual boding.

Last Words

With all due respect to Maestros Strauss and Ebert, we leave the last word to Debussy, who thought about music in a manner quite new:

> I am more and more convinced that music, by its very nature, is something that cannot be cast into a traditional and fixed form. It is made up of colors and rhythms. The rest is a lot of humbug invented by frigid imbeciles riding on the backs of the masters—who, for the most part, wrote almost nothing but period music. Bach alone had an idea of the truth.

Thank you.

Albéniz—*Iberia*
Lecture 18

D espite the fact that Isaac Albéniz was from the north of Spain, the son of a Basque father and a Catalan mother, it was the south—Andalucía—that seduced him with its exotic, multicultural spirit and music. So despite the fact that Albéniz entitled his masterwork for piano *Iberia* (a geographical designation that includes the modern states of Spain, Portugal, and Andorra), 11 of its 12 movements are about Andalucía. The goal of this lecture is to identify musical elements characteristic of Andalusian folk music. This Andalusian musical investigation will be illustrated with examples drawn from Albéniz's *Iberia*.

Stereotypical Aspects of Andalusian Music, Part 1: Mode

- The definition of the term "mode" is seven pitches that can be used as the building bocks for melody and harmony in a given piece of music. The most familiar such seven-pitch modes are "major" and "minor," which together were the principal pitch palette in Western music from roughly 1600 to 1900.

- But there are many other seven-pitch modes, some of which go back to ancient times. One of those modes is today called the Phrygian mode, one of the so-called Church modes, which were used extensively in the plainchant (or Gregorian chant) of the early Christian Church. More recently, the Phrygian mode has come to be identified with the folk music of Spain.

- The identifying sound of the Phrygian mode is a half step between the first and second degree of the collection and a whole step between the seventh and first degree, creating a most characteristic sound. It is an instant Spanish-music melodic stereotype, which is, in truth, an instant Andalusian musical stereotype.

- There are a number of variants of the Phrygian Spanish sound, which should more appropriately be called Phrygian Andalusian sound. For example, we often hear the third degree of the Phrygian mode raised to create music in which the key sonic element is the interval of an augmented second that occurs between the second and third degrees of the collection. This augmented second sounds vaguely Middle Eastern, vaguely Arabic.

- Finally, there's another version of the collection, alternately called the Spanish Gypsy scale or the flamenco scale. This scale has its roots in the music of the Spanish Romanies—the Gypsies—who settled in Andalucía in the 15th century. These Spanish gypsies—known as Gitanos—emigrated from the Punjab and Rajasthan regions of northern India around the year 1000 and arrived in Al-Andalus via northern Africa.

- The music and culture of the Gitanos—part Indian, part Arab, part whatever—melded with the preexisting cultural stew of Andalucía to create a cultural hybrid that is, today, considered the Andalusian identity, an identity crystallized in a music called flamenco.

Stereotypical Aspects of Andalusian Music, Part 2: The Guitar

- Scholars of Spanish folk music refer to the various Phrygian and Gypsy modes as the E modes because, much more often than not, Spanish folk music begins and ends on the pitch E. This might seem odd at first, but not when we consider that the highest and lowest strings on the six-string Spanish guitar—the principal folk instrument of Spain—are both tuned to E.

- In fact, the strings of the Spanish guitar—also known as the classical guitar and the concert guitar—are all tuned to pitches contained within an E Phrygian mode: E, A, D, G, B, and E. It is because of the natural characteristics of the guitar that so much Spanish folk music is set in modes based on the pitch E.

- While the various ancestors of the guitar can be traced to ancient Greece, Persia, North Africa, and western Europe, the guitar as we know it today—a gorgeous, figure-eight-shaped beauty bearing six strings—is a Spanish instrument, an instrument initially created to accompany a song-and-dance music called flamenco. Albéniz's *Iberia* might be a piano piece, but it is nevertheless filled with imitations, evocations, and celebrations of the guitar.

For much of his career as a composer, Isaac Albéniz (1860–1909) was faced with very critical responses to his music.

Stereotypical Aspects of Andalusian Music, Part 3: Flamenco

- "Flamenco" is a genre of Spanish song and dance that originated in Andalucía. Flamenco is an extraordinary hybrid of native Spanish, North African, Arab, and especially Gypsy influences. Flamenco consists of four elements: *cante* (meaning singing), *toque* (which is the especially percussive style of guitar playing typical of flamenco), dancing, and *palmas* (percussive hand clapping).

- Flamenco is considered—along with jazz—the most viscerally exciting music to be found on the planet. The word "flamenco" is Spanish for "flamingo," which is native to southern Spain and is also native to the migratory route followed by the Romani people from India to Spain. While the exact connection between the bird and the artistic tradition is unknown, there can be no doubt that flamenco dancing—with its angular, stylized movements and red costuming—does indeed resemble the flamingo.

- The single most characteristic aspect of flamenco is it rhythmic complexity. By definition, flamenco is a polyrhythmic music, in which various contrasting rhythmic layers—some of them sung, some of them played on guitars, some of them clapped, some of them danced—are layered, one atop the next. From a rhythmic point of view, flamenco has much more in common with African drumming than it does with Western European music. It is a rhythmic complexity and energy that can be found in almost every measure of Albéniz's *Iberia*.

Stereotypical Aspects of Andalusian Music, Part 4: Dances

- If rhythm lies at the heart of flamenco, then so does dance. As we might expect, Albéniz's *Iberia* is a veritable compendium of Andalusian dances.

No. 3: "The Body of Christ in Seville"

- *Iberia* synthesizes every aspect of Albéniz's artistic nature: his passionate love for Andalusian art and music; his nationalistic Spanish pride; his exceptional compositional technique; his prodigious pianism; and his fascination with the contemporary Parisian avant-garde, most notably the music of Claude Debussy. The 12 pieces that make up *Iberia*—"impressions," as Albéniz called them—are grouped into four books of three pieces each.

- Of all 12 pieces in *Iberia*, this is the only one that tells a programmatic story. The story is that of the Feast of Corpus Christi as celebrated in the Andalusian capital of Seville. The "Feast of the Body of Christ" commemorates the ritual of the Eucharist, during which Jesus, at the last supper, instructed his disciples to remember him by blessing and consuming bread and wine that he said were his body and blood. The feast is a solemn occasion and is celebrated on Thursday of Holy Week, the day before Good Friday.

- Albéniz's piece describes the Corpus Christi–day procession as it wends its way through Seville, during which a statue of the Virgin is carried through the streets accompanied by marching bands, singers, and perhaps even a penitential flagellant or two. The piece begins with a series of quiet drum flourishes, as the procession—off in the distance—begins.

- The "march theme" emerges in the distance. It is quiet at first, but as it gets closer, it slowly gets louder. The march continues to build in volume and intensity for roughly another minute, when a climax is reached, as cries of ecstasy resound beneath the march—all of it played fortissississimo.

- The march eventually disappears from view, leaving the "cries of ecstasy" music to take center stage. The middle section of the piece consists of a mystical, gloriously beautiful contemplation of Christ's sacrifice. The melody evokes that most profound of all Andalusian musical styles—the *cante jondo*, meaning the "deep song"—accompaniment by strumming flamenco guitarlike music.

- The march eventually returns, and after a virtuosic climax (during which the march is transformed into an ecstatic three-step dance), the music recedes and quiets, with church bells chiming in the distance. The conclusion is sublime: The stillness of music indicates that while night has come, the magic of the day lingers on.

No. 6: *Triana*
- Triana is a quarter—or *arrabal*—of Sevilla, located on the west bank of the Guadalquivir River. For hundreds of years, Triana was the Gypsy quarter of Sevilla and is considered to be the "cradle" of flamenco.

- The opening of *Triana* is pure flamenco, filled with humor and energy, simulated "guitar strumming," and the percussive clatter of castanets, hand clapping, and heel-to-floor dancing.

No. 8: *El Polo*
- Albéniz indicates in the score that *El polo* is "an Andalusian song and dance" and went so far as to write on his manuscript that the *polo*—which is a type of Spanish song—"should not be confused with the sport of the same name."

- Albéniz's musical *polo* is a melancholy and harmonically complex piece, one that nevertheless betrays its flamenco roots with its dancing rhythm and offbeat accents.

No. 12: *Eritaña*

- The 12th and final piece in the set, *Eritaña* is named for a tavern on the outskirts of Grenada that was famous for its flamenco. The conclusion of *Eritaña* is breathtaking, finger busting, and thrilling.

- *Iberia* contains some of the most difficult, over-the-top virtuosic music ever written for the piano. Albéniz, in the throes of creation, realized how difficult this music was going to be to play, and it aggrieved him no end. *Iberia* is difficult, but in the right hands, it is glorious—among the most gripping works ever composed for the piano.

Albéniz—*Iberia*
Lecture 18—Transcript

We return to *The 23 Greatest Solo Piano Works*. This is Lecture 18. It is entitled Albéniz—*Iberia*

In terms of the abundance, variety, and the preservation of its folk music, Spain stands apart from the rest of Western Europe. To a degree unique in Western Europe, old traditions and festivals have been preserved in Spain, and with them, the music that evolved long ago to accompany those traditions and festivals. Spanish folk music is characterized by an astonishing degree of regional diversity, a diversity created (and maintained) by two factors: geography and invasions. Geographically, the Iberian Peninsula is crisscrossed by mountain ranges. These mountain ranges are effective cultural barriers between regions and have thus intensified the distinctive cultural character of various regions.

Invasions. My friends Spain has been invaded, pillaged and occupied by more races and nationalities than the discount table at your local Wal-Mart. Greeks, Carthaginians, Celts, Romans, North African Berbers, Visigoths, Arabs—among others—have all trundled through and left something of their cultures and genomes behind, there to intermix and congeal into cultures quite new. Jews, gypsies, equatorial Africans, Byzantines, French Troubadours, Italian and English traders, and Native Americans brought back from the colonies in the New World have all passed through as well, leaving something of their lives, genes, and cultural essence behind. Nowhere is this cultural mish-mash more pronounced, and its results more dramatic, than in Andalucía, the southernmost and most populous region in Spain.

In 19 B.C.E., the Romans completed their conquest of the Iberian Peninsula, a region they called Hispania. Hispania quickly became one of the richest of all Roman territories, the breadbasket for much of the empire and a rich source of minerals and metal. It was also a rich source of human capital: Hispanic soldiers were known for their toughness and enterprise, and three Roman soldiers of Hispanic origin went on to become three of Rome's greatest Emperors: Trajan, Hadrian, and Marcus Aurelius.

As all things do, the Roman Empire eventually weakened and died. By the fifth century—the early 400s—Hispania had been ravaged and occupied by a succession of Central European—that is, Germanic—tribes, the Suebi, the Visigoths, and the Vandals among them. But no single foreign invasion was to have a more lasting impact on Spain than the one that occurred between 711 and 718, when Muslim armies conquered nearly all of the Iberian Peninsula. These Muslim conquerors were collectively referred to by Europeans as the Moors. They consisted of Berbers (North Africans), black Africans, and Arabs. The Moorish invaders called their new European territory *Al-Andalus*.

Over time, Christian armies chipped away at Al-Andalus. In 1085, King Alfonso VI of Leon and Castile captured the great cultural city of Toledo, 42 miles south of Madrid. In 1249, the *reconquista*—the re-conquering—of what today is Portugal was complete. Eventually, all that was left of Moorish Spain was the Emirate of Grenada in the south. 1492 was one heckuva year for the Spanish King and Queen Ferdinand and Isabella. Not only did they finance that crazy Genoese fella Christopher Columbus to sail west on the ocean blue, they also oversaw the final *reconquista* of Spain. On January 2 of 1492, after a grinding 10-year war, the Moorish Sultan Muhammad XII surrendered the fortress palace of Grenada—the famed Alhambra itself—directly to the king and queen. With that, nearly 800 years of Muslim rule in Spain came to an end. The last Moorish region of Spain—the Emirate of Grenada—retained its Moorish name, as Al-Andalus became Andalucía.

Muslim rule in Spain was over, but its cultural impact was not. And nowhere is that more true than in Andalucía, with its incredible synthesis of Christian and Muslim, European and African culture. It's a fact that many of the cultural elements that we, today, consider as being quintessentially Spanish—like flamenco, bullfighting, and Moorish-styled architecture—all originated in Andalucía.

Isaac Albéniz as an Honorary Andalusian

Despite the fact that Albéniz was born in the north of Spain, the son of a Basque father and a Catalan mother, it was the south—Andalucía—that seduced him with its exotic, multicultural spirit and music. So despite the fact that Albéniz entitled his masterwork for piano *Iberia* (a geographical designation that includes the modern states of Spain, Portugal, and Andorra), 11 of its 12 movements are about Andalucía. Our first job, then, will be to identify musical elements characteristic of Andalusian folk music. We will illustrate this Andalusian musical investigation with examples drawn from Albéniz's *Iberia*.

Part One: Mode

By "mode," we refer to a collection of seven pitches that can be used as the building bocks for melody and harmony

in a given piece of music. The most familiar such seven-pitch modes are major and minor, which together were the principal pitch palette in Western music from roughly 1600 to 1900. Here's what major sounds like. [**Piano demonstration.**] And minor. [**Piano demonstration.**] But there are many other seven-pitch modes, some of which go back to ancient times. One of those modes is today called the Phrygian mode. The Phrygian mode sounds like this: [**Piano demonstration.**] The Phrygian mode is one of the so-called church modes which were used extensively in the plainchant (or Gregorian chant) of the early Christian church. More recently, the Phrygian mode had come to be identified with the folk music of Spain.

The identifying sound of the Phrygian mode is a half step between the first and second degrees of the collection, and a whole-step between the seventh and first degrees, creating this most characteristic sound. [**Piano demonstration.**]

There you have it: an instant Spanish-music melodic stereotype, which is, in truth, an instant Andalusian musical stereotype. Let's hear some Phrygian mode music from the pen of Señor Albéniz. The following passage comes from the seventh movement of *Iberia*. Entitled *El Albaicin*, it is named for the gypsy quarter of Grenada, which sits on a hill facing the Alhambra. Learning to play this piece takes years. In the interest of mercy, we are using a recording. [**Piano recording:** Albéniz, *Iberia*, "*El Albaicin.*"]

There are a number of variants of this Phrygian Spanish sound, which—again—should more appropriately be called Phrygian Andalusian sound.

For example, we often hear the third degree of the Phrygian mode raised to create this: [**Piano demonstration.**] The key sonic element of this variant is the interval of an augmented second that occurs between the second and third degrees of the collection. [**Piano demonstration.**] If this augmented second sounds vaguely Mid-Eastern, vaguely Arabic to you, well, your ears are on the money. According to the Spanish music scholar Martin Cunningham, "[the] augmented second has been attributed unquestioningly to Arab influence."

Finally, there's another version of the collection, alternately called the Spanish Gypsy scale or the Flamenco scale. It sounds like this. [**Piano demonstration.**] This scale has its roots in the music of the Spanish Romanis—the gypsies—who settled in Andalucía in the 15th century. These Spanish gypsies—known as "Gitanos"—emigrated from the Punjab and Rajasthan regions of northern India around the year 1000, and arrived in Al-Andalus via northern Africa. The music and culture of the Gitanos—part Indian, part Arab, part whatever—melded with the preexisting cultural stew of Andalucía to create a cultural hybrid that is, today, considered the Andalusian identity, an identity crystallized in a music called flamenco.

Now, we'll talk lots more about flamenco in a bit. But first, let's hear the opening of the 11th movement of *Iberia*, a piece called "*Jerez*". The piece is named for the town Jerez de la Frontera located in the Andalusian province of Cádiz . Albéniz's *Jerez* opens with an extended section of music in Phrygian mode followed immediately by a passage using augmented second-bearing Arab and gypsy scales. Note as well that the entire excerpt we're about to hear is underlain by the pitch E, something we'll discuss after we've listened. "*Jerez.*" [**Piano recording:** Albéniz, *Iberia*, "*Jerez*."]

Part Two: The Guitar

Before we listened to that last excerpt, I observed that the entire excerpt is underlain by the pitch E. Indeed, scholars of Spanish folk music refer to the various Phrygian and gypsy modes we discussed earlier as the E Modes, because, way more often than not, Spanish folk music begins and ends on the pitch E. Odd, you say? Nope, not when we consider that the highest and lowest strings on the six-string Spanish guitar—the principal folk instrument of Spain—are both tuned to E. In fact, the strings of the Spanish guitar—also known as the classical guitar and the concert guitar—are all tuned to pitches contained within an E Phrygian mode: E-A-D-G-B-and E. It is because of the natural characteristics of the guitar that so much Spanish folk music is set in modes based on the pitch E.

While the history of the guitar is as complex as the history of Andalucía, we are going to cut to the chase. So, while the various ancestors of the guitar can be traced to ancient Greece, Persia, North Africa, and Western Europe, the guitar as we know it today—a gorgeous, figure eight–shaped beauty bearing six strings—is a Spanish instrument, an instrument initially created to accompany a song and dance music called flamenco. Albéniz's *Iberia* might be a piano piece, but it is nevertheless filled with imitations, evocations, and celebrations of the guitar.

For example: the opening of *El Albaicin* imitates a guitar technique in which the thumb of the plucking hand (the right hand) alternates with the other fingers: [**Piano recording:** Albéniz, *Iberia*, "*El Albaicin*."] Another example of piano-as-guitar comes from the twelfth and final piece in *Iberia*, entitled *Eritaña*. The "Venta Eritaña" was a popular tavern on the outskirts of Grenada, famous for its flamenco. Let's hear the strumming, guitaristic opening of *Eritaña*. [**Piano recording:** Albéniz, *Iberia*, "*Eritaña*."]

Part Three: Flamenco

Flamenco is a genre of Spanish song and dance that originated in Andalucía. Flamenco is an extraordinary hybrid of native Spanish, North African, Arab, and especially gypsy influences. Flamenco itself consists of four elements: *cante* (meaning singing), *toque* (which is the especially percussive style of guitar playing typical of flamenco), dancing, and *palmas* (percussive handclapping that we hear in flamenco performance). In my humble opinion, flamenco is—along with jazz—the most viscerally exciting music to be found on this planet. I would go so far as to suggest that if Andalucía were a media giant equal to the U.S. of A., we'd all be singing and dancing to Flamenco and not that North American–born hybrid called rock 'n' roll. For our information: On November 16, 2010, UNESCO—the United Nations

Educational, Scientific and Cultural Organization—declared Flamenco to be one of the "Masterpieces of the Oral and Intangible Heritage of humanity."

The word *flamenco* is Spanish for "flamingo": a tall, slim, elegant bird with pinkish-white plumage. The flamingo is native to southern Spain and is also native to the migratory route followed by the Romani people from India to Spain. While the exact connection between the bird and the artistic tradition is unknown, there can be no doubt that flamenco dancing—with its angular, stylized movements and its red costuming—does indeed resemble the flamingo.

The single most characteristic aspect of flamenco is it rhythmic complexity. By definition, flamenco is a polyrhythmic music, in which various contrasting rhythmic layers—some of them sung, some of them played on guitars, some of them clapped, some of them danced—are layered, one atop the next. From a rhythmic point of view, flamenco has much more in common with African drumming than it does with Western European music. It is a rhythmic complexity and energy that can be found in almost every measure of Albéniz's *Iberia*.

As but one of many examples of *Iberia's* Flamenco-derived rhythms, we turn to the fourth piece of the set, a movement entitled *Rondeña*, named for the ancient Andalusian town of Ronda, located in the province of Málaga. The *Rondeña* features an almost continuous alternation between compound duple and triple meter. I demonstrate, something that sounds like this: **1**-2-3 **1**-2-3 | **1**—2—3 ||. Let's hear the very opening of *Rondeña*. [**Piano recording:** Albéniz, *Iberia*, "*Rondeña*."]

The fifth piece in *Iberia* is entitled *Almería* and is named for an Andalusian seaport on the Mediterranean. In *Almería* the compound duple and triple meter are not heard consecutively as in *Rondeña*, but simultaneously, creating a complex and constantly shifting polyrhythmic texture. Let's hear the beginning of *Almería*, and let's be aware of the gentle but intricate series of accents and groupings that emerge from the piano: [**Piano recording:** Albéniz, *Iberia*, "*Almería*."]

Part Four: Dances

If rhythm lies at the heart of flamenco, then so does dance. As we might expect, Albéniz's *Iberia* is a veritable compendium of Andalusian dances. Let's sample two more movements and in doing so identify their dance origins. The 10th movement of *Iberia* is entitled *Málaga*. The seaport of Málaga is the second largest city in Andalucía and one of the most ancient cities in the world, having been founded by the Phoenicians around 770 B.C.E. Albéniz's *Málaga* evokes the song-and-dance named for the city, the *Malagueñas*. Here is the opening of *Málaga*. [**Piano recording:** Albéniz, *Iberia*, "*Málaga*."]

The second movement of *Iberia*, entitled *El Puerto* (meaning "the port"), is a zapateado inspired by the port city of Cádiz. *A zapateado is a dance of Mexican Indian origin that was brought back to Spain, there to be claimed by the Spanish* as their own. A spanish zapateado is a brisk, percussive dance in which the dancers strike the heels of their shoes on the floor: a Flamenco tap-dance, as it were. We might have figured that out from the dance's name—zapateado—which is derived from the word *zapato*, the Spanish word for "shoe." Here is the opening of *El Puerto:* [**Piano recording:** Albéniz, *Iberia*, "*El Puerto*."]

A Paucity of Composers

Very little concert music emerged from Spain during the 19th century as there were very few trained, native-born Spanish composers. The list of important, 19th century Spanish composers is a short one; by my count, it consists of only three composers: Juan Arriaga (1806–1826), Enrique Granados (1867–1916), and Isaac Albéniz (1860–1909).

What Spain did have was its amazing folk music. Composers from all over Europe fell in love with Spanish folk music, a love affair evidenced in their own music. It's a fact, Jack: Most of the best stereotypically Spanish concert music written during the 19th century was composed by non-Spanish composers. For example: the opera *Carmen*, composed in 1875 by the French composer Georges Bizet; the Russian composer Nicolai Rimsky-Korsakov's *Capriccio Espagnole* of 1888; the French composer **Édouard**

Lalo's *Symphonie Espagnole* of 1874; and the French composer Emmanuel Chabrier's *España* of 1883.

My friends, Emmanuel Chabrier was a Spanish freak who adored Spain and its music. In 1882 he toured the country for six months. The letters he wrote home to his friends document his fascination with Spanish music. To one friend he wrote, "We make the rounds of the cafés, where they sing the *malagueñas*, the *soledas*, the *zapateados* and the *pateneras*; then the dances, which are positively Arabian. If you could see them wriggling their behinds, twisting and squirming, I don't think you'd [ever] care to leave.")

The list of non-Spanish composers who wrote Spanish-styled music also includes Franz Liszt, Mikhail Glinka, Camille Saint-Saens, Claude Debussy and Maurice Ravel. And while it is an impressive list, it is—in the end—a list of musical tourists, composers who skimmed the Spanish musical surface for color and effect but who did not live and breathe the culture of Spain itself. However, live and breathe Spanish culture Isaac Albéniz did, and his *Iberia*—composed between 1906 and 1909—remains the greatest work ever written by a native Spanish composer.

Albéniz: The Man and his Life

The adult Albéniz was short, round, bearded, and a gentlemen in every sense of the word. The French music critic Georges Jean-Aubry remembered Albéniz this way: "The kindness and generosity of the man were unsurpassable. He was unstinting in his praise of others; his talk was always of friendship, affection, or joy. I never saw him otherwise." The French pianist and teacher Marguerite Long praised him for his "kindness and devotion," while the composer Paul Dukas summed him up as being "a Don Quixote with the manner of [a] Sancho Panza."

If we must fault Albéniz for something, it was that Albéniz—who lived a fascinating life by any standard—had an unfortunate tendency to exaggerate and even fabricate all sorts of biographical data. He was a pianistic child prodigy, although his claim that he ran away from home at 12, stowed away on a ship bound for Buenos Aires, and then—travelling by himself—concertized all over the world is patently false. Likewise, his claim that he was a disciple and piano student of the elderly Franz Liszt is untrue; in all likelihood Albéniz never even met Franz Liszt. To list all of Albéniz's fibs is to waste our good time. So here are the biographical facts, short and sweet.

Albéniz was born on May 29, 1860 in the northern Catalonian town of Camprodon, a few miles from the French border. He first performed publically at the age of four. His concert career began at the age of nine. In 1876, at the age of 16, he studied briefly in Leipzig and Brussels. In 1883, at the age of 23, he began to compose avowedly Spanish works. That same year he married a student of his named Rosina Jordana. Isaac and Rosina had five children, only two of whom survived early childhood. His daughter Laura became a painter and his son Alfonso became a professional soccer player—he played for Real Madrid—before becoming a diplomat. Between 1893 and 1909, Albéniz lived primarily in Paris. (Yes, this arch Spanish nationalist lived in Paris. In Paris he could make the sort of living, enjoy a degree of celebrity, and live in a style impossible back in Spain. So Albéniz joined that long list of expats who extolled the virtues of his own country while living in Paris. None of us should have a problem with that.)

Albéniz composed his magnum opus—*Iberia*—between 1905 and 1908 while living in Paris. He died on May 18, 1909—11 days short of his 49th birthday—in Cambo-les-Bains, a spa town in southwestern France. The immediate cause of death was heart failure, brought on by kidney disease. He is buried in Montjuïc Cemetery in the hills above Barcelona.

Iberia

Walter Aaron Clark, whose biography of Albéniz remains the definitive English-language study of the composer, writes:

> Albéniz's death was a great loss for Spanish music, but one cannot escape the suspicion that in the twelve piano pieces of *Iberia* (completed a year before his death) Albéniz had given the best he had to offer. It is hard to imagine what he could have done to top it; certainly the works he left unfinished at his death held no promise of doing so. In *Iberia* he brought forth a bona fide masterpiece,

without doubt one of the greatest collections of keyboard works ever written, by the foremost Spanish composer in the modern era.

Given his choice, I'm sure Albéniz would have been more than happy to live on and compose works inferior to *Iberia,* but OK, we get Professor Clark's point, and that is that *Iberia* synthesizes every aspect of Albéniz's artistic nature: his passionate love for Andalusian art and music; his nationalistic Spanish pride; his exceptional compositional technique; his prodigious pianism; and his fascination with the contemporary Parisian avant-garde music, most notably the music of Claude Debussy. The 12 pieces that make up *Iberia*—"impressions," as Albéniz called them—are grouped into four books of three pieces each. In our time remaining we're going to sample four more pieces from *Iberia,* one from each "book".

No. 3: "The Body of Christ in Seville"

Of all twelve pieces in Iberia, this is the only one that tells a programmatic story. The "tory is that of the Feast of Corpus Christi as celebrated in the Andalusian capital of Seville. The feast of the body of Christ commemorates the ritual of the Eucharist during which Jesus, at the last supper, instructed his disciples to remember him by blessing and consuming bread and wine that he said were his body and blood. The feast is a solemn occasion, and is celebrated on Thursday of holy week, the day before Good Friday.

Albéniz's piece describes the Corpus Christi–day procession as it wends its way through Seville, during which a statue of the virgin is carried through the streets accompanied by marching bands, singers, and perhaps even a penitential flagellant or two. The piece begins with a series of quiet drum flourishes, as the procession—off in the distance—begins. [**Piano recording:** Albéniz, *Iberia,* "*El Corpus en Sevilla.*"] We are told that when he performed the piece, Albéniz would rest his hands on his rather ample belly during the silences between these drum flourishes!

The march theme now emerges in the distance. It is quiet at first, but as it gets closer it slowly gets louder! [**Piano recording:** Albéniz, *Iberia,* "*El Corpus en Sevilla.*"] The march continues to build in volume and intensity for roughly another minute when a climax is reached, as cries of ecstasy resound beneath the march, all of it played fortissississimo. [**Piano recording:** Albéniz, *Iberia*, "*El Corpus en Sevilla.*"]

The march eventually disappears from view, leaving the cries-of-ecstasy music to take center stage. The middle section of the piece consists of a mystical, gloriously beautiful contemplation of Christ's sacrifice. The melody here evokes that most profound of all Andalusian musical styles, the *cante jondo*—meaning the "deep song"—accompaniment here by strumming flamenco guitar–like music. [**Piano recording:** Albéniz, *Iberia*, "*El Corpus en Sevilla.*"] The march eventually returns, and after a virtuosic climax (during which the march is transformed into an ecstatic three-step dance), the music recedes and quiets, with church bells chiming in the distance. The conclusion is sublime: The stillness of music indicates that while night has come, the magic of the day lingers on.

No. 6: *Triana*

Triana is a quarter—or *arrabal*—of Seville, located on the west bank of the Guadalquivir River. For hundreds of years Triana was the gypsy quarter of *Sevilla* and is considered to be the "radle of flamenco. The opening of *Triana* is pure flamenco, filled with humor and energy, simulated guitar strumming, and the percussive clatter of castanets, hand clapping, and heel-to-floor dancing. We hear its opening minute and a half. [**Piano recording:** Albéniz, *Iberia*, "*Triana.*"]

No. 8: *El Polo*

Albéniz indicates in the score that "*El Polo*" is "an Andalusian song and dance" and went so far as to write on his manuscript that the *polo*—which is a type of Spanish song—"should not be confused with the sport of the same name." Nor with the shirt, we would add. Albéniz's musical polo is a melancholy and harmonically complex piece, one that nevertheless betrays its flamenco roots with its dancing rhythm and off-beat accents. [**Piano recording:** Albéniz, *Iberia*, "*El Polo.*"]

No. 12: *Eritaña*

We sampled *Eritaña* earlier in the lecture, though as the 12th and final piece in the set it deserves to be sampled again. As we observed earlier, the piece is named for a tavern on the outskirts of Grenada that was famous for its flamenco.

We will hear the breathtaking and finger-busting conclusion of *Eritaña* in a moment, but first, a word about its virtusoity. *Iberia* contains some of the most filthy-difficult, over-the-top virtuosic music ever written for the piano. We must ask the question: did Albéniz, in the throes of creation, realize how difficult this music was going to be to play? The answer: Yes he did, and it aggrieved him no end. The Spanish composer Manuel de Falla and pianist Ricart Viñes ran into Albéniz one day on the *rue d'Erlanger* (you see? Everyone did live in Paris!) at the time Albéniz was composing *Iberia*. According to Walter Clark: "They found the master is a state of extreme discouragement. He confided to them that the previous evening he had come close to destroying the manuscripts of the new work because he deemed them unplayable." *Gracias a dios*, Albéniz managed to control that impulse: *Iberia* is hard, but in the right hands, it is not just playable but it is glorious, among the most gripping works ever composed for the piano. With that, let's hear the final, thrilling moments of *Eritaña*. [**Piano recording:** Albéniz, *Iberia*, "*Eritaña.*"]

Conclusion

For much of his career as a composer, Albéniz had to deal with a sort of "damned if you do, damned if you don't" critical response. For many continental critics, the lack of German-styled development in Albéniz's music doomed it to second class status. For these critical wizards, *Iberia* was nothing but a collection of salon pieces, distinguished only by their virtuosity. For many Spanish critics, Albéniz's Chopin-and-Liszt-inspired pianism, his Debussy-inspired harmonic palette, and his pianistic virtuosity made him a sellout: Yes, for these blockheads, his music was too continental to be authentically Spanish. To all these critics we say, "eat lead paint."

Here are the facts. In *Iberia*, Albéniz elevates the "picturesque" to high art. He does this by creating wonderful and entirely original themes, by his superb (and most advanced) harmonic usage, his variational instincts, expressive depth, and incredible pianism. In *Iberia*, the piano is at once an orchestra, a voice, bells, guitars, castanets, and flamenco dancers. What might have become in the hands of a lesser composer a set of exotic salon pieces, "dependent upon repetition and color for their effect," become, in *Iberia*, masterworks of synthesis and intensity, works of the greatest artistic depth, feeling, meaning, and sophistication. My friends, don't let anyone tell you any different.

Thank you.

Ravel—*Valses nobles et sentimentales*
Lecture 19

The waltz is many things: a popular dance; a body of music that employs the rhythm of that dance; and a grand metaphor for the Austrian Empire—its joy, its character, its aspirations, its disintegration and death, and the horrors its disintegration and death wrought on the world. This lecture will examine each of the waltzes in Maurice Ravel's *Valses nobles et sentimentales*. Along with identifying the expressive mood of each waltz, this lecture will identify the particular compositional hook that characterizes each waltz.

The Waltz and *Valses nobles et sentimentales*

- As the waltz gained popularity as a dance, composers wrote evermore waltz music, including "stylized waltzes," waltz music not intended for dancing but, rather, for listening. For example, Frédéric Chopin's 18 waltzes—composed between 1831 and 1849—are stylized dances intended, as they are, for concert performance.

- Chopin notwithstanding, the first major set of stylized waltzes was composed by a native Viennese—Franz Schubert, who wrote roughly 100 waltzes for solo piano between roughly 1815 and 1826. Among the best known of Schubert's waltzes are two collections: the 34 *Valses sentimentales*, Op. 50 (of 1823), and the 12 *Valses nobles*, Op. 77 (of 1826). These waltzes were composed for amateur pianists, and therefore, unlike Ravel's waltzes, they are fairly easy to play.

- However, what Ravel copied from Schubert—aside from his titles— is the spectacular range of Schubert's moods and a concentrated, every-note-counts compositional aesthetic.

- In an autobiographical sketch, Ravel confirmed his inspiration for his *Valses nobles et sentimentales*—or "Waltzes Noble and

Sentimental"—and discussed, as well, its less-is-more aesthetic: "The title *Valses nobles et sentimentales* sufficiently indicates my intention of composing a series of waltzes in imitation of Schubert. The virtuosity [of my earlier piano music] gives way [in the *Valses*] to a markedly clearer kind of writing, which crystallizes the harmony and sharpens the profile of the music." Ravel cut down on the "degree of pianistic difficulty" in the waltzes in favor of "a clearer kind of writing, which crystallizes the harmony and sharpens the profile of the music."

As a composer, Maurice Ravel (1875–1937) was a perfectionist: Every note had to count, and every musical surface had to gleam.

- Ravel's set consists of seven waltzes (some noble and some sentimental, though Ravel does not indicate which), followed by a shimmering, ghostlike epilogue in which the principal themes of the waltzes pass by in a nostalgic haze.

- The first waltz is as much a fanfare as a dance; it kicks things off brilliantly and nobly. It is also a perfect example of the sort of "crystalline harmonic and textural clarity" that Ravel refers to in his autobiographical sketch. The music of the first waltz is dazzling. Its razor edge comes from its sharply accented rhythms and its harmonic language, which, for all its chromaticism, is firmly anchored in G major.

- In Ravel's autobiographical sketch, he describes the premiere of the waltzes on May 9, 1911, at the Salle Gaveau in Paris: "The *Valses nobles et sentimentales* were first performed amid [catcalls] and boos at a concert of the Independent Musical Society, in which the names of the composers were not revealed. The audience voted on the probable authorship of each piece."

- The only person who knew for sure who had composed Ravel's waltzes was its performer (and dedicatee), Louis Aubert. The audience was invited to vote on the authorship of all the works on the program, and the results were published in a periodical called *The Musical Courier* on May 16, 1911, 6 days after the concert.

- The audience—which consisted primarily of professional musicians and critics—did not do a very good job of identifying the composer. The authorship of Ravel's waltzes was credited to, among others, Eric Satie, the Hungarian Zoltán Kodály, the now-forgotten French organist and composer Théodore Dubois, and the French film composer Lucien Wurmser.

- For the 6 days between the concert and the revelation of authorship, Ravel listened deadpan to the jeers leveled at the piece by his friends and the critics, who hadn't a clue that Ravel was the composer. When the truth was revealed, those friends and critics who had trashed the piece suddenly found all sorts of qualities in it that they had somehow failed to notice when they first heard it. In other words, they reversed their negative judgments.

Waltz No. 1
- The mood of the first waltz is noble and fanfare-like. Its compositional hook involves huge, sharply articulated, two-fisted chords that ring and resonate on the piano like clanging bells.

Waltz No. 2
- The mood of the second waltz is sentimental and melancholy. Its compositional hook involves grace notes in the thematic melody that anticipate the beat and that—with exquisite subtlety—desynchronize the pianist's hands and create a dragging sense of world weariness.

Waltz No. 3

- The mood of the third waltz is noble (only because it is certainly not sentimental), light, and playful, with a hint of chinoiserie (meaning stereotypically Chinese-like music).

- Its compositional hook is hemiola, which is a rhythmic device involving a pattern of accents that implies a momentary change of meter. For example, in order to perceive triple meter—or "waltz time," as it is often called—we need to hear some sort of accent every three beats, accents that effectively group the beats into groups of three. A hemiola would put an accent on every second beat, momentarily creating the effect that the meter has changed from triple to duple.

- In the playful opening of Ravel's third waltz, be aware of the hemiola-filled rhythmic pattern: ‖ 1–2–3 | 1–2–3 | 1–2–3 | 1–2–3 | 1–2 | 1–2 | 1–2 | 1–2–3 | 1–2–3 ‖

Waltz No. 4

- The fourth waltz begins without a pause. Its mood is sentimental and gently nostalgic. Its hook is a fluttering, descending melody—the rhythms of which cross the bar line, effectively creating a six-beat metric unit. These six-beat-long metric units create a languorous and floating effect, an effect that stands in polar opposition to the punchy, hemiola-dominated rhythms of the previous waltz.

Waltz No. 5

- The mood of the fifth waltz is sentimental and lyric. The waltz's compositional hook is its intense chromaticism, which creates a sort of blurry smear of harmonic and melodic sound. The result—and Ravel will have to pardon us for using a word he hated—is the most "impressionistic" of the waltzes that make up the piece.

Waltz No. 6

- The mood of the sixth waltz is noble and zippy. The hook is once again rhythmic, as a punchy, rising, triple-meter tune in the pianist's right hand (‖ 1–2–3 | 1–2–3 | 1–2–3 | 1–2–3 ‖) is heard—

as often as not—against a hemiola accompaniment in the left hand (‖: 1–2 | 1–2 | 1–2 :‖).

Waltz No. 7

- The seventh waltz is magnificent, in turns both sentimental and noble. In terms of its compositional hook, this longest waltz in the set is a grand summation of all that has come before it. Over the course of its A–B–A form we will hear the rhythmic complexities of the third, fourth, and sixth waltz; the rippling impressionistic blur of the fifth waltz; and at its climactic moments, the brilliant fanfares of the first waltz.

Waltz No. 8

- The final movement—the eighth waltz—is labeled in score as being an "epilogue." It is a magical and mysterious chunk of music, one that changes entirely our perception of the piece to this point. Up to now, Ravel's *Valses nobles et sentimentales* has been a **suite**—a collection of dances, a piece little different in structure from the dance suites written for harpsichord by Ravel's French compositional ancestors in the 17th century.

- All of that changes in the epilogue. In a ghostly haze, thematic materials from the earlier waltzes drift forward and fade. Like the first waltz, this epilogue is cast in G major. But unlike the first waltz, there is no dance or glide or fanfare here, and the epilogue ends as if in a dream. This epilogue makes it clear that *Valses nobles et sentimentales* is not merely a dance suite but, rather, a piece about the waltz as a metaphor for a vanished world. Nostalgic and ghostlike, this epilogue acknowledges that the Viennese world that created the waltz was, by 1911, but a dream.

Historical Relevance

- Even though Ravel composed *Valses nobles et sentimentales* in 1911, long before the start of World War II and three years before the beginning of World War I, Ravel came to have paradoxical feelings toward the Viennese waltz.

- Ravel was a voracious newspaper reader and was proud of his leftist leanings. He understood what was going on in Europe in 1911. He knew about Mayor Karl Lueger of Vienna and the growing menace of institutional anti-Semitism. Ravel knew about the naval arms race in progress between Great Britain and Imperial Germany.

- He knew that Kaiser Wilhelm II of Germany was as dangerous and unstable as a gunslinger on a 3-day binge. He knew as well that France was spoiling for a fight in order to avenge the humiliation of the Franco-Prussian War and to take back those parts of Alsace and Lorraine that had been ceded to Germany in 1871.

- Maurice Ravel's *Valses Nobles et Sentimentales* is about the coming catastrophe, as it dreams—longingly but vainly—for times past, just as his *La valse*, composed nine years later, is about the catastrophe that did, in fact, occur.

- One can rightly assert that Ravel's *Valses nobles et sentimentales* is simply a great piece of music and that, like all great art, it transcends its time. But taken in its historical context, it becomes a supremely moving historical document as well.

Important Term

suite: A concert work consisting of a collection of dances extracted from a longer ballet.

Ravel—*Valses nobles et sentimentales*
Lecture 19—Transcript

Welcome back to *The 23 Greatest Solo Piano Works*. This is Lecture 19. It is entitled Ravel—*Valses nobles et sentimentales*.

Experienced ballroom dancers aside, I would suggest that most of us consider the waltz to be a stodgy thing, a choreographic burden to be born at weddings and anniversaries during which we shuffle out an approximation of a three-step, attempting to lead a partner who would rather not be led (at least not by me), to the scintillating strains of such triple-meter standards as the *Anniversary Waltz* and *Sunrise, Sunset*.

It is easy, today, to forget that at the time of its creation, the waltz was considered a lewd and lascivious dance, one that led to moral degradation in this world and damnation in the next. Nice! The waltz originated in 18th-century Austria as a peasant's dance. What distinguished it from the beginning were its wide, gliding steps and the fact that the dancers held each other as closely as possible (at a time when courtly dancing forbade almost any touching at all).

The simplicity and physicality of this new, gliding and whirling dance made it extremely popular among the lower classes, who were no more likely to dance the more sophisticated Minuet than Ozzie Osborn a Virginia Reel. By the late 18th century, the gliding and whirling associated with the dance had given it is name: waltzer or waltz, which comes from the German *walzen*, which means "to turn".

The ever-more-popular waltz became the prototypical dance of the enlightenment: a dance in which courtly ritual gave way to sensuality and individual pleasure. By the late 18th century it was being danced by the middle and upper classes, to the great consternation of those self-righteous moralists who made it their business to quash the pleasure of others. Such a paragon of morality named Ernst Arndt was scandalized by what he perceived as "the erotic nature of the waltz" when he saw it danced in 1798 and 1799:

The [men] grasped their partners as closely as possible against them, and in this way the whirling continued in the most indecent positions; the supporting hand lay firmly on the breasts, at each movement making little lustful pressures; the girls went wild. When waltzing on the darker side of the room there were bolder embraces and kisses. 'It is not as bad as it looks' they exclaim, but now I understand why in parts of Swabia and Switzerland the waltz has been prohibited!

In 1804, a tourist in Paris was appalled by the waltzing he witnessed there: "This love for the waltz is quite new, and has become one of the vulgar fashions since the [Revolution], like smoking." Merry old England was the last Western European country to succumb to the charms of the waltz. In July of 1816, a waltz was included in a ball given in London by the prince regent himself. A few days later, an editorial appeared in *The Times*:

We remarked with pain that the indecent foreign dance called the Waltz was introduced at the English court on Friday last. It is quite sufficient to cast one's eyes on the voluptuous intertwining of the limbs and close compressure of the bodies in [this] dance, to see that it is, indeed, far removed from the modest reserve which has hitherto been considered distinctive of english females. So long as this obscene display was confined to prostitutes and adulteresses, we did not think it deserving of notice; but now that it is to be forced on the respectable classes of society, we feel it a duty to warn every parent against exposing his daughter to so fatal a contagion.

There is the story of the old English dowager watching a young couple waltzing: wide-eyed, outraged and—we would hope—fanning herself spastically as she asked incredulously, "Are they married?" Well honey, loosen your corset and untie yer skivvies, 'cause like-it-or-not, by the mid-19th century, the waltz had become the single most popular ballroom dance in the Western world. In 19th -century Vienna, the waltz became an industry: Joseph Lanner and Johann Strauss I composed hundreds of waltzes that were heard not just in Vienna but throughout Europe. Johann Strauss's son, Johann Strauss II, picked up where his father left off, and raised the waltz to a level of high art. Appropriately known as the waltz king, Johann Strauss the younger—who lived from 1825 to 1899—created some of the best-known and best-loved music of the 19th century, including *The Blue Danube Waltz, Tales from the Vienna Woods,* and the operetta *Die Fledermaus.*

Thanks primarily to the Strausses, father and son., the waltz came to be uniquely linked with the spiritual essence—the zeitgeist—of late 19th and early 20th century Vienna. On one hand, that Viennese spirit was one of joy and abandon, of living for the moment, of escapism. On the other hand, there was distinct feeling in late 19th-century Vienna of impending disaster. The Austrian Empire—with Vienna as its capitol—was beginning to unravel. The Austro-Prussian War of 1866—which Austria lost—seriously weakened Austrian influence in Europe. The unification of Germany in 1871 further diminished Austria's political clout and economy; almost overnight, Austria was reduced from Great Power status to a second-class state. Vienna was a dying capital, one that was about to become what Karl Kraus called "the proving-ground for world destruction".

Demagogues began to crawl out from under their rocks to lay blame for Austria's woes. Appealing to the fears and prejudices of the working classes, they blamed everyone but themselves for Austria's problems: They blamed the Slavs; they blamed the gypsies; they blamed immigrants and seasonal workers; they blamed the intellectuals. But mostly, they blamed the Jews. On April 8, 1897, a virulently anti-Semitic lawyer named Karl Lueger was elected mayor of Vienna. He remained in office until 1910. Adolf Hitler—who lived in Vienna from 1907 until 1913—paid Lueger tribute in *Mein Kampf*, calling Lueger's anti-Semitism an "inspiration."

Through it all, the Viennese waltzed. The ability of the Viennese to dance in the face of disaster is legendary. Call it survival, call it denial, whatever; the old Viennese joke says: "The situation is desperate but not serious." The composer Johannes Brahms—who had moved to Vienna as a young man—chose not to waltz. Like many others—including, as we will discuss, Maurice Ravel—he saw what was coming. In 1881 Brahms wrote his friend and publisher Franz Simrock: "In a city and a land where everything is [going] downhill, you can't expect music to fare better. Really, it's a pity and a crying shame, not only for music but for the whole beautiful land and the beautiful, marvelous people. I think real catastrophe is coming."

That it was. World War I destroyed the Austrian Empire, and World War II destroyed Vienna. No, not the buildings; the buildings are still there. But the spirit and creativity of what was an amazing, melting-pot city is gone forever. While Vienna remains a lovely tourist destination, it is no longer a hotbed of art and science, of philosophy and design, of literature and intellectual activity, of philanthropy and liberalism and music, primarily because Vienna's Jews are all gone.

According to the 1923 census, there were 201,513 Jews in Vienna, roughly 11 percent of the population. According to the 1934 census, that 11 percent of the population supplied 52 percent of Vienna's doctors; 75 percent of its bankers; 34 percent of its photographers; 40 percent of its café operators; 63 percent of its theater owners; 85 percent of its lawyers; 70 percent of its petrol dealers, wood and paper sellers, and shoemakers; 85 percent of its furniture manufacturers; 73 percent of its textile manufacturers; 80 percent of its radio dealers; 74 percent of its wine merchants; and, for what it's worth, 100 percent of its scrap-metal dealers.

The Nazis goose-stepped into Austria in March of 1938. By the end of 1941, 130,000 Jews had managed to get out of Vienna. But more than 65,000 did not, and they were, to a person, deported to the camps. Of that 65,000, only 2,000 survived the war. For many in the postwar era, the Viennese Waltz came—paradoxically—to encapsulate all of this: joy and sorrow; beauty and vulgarity; civility and unspeakable tragedy.

Now: Maurice Ravel composed *Valses nobles et sentimentales* in 1911, long before the start of World War II and three years before the beginning of World War I. Nevertheless, I do believe Ravel came to have the same paradoxical feelings towards the Viennese waltz that I just described. My evidence for that statement is a piece of music Ravel composed in 1919 and 1920—immediately after the end of World War I—a piece of music entitled *La Valse*: "The Waltz." Ravel described *La Valse* as being a tribute to the waltz, but it is much more than that. Using melodic motives drawn from *Valses nobles et sentimentales*, *La Valse* builds up to a vicious, concluding climax of frenzy and disintegration. According to the English composer and music theorist George Benjamin: "Whether or not it was intended as a metaphor for the predicament of European civilization in the aftermath of the

Great War, its one-movement design plots the birth, decay and destruction of a musical genre: the waltz."

The waltz, then, is many things: a popular dance; a body of music that employs the rhythm of that dance; and a grand metaphor as well, a metaphor for the Austrian empire: its joy; its character; its aspirations; its disintegration and death, and the horrors its disintegration and death wrought on the world. Let us not forget that it was the assassination of the Austrian crown-prince, Archduke Franz Ferdinand, that precipitated the outbreak of World War I, and a deranged, Austrian-born foot-soldier who instigated World War II.

Maurice Ravel (1875–1937)

Maurice Joseph Ravel was born on March 7, 1875 in Ciboure, in southwestern France, near Biarritz. He died in Paris on December 28, 1937. His mother, Marie, was a native Basque and his father—Pierre-Joseph Ravel—was a Swiss-born engineer. Ravel himself would have made a heck of an engineer. He was meticulous in every aspect of his life, from the design of his home to the clothes he wore and the food he cooked. As a composer he was a perfectionist: Every note had to count and every musical surface had to gleam. His friend, the poet *Léon*-Paul Fargue, wrote that, "He liked to do and do well everything. Everything that came from his brain carries the mark of perfection. His passion was to offer to the public finished works polished to a supreme degree." Speaking to both Ravel's workmanship and his father's Swiss origins, Igor Stravinsky referred to him as "a Swiss watchmaker."

The Ravel family moved to Paris three months after Maurice was born, and it was there that Ravel grew up during one of the great epochs in that arguably greatest of all cities' history. A talented pianist but not a prodigy, Ravel entered the Paris Conservatory in 1889, at the age of 14. He studied there on and off for 16 years, and completed his education as a composition protégé of Gabriel *Fauré*.

Maurice Ravel was neither a loudmouth nor a jerk. Nevertheless, he drove his teaches at the Conservatory nuts. The "problem" was that Ravel began to experience real success as a composer while he was still a studen. Think about it: what can a academic pedant tell a 23-year-old student who has already garnered more artistic fame and respect than the pedant ever will? The directors of the Conservatory came to loathe Ravel and decided that their best course was to knock him down a few pegs. So despite his talent and success, Ravel was never awarded any of the departmental prizes that were considered so important to a student's future success.

Ravel had the last laugh, because in the end, his ongoing failure to win a *Prix de Rome*—the "Rome Prize"—created a scandal that brought down the leadership of the Conservatory! Here's the scoop: In 1900—at a time his music was being talked about across Paris—Ravel was not even allowed to participate in the competition. In 1901 Ravel was deemed worthy to enter the competition, which was to compose a cantata based on a text given him by the competition committee. On a lark, Ravel—who thought the text was idiotic—composed a cantata that was set almost entirely as a waltz.

The judges were not amused; they wrote: "Monsieur Ravel should not think [that] he can ridicule us. Monsieur Ravel may well consider us flat-footed pedants, but he will not go unpunished for taking us as imbeciles." Needless to say, Ravel was not awarded the *Prix de Rome* in 1901, which instead went to someone named André Caplet. Neither was he awarded the prize in 1902 or 1903. In 1904 Ravel did not compete and in 1905 he was not allowed to compete because he had turned 30 earlier that year.

Well, to tell you the truth, by 1905, the 30-year-old Ravel didn't need no stinkin' prize. He was famous and had come to be considered—along with Claude Debussy—the most important young composer in France. Given Ravel's fame, his treatment by the directors of the *Conservatoire* created a scandal. Called "*L'affaire Ravel*", the scandal led to the resignation of the director of the Conservatory—Theodore Dubois—and the appointment of Ravel's friend and teacher—Gabriel *Fauré*—in Dubois's place. My friends, this we've got to love!

Ravel's Friends

If the mark of a man is his friends, then Ravel receives the highest possible marks, an A++, in bonhomie. His many friends included many of France's greatest artists and intellectuals, and to a person they left the sort of reminiscences of Ravel that we'd all like to inspire. According to the pianist Marguerite Long:

> Ravel combined Schubert's friendliness, Mendelssohn's courtesy, Liszt's generosity, and Albéniz's delicacy. He was a typical Basque; small, thin, the bone structure of his face strongly marked. His hair was wavy, and having turned early to silver gave an expression of gentleness to his features. A tireless walker, he was much given to walking about Paris.

> He was something of a dandy, anxious to follow fashion or even set it. He has a penchant for nice ties, the choice of which was often the subject of endless discussion. This meticulous elegance helped Ravel create an appearance and to carry the mask he ever used to thwart all invasion of his privacy. His small stature troubled him much [he was about 5'3"], [though he was wont to point out that] 'some composers were small: think of Beethoven and Mozart.' Ravel's integrity and loyalty were beyond reproach. He was always free from untruth and malice. So far as manners were concerned he was a complete thoroughbred. He had the same consideration for people of little importance as for the great, to whom he showed no special regard.

Ravel's friend Louis Aubert—who is the dedicatee of the *Valses Nobles et Sentimentales*—gave the premiere performances in May, 1911. He remembered Ravel as a man virtually without artistic pretense: "No one was freer than he was from obvious vanity. Certainly he set great store by extreme elegance in his clothes. But I wonder whether this was out of a desire to lose himself in the anonymity of a certain bourgeois correctness, ands thus avoid the appearance of being an 'artiste' which was then all the rage." The composer and critic Alexis Roland-Manuel remembered that:

> In any discussion of the discrepancies in the allotment of talent he would shrug his shoulders [and say]: "Everybody's talented; I'm no more so than anyone else. With a little application each of you could do what I do." If it is true that all art involves imitation, then no artist believed the dictum more than Ravel did. He never tired of saying that one must not be afraid of continual imitation. He was quite

happy, therefore, to compare his *Valses* with those of Schubert from whom he had borrowed the epithets "noble" and "sentimental."

Valses nobles et sentimentales (1911)

Let us begin our examination of the "waltzes noble and sentimental" with the just-quoted observation regarding the influence of Franz Schubert's waltzes on Ravel's. As the waltz gained popularity as a dance, so composers wrote ever more waltz music, including stylized waltzes: waltz music not intended for dancing, but rather for listening. For example, Frédéric Chopin's 18 waltzes—composed between 1831 and 1849—were stylized dances, intended—as they are—for concert performance.

Chopin notwithstanding, the first major set of stylized waltzes was composed by a native Viennese: Franz Schubert, who wrote roughly 100 waltzes for solo piano between roughly 1815 and 1826. Among the best known of Schubert's waltzes are two collections: the 34 *Valses Sentimentales*, Op. 50 (of 1823) and the 12 *Valses Nobles*, Op. 77 (of 1826). These waltzes were composed for amateur pianists, and therefore, unlike Ravel's waltzes, they are fairly easy to play. However, what Ravel did copy from Schubert— aside from his titles—is the spectacular range of Schubert's moods and a concentrated, every-note-counts compositional aesthetic.

In an autobiographical sketch, Ravel confirmed his inspiration for his *Valses nobles et sentimentales* and discussed, as well, its less-is-more aesthetic: "The title *Valses nobles et sentimentales* sufficiently indicates my intention of composing a series of waltzes in imitation of Schubert. The virtuosity [of my earlier piano music] gives way [in the *Valses*] to a markedly clearer kind of writing, which crystallizes the harmony and sharpens the profile of the music."

Let's dwell on that last statement: that Ravel cut down on the "degree of pianistic difficulty" in his waltzes in favor of "a clearer kind of writing, which crystallizes the harmony and sharpens the profile of the music." Ravel's set consists of seven waltzes (some noble and some sentimental, though Ravel does not indicate which), followed by a shimmering, ghostlike epilogue in which the principal themes of the waltzes pass by in a nostalgic haze.

The first waltz is as much a fanfare as a dance; it kicks things off brilliantly and nobly. It is also a perfect example of the sort of "crystalline harmonic and textural clarity" that Ravel refers to in his autobiographical sketch. Let's hear it: Ravel, *Valses nobles et sentimentales*, waltz no. 1. [**Piano performance:** Ravel, *Valses nobles et sentimentales*, waltz no. 1.]

That music is as dazzling as a Cartier diamond; as clear and razor-edged as a crystal Baccarat chandelier. Its edge comes from its sharply accented rhythms and from its harmonic language that, for all its chromaticism, is firmly anchored in G Major.

We return to Ravel's autobiographical sketch, and his description of the premiere of the waltzes on May, 9 1911 at the Salle Gaveau in Paris. "The *Valses Nobles et Sentimentales* were first performed amid [catcalls] and boos at a concert of the independent musical society, in which the names of the composers were not revealed. The audience voted on the probable authorship of each piece." Talk about an audience participation event! The only person who knew for sure who had composed Ravel's waltzes was its performer (and dedicatee), Louis Aubert. In the spirit of name-that-tune, the audience was invited to vote on the authorship of all the works on the program, and the results were published a periodical called "The Musical Courier" on May 16, 1911, six days after the concert.

That audience—which consisted primarily of professional musicians and critics—did not do a very good job of identifying the composer. The authorship of Ravel's waltzes was credited to, among others, Eric Satie, the Hungarian Zoltán Kodály, the now-forgotten French organist and composer, *Théodore* Dubois and the French film composer, Lucien Wurmser. In his wonderful biography of Ravel, Ravel's friend Alexis Roland-Manuel observes that, "Such howlers are surprising. But they are explained by the peculiar audacity of the work which, by the very brilliance of its originality, could blind the music lovers of 1911."

Blind them it did. For the six days between the concert and the revelation of authorship, Ravel listened deadpan to the jeers leveled at the piece by his friends and the critics, who hadn't a clue that Ravel was the composer. When the truth was revealed, those friends and critics who had trashed the piece suddenly found all sorts of qualities in it that they had somehow failed to notice when they first heard it. To a person they reversed their negative judgments. According to Ravel biographer Madeline Goss, "This experience proved a lesson to Ravel in the true value of criticism." I'll bet.

Let's examine each of the waltzes. Along with identifying the expressive "mood" of each waltz we will identify—as well—the particular compositional hook that characterizes each waltz. Waltz number one (which we've already heard). Mood: noble and fanfare-ish. Compositional hook: huge, sharply articulated, two-fisted chords that ring and resonate on the piano like clanging bells. [**Piano demonstration.**] Waltz number two. mood: sentimental and melancholy. Compositional hook: grace notes in the thematic melody that "anticipate" the beat and that—with exquisite subtlety—desynchronize the pianist's hands and create a dragging sense of world weariness For example: [**Piano demonstration.**] We hear the first half of waltz number two. [**Piano performance:** Ravel, *Valses nobles et sentimentales*, waltz no. 2.]

Waltz number three. Mood: noble (only because it is certainly is not "sentimental"), light and playful, with a hint of *Chinoiserie* (meaning stereotypically "Chinese-like" music). Compositional hook: hemiola. "Hemiola." I will be the first to admit that "hemiola" is an excessively unattractive word, on par with "phlegm," "mucus," and "smegma." However, unlike those words, "hemiola" does not refer to icky bodily stuff, but rather to a rhythmic device. A hemiola is a pattern of accents that implies a momentary change of meter. For example, in order to perceive triple meter—or waltz time, as it is often called—we need to hear some sort of "ccent every three beats, accents which effectively group the beats into three: 1-2-3, 1-2-3, 1-2-3.

A hemiola would put an accent on every second beat, momentarily creating the effect that the meter has changed from triple to duple. 1-2-3, 1-2-3, 1-2-1-2-1-2-3, 1-2-3, 1-2-1-2-1-2 and so forth. Let's hear the playful opening of Ravel's waltz number three, and let's be aware of the hemiola-filled rhythmic pattern: 1-2-3, 1-2-3, 1-2-3, 1-2-3, 1-2-1-2-1-2, 1-2-3. [**Piano performance:** Ravel, *Valses nobles et sentimentales*, waltz no. 3.] With our rhythmic antennae now fully extended, let's kick back and hear number three in its entirety. [**Piano performance:** Ravel, *Valses nobles et sentimentales*, waltz no. 3.]

Waltz number four begins without a pause. Its mood is sentimental and gently nostalgic. Its hook is a fluttering, descending melody the rhythms of which cross the bar line, effectively creating a six beat metric unit. Here's that melodic rhythm. [**Demonstration.**] These six-beat-long metric units create a languorous and floating effect, an effect that stands in polar opposition to the punchy, hemiola-dominated rhythms of the previous waltz. Let's hear it, waltz number four. [**Piano performance:** Ravel, *Valses nobles et sentimentales*, waltz no. 4.]

Waltz number five. The mood is sentimental and lyric. The waltz's compositional hook is its intense chromaticism, which creates a sort of blurry smear of harmonic and melodic sound. The result—and Ravel will have to pardon us for using a word he hated—the result is the most impressionistic of the waltzes that make up the piece. Waltz number five: [**Piano performance:** Ravel, *Valses nobles et sentimentales*, waltz no. 5.]

Waltz number six. Mood: noble and zippy. The hook is once again rhythmic, as a punchy, rising, triple meter tune in the pianist's right hand (1-2-3, 1-2-3, 1-2-3, 1-2-3) is heard —as often as not—against a hemiola accompaniment in the left hand (1-2, 1-2, 1-2, 1-2). Waltz number six. [**Piano performance:** Ravel, *Valses nobles et sentimentales*, waltz no. 6.]

Waltz number seven is magnificent, in turns both "sentimental" and "noble." Compositional hook: This longest waltz in the set is a grand summation of all that has come before it. Over the course of its A-B-A form we will hear the rhythmic complexities of waltzes numbers three, four, and six; the rippling impressionistic blur of waltz number five; and at its climactic moments, the brilliant fanfares of waltz number one. Number seven: [**Piano performance:** Ravel, *Valses nobles et sentimentales*, waltz no. 7.]

The final movement—number eight—is labeled in score as being an epilogue. It is a magical and mysterious chunk of music, one that changes entirely our perception of the piece to this point. Up to now, Ravel's *Valses nobles et sentimentales* has been a suite: a collection of dances, a piece little different in structure from the dance suites written for harpsichord by Ravel's French compositional ancestors back in the 17th century.

Well, all of that changes in the epilogue. In a ghostly haze, thematic materials from the earlier waltzes drift forward and fade. Like the first waltz, this epilogue is cast in G major. But unlike that first waltz, there is no dance or glide or fanfare here, and the epilogue ends as if in a dream. This epilogue makes it clear that *Valses nobles et sentimentales* is not merely a dance suite, but rather, a piece about the waltz as a metaphor for a vanished world. Epilogue: [**Piano performance:** Ravel, *Valses nobles et sentimentales*, waltz no. 8.] Nostalgic and ghostlike, this epilogue acknowledges that the Viennese world that created the waltz was, by 1911, but a dream.

Ravel was a voracious newspaper reader and proud of his leftist leanings. He understood what was going on in Europe in 1911. He knew about Mayor Karl Lueger of Vienna and the growing menace of institutional anti-Semitism. Ravel knew about the naval arms race in progress between Great Britain and Imperial Germany. He knew that Kaiser Wilhelm II of Germany—with his shriveled left arm and his huge moustache and his strutting, militant machismo—was as dangerous and unstable as a gunslinger on a three-day binge. He knew as well that France was spoiling for a fight in order to avenge the humiliation of the Franco-Prussian War and to take back those parts of Alsace and Lorraine that had been ceded to Germany back in 1871.

Maurice Ravel's *Valses nobles et sentimentales* is about the coming catastrophe, as it dreams—longingly but vainly—for times past, just as his *La Valse*—composed nine years later—is about the catastrophe that did, in fact, occur. Yes, one can rightly assert Ravel's *Valses nobles et sentimentales* is simply a great piece of music, and that like all great art, it transcends its time. But taken in its historical context, it becomes a supremely moving historical document as well.

Thank you.

Scriabin—Piano Sonata No. 5
Lecture 20

Aleksandr Scriabin's 10 piano sonatas, written across the span of his compositional life, are collectively his defining works. This single set of compositions demonstrates his fascinating and sometimes unsettling artistic trajectory, from a late-romantic composer of tonal music to a brilliant (if slightly crazed) modernist. Composed in 1907, Scriabin's Piano Sonata no. 5—the focus of this lecture—is cast as a single movement and is about 12 minutes in length. Although the piece uses traditional key signatures, it exists, in truth, at the very outer limits of traditional tonality.

Tonal Centricity: Consonance and Dissonance

- Scriabin's Piano Sonata no. 5 of 1907 is the most frequently recorded of Scriabin's 10 piano sonatas. The great Soviet pianist Sviatoslav Richter once described it as the most difficult piece in the entire piano repertoire. At the time he completed it, Scriabin himself considered it the best piano piece he had ever composed. Amazingly, he composed the sonata in an astonishingly fast 6 days.

- The roiling opening of the introduction is intended to depict the secret yearnings Scriabin summons forth from the dark depths in order to bring them to life. The introductory music lies completely outside traditional tonal practice; it lacks entirely any sense of traditional tonal centricity, meaning harmonic gravity.

- Tonal centricity is created when harmonic instability—dissonance—resolves to harmonic stability—consonance. However, Scriabin's introduction is uniformly dissonant. It employs harmonic and melodic ideas filled with intervals—pitch relationships—that in traditional tonal music would be considered as unstable.

- The oscillating tremolo in the deep bass outlines a dissonant interval called a tritone. Layered atop the tritone is a trill, pitched a dissonant minor second above the bottom note of the triton. And all of that is interspersed with upward-ripping gestures that outline yet another dissonant interval called a major seventh.

- "Dissonance" is not an absolute term but, rather, a relative term; dissonance only means something relative to consonance. Lacking any relative consonance, Scriabin's introductory passage, then, creates a nontonal environment, in which its gestural character—as it shreds the piano from bottom to top—is its essence.

- Much of Scriabin's Piano Sonata no. 5 is grounded in harmonic tradition, so what we have is a very modern piece of music, one in which tonal music and nontonal music coexist, a product of Scriabin's theosophical belief that his musical imagination can and must synthesize all of nature in order to experience divine revelation.

Sonata Form

- For all its outward modernity, Scriabin's one-movement Piano Sonata no. 5 is cast in sonata form, a formal procedure invented in the mid-18th century. A sonata form movement is one in which two or more principal, contrasting themes are presented, developed, and ultimately reconciled to each other.

- The opening section of a sonata form movement—during which the multiple, contrasting themes are introduced—is called the exposition. Materials from the exposition are then developed in a section called the development, after which the themes return in their original order (but with important changes) in a section called the recapitulation. A coda will usually bring such a movement to its conclusion.

- The formal orthodoxy, or template, of sonata form serves Scriabin well in his Piano Sonata no. 5, because it helps to give coherence and a measure of tradition to Scriabin's otherwise most untraditional musical materials. The goal of your listening is to perceive exactly this dichotomy of new and old—the idiosyncratic nature of Scriabin's musical materials and how those materials are deployed in sonata form.

Exposition

- Theme 1—labeled "*presto con allegrezza*," meaning "very fast, and with joy"— is a bouncing, ecstatic theme set in the key of F-sharp major. Using the terminology of sonata form, the passage that follows is the modulating bridge, a chunk of music tasked with transiting to the second theme and changing the key in anticipation of that second theme.

The piano and orchestral music of Aleksandr Scriabin (1872–1915) is known for its uncustomary harmonies.

- In a harmonic environment as fluid as this one, perceiving modulation—that is, key change—will be difficult. Scriabin's bridge alternates a long-breathed melodic idea that anticipates theme 2 with pulsating chords drawn from theme 1.

- As we would expect in a sonata form movement, theme 2, set here in B-flat major, is the more lyric of the two principal themes. Lush, leisurely, and luxuriant, the theme features sinuous accompanimental lines that are the aural equivalent of the plant-inspired vocabulary of art nouveau, an art movement with which this sonata is exactly contemporary.

The "Mystic Chord"

- Underpinning much of the magical second theme is a harmony that is an ever-so-slight variant of a harmony that has come to be known as Scriabin's "mystic chord." As he matured, Scriabin's melodies and harmonies were increasingly built from variants of the mystic chord.

- At a time when composers like Debussy, Schoenberg, and Stravinsky were all trying to break away from the expectations of traditional tonality, the mystic chord and its various permutations were Scriabin's harmonic solution, his way of creating a basic harmonic sound that existed outside of traditional tonality.

- The mystic chord doesn't seem to imply consonance or tonal centricity—that is, not one of its pitches can be perceived as representing a state of rest. But neither is Scriabin's mystic chord dissonant in a tonal sense, in that it does not sound as if it needs to resolve. In truth, the mystic chord is neither consonant nor dissonant; it represents neither rest nor tension—it just exists.

- The tonal harmonic system had been the solar plexus of the Western musical language since the 15th century. At its most basic, the tonal system is a metaphor for the complementary opposites that frame our existence: rise and fall, tension and release, activity and inactivity, struggle and repose, the turmoil of life and the eternal rest of death.

- At the heart of the tonal system are two harmonies or chords, one that represents tension and the other rest. Scriabin's mystic chord is constructed in such a way as to imply neither tension nor rest.

- Scriabin himself did not call this harmony the "mystic chord," which is a term that was coined in 1916—after Scriabin's death—by the English music critic Arthur Hull. Scriabin called it "the chord of the pleroma."

- Much of Scriabin's late music—reliant, as it is, on the mystic chord—is going to be characterized more by harmonic stasis than forward motion. In its mystic chord–created harmonic stasis, Scriabin's music will remind us of Debussy's on one hand and, philosophically at least, the mantra-like music of India on the other.

- The exposition of Scriabin's Piano Sonata no. 5 is brought to its conclusion with a rousing bit of closing music based loosely on theme 1.

Development Section
- The development section is cast in three large parts. The first part features the introduction and theme 1; the second part features the introduction and theme 2; and the third part further expands on theme 2, as well as the closing material that concluded the exposition.

- Part 3 of the development section begins with an expansion of the closing material heard at the conclusion of the exposition and then concludes with a magisterial, teeth-rattling version of theme 2 that brings the development to its climax.

Recapitulation
- On paper, Scriabin's recapitulation is a textbook affair: Theme 1 returns, followed by the modulating bridge, theme 2, and the closing material. However, there is nothing "textbook" about the way the recap sounds. Scriabin compresses everything: The introductory music is gone, and everything that follows is compressed and intensified, building inexorably to the grand climax that is the sonata-concluding coda. In the compressed recapitulation, what took roughly four minutes to pass in the exposition now takes just over two minutes in the recapitulation.

Coda
- Scriabin indicates that the coda be played "*con luminosita*," meaning "with luminosity." Scriabin just loved to use expressive designations that referred to light and color. According to some commentators, such designations were not just expressive directives but references to Scriabin's synesthesia.

- Much has been made about Scriabin's presumed synesthesia, a condition whereby Scriabin purportedly saw colors while listening to music. Scriabin had a lot of issues, but synesthesia was not one of them. The color system he invented and for which he is known—a system that associated certain colors with certain pitches—was a carefully worked out scheme based on the circle of fifths and the primary colors as described by Sir Isaac Newton in his *Opticks*, otherwise known as "ROY G. BIV": red, orange, yellow, green, blue, indigo, violet.

- In Scriabin's system, C was red, G (a fifth above C) was orange, D (a fifth above G) was yellow, A was green, E was blue, B was indigo, and F-sharp was violet. The remaining five pitches described shades of purple progressing to rust, leading back to the red of the pitch C.

- So much for Scriabin's storied color synesthesia: In reality, his color system was invented so that in the course of a musical performance, colors could be projected that corresponded with the pitches being heard. To this end, he worked with an inventor named Alexander Mozer to create a color organ, which, like so many of Scriabin's plans, never quite worked.

- The coda of Scriabin's Piano Sonata no. 5 is cast in four brief parts. The first part is based on theme 1; the second features a magisterial and throbbing version of theme 2; the third part—marked *"presto,"* meaning "very fast"—returns to theme 1; and the fourth part, which flies by in the blink of an eye, features the upward-ripping, dissonant gesture that began the sonata back in the introduction. Taken all together, this coda constitutes an apotheosis: an ecstatic, barely disguised instance of excitement that brings the sonata to its conclusion.

- While the formal structure of Scriabin's Piano Sonata no. 5 might be traditional, its musical content is something altogether different—or, in other words, original. There's nothing else that sounds like this music.

Scriabin—Piano Sonata No. 5
Lecture 20—Transcript

We return to *The 23 Greatest Solo Piano Works*. This is Lecture 20. It is entitled Scriabin—Piano Sonata No. 5.

Aleksandr Nikolayevich Scriabin (1872–1915). Aleksandr Scriabin was not just the odd man out of turn-of-the-20th-century Russian composers; he was, arguably, the oddest-man-out in the history of Western music. Scriabin didn't start out life as a world-class oddball. He was born in Moscow and was a piano prodigy. He was a friend and classmate of Sergei Rachmaninoff, first in the piano studio of Nikolai Zverov, and later at the Moscow Conservatory. They graduated together in 1892, ranked numbers one and two. Rachmaninoff received the "Great Gold Medal" and Scriabin the "Little Gold Medal." (Oh my goodness. The Moscow Conservatory Class of 1892: pretty darned impressive!)

Scriabin began his career as a touring pianist and composed charming piano miniatures a la Chopin. He married and quickly fathered four children. When he wasn't on tour he taught at the Moscow Conservatory. Then, in 1902—at the age of 30—something in his mind sparked and fizzled, bzzzzt. Suddenly preoccupied with issues philosophical and mysterious, Scriabin quit his teaching job, took up with a former student named Tatiana Schloezer, and abandoned his family, telling his wife Vera that he was going to live with Tatiana as "a sacrifice to art." Gentlemen: Don't even think of what would happen to you if you tried that line on your wives.

Depending upon who you talk to, Scriabin went on to become either one of the great visionaries in the history of music or a total crackpot. However, one thing we can all agree on is that Scriabin proceeded to create a truly unique body of musical work.

Behavioral Issues

It is pretty much agreed upon that after his epiphany (or whatever it was) in 1902, Aleksandr Scriabin became a certifiable narcissistic megalomaniac. Some writers attribute his epiphany to mental illness. Others attribute it to overcompensation for his diminutive size (he could not reach more than an octave in either of his hands). Still others claim that his narcissism and megalomania were built into his personality, the result of his upbringing.

For our information: Scriabin's mother died of tuberculosis when he was just one year old, and his father, who was a member of the Russian consular service, was posted to Turkey. As a result, according to the English musicologist Hugh Macdonald, "Scriabin was brought up by his Aunt Lyubov, his grandmother and his great aunt, all of whom doted passionately on the boy, pampered him endlessly and set his mind towards the egocentricity of his later years as well as giving him a certain effeminacy in his manners[!]."

Scriabin spent the years after 1902 contemplating the work that would be his magnum opus: an apocalyptic, Wagner-inspired, all-inclusive artwork-on-growth-hormone entitled *Mysterium*, a no-holds-barred, everything-including-the-kitchen-sink happening that would synthesize "all the arts, loading all the senses in a hypnoidal, many-media extravaganza of sound, sight, smell, feel, dance, décor, orchestra, piano, singers, light, sculptures, colors [and] visions." Scriabin planned its premiere for a yet-to-be built, hemispherical temple at the base of the Himalayan Mountains. In order to prepare himself for his residency in India, Scriabin went so far as to buy himself a pith helmet, a white tropical suit, and a book on Sanskrit grammar! A real Boy Scout he was: Be prepared!

According to Scriabin, the climax of *Mysterium* would bring about nothing less than the collapse of the universe, after which men and women would be reborn as androgynous astral souls, relieved not only of their sexual differences but any other physical limitations as well. As for himself, Scriabin claimed that, "I shall not die; I shall suffocate from ecstasy after *Mysterium*." It's right about here that the venerable Cheech Marin would inquire, "What're you smokin', man?"

Well, part of what Scriabin was smokin' was the music and megalomania of the German composer Richard Wagner. Point in fact: Scriabin was pretty much the only contemporary Russian composer to take Wagner seriously, and there's no doubt that when it came to *Mysterium*, he wanted to "be

371

like Dick." But in reality, Scriabin's plans for *Mysterium*—which were never realized (oh, really?)—made Wagner look like a small-time piker by comparison.

Scriabin's Piano Sonatas

The jewels in the crown of Scriabin's compositional output are his 10 piano sonatas. Scriabin would be most annoyed to hear me say that. Not that it isn't true, and not that he privately wouldn't agree; no, the issue is that he didn't want to be known merely as a composer for the piano. He did indeed write some outstanding orchestral music, including a piano concerto and three symphonies (I would direct your attention, in particular, to his Third Symphony of 1904, entitled "The Divine Poem"). His two late orchestral works, *Poem of Ecstasy* of 1907 and *Prometheus* of 1910, are likewise superb.

Having said that, it is Scriabin's piano sonatas, written across the span of his compositional life, that are collectively his defining works: that single set of compositions that demonstrate his fascinating and sometimes unsettling artistic trajectory, from a late-romantic composer of tonal music to a brilliant (if slightly crazed) modernist. He composed his first piano sonata in 1892, at the age of 20, and completed his tenth and final sonata in 1913, at the age of 41. He died two years later under circumstances so ridiculous that we can only shake our heads. We will talk about that in due time.

Scriabin's Piano Sonata No. 5—the focus of this lecture—was composed in 1907. It is cast as a single movement, about 12 minutes in length. Although the piece uses traditional key signatures it exists, in truth, at the very outer limits of traditional tonality.

The introductory material that begins the sonata dwells far beyond tonal tradition, as a series of roiling, trilling, ripping musical gestures rise from the depth of the piano followed by a shimmering and mysterious passage. Let's hear this most modern-sounding introductory music. [**Piano performance:** Scriabin, Piano Sonata No. 5.]

Theosophy and Revelation

The mystical, esoteric philosophy called theosophy that Scriabin went just a little crazy over around 1902 considered visual and musical art to be vehicles for revelation: that is, capable of imparting divine knowledge unmediated by words or the intellect. Late 19th- and early 20th-century theosophy was characterized by three central beliefs. Belief number one: that the cosmos consists of three inter-related elements, all of which are fully alive: nature, the divine, and humanity. Belief number two: the creative impulse—and all the myths and symbols and sounds and images it employs—synthesizes nature, the divine, and the human into a singularity understood to be "The Mind." Belief number three: The creative impulse gives humanity the ability to penetrate and become one with nature and the divine. The creative process gives humanity access to all levels of reality, "to co-penetrate the human with the divine and to bond to all reality and experience a unique inner awakening."

If you found that most brief explanation of theosophical dogma just a bit confusing, well, welcome to my neighborhood. Like most such mystical philosophies, close encounters with theosophy by the uninitiated like myself will cause eyes to cross, heads to ache, and steam to emerge from ears. Russia's most important mystical-symbolist poet, Vyacheslav Ivanov (1866–1949) was a close friend of Scriabin and was downright jealous of the power of music to synthesize experience and reveal the deepest truths. Ivanov wrote:

> Where we poets monotonously blab the word "sadness", music overflows with thousands of particular shades of sadness, each so ineffably novel that no two of them can be called the same feeling. [Music is therefore] the unmediated pilot of our spiritual depths, the most sensitive of the arts and inherently prophetic, the womb in which the Spirit of the Age in incubated.

Despite the fact that Ivanov wrote those words in 1915, they represent pure 19th-century romantic dogma. A full 100 years before, the German author, composer, and critic E.T.A. Hoffmann had written that, "Music is the secret sanskrit of nature expressed in tones which fill the human heart with endless longing, and only in music does one understand the songs of trees, flowers, animals, stones and floods!" In a style as purple as the Joker's jockey shorts, Hoffmann expressed exactly what both Ivanov and Scriabin continued to believe a century later: that music could evoke the sublime in a manner and to a depth beyond that of any other non-pharmaceutical construct.

So back to Scriabin, and his philosophical epiphany. The older he got, the more he came to believe in the post-Beethoven, romantic-era ideal that considered musical composition to be a vehicle for self- revelation. At the same time, like so many early 20th-century composers, he came to realize that in order to make the sorts of bold and original expressive statements his revelatory expressive vision demanded, he had to go ever more beyond the tradition tonal system in order to make them.

Scriabin, Sonata No. 5, Op. 53

Scriabin's Piano Sonata No. 5 of 1907 is a work of superlatives. It is the most frequently recorded of Scriabin's 10 piano sonatas. The great Soviet pianist Sviatoslav Richter once described it as the most difficult piece in the entire piano repertoire. At the time he completed it, Scriabin himself considered it the best piano piece he had ever composed. In a letter dating from December 1907 he wrote, "Today I have almost finished my 5th Sonata. I deem it the best piano composition I have ever written. I do not know by what miracle I accomplished it." We would echo Scriabin's amazement at the speed with which he composed the sonata: an astonishingly fast six days.

Across the top of the score of the sonata, Scriabin placed the following poetic inscription, an inscription drawn from his own "Poem of Ecstasy":

> I summon you to life, secret yearnings!
> You who have been drowned in the dark depths
> Of the creative spirit, you timorous
> Embryos of life, it is to you that I bring daring!

The roiling opening of the introduction—sampled previously—is intended to depict the "secret yearnings" Scriabin summons forth from the "dark depths" in order to bring them to life. Let's hear this roiling opening, and then let's talk about it. [**Piano performance:** Scriabin, Piano Sonata No. 5.] That introductory music lies completely outside traditional tonal practice: It lacks entirely any sense of traditional tonal centricity, meaning harmonic gravity.

I explain. Tonal centricity is created when harmonic instability—dissonance—resolves to harmonic stability—consonance. For example, dissonance. [**Piano demonstration.**] Consonance. [**Piano demonstration.**] However, Scriabin's introduction is uniformly dissonant. It employs harmonic and melodic ideas filled with intervals—pitch relationships—that, in traditional tonal music, would be considered as unstable as a one-legged chair. Check it out: The oscillating tremolo in the deep bass that begins the sonata outlines a dissonant interval called a tritone. [**Piano demonstration.**] Layered atop that tritone is a trill, pitched a dissonant minor second above the bottom note of the tritone! [**Piano demonstration.**] And all of that is interspersed with upward-ripping gestures that outline yet another dissonant interval, this one called a major seventh. [**Piano demonstration.**] Let's hear all of that in context once again. [**Piano performance:** Scriabin, Piano Sonata No. 5.]

Now, moments ago we observed that that passage is uniformly dissonant. Let us now modify that statement, because in fact, "dissonance" is not an absolute term, but rather a relative term. Just as "pleasure" only means something relative to "pain," just as "wealth" only means something relative to "poverty," so "dissonance" only means something relative to "consonance."

Lacking any relative consonance, Scriabin's introductory passage, then, creates a non-tonal environment, in which its gestural character—as it literally shreds the piano from bottom to top—is its essence. [**Piano performance:** Scriabin, Piano Sonata No. 5.] Now, please, there's no need to run for the hills: Much of Scriabin's Piano Sonata No. 5 is grounded in harmonic tradition. So what we have here is a very modern piece of music, one in which tonal music and non-tonal music coexist, a product of Scriabin's theosophical belief that his musical imagination can and must synthesize all of nature in order to experience divine revelation. Yes, we'll need to chew on all that for a while. But for now, we move on.

Sonata Form

For all its outward modernity, Scriabin's one-movement Piano Sonata No. 5 is cast in sonata form, a formal procedure invented back in the mid-18th century. A sonata form movement is one in which two or more principal, contrasting themes are presented, developed, and ultimately reconciled to each other. The opening section of a sonata form movement—during which the multiple, contrasting themes are introduced—is called the exposition. Materials from the exposition are then developed in a section called the development, after which the themes return in their original order (but with important changes) in a section called the recapitulation. A coda, or tail section, will usually bring such a movement to its conclusion.

OK: That's the formal orthodoxy, the template of sonata form. It's a template that serves Scriabin well here in his fifth piano sonata, because it helps to give coherence and a measure of tradition to Scriabin's otherwise most untraditional musical materials. The goal of our listening will be to perceive exactly this dichotomy of new and old: the idiosyncratic nature of Scriabin's musical materials and how those materials are deployed in sonata form. We heard the great bulk of the introduction at the beginning of the lecture, with its ripping, tearing opening and then the languid passage that follows. Let us move forward, then, to the—

Exposition

I strongly suggest we all put on a good pair of sunglasses (or at least some sun block) before we hear theme one, because this halogen-bright theme might otherwise toast us if we're not careful. Labeled *"presto con allegrezza,"* meaning "very fast, and with joy," this bouncing, ecstatic theme is set in the key of F-sharp Major. Let's hear it. [**Piano performance:** Scriabin, Piano Sonata No. 5, exposition.]

Using the terminology of sonata form, the passage that follows is the modulating bridge: a chunk of music tasked with transiting to the second theme and changing the key in anticipation of that second theme. In a harmonic environment as fluid as this one, perceiving modulation—that is, key change—will be difficult at best. Scriabin's bridge alternates a long-breathed melodic idea that anticipates theme two, a melodic idea that sounds like this—[**piano demonstration**]—with pulsating chords drawn from theme one. Let's hear it, the modulating bridge. [**Piano performance:** Scriabin, Piano Sonata No. 5, modulating bridge.]

As we would expect in a sonata form movement, theme 2—set here in B-flat Major—is the more lyric of the two principal themes. Lush, leisurely and luxuriant, it features a melody that begins this way. [**Piano demonstration.**] The theme features as well sinuous accompanimental lines that are, to my ear, the aural equivalent of the plant-inspired vocabulary of *art nouveau,* an art movement with which this sonata is exactly contemporary. Let's hear theme 2, after which we'll talk a bit about its harmonic language. Theme 2: [**Piano performance:** Scriabin, Piano Sonata No. 5, theme 2.]

Underpinning much of this magical second theme is the following harmony. [**Piano demonstration.**] Again. [**Piano demonstration.**] This harmony is an ever so slight variant of a harmony that has come to be known as Scriabin's "mystic chord." Here's the mystic chord. [**Piano demonstration.**] Again. [**Piano demonstration.**] Man oh man, if we all had a dollar for all the words that have said and written about Scriabin's mystic chord, not a one of us would ever have to work again. Let's add our words to the pot.

The "Mystic Chord"

As he matured, Scriabin's melodies and harmonies were increasingly built from variants of what has come to be known as the mystic chord. [**Piano demonstration.**] At a time when composers like Debussy, Schoenberg, and Stravinsky were all trying to break away from the expectations of traditional tonality, the mystic chord and its various permutations were Scriabin's harmonic solution, his way of creating a basic harmonic sound that existed outside of traditional tonality. [**Piano demonstration.**] The mystic chord just kind of sits there, doesn't it? It doesn't seem to imply consonance or tonal centricity; that is, no one of its pitches can be perceived as representing a state of rest. [**Piano demonstration.**] But neither is Scriabin's mystic chord dissonant in a tonal sense, in that it does not sound as if it needs to resolve. [**Piano demonstration.**]

In truth, the Mystic Chord is neither consonant nor dissonant; it represents neither rest nor tension; it just is. I explain. The tonal harmonic system had been the "sonar plexus" of the Western musical language since the 15th century. At its most basic, the tonal system is a metaphor for the complementary opposites that frame our existence: rise and fall, tension and release, activity and inactivity, struggle and repose, the turmoil of life and the eternal rest of death. At the heart of the tonal system are two harmonies or chords, one that represents tension. [**Piano demonstration.**] And the other, rest. [**Piano demonstration.**] Again, tension. [**Piano demonstration.**] Rest. [**Piano demonstration.**] Scriabin's mystic chord is constructed in such a way as to imply neither tension nor rest. [**Piano demonstration.**]

Scriabin himself did not call this harmony the mystic chord; that term was coined in 1916—after Scriabin's death—by the English music critic Arthur Hull. Scriabin called it "the chord of the pleroma." The chord of the pleroma? The Russian music scholar Richard Taruskin tries to help by explaining that:

> The *pleroma*, a Christian Gnostic term derived from the Greek for "plentitude," was the all-encompassing hierarchy of the divine realm, located entirely outside the physical universe, at immeasurable distance from man's earthly abode, totally alien and essentially "other" to the phenomenal world and whatever belongs to it. The "mystic chord", then, was designed by Scriabin to afford instant apprehension of—that is, to reveal, in the biblical sense— what was in essence beyond the mind of man to conceptualize. Its magical stillness was a mystical or Gnostic intimation of a hidden otherness, a world wholly above and beyond rational or emotional cognition, a musical symbol that establishes a nexus between external phenomenal reality and the higher nouminal reality called *realiora*, the "more real", the immobile non-temporal world of essences.

My friends, does that help? What all this means in real musical terms is that much of Scriabin's late music—reliant, as it is, on the mystic chord—is going to be characterized more by harmonic stasis than forward motion. In its mystic chord–created harmonic stasis, Scriabin's music will remind us of Debussy's on one hand and, philosophically at least, the mantra-like music of

India on the other. Back please to the exposition of Scriabin's Piano Sonata No. 5. Scriabin brings the exposition to its conclusion with a rousing bit of closing music based loosely on theme 1. Let's hear it. [**Piano performance:** Scriabin, Piano Sonata No. 5, exposition.]

Development Section

The Development Section is cast in three large parts. The first part features the introduction and theme 1; the second part features the introduction and theme t2; and the third part further expands on theme 2 as well as the closing material that concluded the exposition. Let's advance directly to part three.

Part three of the Development Section begins with an expansion of the closing material heard at the conclusion of the exposition and then concludes with a magisterial, teeth-rattling version of theme 2 that brings the development to its climax. Development section, part three. [**Piano performance:** Scriabin, Piano Sonata No. 5, development.]

Recapitulation

On paper, Scriabin's recapitulation is a textbook affair: Theme 1 returns, followed by the modulating bridge, theme 2, and the closing material. However—and I know you knew I was going to say this—there is nothing textbook about the way the recap actually sounds. Scriabin compresses everything: The introductory music is gone, and everything that follows is compressed and intensified, building inexorably to the grand climax that is the sonata-concluding coda. Let's hear the compressed recapitulation: What took roughly four minutes to pass in the exposition now takes just over two minutes to pass in the recapitulation. [**Piano performance:** Scriabin, Piano Sonata No. 5, recapitulation.]

Coda

Scriabin indicates that the Coda be played *con luminosita*, meaning "with luminosity." (Given its be-everywhere-on-the-keyboard-at-once virtuosity, one might suggest that the luminosity generated by the coda will be a result of digital ignition, as the pianist's arms and fingers combust.) Scriabin just loved to use expressive designations that referred to light and color. According to some commentators, such designations were not just expressive directives but references to Scriabin's presumed synesthesia.

Sidebar: Seeing Things

Much has been made about Scriabin's presumed synesthesia, a condition whereby Scriabin purportedly saw colors while listening to music. OK, Scriabin had a lot of issues my friends, but synesthesia was not one of them. The color system he invented and for which he is known—a system which associated certain colors with certain pitches—was a carefully worked-out scheme based on the circle of fifths and the primary colors as described by Sir Isaac Newton in his *Optics*, otherwise known as "ROY G. BIV": red, orange, yellow, green, blue, indigo, violet. In Scriabin's system, the note C was red; G (a fifth above) was orange; D (a fifth above G) was yellow; A was green, E was blue; B was indigo; and F-sharp was violet. The remaining five pitches of the chromatic collection described shades of purple progressing to rust, leading back to the red of the pitch C. (Which makes us wonder why there's no taupe.)

So much for Scriabin's storied color synesthesia; in reality, his color system was invented so that in the course of a musical performance colors could be projected that corresponded with the pitches being heard. To this end, he worked with an inventor named Alexander Mozer to create a "color organ" which, like so many of Scriabin's best-laid plans, never quite worked.

Back to the Coda

The coda is cast in four brief parts. The first part is based on theme 1; the second features a magisterial and throbbing version of theme 2; the third part—marked *presto*, meaning "very fast"—returns to theme 1; and the fourth part—which flies by in the blink of an eye—features the upward-ripping, dissonant gesture that began the sonata back in the introduction! Taken altogether, this coda constitutes an apotheosis: an ecstatic, barely disguised multiple orgasm that brings the Sonata to its conclusion. The coda: [**Piano performance:** Scriabin, Piano Sonata No. 5, coda.] Wow, wow, and wow. While the formal structure of Scriabin's piano sonata might be traditional, its musical content is something altogether different! My friends, crazy or no, Scriabin was an original. There's nothing else that sounds like this music.

A Man on a Mission

By the last years of his life, Aleksandr Scriabin had begun to identify more with God than with his fellow mortals. He kept diaries and notebooks in which he'd jot down his thoughts and ideas in a sort of poetic prose, writing things that seemed to indicate that he was indeed a few Bradys short of a bunch. For example:

> I am freedom, I am life, I am a dream, I am weariness, I am feeling,
> I am unceasing burning desire, I am bliss, I am insane passion, I am
> nothing, I am atremble, I am the world. I am wild flight, I am desire,
> I am light, I am creative ascent that tenderly caresses, that captivates,
> that sears, destroying, revivifying. I am raging torrents of unknown
> feelings, I am the boundary, I am the summit. I am nothing.

> I am God!

> I am nothing, I am play, I am freedom, I am life. I am the boundary,
> I am the peak.

> I am God!

> I am the blossoming,
> I am the bliss,
> I am all-consuming passion, all engulfing,
> I am fire enveloping the universe,
> Reducing it to chaos.
> I am the blind play of powers released.
> I am creation dormant, Intellect quenched.

And koo-koo ka-choo. The issue of Scriabin's post-1902 mental health raises a difficult question. Was the ongoing development of his messianic megalomania the necessary precondition for the sublime, amazing, and often revolutionary music he composed during the second half of his life? Like Beethoven's hearing disability, did mental health issues free Scriabin from the musical and social strictures of his time, and thus allow him to find a voice and inspiration within himself that he would never otherwise have found? Good questions. The musicologist and Scriabin scholar Hugh Macdonald offers this point of view on Scriabin's late music:

> There is clearly a close relation between the egomania of Scriabin's personality and the development of his music from the derivative, charming style of his youth to the powerfully progressive works of his last years. The weaknesses of his character—his capacity for self-delusion, his overbearing demands on others, and his undisguised conceit—are not to be imputed as weaknesses to his music. Scriabin believed in the coming regeneration of the world through a cataclysmic event; [and that] the new Nirvana would spring from his own promethean creativity. He even welcomed the outbreak of [World War I] in 1914 as an initial step towards cosmic regeneration.

One wonders, had Scriabin lived past 1915, if he would have continued to enthusiastically embrace the war, especially given its disastrous outcome for Russia.

What a Way to Go

For someone who came to consider himself a creative god, one whose music would bring an end to the universe as we know it and effect the transition to nirvana, Scriabin's death could not have been more absurdly mundane. On Saturday, April 4, 1915 Scriabin noticed a little pimple just above the upper right side of his lip. According to one writer, "The pimple became a pustule, then a carbuncle and again a furuncle." Meaning, my friends, a deep folliculitis: an infection of the hair follicle, most probably caused by the bacterium staphylococcus aureus.

Whatever we call what was a big, honkin' zit, in less than a week—on April 10—Scriabin was bedridden with a 106° fever. In those days before antibiotics, he was as good as dead. Attempts to drain the infection only made things worse, and he died of septicemia—blood poisoning—on April 14, 1915. Scriabin was just 43 years old. When the sculptor Merkulov arrived to make a death mask he could not, so swollen and scarred was Scriabin's face. So he made a cast of his right ear and right hand instead.

Thank you.

Rachmaninoff—*Études-tableaux*
Lecture 21

Sergey Rachmaninoff is often referred to as Tchaikovsky's "heir" and the last of the Russian romantic composers. Like Tchaikovsky, Rachmaninoff's music is dominated by its luxuriant thematic melody. Unlike Tchaikovsky, Rachmaninoff's melodic palette leans toward the elegiac—more often than not, dark and brooding—and in this way, it sounds stereotypically "Russian." In this lecture, you will be exposed to a selected number of the **études** in Rachmaninoff's *Études-tableaux* by first identifying their programmatic content and then observing—where appropriate—what aspect, or aspects, of pianism are exploited in each work.

A Study of Pictures

- A piece of music called an étude—or "study"—is one that exploits some aspect or aspects of instrumental technique. Before the 19th century, keyboard études were nothing but finger exercises. That all changed in the 1830s with the piano études of Frédéric Chopin and Franz Liszt, whose études are both technical studies and superbly wrought musical compositions.

- Sergey Rachmaninoff (1873–1943) took things yet another step in his two sets of *Études-tableaux*—"picture studies"—of Opus 33 and 39, completed in 1911 and 1917, respectively. Each of the 17 études (eight in Op. 33 and nine in Op. 39) is, in some way, programmatic: Each evokes a particular mood, paints a picture, or tells a story.

- In a letter to the Italian composer Ottorino Respighi, Rachmaninoff indicated, for example, that Op. 33, no. 7 represents a fair; Op. 39, no. 2 depicts the sea and seagulls; and Op. 39, no. 6 depicts the story of Little Red Riding Hood.

- No matter what the mood or picture being painted, Rachmaninoff's *Études-tableaux* are filled through and through with his extraordinary pianism. Rachmaninoff was one of the greatest pianists who ever lived, and at six feet and six inches tall, he had the frame and the hands to seemingly cover the entire keyboard all at once.

- Rachmaninoff's title, *Études-tableaux*, indicates that these compositions are both keyboard "studies" and programmatic works. Rachmaninoff, who was generally loath to identify programmatic specifics in his music, did indeed identify the programmatic content of 5 of the 18 études in a letter to the Italian composer Ottorino Respighi, who orchestrated them in 1929 at the request of Serge Koussevitzky, the conductor of the Boston Symphony Orchestra. Our thanks to Maestro Rachmaninoff for thus making things easy for us, as we will examine the five études he identified.

Sergey Rachmaninoff (1873–1943) was a piano prodigy, with a phenomenal memory and the ability to almost instantly memorize any music.

© Etincelles/Wikimedia Commons/Public Domain.

Étude-tableau, Op. 39, No. 6: "Little Red Riding Hood and the Wolf"

- The sixth étude of Op. 39, which depicts the story of Little Red Riding Hood, is an example of Rachmaninoff's picture painting and his pianism. The étude begins with two snarls low in the piano. A skittish Little Red Riding Hood is depicted high in the piano, with rapid right-hand figuration.

- After Little Red Riding Hood's entrance and her initial "conversation" with the wolf, for the next minute and a half or so, the wolf does most of the "talking." As the étude proceeds, a sense of terrible danger increasingly pervades its expressive atmosphere. The piece concludes with Little Red Riding Hood's increasingly panicked music, followed by one last ominous bit of the wolf's music.

- In the version of the story Rachmaninoff sets, there's no woodsman conveniently strolling by to rescue Little Red Riding Hood. The wolf has the last word—or snarl, as the case may be—as he swallows the inquisitive little girl whole, followed by a self-satisfied belch.

Étude-tableau, Op. 33, No. 6: "The Fair"

- Like almost all of the *Études-tableaux*, Op. 33, no. 6 is cast as a three-part, A–B–A form. We can assume, based on the joyful character of this étude, that Rachmaninoff liked fairs.

- The étude projects two programmatic elements. The first is the hustle and bustle of activity of the fair itself: a sensory feast depicted by a tremendous amount of musical activity, in particularly long swatches of rapidly moving chords and tremolos in the pianist's right hand. The second programmatic element is quite personal, and that would be Rachmaninoff's own emotional reaction to the sights and sounds of the fair: a joyful excitement projected by the fanfare-like nature of the thematic material and the key of E-flat major, in which the étude is set.

- The B section that follows offers a playful contrast before the rocking-and-rolling return of the final A section brings the étude to its conclusion.

- As an étude, Op. 33, no. 6 is primarily a study in endurance—those long, rapid tremolos and shifting chords in the right hand are oxygen-depleting, lactose acid–inducing killers—and balance, as the pianist must project all the myriad parts of the piece (of the "fair") without garbling them into a mass of undifferentiated slop (which is no small challenge).

Étude-tableau, Op. 39, No. 2: "The Sea and the Seagulls"

- The expressive mood Rachmaninoff projects in this étude is the polar opposite of "The Fair"; in "The Sea and the Seagulls," he projects a mood of bleak desolation.

- The construction of this étude is simplicity itself. It consists of two basic elements. The first is a steady, rolling triplet line heard initially in the pianist's left hand.

- These sorts of steady-state triplets are stereotypical water-and-wave music, and they are heard—in one hand or the other—throughout almost the entire étude. Hints of the *Dies Irae*, the Catholic prayer for the dead, imbue this water-and-wave music with a deathly pallor.

- The second element of the étude is "the birds," which are depicted in a long-breathed melody that virtually floats above the triplets. Rachmaninoff achieves this floating effect by projecting two separate rhythmic strata: The melody representing the birds does not line up rhythmically with the water-and-wave triplets below.

- Slowly but inexorably, this melancholy music builds up to a despairing, angst-filled climax, and increasingly quiet music follows. From that point, the étude concludes as it began, hushed and desolate.

Étude-tableau, Op. 39, No. 7: "Funeral March"

- In his letter to Ottorino Respighi, Rachmaninoff described this étude as: "A funeral march. The initial theme is a march; the other theme represents the singing of a choir. Beginning with the sixteenth notes in C Minor, a fine rain is suggested, incessant and hopeless. This movement culminates [in] the chimes of a church."

- The opening theme represents the funeral march, and the second theme represents the singing of the chorus. It is the rain—a rain of tears, one that starts out as a drizzle but becomes a cataclysmic torrent—that drives this étude to its climax.

- The harmonic language of the funeral march sections is extremely advanced. It is a harmonic language most reminiscent of that employed by Rachmaninoff's friend and Moscow Conservatory classmate, the pianist and composer Alexander Scriabin.

- In fact, the musical connection between this étude and Scriabin's music is not coincidental. Something Rachmaninoff failed to tell Respighi was that this étude was inspired by Scriabin's funeral, which occurred not long before Rachmaninoff composed the étude.

- Rachmaninoff biographers Sergei Bertesson and Jay Leyda wrote: "On April 14, [1915], Alexander Scriabin died of blood poisoning. Years later, Rachmaninoff [still] recalled the minute details of Scriabin's funeral—the rain, the crowd, the fresh grave—and his decision that day to devote his tour of the coming season to Scriabin's piano works."

Étude-tableau, Op. 39, No. 9: "March"

- This march, heroic and virtuosic, provides a fittingly explosive conclusion to the *Études-tableaux*. Once it gets off the ground, the march features a single rhythmic idea: an eighth note followed by two sixteenth notes. This rhythm is punched out over and over again with the ferocity of a Muhammad Ali left jab.

- However, the rhythm keeps shifting relative to the meter; sometimes the eighth note falls on the beat, and sometimes the sixteenth note falls on the beat. The result is a fabulous concoction of rhythmic ambiguity and shifting accent—a powerfully rhythmic march that can't quite seem to stay in rhythm.

Rachmaninoff—*Études-tableaux*
Lecture 21—Transcript

Welcome back to *The 23 Greatest Solo Piano Works*. This is Lecture 21. It is entitled Rachmaninoff—*Études-tableaux*.

A piece of music called an étude—or "study"—is one that exploits some aspect or aspects of instrumental technique. Before the 19th century, keyboard études were really nothing but finger exercises. That all changed in the 1830s with the piano études of Frédéric Chopin and Franz Liszt, whose études are both technical studies and superbly wrought musical compositions.

Sergei Rachmaninoff (1873–1943) took things yet another step in his two sets of *Étude-tableaux*—"picture studies"—of Op. 33 and 39, completed, respectively, in 1911 and 1917. You see, each of the 17 études (eight in Op. 33 and nine in Op. 39) is, in some way, programmatic: Each evokes a particular mood, paints a picture, or tells a story. In a letter to the Italian composer Ottorino Respighi, Rachmaninoff indicated, for example, that Op. 33, No. 7 represents a fair; Op. 39, No. 2 depicts the sea and seagulls; and that Op. 39, No. 6 depicts the story of Little Red Riding Hood. No matter what the mood or picture being painted, Rachmaninoff's Étude Tableaux are rent through and through with his extraordinary pianism. Rachmaninoff was one of the greatest pianists who ever lived, and at six-foot-six he had the frame and the hands to seemingly cover the entire keyboard all at once.

Now I suspect you stopped listening carefully when I told you that the sixth étude of Op. 39 depicts the story of Little Red Riding Hood, so let's immediately turn to that étude as an example of Rachmaninoff's "picture painting" and his pianism. The étude begins with two snarls low in the piano: "So nice to see you, my dear!" [**Piano performance:** Rachmaninoff, *Études-tableaux*, Op. 39, No. 6.] A skittish Little Red Riding Hood is depicted high in the piano, with rapid right-hand figuration. Let's hear her entrance and her initial conversation with the wolf, from the beginning. [**Piano performance:** Rachmaninoff, *Études-tableaux*, Op. 39, No. 6.]

For the next minute and twenty seconds or so, the wolf does most of the talking: "Mm-mm, you do smell fine … a plumpalicious happy meal on two legs. Come on over here and let grandmamma give you a little bite … I mean kiss!" Yes indeed: As the étude proceeds, a sense of terrible danger increasingly pervades its expressive atmosphere! **[Piano performance:** Rachmaninoff, *Études-tableaux*, Op. 39, No. 6.]

The piece concludes with Little Red Riding Hood's increasingly panicked music—"what large incisors you have, Grandma!"—followed by one last, ominous bit of the wolf's music: "Big teeth I've got, toots … now, snack time!" In the version of the story Rachmaninoff sets, there's no woodsman conveniently strolling by to rescue Red Riding Hood. The wolf has the last word—or snarl, as the case may be—as he swallows the inquisitive little girl whole, followed by what I take to be a self-satisfied belch. **[Piano demonstration.]** **[Piano performance:** Rachmaninoff, *Études-tableaux*, Op. 39, No. 6.]

Early Life

Sergei Vasilievich Rachmaninoff was born on April 1 (some sources say April 2), 1873 in the Russian village of Semyonovo, roughly 100 miles south of St. Petersburg. He died—as did so many Europeans artists of his generation—an expatriate, in Beverly Hills, California, on March 28, 1943. His family had been in the service of the Tsars since the 1500s. As such, they were considered to be of the old aristocracy, although by the time Sergei was born most of the family money was gone.

Sergei's father Vasily was an army officer and an amateur pianist; his mother Lyubov was an accomplished amateur pianist as well. Altogether, Vasily and Lyubov had six children: three boys and three girls. Sergei was the middle of the three boys. History has been unkind to Rachmaninoff's father; sources refer to him variously as "a wastrel," a "skirt chaser," a "pathological liar," a "compulsive gambler," "always conceiving grandiose projects, usually of a business nature, which cost him vast sums of money and were either never realized or suffered sudden collapse." It was in this way that Vasily Rachmaninoff squandered what was left of the family's property. In 1882— when Sergei was just nine—the last of that property was sold in a public auction and the family moved to a small flat in St. Petersburg.

Sergei had begun piano lessons five years earlier, at the age of four. By the time he moved to St. Petersburg, his prodigious talent was obvious to everyone. Sergei's mother wanted him to attend the St. Petersburg Conservatory, something that his father was adamantly against. Rachmaninoff remembered, "[For my father], the thought that [I] should become a musician was intolerable, [claiming that] this 'proletarian profession' was entirely unsuited for the son of a nobleman."

Vasily wanted Sergei to go to military school. But military school was expensive: Bribes had to be paid for admission; a commission had to be purchased and the requisite equipment and clothing had to be bought. And Vasily Rachmaninoff was broke. So in 1883, the 10-year-old Sergei was indeed admitted to the St. Petersburg Conservatory. His father, mortified by the turn of events, walked out and moved to Moscow. Rachmaninoff's parents did not divorce—that was out of the question given the strictures of the Orthodox Church—but they never saw each other again.

I wish I could tell you that Rachmaninoff's three years at the St. Petersburg Conservatory saw one triumph after another, but I cannot. He missed his father. He hated living in a little flat in the middle of a stinking city after having grown up on an estate with servants. His mother became clinically depressed, and so he was increasingly cared for by his maternal grandmother, who spoiled him rotten. He stopped practicing; played hooky (and possibly hockey as well; Rachmaninoff was an avid skater); he failed his general education classes and then attempted to cover it all up by altering his report cards, grade hacking by any other name. Professor Nikolai Rimsky-Korsakov called it all an act of "purely Russian self-delusion and laziness."

At wits' end, Rachmaninoff's mother consulted with Alexander Siloti, Sergei's first cousin and a former student of none other than Franz Liszt. She asked what she could possibly do. Siloti's concise answer was as follows: "There is only one person who can help; it is my former teacher, [Nikolai] Sverev, in Moscow. The boy must come under his discipline." Madame Rachmaninoff meekly accepted this oracular sentence. She decided to place the boy under Sverev's rod of correction at the Moscow Conservatory the following autumn.

In August of 1885, the 12-year-old Rachmaninoff was packed off to Moscow where he moved into Sverev's house. He later recalled, "I entered [the] house with a faint heart, having heard a great deal about his unbridled severity. I felt that my golden days of youth and freedom had come to an end." Rachmaninoff need not have worried. Sverev might have been a despot with a temper, but he was also a humane, intelligent, and generous man. (For our information, Sverev never accepted a ruble for Rachmaninoff's board and lessons; he bought his students their school uniforms and took them to every concert and opera that he himself attended.)

OK, now we can say it: Rachmaninoff's years at the Moscow Conservatory were marked by one triumph after another. Rachmaninoff was a piano prodigy, with a phenomenal memory and the ability to sight-read and almost instantly memorize any music. His classmate Alexander Goldenweiser remembered, "Whatever composition was ever mentioned—piano, orchestra, operatic, or other—by a classical or contemporary composer, if Rachmaninoff had at any time heard it, he played it as if it were a work he had studied thoroughly."

Rachmaninoff impressed everyone he met in Moscow, including Peter Tchaikovsky, whom Rachmaninoff claimed was his single greatest influence as a composer. (The respect was mutual. In 1886, when Rachmaninoff was just 13, Tchaikovsky sat on the jury of a composition competition in which Rachmaninoff was participating. The highest possible grade was a 5. Tchaikovsky gave Rachmaninoff a 5, and then put four plusses around the 5—one above, one below, and one on either side. As Rachmaninoff later—and proudly—recalled: "This five with four plus marks—a unique occurrence in the annals of the Conservatory—was naturally much discussed, and the story made the round of all Moscow.") When Rachmaninoff graduated from the Conservatory at the age of 19 in 1892, he became only the third person to receive the "Great Gold Medal" upon graduation.

The "Modern" Piano

In 1851, a German cabinet maker named Heinrich Engelhard Steinweg and four of his sons emigrated from the German city of Braunschweig to New York City. Two years later—in 1853—he and his sons founded a piano company and dubbed it Steinway and Sons. In 1872, Steinway bridged the technological gap between proto-modern pianos and what today is considered the fully modern piano when it patented something called duplex scaling, which enhanced the power and resonance of the piano by lengthening the strings and allowing the undamped portion of the strings to vibrate sympathetically.

When Rachmaninoff was born in 1873, no one there in Semyonovo would have guessed that half a world away an event was taking place that would significantly shape Rachmaninoff's future life as an artist. The event? Steinway opened a piano factory in Astoria, in the northwest corner of what today is the borough of Queens, to manufacture its modern pianos, pianos that would ultimately define Sergei Rachmaninoff as both a composer and as a pianist.

Some background. The first pianos were made by a harpsichord builder named Bartolomeo Cristofori around the year 1700. These instruments were small, tinny-sounding, and breakable. The history of the piano between 1700 and 1860—between Cristofori and Heinrich (or "Henry") Steinway—was about making the instruments bigger, more resonant, and more sturdy.

The great experimental decade of the piano was the 1820s, when builders began making iron harp frames (called plates) that allowed for thicker and more numerous strings. (For our information: In a modern concert grand piano, string tension exceeds 20 tons. Let's not even think about what would happen to a wooden harp frame if it had to resist 40,000 pounds of tension!) By 1860, Steinway's almost-modern pianos were taking the American market by storm. In 1860 the following notice appeared in *Frank Leslie's Illustrated News*, the *Time* magazine of its day.

Until the last three of four years Erard's Grand Pianos took the first rank in the world. A large number were imported to this country, and they held undisputed sway in the concert-room. The Steinways commenced making grand pianos about four years [ago], and succeeded well with the very first, since which time they have added improvement after improvement, until at this time [they] have completely overshadowed the fame of the Erards and almost driven it out of the market. In depth, volume, and brilliance of tone they surpass the Erard's, while in point of 'touch'—in which Erard's were supposed to be unapproachable—[the Steinways] are fully its equal. Steinway's grands are really grand in every point of view, and cannot be surpassed by any similar instrument in the world.

Lest we think this just gratuitous ad copy, let's reflect on Steinway's two great competitors at the time: Erard of Paris and Chickering of Boston. Has anyone within earshot of my voice ever played an Erard? A Chickering? After years of decline, Erard went out of business in 1971 and its name was bought by the German maker Schimmel. Chickering was bought out by the American Piano Company (also known as "Ampico") in 1908. While "Chickering" lives on as a trade name, the Chickering piano company does not.

We have spent this bit of time talking about the firm of Steinway & Sons because Steinway pianos—those built in New York and later in Germany—were the instruments that more than any other defined the so-called Russian School of piano playing, a school in which Rachmaninoff was arguably the greatest member. The Russian School of piano playing began with Anton Grigorevich Rubinstein, who lived from 1829 to 1894. As a pianist, Rubinstein is ranked beside Franz Liszt as one the great virtuosos of the 19th century. A man and musician of intelligence, he was known for the primal power of his playing, a pianistic force of nature he was. According to Harold Schonberg, Rubinstein's playing was characterized by "extraordinary breadth, virility and vitality, immense sonority and technical grandeur." In 1886, the 13-year-old Rachmaninoff had the opportunity to hear Rubinstein perform his famous historical concerts. We'll let Rachmaninoff tell the story:

He presented a complete survey of the works of Bach, the old Italians, Mozart, Beethoven, and Chopin, up to Liszt and the Russian Moderns. The concerts took place on seven Tuesday evenings. On Wednesday mornings he repeated the whole program for the benefit of students. [I] was present at both series of performances [and thus] heard the programs twice. I stored up wonderful memories, with which no others in my experience can compare.

It was not so much his magnificent technique that held one spellbound as [it was his] profound, spiritually refined musicianship, which spoke from every note and every bar he played, and singled him out as the most unequalled pianist in the world. Naturally I never missed a note, and I remember how deeply affected I was. One listened entranced, so unique was the beauty of tone he drew from the keys.

Rubinstein's impact on the Russian piano community was singular. He founded the St. Petersburg Conservatory in 1862 and oversaw the founding of the Moscow Conservatory in 1866. His views regarding piano pedagogy and piano playing and interpretation became gospel at both institutions, and remain so in Russia to this day. Rubinstein's piano? Starting in 1872, a Steinway.

In 1872 and 1873, Rubinstein toured the United States, giving 215 concerts in 239 days. The tour was arranged by Steinway & Sons, and—of course—he played Steinway pianos. In doing so, he became the first "Steinway Artist": the first pianist who contractually obligated himself to publicly perform on a Steinway piano if one was available. Rubinstein's style of playing was perfectly served by the Steinways, which were (and are) as robust and nuanced as his playing. Thus the style of playing that Rubinstein initiated—known today as the Russian piano school—was predicated on having an instrument capable of the extremes of expression defined by the school. That instrument was the modern piano, and the first fully modern piano was a Steinway.

Rachmaninoff: The Man and Composer

Rachmaninoff is often referred to as Tchaikovsky's heir and the last of the Russian romantic composers. As far as generalizations go, we can live with both of these. Like Tchaikovsky, Rachmaninoff's music is dominated by its luxuriant thematic melody. Unlike Tchaikovsky, Rachmaninoff's melodic palette leans towards the elegiac—more often than not, dark and brooding—and in this way it sounds stereotypically "Russian" (my friends, can we imagine comedy skits by Rachmaninoff's spiritual brothers Tolstoy and Dostoevsky? *Nyet*!). Rachmaninoff—a rather grim and extremely quiet man—himself admitted "bright [expressive] tones do not come easily to me." Rachmaninoff's taciturn nature is wonderfully described by his fellow Russian, the composer Igor Stravinsky, who recalled:

> The last time I saw that awesome man he had come to my house in Hollywood [California] bearing me the gift of a pail of honey. I was not especially friendly with Rachmaninoff at the time, nor, I think, was anyone else: social relations with a man of Rachmaninoff's temperament require more perseverance than I can afford: he was merely bringing me some honey. It is curious, however, that I should meet him NOT in Russia, though I OFTEN heard him perform there in my youth, but in Hollywood. Some people achieve a kind of immortality just by the totality with which they possess some characteristic. Rachmaninoff's immortalizing totality was his scowl. He was a six-and-a-half-foot-tall scowl. I suppose my conversations with him, or rather, with his wife—for he was always silent—were typical:
>
> Madame Rachmaninoff: "[Monsieur Stravinsky], what is the first thing you do when you rise in the morning?"
>
> [My response]: "For fifteen minutes I do exercises taught me by a Hungarian gymnast and maniac or, rather, I did them until I learned that the Hungarian had died very young and very suddenly. Then I take a shower."
>
> Madame Rachmaninoff: "You see, Sergei, Stravinsky takes showers. How extraordinary! [Sergei], do you still say that you are afraid of them? And you heard Stravinsky say that he exercises? What do you think of that? Shame on you who will hardly take a walk!"
>
> [Rachmaninoff's response]: (Silence).

We must assume that Rachmaninoff saved his mojo for his compositions and the concert stage. Harold Schonberg—senior music critic of the *New York Times* for 20 years—had the opportunity to hear Rachmaninoff in concert when he—Schonberg—was a young man. Writing many years later, Schonberg was still all aglow:

> There was nobody like him. Rachmaninoff would come on stage stiff and severe, never smiling, with his hair cropped as close as a convict's. With terrible dignity he would seat himself and wait for the audience to quiet. He played with a minimum of physical exertion, brooding over the keys. From his fingers came an indescribable tone: warm, projecting into every corner of the hall, capable of infinite modulation. When Rachmaninoff played, everything was perfectly planned, perfectly proportioned. Melodies were outlined with radiant authority; inner voices were brought out in chamber music style. And those marvelous fingers seemed incapable of striking a wrong note. In an age of spectacular technicians, Rachmaninoff was peerless.

Rachmaninoff: *Études-tableaux*

Rachmaninoff's title—*Études-tableaux*—indicates that these compositions are both keyboard studies and programmatic works. We will approach a selected number of the études from both points of view by first identifying their programmatic content and then observing—where appropriate—what aspect (or aspects) of pianism are exploited in each work.

As we observed early on in this lecture, Rachmaninoff—who was generally loath to identify programmatic specifics in his music—did indeed identify the programmatic content of five of the 18 études in a letter to the Italian composer Ottorino Respighi, who orchestrated them in 1929 at the request of Serge Koussevitzky, the conductor if the Boston Symphony Orchestra. Our thanks to Maestro Rachmaninoff for thus making things easy for us, as we will examine the five études he identified. We've already looked at and listened to Op. 39, No. 6: "Little Red Riding Hood and the Wolf"; onward then to the other four.

Études-tableaux Op. 33, No. 6: "The Fair"

Some editions call this No. 7. Six or 7, we will call it "The Fair." Like most all of the *Études-tableaux*, Op. 33, No. 6 is cast as a three-part, A-B-A form. We can assume, based on the joyful character of this étude, that Rachmaninoff liked fairs. The étude projects two programmatic elements. The first is the hustle and bustle of activity of the fair itself: a sensory feast depicted by a tremendous amount of musical activity, in particular long swatches of rapidly moving chords and tremolos in the pianist's right hand. The second programmatic element is quite personal, and that would be Rachmaninoff's own emotional reaction to the sights and sounds of the fair: a joyful excitement projected by the fanfare-like nature of the thematic material and the key of E-flat Major in which the étude is set. Let's hear the opening A section of Op. 33, No. 6: "The Fair." For these excerpts, we've used a licensed recording. [**Piano recording:** Rachmaninoff, *Études-tableaux*, Op. 33, No. 6.] The B section that follows offers up a playful contrast before the rockin' and rollin' return of the final A section brings the étude to its conclusion. Let's hear the remainder of the étude, starting with the playful B section.

As an étude, Op. 33, No. 6 is primarily a study in endurance—those long, rapid tremolos and shifting chords in the right hand are oxygen-depleting, lactose acid–inducing killers—and balance, as the pianist must project all the myriad parts of the piece (of the fair) without garbling them into a mass of undifferentiated slop. No small challenge, that.

Études-tableaux Op. 39, No. 2: "The Sea and the Seagulls"

The expressive mood Rachmaninoff projects in this étude is the polar opposite of "the fair"; in "the sea and seagulls" he projects a mood of bleak desolation. The construction of this étude is simplicity itself (but then again, so is the construction of a light bulb: Shove some electrons through a tungsten filament and light is emitted in a de facto continuous spectrum; duh). The étude consists of two basic elements. The first is a steady, rolling, triplet line heard initially in the pianist's left hand. [**Piano demonstration.**]

These sorts of steady-state triplets are stereotypical water-and-wave music, and they are heard—in one hand or the other—throughout almost the entire étude. Hints of the *Dies Irae*—the Catholic prayer for the dead—imbue this water-and-wave music with a deathly pallor. [**Piano demonstration.**]

The second element of the étude is the birds: They are depicted in a long-breathed melody that virtually floats above the triplets. Rachmaninoff achieves this floating effect by projecting two separate rhythmic strata: You see, the melody representing the birds does not line up rhythmically with the water-and-wave triplets below. Let's listen to the opening of the étude and you'll hear exactly what I'm talking about. [**Piano performance:** Rachmaninoff, *Études-tableaux*, Op. 39, No. 2.] Slowly but inexorably, this melancholy music builds up to a despairing, angst-filled climax. Let's hear that climax and the increasingly quiet music that follows. [**Piano performance:** Rachmaninoff, *Études-tableaux*, Op. 39, No. 2.] From that point the étude concludes as it began, hushed and desolate.

Études-tableaux Op. 39, No. 7: "Funeral March"

In his letter to Ottorino Respighi, Rachmaninoff described this étude as "a funeral march. The initial theme is a march; the other theme represents the singing of a choir. Beginning with the sixteenth notes in C Minor, a fine rain is suggested, incessant and hopeless. This movement culminates [in] the chimes of a church." The opening theme—the one that represents the funeral march—begins this way. [**Piano performance:** Rachmaninoff, *Études-tableaux*, Op. 39, No. 7.] The second theme—the one that would represent the singing of the chorus—begins this way. [**Piano performance:** Rachmaninoff, *Études-tableaux*, Op. 39, No. 7.]

It is the rain—a rain of tears, one that starts out as a drizzle but becomes a cataclysmic torrent—that drives this étude to its climax. Here's how the rain begins. [**Piano performance:** Rachmaninoff, *Études-tableaux*, Op. 39, No. 7.] And here's the torrential climax and conclusion of the étude. [**Piano performance:** Rachmaninoff, *Études-tableaux*, Op. 39, No. 7.]

The harmonic language of the funeral march sections is extremely advanced. It is a harmonic language most reminiscent of that employed by

Rachmaninoff's friend and Moscow Conservatory classmate, the pianist and composer Alexander Scriabin. In fact, the musical connection between this étude and Scriabin's music is not coincidental. Something Rachmaninoff failed to tell Respighi was that this étude was inspired by Scriabin's funeral, which occurred not long before Rachmaninoff composed the étude. Rachmaninoff biographers Sergei Bertesson and Jay Leyda wrote: "On April 14, [1915], Alexander Scriabin died of blood poisoning. Years later, Rachmaninoff [still] recalled the minute details of Scriabin's funeral—the rain, the crowd, the fresh grave—and his decision that day to devote his tour of the coming season to Scriabin's piano works."

Études-tableaux Op. 39, No. 9: "March"

This march—heroic and finger-bustingly virtuosic—provides a fittingly explosive conclusion to the *Études-tableaux*. Once it gets off the ground, the march features a single rhythmic idea: an eighth-note followed by two sixteenth notes. [**Demonstration.**] This rhythm is punched out over and over again with the ferocity of an Ali left jab. However, the rhythm keeps shifting relative to the meter; sometimes the eighth-note falls on the beat [**demonstration**], and sometimes the sixteenth notes fall on the beat [**demonstration**]. The result is a fabulous concoction of rhythmic ambiguity and shifting accent: a powerfully rhythmic march that can't quite seem to stay in rhythm! Let's hear the étude—this "study in sheer difficulty"—in its entirety. [**Piano performance:** Rachmaninoff, *Études-tableaux*, Op. 39, No. 9.]

Final Words

Rachmaninoff maintained his base of operations in Moscow until 1917. Following the Bolshevik Revolution in October of 1917, Rachmaninoff knew his days in Russia were numbered. On December 22, 1917, he left Russia with his family, never to return. After brief stops in Stockholm and Copenhagen, the clan put down their roots in the United States, first in New York City and finally in Beverly Hills, where Rachmaninoff bought a house at 610 Elm Drive (yes, it's still there). He died in Beverly Hills—of acute melanoma—on March 28, 1943. He had become an American citizen exactly eight weeks before, on February 1.

He was buried in Kensico Cemetery, in Valhalla New York, in Westchester County. Kensico was a well-known final resting place for the rich and the famous, and among Rachmaninoff's neighbors are Anne Bancroft, Paddy Chayevsky, Tommy Dorsey, Danny Kaye, Ayn Rand, Beverly Sills, Florenz Ziegfeld, and Lou Gehrig. While we would hope that Rachmaninoff would be pleased to rest in such company, we suspect that—in fact—he continues to scowl.

Thank you.

Prokofiev—Piano Sonata No. 7
Lecture 22

Not including six juvenile piano sonatas and one left unfinished at his death, Sergey Prokofiev completed nine numbered piano sonatas. They are, collectively, the cornerstone of the 20th-century piano sonata literature. Prokofiev composed his Piano Sonata no. 7 in 1942. On paper, it looks like a traditional, classically proportioned piano sonata. Like Mozart's piano sonatas, it is cast in three movements, with a first movement in sonata form, a slow second movement, and a brilliant third movement finale. In terms of its actual musical content, Prokofiev's Piano Sonata no. 7 has nothing to do with 18th-century classicalism—it is new 20th-century music.

Prokofiev's Public versus Private Works

- By 1939, Prokofiev had come to realize that he was going to have to be two composers in one: With one hand, he would write explicitly "Soviet" works—public works that satisfied the ideologues—while, with the other hand, he would compose the music that he wanted to compose—private works that would be tolerated in light of the more patriotic stuff.

- In the fall of 1939, Prokofiev was working on a cantata for chorus and orchestra subtitled "Hail to Stalin," a work intended as a tribute to "the great leader and teacher" on the occasion of his 60th birthday. At the same time, he was composing his Piano Sonatas nos. 6, 7, and 8, each of which is pure modern Prokofiev and a masterwork.

- These three sonatas are generally referred to as Prokofiev's "War Sonatas," despite the fact that he began all of them long before the Soviet Union went to war with Germany in June of 1941. Piano Sonata no. 6 was completed in 1940, no. 7 in 1942, and no. 8 in 1944. They remain among the most modernistic piano works Prokofiev ever composed.

- Some commentators—running with the "War Sonata" idea for all its worth—attempt to ascribe their astringent musical language and expressive power to the war itself. For example, the pianist and Yale School of Music professor Boris Berman writes in his book *The Piano Sonatas of Prokofiev* that: "While the Sixth Sonata reflects the nervous anticipation of World War II and the Eighth looks back to those terrible events retrospectively, the Seventh Sonata projects the anguish and the struggle of the war years as they were experienced in real time."

At the age of 13, Sergey Prokofiev (1891–1953) and his mother moved to St. Petersburg so that he could attend the St. Petersburg Conservatory, where he spent 10 years.

- Whatever "anguish" Prokofiev might have been feeling when he began his Piano Sonata no. 7 in 1939 had nothing to do with a war that hadn't yet begun—but it might very well have had a lot to do with a war for his own soul.

- Prokofiev completed the Piano Sonata no. 7 in April of 1942. Despite the titular claim that the piece is in "B-flat major," the sonata is overall dark and ominous in mood. The sonata is cast in three movements.

Movement 1

- The first movement is set in sonata form, meaning that two contrasting themes will be presented in the opening section (the exposition), and they will then, in some way, be developed in the development section and recapitulated in the recapitulation.

- Prokofiev's theme 1 is an angular, ferocious, and grotesque march that begins without an introduction and sounds nothing like the home key B-flat major.

- Among Prokofiev's oldest friends and most important artistic collaborators was the theater director, actor, and producer Vsevolod Meyerhold. In 1938, Meyerhold and Prokofiev began a collaboration to create a new opera entitled *Semyon Kotko*. On June 20, 1939—just as Prokofiev was completing the score—the 65-year-old Meyerhold was arrested, a victim of Stalin's Great Terror. He was brutally tortured and then executed by firing squad seven-and-a-half months after his arrest, on February 3, 1940.

- Meyerhold's wife, the actress Zinaida Raikh, fared even worse. On the night of July 15, 1939, 25 days after Meyerhold's arrest, "unknown assailants" broke into her apartment. Dmitri Shostakovich describes what happened: "They killed her. Seventeen knife wounds; she was stabbed in the eyes. Raikh screamed for a long time, but none of the neighbors came to her aid. No one dared go into Meyerhold's apartment."

- Nothing was taken from the apartment. The assailants—of course—were never found. Instead, the apartment was split into two, and the "new" apartments were given to two ranking members of the NKVD, the precursor to the KGB.

- Prokofiev was stunned by the deaths of Meyerhold and Raikh. If he had chosen "not to see" before, he could not hide from the truth now: that he had voluntarily returned to a society of unspeakable brutality and that in doing so he had put not just himself but his family—his wife and two sons—in terrible danger.

- Just weeks after Zinaika Raikh's murder, Prokofiev was "informed" that he would compose a cantata entitled "Hail to Stalin" in celebration of Stalin's 60th birthday. And just weeks after that, Prokofiev began composing his Piano Sonatas nos. 6, 7, and 8. It is the opinion of Prokofiev biographer David Jaffé that: "having forced himself to compose a cheerful evocation of the 'nirvana' Stalin wanted everyone to believe he had created [in "Hail to Stalin," Prokofiev then, in these three sonatas], expressed his true feelings."

- Back to the first movement, in sonata form, of Prokofiev's Piano Sonata no. 7. Following a relatively quiet modulating bridge, an expansive and introspective theme 2 emerges. Like theme 1, theme 2 is essentially nontonal, and the themes share a similar opening contour. Here's the melodic "contour" that initiates theme 1.

- The resemblance between the themes notwithstanding, there is a fundamental contrast between them. Theme 1 is a grotesquerie, a caricature of brutal, militant force. Theme 2 is a pained and personal rumination on that brutality, entirely introverted in its expressive effect.

- A thrumming, increasingly loud and dramatic passage of closing music concludes the exposition and leads directly into the dissonant, frenzied, theme 1–dominated development section, music that can—without any fear of overstatement—be equated to Prokofiev's battle for his own soul.

- The recapitulation begins not with theme 1 but, rather, with the modulating bridge. An abbreviated version of theme 2 follows. The coda that concludes the movement, based on theme 1, ends not with a bang but with an unsettling whimper. "Exhaustion" is the word that best fits these final moments—physical and spiritual exhaustion.

Movement 2

- Prokofiev's second movement is a 6-minute-long cry of pain. The opening and closing A sections are based on a song by Robert Schumann entitled "Sadness," from his cycle *Liederkreis*, Op. 39 of 1840. Prokofiev's second movement and Schumann's song begin the same way—set in the same key, E major.

- The words of Schumann's song—and, therefore, the words Prokofiev tacitly implies at the beginning of the second movement—would seem to have been custom made for Prokofiev's own state of mind. The following are the words, by the poet Joseph Eichendorff.

> I can sometimes sing
> as if I were happy,
> but secretly tears well up.
>
> The nightingales
> sing their songs of unfulfilled longing
> from the depths of their dungeons.
>
> Everyone delights who listens,
> because they do not understand the pain:
> the deep sorrow of the song.

- As the second movement progresses, the quiet, Schumann-inspired opening evolves into a terrible and sustained cry of pain and sorrow. This climactic shriek is followed by the slow fadeaway to the opening music and, finally, the conclusion of the movement.

Movement 3

- For all its diabolic power, this third movement comes as a tremendous relief after the emotional intensity of movements 1 and 2. This third movement is a toccata, meaning a fast, virtuosic movement intended to show off the digital dexterity of the performer.

- The theme of this movement is its rhythm—an unrelenting 7/8 meter that plows forward regardless, a 7/8 meter that is subdivided in a 2 + 3 + 2. The closest thing to a melodic theme in the movement is an ostinato—a repeated pattern of notes—heard in the bass at various points of the movement.

- Despite its brevity (it runs just a bit over three minutes), this third movement is a showstopper, among the most rousing finales in the entire piano repertoire.

Prokofiev—Piano Sonata No. 7
Lecture 22—Transcript

Welcome back to *The 23 Greatest Solo Piano Works*. This is Lecture 22. It is entitled Prokofiev—Piano Sonata No. 7.

Not including six juvenile piano sonatas and one left unfinished at his death, Prokofiev completed nine numbered piano sonatas. They are, collectively, the cornerstone of the 20th-century piano sonata literature. Prokofiev composed his Piano Sonata No. 7 in 1942, when he was 51 years old. On paper, it looks like a traditional, classically proportioned piano sonata. Like Mozart's piano sonatas, it is cast in three movements, with a first movement sonata form, a slow second movement, and a brilliant third movement finale.

Of course, in terms of its actual musical content, Prokofiev's Piano Sonata No. 7 has nothing to do with 18th -century classicism. It is new music, 20th-century music, machine-age music by a composer who loved cars and techno-gadgets almost as much as he loved music! Nowhere is the machine-age spirit more apparent than in Prokofiev's treatment of the piano. Now, the piano is technically a percussion instrument because it creates its sound by striking one object against another; in the case of the piano, a hammer against a string. Nevertheless, from the time of its invention around the year 1700 through the 19th century, the piano was conceived of as being primarily a stringed instrument, an instrument born to sing.

While Prokofiev could compose as lyrically as anyone, he considered the piano to be, primarily, an 88-drum trap set, and his percussive instincts as both a pianist and composer inform his piano music with a punch, a snap-crackle-pop, a go-go-go physicality and rhythmic thrust that are entirely 20th century! As an example, let's hear the opening of the third movement of Prokofiev's Piano Sonata No. 7, and while we listen, let us think drums. [**Piano performance:** Prokofiev, Piano Sonata No. 7 in B-flat Major, Op. 83.] It was just such music that caused the critic Richard Aldrich of the New York Times to write:

New ears for new music! The sonata contains no sustained musical development. The final movement of the work evoked visions of a charge of mammoths on some vast immemorial Asiatic plateau. Prokofiev uses, like Arnold Schoenberg, "modern harmonies". He is a psychologist of the uglier emotions. Hatred, contempt, rage—above all, rage—disgust, despair, mockery and defiance legitimately serve as models for [his musical] moods.

Oh please: This clueless dude just didn't get it at all. The expressive issue he refers to as "rage—above all, rage" is nothing of the sort. it is energy: the gut-busting, rip-roaring, nonstop rock 'n' roll energy of the 20th century.

Life and Personality

Prokofiev was born on April 11, 1891 in the village of Sontsovka, in Ukraine. His father managed a large estate, and it was on that estate that Prokofiev grew up an isolated, lonely, only child. He was homeschooled and rarely associated with the local children, who were considered by the Prokofievs to be "social inferiors."

Sergei's talent as a pianist manifested itself early, and in 1904—at the age of 13—he and his mother moved to St. Petersburg so that he could attend the St. Petersburg Conservatory, where he spent 10 years. By the time he graduated in 1914—first in his class—Prokofiev was already well on his way to fame. Between 1913 and 1918 he composed a series of outstanding works in an wide range of styles, from his post-romantic Piano Concerto No. 1 of 1913, to the Fauvist primitivism of the *Scythian Suite* of 1915, to the Haydn-inspired classicism of his Symphony No. 1 of 1917, to the musically and dramatically strident operas *Maddalena* (of 1913) and *The Gambler* (of 1917).

All of these works were written against the backdrop of World War I. The war began on July 28, 1914, just a couple of months after Prokofiev graduated from the Conservatory. As the only son of a widow, he was not called up into the military, a mercy for which we must be grateful as Russia suffered nearly four million deaths during the war, equal to the combined deaths suffered by France, Great Britain, and Belgium.

Incredibly, even as Russia plunged towards revolution, Prokofiev's career was thriving. In the fall of 1916, he performed his Piano Concerto No. 1

in Kiev. In the audience was a young composer named Vladimir Dukelsky, who later would become one of Prokofiev's best friends. Dukelsky was star-struck and left us with this description of Prokofiev:

> He had white-blonde hair, a small head with very thick lips, and very long, awkwardly dangling arms, terminating in a bruiser's powerful hands. Prokofiev wore dazzlingly elegant tails, a beautifully cut waistcoat, and flashing black pumps. The strangely gauche manner in which he traversed the stage was no indication of what was to follow; after sitting down and adjusting the piano stool with an abrupt jerk, Prokofiev let go with an unrelentingly muscular exhibition of a completely novel kind of piano playing. There was no sentiment, no sweetness [in it]—nothing but unrelenting energy and athletic joy. There was frenetic applause. Prokofiev bowed clumsily, dropping his head almost to his knees and recovering with a yank.

Unfortunately, current events were about to cream Prokofiev's developing career like a bass in a blender. Violent frustration over the Russian war effort led Czar Nicholas II to abdicate on March 2, 1917. An armed insurrection brought Vladimir Lenin's Bolshevik Party to power in November of 1917, and the Russian Civil War began. The civil war would last for five horrific years. It is estimated that an additional nine million Russians died during the civil war, and the Russian economy was destroyed. One could argue that it still has yet to completely recover.

In March of 1918, the Bolshevik regime made a separate peace with the Central Powers. Four months later—on the night of July 16 and 17, 1918, Nicholas II, his wife, his son, his four daughters, his footman, his wife's maidservant, his family's doctor and his cook were slaughtered in a basement room in the central Russian city of Ekaterinburg. The 27-year-old Prokofiev did his level best to ignore all of these events that were occurring around him. But events would not ignore him, and he decided that he could not ply his trades as a composer and pianist in such an environment. So he decided that the time was right for a brief trip abroad. Prokofiev later wrote, "On May 7, 1918, I started my journey, which was to take me abroad for only a few months ... or so I thought." In reality, it would be nine years before Prokofiev returned. Writes Harlow Robinson:

Like so many other Russians of his upbringing and education, Prokofiev failed to grasp the scope of the social and cultural transformation that was to come. Prokofiev's time abroad turned into years. By the early 1920s Russia had lost (to name only [a few]), Nabokov and Bunin in literature; Kandinsky and Chagall in painting; Stravinsky, Rachmaninoff, and Prokofiev in music. Many of these artists believed—like Prokofiev—that they were leaving Russia only temporarily. Some were confident that [the] Bolshevik hoodlums would soon be thrown out of power; others were simply waiting for the situation to settle down.

So Prokofiev decided to go to New York. Since war was still raging in Europe, he took the long way around. Travelling across Russia he arrived in Vladivostok. From there he took a steamer to Yokohama, Japan. From Yokohama he took a steamer to San Francisco. When he arrived in San Francisco he was detained on Angel Island by immigration officials who suspected him of being a Bolshevik spy. Prokofiev remembered:

> They wouldn't let me on shore right away, since they knew that in Russia the Bolsheviks were in power. After holding me for three days on the island and interrogating me in detail ("Have you been in prison?'—"Yes, I have."—"That's bad. Where?"—"Here, on your island."—"Oh, so you like to make jokes!") After holding me for three days they let me into the Unites States. In early September of 1918 I arrived in New York.

In the United States, Prokofiev was admired but not liked. According to Harold Schonberg:

> He was stubborn, ill-tempered, obstinate, and surly. he had pink skin that would turn red when he was in a rage (which was often). He disturbed everybody: always ready with a crushing repartee, with an irritating chuckle and a celebrated leer. He was a man who never could temporize, and he did not suffer fools gladly.

In 1923 Prokofiev decamped for Paris, which remained his home base for 13 years, until 1936. And while Prokofiev experienced genuine success in both the United States and France, he never felt fully appreciated or at home in either location. One reason for this was his compositional eclecticism: His music swung back and forth between starkly modern works, classical lyricism, and folkloric works. Neither the conservatives nor the avant-garde knew quite what to make of him.

Another problem was Prokofiev's personality. The people around him never ceased to be amazed by his incredible rudeness, which, according to his pal Nicholas Nabokov, "bordered on sadistic cruelty." My friends, I can think of no other composer in the entire history of Western music who had so many fights, conducted as many feuds, initiated as many lawsuits, and made so many enemies as did Sergei Prokofiev. Prokofiev's personality goes a long way towards explaining why he had problems in the United States and France. Even more, it is Prokofiev's narcissism that explains the single biggest mistake he ever made, a mistake he shared with Napoleon and Hitler: his belief that he could march on Moscow and, having done so, live there in triumph.

Back in the U.S.S.R.

On January 18, 1927, Prokofiev set foot in what was now the Soviet Union for the first time in nearly nine years. He had been invited to concertize, and the tour was a triumph. Prokofiev returned again in 1929, 1932, and twice in both 1933 and 1934. The success of these tours convinced Prokofiev to return permanently in 1936 and become a Soviet citizen. The Russian émigré community was scandalized, and Igor Stravinsky spoke for many when he declared:

> Prokofiev was always very Russian minded. But in my opinion [this] had little to do with his return to Russia, [which was] a sacrifice to the bitch goddess [of greed] and nothing else. He had no success in the United States or Europe for several seasons, while his visits to Russia had been triumphs. He was politically naïve, [so] he returned to Russia, and when finally he understood his position there, it was too late.

Oh, at first, everything was hunky dory. Prokofiev's return was a public-relations bonanza for Stalin's regime: The "worker's paradise" had reclaimed a prodigal son. Prokofiev was honored and celebrated and, for a couple of years, he was even allowed to travel abroad. On one such trip to New York in 1937, Prokofiev visited the Russian émigré composer Vladimir Dukelsky (who, under the pseudonym "Vernon Duke" composed, among other ditties, the songs "I Can't Get Started," "April in Paris," and "Autumn in New York"). Dukelsky recalled:

> I asked Sergey a difficult question. I wanted to know how he could live and work in the atmosphere of Soviet totalitarianism. Sergey was quiet for a moment and then said: "Here is how I feel about it: I care nothing for politics—I'm a composer first and last. Any government that lets me write my music in peace, publishes everything I compose before the ink is dry, and performs every note that comes from my pen, is all right with me."

Nothing more starkly underlined Prokofiev's epic naïveté than the blue Ford sedan he bought while on tour in the United States and had shipped back to Moscow. Private cars were an unheard-of luxury in Moscow in 1937, and boy oh boy, did his Soviet colleagues hate him for having it. It was a reminder to everyone of Prokofiev's privileged status in what was, presumably, a socialist society. But Prokofiev—naïve to the point of absurdity—was accustomed to material luxuries, and he saw no reason why he should have to give them up.

What turned out to be Prokofiev's last trip out of the Soviet Union was a North American tour in 1938. While in New York, Prokofiev asked Vladimir Dukelsky to go shopping with him. Dukelsky remembered:

> [He asked] "will you come to Macy's with me? I've got to buy a roomful of things you can't get in Russia—just look at [my wife] Lina's list." The list was imposing, and we went to Macy's, [allegedly] another sample of capitalistic bait designed by the lackeys of Wall Street to be swallowed by oppressed workers. Sergei enjoyed himself hugely in the store—he loved gadgets and trinkets of every description. Suddenly he turned to me, his eyes moist, [and said]: "You know, Dima, it occurred to me that I may not be back for some time. I don't suppose it would be wise for you to come to Russia,

would it?" "No, I don't suppose it would," I answered. I never saw Prokofiev again.

That's because Prokofiev was never again allowed to leave the Soviet Union. We can only shake our heads. Did Prokofiev not read the papers? Was he entirely unaware of the collectivization and forced starvations that killed millions of Soviet citizens? Was he unaware of the show trials and reign of terror that corresponded precisely with his return? Was he not aware of the possibly fatal censure of Dmitri Shostakovich and his opera *Lady Macbeth* in January of 1936? Did he not understand that the role of music in the Soviet Union was to promote the state and not to gratify the expressive desires of its composers? Yes, Prokofiev knew about all of this. But he believed that none of it had anything to do with him. Well, of course he was wrong. Dmitri Shostakovich understood Prokofiev's true position with painful clarity:

> Prokofiev was an inveterate gambler [who] thought he had calculated perfectly. For some 15 years Prokofiev sat between two stools: in the west he was considered a Soviet and in Russia they welcomed him as a Western guest. And [then] Prokofiev decided that it would be more profitable for him to move to the U.S.S.R. Such a step would only raise his stock in the West, because things Soviet were becoming fashionable just then; [and] they would stop considering him a foreigner in the U.S.S.R., and therefore he would win all around.

And this is where Prokofiev landed like a chicken in soup. He came to Moscow to teach them, and they started teaching him.

Piano Sonata No. 7 in B-Flat Major, Op. 83

By 1939, Prokofiev had come to realize that he was going to have to be two composers in one. With one hand, he would write explicitly Soviet works: "public" works that satisfied the ideologues, while, with the other hand, he would compose the music that he wanted to compose, "private works" that would be tolerated in light of the more patriotic stuff.

413

So it was that in the fall of 1939, Prokofiev was hard at work on a cantata for chorus and orchestra subtitled "Hail to Stalin," a work intended as a tribute to "the great leader and teacher" on the occasion of his 60th birthday. At the same time, he was composing his Sixth, Seventh, and Eighth piano sonatas, each of which is pure, modern Prokofiev and a masterwork. These three sonatas are generally referred to as Prokofiev's "War Sonatas," despite the fact that he began all of them long before the Soviet Union went to war with Germany in June of 1941. The Sixth was completed in 1940; the Seventh in 1942; and the Eighth completed in 1944. They remain among the most modernistic piano works Prokofiev ever composed.

Some commentators—running with the "War Sonata" idea for all its worth—attempt to ascribe their astringent musical language and expressive power to the war itself. For example, the pianist and Yale School of Music professor Boris Berman writes in his book about the piano sonatas of Prokofiev that, "While the Sixth Sonata reflects the nervous anticipation of World War II and the Eighth looks back to those terrible events retrospectively, the Seventh Sonata projects the anguish and the struggle of the war years as they were experienced in real time."

With all due respect, that's nothing but liner-note gibberish. Whatever anguish Prokofiev might have been feeling when he began the Seventh Sonata in 1939, it had nothing to do with a war that hadn't yet begun. But it might very well have had a lot to do with a war for his own soul. Before we talk about that war, let's do some listening. Prokofiev completed the Piano Sonata No. 7 in April of 1942. Despite the titular claim that the piece is in B-flat Major, the sonata is overall dark and ominous in mood. The sonata is cast in three movements.

Movement One

The first movement is set in sonata form, meaning that two contrasting themes will be presented in the opening section (called the exposition), they will then, in some way, be developed in a section called the development and recapitulated in a section called the recapitulation. Prokofiev's theme 1 is an angular, ferocious, and grotesque march that begins without an introduction and sounds as much like the home key of B-flat Major as your front teeth do when scraped across a blackboard. [**Piano performance:** Prokofiev, Piano Sonata No. 7 in B-flat Major, Op. 83.]

Back, then, to the war for Prokofiev's own soul. Among Prokofiev's oldest friends and most important artistic collaborators was the theater director, actor, and producer Vsevolod Meyerhold. In 1938, Meyerhold and Prokofiev began a collaboration to create a new opera entitled *Semyon Kotko*. On June 20, 1939—just as Prokofiev was completing the score—the 65-year-old Meyerhold was arrested, a victim of Stalin's Great Terror. He was brutally tortured and then executed by firing squad seven-and-a-half months after his arrest, on February 3, 1940. Meyerhold's wife, the actress Zinaida Raikh, fared even worse. On the night of July 14–15 1939, 25 days after Meyerhold's arrest, "unknown assailants" broke into her apartent. Dmitri Shostakovich describes what happened: "They killed her. Seventeen knife wounds; she was stabbed in the eyes. Raikh screamed for a long time, but none of the neighbors came to her aid. No one dared go into Meyerhold's apartment." Nothing was taken from the apartment. The assailants—of course—were never found. Instead, the apartment was split into two, and the new apartments were given to two ranking members of the NKVD, the precursor to the KGB.

Prokofiev was stunned by the deaths of Meyerhold and Raikh. If he had chosen not to see before, he could not hide from the truth now: that he had voluntarily returned to a society of unspeakable brutality, and that in doing so he had put not just himself but his family—his wife and two sons—in terrible danger. Just weeks after Zinaika Raikh's murder, Prokofiev was "informed" that he would compose a cantata entitled "Hail To Stalin" in celebration of Stalin's 60th birthday. And just weeks after that, Prokofiev began composing his Piano Sonatas Nos. 6, 7, and 8. It is the opinion of Prokofiev biographer Daniel Jaffé—an opinion that I share—that, "having forced himself to compose a cheerful evocation of the "nirvana" Stalin wanted everyone to believe he had created [in "Hail to Stalin," Prokofiev then, in these three sonatas], expressed his true feelings."

Back to the first movement sonata form of Prokofiev's Piano Sonata No. 7. Following a relatively quiet modulating bridge, an expansive and introspective theme 2 emerges. Like theme 1, theme 2 is essentially non-tonal, and the themes share a like opening contour. Here's the melodic contour that initiates theme 1. [**Piano demonstration.**] And now the melodic contour that initiates theme 2: [**Piano demonstration.**] Again, theme 1. [**Piano demonstration.**] Theme 2. [**Piano demonstration.**]

The resemblance between the themes notwithstanding, I'd point out that there is a fundamental contrast between them. Theme 1 is a grotesquerie, a caricature of brutal, militant force. Theme 2 is a pained and personal rumination on that brutality, entirely introverted in its expressive effect. Theme 2: [**Piano performance:** Prokofiev, Piano Sonata No. 7 in B-flat Major, Op. 83.] A thrumming, increasingly loud and dramatic passage of closing music concludes the exposition and leads directly into the dissonant, frenzied, theme 1-dominated development section, music that can—without any fear of overstatement—be equated to Prokofiev's battle for his own soul. [**Piano performance:** Prokofiev, Piano Sonata No. 7 in B-flat Major, Op. 83.]

The recapitulation begins not with theme 1, but rather with the modulating bridge. An abbreviated version of theme 2 follows. The coda that concludes the movement—based on theme 1—ends not with a bang but with an unsettling whimper. "Exhaustion" is the word that best fits these final moments: physical and spiritual exhaustion. Here's the coda: [**Piano performance:** Prokofiev, Piano Sonata No. 7 in B-flat Major, Op. 83.]

Movement Two

Prokofiev's second movement is a six-minute-long cry of pain. The opening and closing A sections are based on a song by Robert Schumann entitled "Sadness," from his song cycle *Liederkreis,* Op. 39 of 1840. Prokofiev's second movement begins this way: [**Piano performance:** Prokofiev, Piano Sonata No. 7 in B-flat Major, Op. 83.] Schumann's song, set in the same key—E Major—begins this way. [**Piano demonstration.**]

The words of Schumann's song—and therefore, the words Prokofiev tacitly implies here at the beginning of the second movement—would seem to have been custom made for Prokofiev's own state of mind. Here are the words, by the poet Joseph Eichendorff:

I can sometimes sing
as if I were happy,
but secretly tears well up.

The nightingales
sing their songs of unfulfilled longing
from the depths of their dungeons.

Everyone delights who listens,
because they do not understand the pain:
the deep sorrow of the song.

As this second movement progresses, the quiet, Schumann-inspired opening evolves into a terrible and sustained cry of pain and sorrow. Let us hear that climactic shriek followed by the slow fade away to the opening music and finally, the conclusion of the movement. [**Piano performance:** Prokofiev, Piano Sonata No. 7 in B-flat Major, Op. 83.]

Movement Three

Fall all its diabolic power, this third movement comes as a tremendous relief after the emotional intensity of movements one and two. This third movement is a toccata, meaning a fast, virtuosic movement intended to show off the digital dexterity of the performer. The theme of this movement is its rhythm: an unrelenting 7/8 meter that plows forward regardless, a 7/8 meter that is subdivided into a 2+3+2. [**Vocal demonstration.**] The closest thing to a melodic theme in the movement is an ostinato—a repeated pattern of notes—heard in the bass at various points of the movement. That ostinato sounds like this. [**Piano demonstration.**] Despite its brevity—it runs just a bit over three minutes—this third movement is a show stopper, among the most rousing finales in the entire piano repertoire. Let's hear it in its entirety. [**Piano performance:** Prokofiev, Piano Sonata No. 7 in B-flat Major, Op. 83.]

1948: The Beginning of the End

The German invasion of the Soviet Union—which began on June 20, 1941—destroyed most of Soviet Europe. As an official "treasure" of the Soviet

Union, Prokofiev was packed off to various artist colonies in order to keep him as far from the fighting as possible. Incredibly, Prokofiev thrived during the war years. He separated from his wife Lina and moved in with a writer named Mira Mendelson. He wrote some of his greatest music during these years despite the physical hardships with which he lived. Most remarkable was that Prokofiev seemed—for the first time in his life—to be genuinely happy. With no small bit of amazement, his friend Olga Lamm wrote:

> Despite the depressed mood of those who surrounded him, and despite a life that was far from easy materially, he was happy, and this happiness was written on his face: he was always beaming. He was composing a great deal and with enormous inspiration, and, like all happy people, was filled with a sort of amazingly affectionate and kind attitude toward those around him. We were astonished: what had happened to the condescending attitude towards others?

OK, in truth, Prokofiev could still be a real jerk. Nevertheless, he had changed. Part of it was the war itself: it infused people with a sense of common purpose that transcended their individual lives. In the Soviet Union, part of it was knowing, for a change, that the enemy was an outsider and not your own government. And part of it, for Prokofiev, was maturity. He turned 50 in 1941, and he was mellowing. The war was good for Prokofiev, but it could not go on forever.

The war in Europe ended on May 8, 1945. Any hopes that Stalin would allow his exhausted people a respite after the horrors they had endured were quickly squashed, as he reinstituted the terror, intent—once again—on destroying his presumed enemies before they knew they were his enemies! Having first purged his officer's corps, returning prisoners of war, the Jewish community, and the theatrical, literary, cinematic, and academic communities, it was time—in 1948—to terrorize the musical community. And unlike the purges of the late 1930s, when the newly returned Sergei Prokofiev was given a free pass, this time the apparatchiks had him sighted firmly in their crosshairs. On February 10, 1948 the Central Committee of the Communist Party accused the leading Soviet composers—with Prokofiev and Shostakovich in the forefront—of writing unnecessarily dissonant, overtly self-expressive and anti-Soviet music.

A week later, on February 17, Prokofiev's recent music—including his Piano Sonata No. 7—was branded as being "worthless and even evil."

Like his colleagues, Prokofiev was forced to write a pathetic apology, confessing his compositional "sins" and begging forgiveness. Prokofiev concluded his apology this way: "I would like to express my gratitude to our Communist Party for the concrete directives of its decree which are helpful in my search for a musical language clear and close to our people, a language worthy of our people and of our great country."

But Prokofiev's censure and humiliation were not enough. The authorities needed an insurance policy that would guarantee Prokofiev's ongoing cooperation and protect against recidivism. So on February 20, 1948 his estranged wife Lina—the mother of his two sons—was arrested and thrown into prison. Tried for espionage, she was sentenced to 20 years and sent to the Gulag, where she could only dream about her life in Paris. (She, by the way, was released in 1956 during Khrushchev's "thaw." She left the Soviet Union in 1974 never to return, and died in London in 1989 at the age of 91.)

1948 marked the beginning of the end for Prokofiev. His health deteriorated rapidly. Many of his works were banned. The impression of privilege was smashed. Despite his attempts to soldier on, his final five years were filled with rejection, stifling official criticism, disappointment, illness, and in the end, fear.

He died of a cerebral hemorrhage on March 5, 1953, aged 61 years, just about one hour before Joseph Stalin died. In the April, 1953 issue of *Sovietskaya Muzyka*—"Soviet Music," the official publication of the Union of Soviet Composers—Prokofiev's death was reported in a blurb on page 117. The first 116 pages were devoted entirely to the death of Stalin.

Thank you.

Copland—*Piano Variations*
Lecture 23

Aaron Copland's *Piano Variations* is an epochal piece. It is "American" to its bones, a piece of music that combines Copland's formal training and a modernist compositional impulse with a ragtime- and jazz-inspired approach to rhythm, melody, and harmony and the relentless, machine-age energy, pace, and power that radiated from New York City in the 1920s. By the mid-1930s, Copland's spare and angular compositional style had come to be perceived as a perfect musical metaphor for the "wide open spaces" and pioneer spirit of America.

"American" Music Comes of Age

- Eclecticism is as American as apple pie. In a culture defined by its racial and ethnic multiplicity, any music that claims to be "American" must, somehow, reflect that multiplicity. Such an American concert music emerged during the first decades of the 20th century, when American-born composers began to synthesize jazz, ragtime, Anglo American and Hispanic folk music, popular song, and elements of American musical theater into their concert works.

- The music of Aaron Copland exemplifies this emergence. Copland, formally trained in the European concert tradition, was determined to create a uniquely "American" body of work. To that end, his music drew freely from such diverse traditions as jazz, North American and Latin America folk music and dance, and European modernism.

- Copland composed his *Piano Variations* in 1930, when he was 30 years old. For all the popularity of his "populist" ballet scores like *Appalachian Spring*, for all the patriotic bombast of his *Fanfare for the Common Man*, for all his film scores and chamber compositions, *Piano Variations* is Copland's great masterwork—the most important piano work by an American composer. Its greatness rests on two pillars.

- The first is purely self-referential, and that is the beauty, power, and invention of the music itself. The second pillar of greatness is what the piece represents historically and stylistically: a diamond-hard synthesis of Western European musical modernism; a steely, New York City skyline–inspired, art deco–like angularity and clarity; west African microtonal melody; and ragtime- and jazz-inspired rhythmic practice, themselves derived from west African drumming.

- In every sense, Copland's *Piano Variations* is the great American piano work, written at precisely the time American composers were attempting to define what constituted "American music."

- A distinctly American compositional music tradition emerged in the 1920s for four main reasons. The first reason had to do with the maturation of American culture and society. With westward expansion and industrialization complete, the American public increasingly turned its attention to quality-of-life issues. As we know, few things can elevate our quality of life more completely than music.

- The second reason is that the long-standing bias in favor of German and Austrian music was undone by America's participation in World War I against Germany and Austria.

- The third reason was the isolationist spirit that followed World War I, a spirit that focused on things homegrown, such as ragtime, jazz, American musical theater, and American folk music.

- Finally, by the 1920s, such indigenous American music as ragtime, jazz, American musical theater, and folk music had developed and been codified to the point that they could be embraced and synthesized into an American concert music.

- More than anything else, it was the musical synthesis of west Africa and Europe that came to define American music, a synthesis that produced the spiritual, blues, ragtime, jazz, and rock 'n' roll. This synthesis of Africa and Europe lies at the very heart of Copland's *Piano Variations*.

Theme

- Copland's *Piano Variations* was composed in 1930, at just the time that jazz was solidifying its hold on the mainstream consciousness of America. Copland's theme—melodically angular, rhythmically irregular, and constantly shifting between major and minor—is a brilliant abstraction and intensification of west African polyrhythm and microtonal melody, music conditioned by Copland's absorption of the language of ragtime and jazz.

- In the score, Copland indicates that the player should: "strike each note sharply." The effect is percussive, and each note stands in the highest relief. In a ragtime or jazz performance, it is just such percussive accentuations that serve to create a polyrhythmic layer above the regular beat created by the bass line.

- Copland conceived his theme with a jazz-inspired vision of explosive percussivity and then stripped away everything but the high-relief accented notes. It is in this way that Copland's theme becomes an abstraction and an intensification of the sort of rhythms and articulation characteristic of jazz and ragtime.

- The thematic melody is cast in three phrases, with each phrase longer than the previous one. This thematic melody is based on a four-note motive that will drive the entire piece. It's a melodic idea that implies a harmonic alternation of C major, C minor, and C-sharp minor.

- The net effect of the constant oscillation between major and minor that we hear from the first page to the last of Copland's *Piano Variations* is to evoke exactly the "blue notes"—the simultaneously major and minor notes—that grew out of west African melodic practice. This is particularly apparent in the harmonic language of the piece, in which these major and minor intervals are heard simultaneously.

- For example, as the theme draws to its conclusion, an explosive harmony punctuates the conclusion. The harmony is a blues chord—a simultaneously C major and minor harmony that has no precedent in Western European harmonic practice but many, many precedents in blues and jazz practice.

- Copland's *Piano Variations* is not blues, nor is it jazz. Instead, it is profoundly influenced by the rhythmic, melodic, and harmonic language of blues and jazz. In fact, it is a musical synthesis that mirrors, in some way, the racial and ethnic synthesis that is the American nation.

American composer Aaron Copland (1900–1990) composed in an expressive modern style that incorporated the contemporary trends.

Variations

- Copland's angular theme is followed by 20 variations and a closing section called a coda. Copland's variations are cumulative, which means that each new variation builds on the one that preceded it so that the piece is characterized by constant developmental momentum.

- Keep in mind that Copland's theme and the subsequent variations are based on a four-note motive that will be heard melodically as well as harmonically. In varying this motive melodically, Copland employs a technique throughout the variations called octave displacement, which means shifting a melody note (or notes) into higher or lower octaves. The leaping about due to octave displacements has much to do with the angularity and abruptness that is so characteristic of the *Piano Variations*.

- Variation 1 starts low on the keyboard and gradually expands upward. It is set initially as a canon; the theme begins in the pianist's right hands and then follows, four beats later, in the left hand.

- In variation 2, the basic motive begins to be heard harmonically.

- Variations 4, 5, 6, and 7 together constitute a large dramatic buildup and bring the first large part of the piece to its climax. Copland achieves this buildup and climax a number of ways: Rhythms become more incisive and varied; more and more registral space is enveloped; and huge, dissonant harmonies built from the basic motive explode. Variation 7 concludes—and with it, the first large part of the piece—with a brilliant and piercing E-major chord.

- Variations 8 through 13 are, in turn, mysterious, lyric, majestic, melancholy, and playful. Together, these six variations represent the central section of the piece.

- The third and final large group of variations—numbers 14 through 20—feature some of the most influential piano writing of the 20th century. Copland, who was always a less-is-more sort of composer (he liked to refer to his compositional style as being "thrifty"), strips away all nonessentials in these variations and, in doing so, creates piano textures of diamond hardness and clarity.

- In variation 14, upward-rippling arpeggios alternate with accented, quarter-note basic motives; low C pedal tones; and skittering, rhythmically irregular eighth-note lines.

- In variation 15, skittering, irregular eighth-note lines alternate with rippling chords and arpeggios.

- In variation 16, various permutations of the basic, four-note motive alternate with gunshot-like chords built from the basic, four-note motive.

- In variation 17, skittering octaves played fortissimo alternate with scurrying four-note motives and quietly repeated E-major chords.

- Variation 18 offers a last bit of quiet before the final onslaught, as rippling sixteenth-note basic motives (played pianissimo) alternate with widely spaced versions of the basic motive (played piano).

- Variation 19 features sonorous, chordal music that starts slowly and quietly but gathers tremendous force as it progresses.

- Variation 20—the longest in the set—is filled with **syncopations**, virtuosic octaves and concludes explosively deep in the piano.

- The coda builds to a huge, sonorous climax and concludes with a magisterial version of the theme.

Important Term

syncopation: Displacement of the expected accent from a strong beat to a weak beat and vice versa.

Copland—*Piano Variations*
Lecture 23—Transcript

Welcome back to *The 23 Greatest Solo Piano Works*. This is Lecture 23. It is entitled Copland—*Piano Variations*.

Eclecticism is as American as apple pie. In a culture defined by its racial and ethnic multiplicity, any music that claims to be American must, somehow, reflect that multiplicity. Such an American concert music emerged during the first decades of the 20th century, when American-born composers began to synthesize jazz, ragtime, Anglo-American and Hispanic folk music, popular song, and elements of American musical theater into their concert works.

The music of Aaron Copland exemplifies this emergence. Copland, formally trained in the European concert tradition, was determined to create a uniquely American body of work. To that end he drew freely in his music from such diverse traditions as jazz, North American and Latin American folk music and dance, as well as European modernism.

Copland composed his *Piano Variations* in 1930, when he was 30 years old. For all the popularity of his "populist" ballet scores like *Appalachian Spring*; for all the patriotic bombast of his *Fanfare for the Common Man*; for all his film scores and chamber compositions, the *Piano Variations* is Copland's great masterwork; in my opinion the most important piano work by an American composer. Its greatness rests on two pillars.

The first is purely self-referential, and that is the beauty, power, and invention of the music itself. The second pillar of greatness is what the piece represents historically and stylistically: a diamond-hard synthesis of Western European musical modernism; a steely, New York City skyline–inspired, art deco–like angularity and clarity; West African microtonal melody; and ragtime and jazz-inspired rhythmic practice, themselves derived from West African drumming. In every sense, Copland's *Piano Variations* is "the great American piano work," written at precisely the time American composers were attempting to define what constituted "American music."

Some music. Let us hear the angular and explosive theme of Copland's *Piano Variations*, a theme we will come to love by the conclusion of this lecture! [**Piano performance:** Copland, *Piano Variations*, theme.]

"American" Music Comes of Age

A distinctly American compositional music tradition emerged in the 1920s for four main reasons. Reason number one had to do with the maturation of American culture and society. With westward expansion and industrialization complete, the American public increasingly turned its attention to quality-of-life issues. As we know, few things can elevate our quality of life more completely than music. Reason number two: The long-standing bias in favor of German and Austrian music was undone by America's participation in World War I against Germany and Austria.

Reason number three was the isolationist spirit that followed World War I, a spirit that focused on things homegrown: like Ragtime, Jazz, American musical theater and American folk music. Finally, reason number four: by the 1920s, such indigenous American musics as ragtime, jazz, American musical theater and folk music had developed and been codified to the point that they could be embraced and synthesized into an American concert music. More than anything else, it was the musical synthesis of West Africa and Europe that came to define American music, a synthesis that produced the spiritual, blues, ragtime, jazz, and rock 'n' roll. This synthesis of Africa and Europe lies at the very heart of Copland's *Variations for Piano*. Let us, then, identify it.

West Africa

Some dates and numbers. 1619: the British import the first slaves to North America to work in the colony of Virginia. Two-hundred and forty-one years later: the 1860 census reveal 3,953,760 slaves living and working in the United States. The great bulk of these unfortunate Africans came from West Africa: from the Gold Coast (what today is the nation of Ghana), and from the ancient kingdom of Dahomey, today the southern part of Benin. Despite the varied cultural backgrounds of these West Africans, we can make three generalizations about the music they brought with them to the Americas, generalizations that distinguish West African music from European music.

The first distinguishing aspect of West African music has to do with rhythm. In West African music, various layers of drummed and sung rhythms are stacked one atop the next, weaving a complex composite of contrasting beats and accents. We call such a multi-layered rhythmic entity a polyrhythm.

For example, I will—roughly but enthusiastically—perform a piece called *Gota* from the kingdom of Dahomey. It consists of three rhythmic layers. The lowest layer is the control element: a steady state rhythm that is the foundation of the polyrhythm. [**Drum example.**] The next rhythmic layer sounds like this. [**Drum example.**] Finally, the third layer sound like this. [**Drum example.**] Put 'em all together and here's what we've got. [**Drum example.**] So, distinguishing aspect number one of West African music is polyrhythm.

The second distinguishing aspect of West African music has to do with the nature of its melodies, which are based on microtonal collections of pitches (or scales) that listeners raised in the European musical tradition hear as a combination of major and minor. For example, here's a tune called *Kpatsa* with words added by yours truly. Here's what *Kpatsa* would sound like if it were in major. [**Musical example.**] And here's what it would sound like if it were in minor. [**Musical example.**] And here's how it really sounds, in a microtonal melody that would seem to simultaneously combine major and minor. [**Musical example.**] So, distinguishing aspect number two of West African music: microtonal melody.

Distinguishing aspect number three is a performance technique: West African songs are typically sung communally, using a technique called call-response or responsorial singing. [**Musical example.**]

Synthesis

Slaves in the North American colonies adapted the call-response technique to their work routines, social activities and religious gatherings. White Americans called these field hollers and shouts. But much more important is what happened when the microtonal melodies and call-response technique of West African music were synthesized with the English Protestant church hymns of the slave owners. An entirely new genre of music came into being, one that represented a unique combination of African and European musical elements. This genre is the spiritual. My friends, the spiritual tradition became the gospel tradition, which in turn gave birth to soul; such great opera and soul singers as Jessye Norman, Aretha Franklin, Marian Anderson, Patti LaBelle all cut their musical teeth singing gospel music.

Blues

Blues was born during the second half of the 19th century out of the synthesis of three elements. Element one of blues is its West African heritage: West African polyrhythm, microtonal melody, and call-response technique. Element number two of blues is European: European harmonic practice and musical instruments. Element number three is the angst and humor of the post–Civil War African American community, the community that created the blues. A piece of music identified as a blues will exhibit three characteristics: a particular mood, a particular musical structure, and a characteristic sound. One at a time.

Mood. Since the 1500s, the word "blue" has been associated with low emotional spirits. By definition, then, blues is music of protest, of lost love, lost opportunity, lost credit cards, whatever. Having said that, I would point out that playing and listening to the blues are entirely different than "having the blues." Playing and listening to the blues are cathartic acts. The blues, my friends, should make us smile and, paradoxically, give us joy!

Structure. Blues music is based on a three-line poetic construct, which in turn is based on West African call-response technique, a poetic construct consisting of a call, an answer, and a punch line. For example: Call: You can call it *Great Courses*, it's still Teaching Company to me. Answer: You can call it *Great Courses*, it's still Teaching Company to me. Punch line: After 20 years recording, that's just how it's got to be.

Call: When I'm here in Chantilly, I record four lectures a day. Answer: When I'm here in Chantilly, I record four lectures a day. Punchline: That's the most I can do, keeps the quality high that way.

I would tell you that a three-chord harmonic structure—based on European harmonic practice—evolved to delineate this three-line poetic structure. We call this harmonic structure 12-bar blues because—by definition—a Blues will follow this 12-bar—or 12-measure—harmonic structure. I'll demonstrate this harmonic structure and count the 12 measures for you. [**Musical demonstration.**] By definition, a blues is 12 measures long and follows that harmonic structure. Let's put it all together: the "Great Courses Blues"! [**Musical demonstration.**]

We observed that by definition, the genre blues is three things: a mood, a harmonic structure, and a sound. Let's talk about sound. OK, we go to a piano bar and hear a pianist tinkling on the keys (a terrible phrase, really, one that conjures up rusty pedals and yellow socks). Anyway, the pianist noodles something like this. [**Piano demonstration.**] And we might say "that's really 'bluesy' piano playing." Now, what's "bluesy"—or "blues-like"—really mean? What we're hearing is an attempt by the piano player to evoke microtones by playing in major and minor at the same time! [**Piano demonstration.**] Such major/minor notes are called blue notes or crushed notes. In fact, when we identify a pianist as being bluesy, what we're really doing is saying "that sounds like an attempt to evoke West African microtonal melody on a European instrument that, in reality, is incapable of playing microtones!"

Ragtime

Parallel to the development of blues was the birth and development of a piano music called ragtime. Ragtime, like blues, was developed by African American musicians. Ragtime, like blues, is a composite music, a synthesis of vastly different elements. Element number one of ragtime is the moderate duple meter and musical form of the marching band music—music that grew out of the Western European musical traditions—that was so fabulously popular around the turn of the 20th century. For example, John Philip Sousa's iconic *The Stars and Stripes Forever* was composed in 1896.

[**Musical demonstration.**] That's element number one of ragtime—marching band music.

Element number two of ragtime is of West African origin. In ragtime, the complex polyrhythmic layers of West African drumming are transferred to the piano. In ragtime, a marching, on-the-beat left hand supports the off-the-beat, syncopated right hand layered atop, a layer that is actually a polyrhythmic layer, a layer that does not line up with the march beat. For example, let's hear as in Scott Joplin's iconic *Maple Leaf Rag* of 1899, and let's be aware to the degree we can that the rhythms in the right hand don't quite line up with those in the left. [**Piano demonstration.**]

Ragtime was the first African American music to enter the mainstream of American culture. However, it was not the brilliant instrumental rags of black composers like Scott Joplin that did so, but rather, rag-sploitation songs churned out by the New York–based pop song industry, the most famous of which was Irving Berlin's *Alexander's Ragtime Band* of 1911. It was music like *Alexander's Ragtime Band* that Aaron Copland referred to when he wrote:

> Music was the last thing anyone would have connected with [my family, although] I don't want to give the impression that there was no music in my house. My oldest brother played the violin to my sister's accompaniments, and I remember a considerable amount of ragtime on top of the piano for "lighter moments."

Exploitative or not, it was the ragtime songs of New York's Tin Pan Alley that captured the ears and hearts of such young American composers as Aaron Copland and George Gershwin (to mention just two of many), songs that helped predispose these young composers towards a West African–inspired rhythmic palette.

Jazz

It was just a matter of time before West African–inspired polyrhythms and microtonal melody were grafted into the music of larger instrumental ensembles. That event took place during the first years of the 20th century in the marching bands of New Orleans. Your typical New Orleans–style band consists of two basic elements. The first is played by a banjo, a tuba, maybe a drum, whose collective job is to play the bass line, harmonies, and provide the underlying beat of the music. These instruments are the equivalent of a ragtime pianist's left hand, the rhythm section, the control element, against which is heard the second basic element of New Orleans Jazz: a trumpet or cornet, a clarinet, trombone, which would play and improvise simultaneously, creating the characteristic sound of New Orleans Jazz: the multiple layers of group improvisation layered atop the rhythm section evolved from the polyrhythmic layers of West African drumming.

By the 1930s, the essential elements of jazz as we understand it today were in place. The rhythm section (the control element) had become standardized: a piano, a bass, and a set of drums supplied the bass line, harmonies, and beat. [**Piano demonstration.**] Above the rhythm section, the improvising instruments—now soloing one at a time—layer their rhythmically contrasting lines, creating a rhythmic tension called swing (which is just another word for "polyrhythm"). [**Piano demonstration.**]

Variation for Piano, Theme

The *Variations* was composed in 1930, at just the time that jazz was solidifying its hold on the mainstream consciousness of America. Copland's theme—melodically angular, rhythmically irregular, and constantly shifting between major and minor—is a brilliant abstraction and intensification of West African polyrhythm and microtonal melody, music conditioned by Copland's absorption of the language of ragtime and jazz. Once again, we hear the theme in its entirety. [**Piano performance:** Copland, *Piano Variations*, theme.]

In the score, Copland indicates that the player should "strike each note sharply." The effect is percussive, and each note stands in the highest relief. [**Piano demonstration.**] In a ragtime or jazz performance, it is just such percussive accentuations that serve to create a polyrhythmic layer above the regular beat created by the bass line. [**Piano demonstration.**] Copland conceived his theme with a jazz-inspired vision of explosive percussivity, and then striped away everything but the high-relief accented notes. Thus, a jazz line that might sound something like this—[**piano demonstration**]—becomes this if we strip away everything but the accentuations: [**piano demonstration**]. It is in this way that Copland's theme becomes an abstraction and an intensification of the sort of rhythms and articulation characteristic of jazz and ragtime.

Back, please, to the theme. The thematic melody is cast in three phrases, with each phrase longer than the previous one. Phrase one. [**Piano demonstration.**] Phrase two. [**Piano demonstration.**] Phrase three. [**Piano demonstration.**] This thematic melody is based on a Jack Sprat lean four-note motive that sounds like this. [**Piano demonstration.**] Again. [**Piano demonstration.**] That motive will drive the entire piece, so it behooves us to really know it. [**Piano demonstration.**] It's a melodic idea that implies a harmonic alternation of C Major, C Minor, and C-sharp Minor. [**Piano demonstration.**]

The net effect of the constant oscillation between major and minor that we hear from the first page to the last of Copland's *Variations* is to evoke exactly the blue notes—the simultaneously major and minor notes—that grew out of West African melodic practice. This is particularly apparent in the harmonic language of the piece, in which these major and minor intervals are heard simultaneously. For example, as the theme draws to its conclusion, an explosive harmony punctuates that conclusion. Here is that harmony. [**Piano demonstration.**] That, my friends, is a blues chord: a simultaneously C Major and Minor harmony that has no precedent in Western European harmonic practice, but a zillion-and-one precedents in blues and jazz practice.

So. Is Copland's *Piano Variations* a blues? No. Is it jazz? No. Is it profoundly influenced by the rhythmic, melodic, and harmonic language of blues and jazz? You betcha. Is it a musical synthesis that mirrors, in some way, the racial and ethnic synthesis that is the American nation? Absolutely.

Aaron Copland (1900–1990)

Aaron Copland was born in Brooklyn, New York on November 14, 1900, the youngest of five children. His parents had immigrated to the United

States from Lithuania and en route, his father had Anglicized the Jewish family name of "Kaplan" to "Copland." Copland's father Harris was your prototypical motivated immigrant. He opened a clothing store which Aaron described as "a kind of neighborhood Macy's." Copland wrote, "My father was justifiably proud of what he had accomplished in the business world. But above all, he never let us forget that it was America that had made all this possible."

Copland began taking piano lessons at the relatively "advanced" age of 13 In 1921—two years after graduating from Brooklyn's Boys High School— Copland travelled to Fontainebleau, outside of Paris, where he completed his music education with the formidable Nadia Boulanger. Copland remained in Europe for three years, during which time he learned his trade, toured the continent and seems to have met and charmed pretty much everyone, including such fellow Montparnasse-dwelling expats as Gertrude Stein, E. E. Cummings, Ernest Hemingway, Sherwood Anderson, Sinclair Lewis, and Archibald MacLeish. Paris in the 1920s. Good times.

Copland returned to the Unites States in June of 1924 at a most auspicious moment: just four months after the premiere of George Gershwin's *Rhapsody in Blue* at a concert dedicated to incorporating jazz into concert music. Copland later wrote:

> I was anxious to write a work that would immediately be recognized as "American" in character. This desire to be "American" was symptomatic of the period. I had experimented with the rhythms of popular music in several earlier compositions, but now I wanted frankly to adopt the jazz idiom and see what I could do with it.

The first piece Copland wrote on returning to the United States was the jazz- and Broadway-inspired *Music for the Theater*, a suite for a theater-sized orchestra that incorporated elements of both jazz and theater music. Many years later, Copland wrote:

> The jazz element in *Music for the Theater* was further developed in my next work, a Concerto for Piano and Orchestra. This proved to be the last of my "experiments" with jazz. With the Concerto I felt

I had done all I could with the idiom. True, it was an easy way to "be American" in musical terms, but all American music could not possibly be confined to [the] two dominant jazz moods—the blues and the snappy number.

We must consider Copland's words very carefully, because it's easy to be misled by his assertion that his Concerto for Piano and Orchestra of 1926 was his last "experiment" with jazz. In truth, much of the music Copland composed for the remainder of his long life—he lived until 1990—was powerfully influenced by the rhythmic snap and microtonal (or "bluesy") elements of jazz, no more so than in his *Piano Variations* of 1930.

The Variations

Copland's angular theme is followed by 20 variations and a closing section called a coda. Copland's variations are cumulative. What that means that each new variation builds on the one that preceded it, so that the piece is characterized by constant developmental momentum. As a reminder: Copland's theme and the subsequent variations are based on a four-note motive. [**Piano demonstration.**]

This four-note motive will be heard melodically. [**Piano demonstration.**] As well as harmonically: [**Piano demonstration.**] In varying this motive melodically, copland employs a technique throughout the variations called octave displacement. "Octave displacement" means shifting a melody note (or notes) into higher or lower octaves. For example, if we displace a note from the opening of *Happy Birthday*, we go from this. [**Piano demonstration.**] To this: [**Piano demonstration.**] Thus Copland's basic, four-note motive, which in its non-displaced state sounds like this: [**Piano demonstration.**] Might, if we start displacing its notes, also sound like this. [**Musical demonstration.**] Or perhaps, like this. [**Piano demonstration.**] The leaping about due to octave displacements has much to do with the angularity and abruptness that so characteristic of the *Piano Variations*.

Variation 1: Variation 1 starts low on the keyboard and gradually expands upwards. It is set initially as a canon: The theme begins in the pianist's right hand and then follows, four beats later, in the left hand. Variation 1:

[**Piano performance:** Copland, *Piano Variations*, variation 1.] In variation 2, the basic motive begins to be heard harmonically. Variation 2: [**Piano performance:** Copland, *Piano Variations*, variation 2.]

Variations 4, 5, 6, and 7 together constitute a large dramatic buildup and bring the first large part of the piece to its climax. Copland achieves this buildup and climax a number of ways: Rhythms become more incisive and varied; more and more registral space is enveloped; and huge, dissonant harmonies built from the basic motive explode like a lava lamp in a microwave.

Variation 7 concludes—and with it, the first large part of the piece—with a brilliant and piercing E Major chord. I will indicate the advent of variations 4 through 7 as each one begins. [**Piano performance:** Copland, *Piano Variations*, variations 4–7.] Variations 8–13 are, in turn, mysterious, lyric, majestic, melancholy, and playful. Together, these six variations represent the central section of the piece.

Time demands that we move on to the third and final large group of variations: numbers 14–20. These variations feature some of the most influential piano writing of the 20th century. Copland, who was always a less-is-more sort of composer (he liked to refer to his compositional style as being "thrifty"), strips away all nonessentials in these variations and in doing so, creates piano textures of diamond hardness and clarity.

Variation 14: Upwards-rippling arpeggios alternate with accented, quarter-note basic motives, low-C pedal tones and skittering, rhythmically irregular eighth-note lines. Variation 14:   [**Piano performance:** Copland, *Piano Variations*, variation 14.] Variation 15: skittering, irregular eighth-note lines alternate with rippling chords and arpeggios. Variation 15: [**Piano performance:** Copland, *Piano Variations*, variation 15.] Variation 16: various permutation of the basic, four-note motive alternate with gunshot-like chords built from the basic, four-note motive. Variation 16: [**Piano performance:** Copland, *Piano Variations*, variation 16.]

Variation 17: skittering octaves played fortissimo alternate with scurrying four-note motives and quietly repeated E Major chords. Variation 17: [**Piano performance:** Copland, *Piano Variations*, variation 14.] Variation 18 offers a last bit of quiet before the final onslaught, as rippling sixteenth-note basic motives (played *pianissimo*) alternate with widely-spaced versions of the "basic motive" (played *piano*). Variation 18: [**Piano performance:** Copland, *Piano Variations*, variation 18.]

Variation 19 features sonorous, chordal music that starts slowly and quietly but gathers tremendous force as it progresses. Variation 20—the longest in the set—is filled with syncopations, virtuosic octaves, and concludes explosively deep in the piano. Variations 19 and 20: [**Piano performance:** Copland, *Piano Variations*, variations 19 and 20.] The coda now builds to a huge, sonorous climax and concludes with a magisterial version of the theme. The coda: [**Piano performance:** Copland, *Piano Variations*, coda.]

Copland's *Piano Variations* is an epochal piece. It is American to its bones, a piece of music that combines, (1) Copland's formal training and a modernist compositional impulse with (2) a ragtime- and jazz-inspired approach to rhythm, melody, and harmony and (3) the relentless, machine-age energy, pace, and power that radiated from New York City in the 1920s. By the mid-1930s, Copland's spare and angular compositional style had come to be perceived as a perfect musical metaphor for the wide-open spaces and pioneer spirit of America, no small irony given that he grew up in a Jewish, New York household, the son of Lithuanian immigrants. But then, that is the American experience: the melting pot in action!

Thank you.

The A-List
Lecture 24

U p until this lecture, this course has excluded the sort of short, relatively easy piano works that are the mainstay of the pedagogic and amateur repertoire. Accordingly, the works that you will explore in this lecture represent—collectively—a "single" conceptual work: piano pieces intended primarily for amateurs. As such, the title of this lecture, "The A-List," refers—with no disparagement implied—to "The Amateur List." Specifically, this lecture will survey nine works chronologically, from Mozart's Piano Sonata in C Major of 1788 to Debussy's "Clair de Lune" of 1890.

Mozart: Piano Sonata in C Major, K. 545

- Mozart's Piano Sonata in C Major is the 16th of Mozart's 19 numbered piano sonatas. Mozart entered the work into his thematic catalog on June 26, 1788, when he was 32 years old. In the catalog, he described the piece as being *"eine kleine Klavier Sonate für Angfänger,"* meaning "a little piano sonata for beginners." While it is the single best-known piano work by Mozart today, it was unknown in his lifetime and wasn't published until 1805, 14 years after his death.

- Mozart's sonata is a perfect example of the cliché that big things come in small packages. The first movement is a crystal-clear sonata form, in which the essential pedagogic element—rising and falling scales—are heard during the modulating bridge and development section. Mozart's principal themes are models of brevity, memorability, and elegance.

- Theme 1 is but four measures long and consists of just two phrases and 15 notes—but it might very well be the most succinct and memorable thematic melody ever composed, with enough rhythmic variety and harmonic interest to power a tune four times longer.

- It is not unusual for composers to compose pedagogic music, and some composers built their entire careers around writing pedagogic music. In Mozart's Piano Sonata in C Major, K. 545, the highest of art and pedagogic utility coexist in perfect balance.

Beethoven: "Für Elise"

- "Für Elise" (Bagatelle no. 25 in A Minor) is cast as a rondo, which means that a principal theme—the rondo theme—returns periodically after various contrasting episodes. Along with the opening theme of Beethoven's Symphony no. 5 and the "Ode to Joy Theme" from the Symphony no. 9, the rondo theme of "Für Elise" is the most famous melody Beethoven ever composed.

- "Für Elise" was first published in 1867, 40 years after Beethoven's death. The manuscript had been discovered by a German music scholar named Ludwig Nohl, who noted that Beethoven's manuscript was inscribed "For Elise on 27 April as a memento from L. v. Beethoven."

- But who is Elise? The two principal candidates are a German soprano named Elisabeth Röckel and a rich, titled Austrian lady named Therese Malfatti. According to the German musicologist Klaus Kopitz, Elisabeth Röckel was part of Beethoven's inner circle around the year 1810 and might have gone by the nickname "Elise."

- However, the general consensus is that "Elise" is Therese Malfatti. She was a competent musician who was proposed to by Beethoven in 1810, when she was 18 years old. Her rejection was immediate and absolute.

- The likely story is that "Für Elise" was composed as an offering for Therese during Beethoven's abortive courtship. As for the title, the speculation is that given Beethoven's nearly illegible handwriting, Nohl simply misread and then miscopied the inscription, turning "Für Therese" into "Für Elise."

Beethoven: Minuet in G Major, WoO 10, No. 2

- In *The Music Man*, Professor Harold Hill is a bogus music teacher. His teaching "method" is something he calls "the think system": He tells his students that if they can think hard enough about a piece of music, they will be able to play it. The piece of music about which they are instructed to think is Beethoven's Minuet in G Major, WoO 10, no. 2.

Schumann: "Traumerei," from *Kinderscenen*, Op. 15

- In 1945, Schumann's "Traumerei"—which means "Dreaming"—was selected by some forgotten apparatchik at Radio Moscow to be played in the background during a moment of silence at 6:55 pm on May 8, 1945, in memory of the victims of the Soviet Union's war against Nazi Germany.

- Schumann's work evokes a mood of aching melancholy, loss, and nostalgia—a mood very different from that evoked by the military or funeral music that might well have been chosen. Schumann's "Traumerei" was immediately embraced by the Soviet people, who felt in its sweetness and longing not just their own grief but a healing sense of peace as well.

- "Traumerei" became the go-to piece played by Soviet military bands at World War II memorial ceremonies. According to the soprano Galina Vishnevskaya, it was even performed at Stalin's funeral.

- It is fascinating that the music of a 19th-century German composer should become a memorial to the 26.6 million Soviets who lost their lives in a war against Germany. But, really, it's just another example of the universal power of great art, which knows no boundaries or borders.

Mendelssohn: "Spring Song," Op. 62, No. 6

- For many people who grew up in the United States in the 1930s, 1940s, and 1950s, their first exposure to opera and concert music was not in an opera house or a concert hall but, rather, through the cartoons that used to be played at movie houses before the featured movie. The repertoire of opera and concert music provided a huge, preexisting catalog of out-of-copyright music that could be used to accompany the new, synchronized-sound cartoons that were introduced the late 1920s.

- The most used of all concert works in the cartoon world is Felix Mendelssohn's *Songs without Words*, Op. 62, no. 6 of 1842, also known as "Spring Song." The first cartoon to use the "Spring Song" in its soundtrack was released in 1931. Appropriately entitled "Mendelssohn's Spring Song," it was directed by Cy Young (of Disney fame) and animated by Lillian Freedman. It features various small critters—a family of birds, a butterfly, amorous spiders, a caterpillar, and a frog—all cavorting to the music.

- At Warner Bros, the legendary team of cartoonist Tex Avery (who created—among other characters—Bugs Bunny, Porky Pig, and Daffy Duck) and his music director Carl Stalling used the "Spring Song" as a sort of leitmotif throughout their cartoons. Idyllic, out-of-doors scenes were almost inevitably accompanied by the "Spring Song," and many of the hunting sequences featuring Elmer Fudd use the "Spring Song" as well.

Chopin: "Minute Waltz" (Waltz in D-flat Major, Op. 64, No. 1)

- While it is theoretically possible to play the notes of Chopin's Op. 64, no. 1 in one minute, such a pace cannot constitute anything resembling a musical performance or anything approaching Chopin's artistic intent. In fact, the piece—entitled "Minute Waltz"—wasn't intended to be played in a minute; it is a case of an epic mispronunciation.

- The piece was known as the "small" or "miniscule" waltz almost from the moment of its publication in 1847 by the Leipzig-based house of Breitkopf & Härtel. An early English edition entitled the piece the "Minute Waltz"—as in "small" or "brief"—not as in 60 seconds.

- Actually, the waltz has a legitimate, Chopin-sanctioned nickname: "Waltz of the Little Dog." This nickname was bestowed on the waltz by Chopin's beloved, the writer George Sand (whose birth name was Amantine Dupin). The little dog in question was George Sand's pooch, named Marquis, and its title was inspired by the dog's proclivity to chase his own tail.

Anton Rubinstein (1829–1894) was one of the most important Russian musicians of the 19th century.

Rubinstein: Melody in F

- Anton Rubinstein (who lived from 1829 to 1894) was one of the most important Russian musicians of the 19th century—a pianist, a conductor, and an educator of the highest renown. He founded the St. Petersburg Conservatory in 1862 and, by doing so, put Russia on the European musical map.

- Rubinstein composed 20 operas, 6 symphonies, 5 piano concertos, 2 'cello concertos, and a violin concerto; numerous other orchestral works and **tone poems**; oratorios, a ballet, a copious number of songs and chamber works; and many, many works for solo piano. The only one of Rubinstein's works consistently heard outside of Russia today is his Melody in F, Op. 3, no. 1, a modest little piano piece written in 1852, when he was just 23 years old.

Dvořák: *Humoresques*

- Antonin Dvořák (born in 1841 and died in 1904) was a compositional synthesist, who blended the melodic and rhythmic sensibilities of his native Czech music with a high-end Germanic compositional technique and the expressive palette of romanticism. The result is an irresistibly tuneful, technically polished, expressively powerful body of music. In his own lifetime, Dvořák was the single most popular composer of instrumental music.

- It was Dvořák's international popularity and his reputation as a "nationalist" composer that led him to be hired in 1892 as director of the National Conservatory of Music in New York City, where he worked for 3 years.

- During his stay in the United States, he composed some of his greatest music, including his Symphony in E Minor (known today as "The New World Symphony"), the **String Quartet** in F Major (known as the "American Quartet"), the String Quintet in E-flat Major, and the 'Cello Concerto in B Minor.

- In 1894, Dvořák returned home to Bohemia for summer break. He carried with him a sketchbook filled with themes presumably inspired by his American experience. During that summer of 1894, he composed a set of eight humoresques based on these "American" themes. He completed the set on August 27, 1894, and it was published a few months later.

- A humoresque is a genre of light music characterized by a mood of fanciful humor. Dvořák's *Humoresques* are brilliant, none more so than the seventh, which is, according to the American music critic David Hurwitz, "probably the most famous small piano work ever written after Beethoven's 'Für Elise.'"

Debussy: "Clair de Lune"
- In 1890, the 28-year-old Debussy composed a set of four piano pieces, which he entitled *Suite Bergamasque*. The third of the four pieces was a slow, atmospheric piece called "Promenade Sentimental." Having completed the *Suite Bergamasque*, Debussy put it on the shelf, where it sat for 15 years, until 1905.

- In the 15 years between 1890 and 1905, Debussy went from being a relative unknown to a famous composer. By 1905, there was a big demand for Debussy's music, and so it was that the Paris-based publishing house of E. Fromont approached Debussy with a request to publish the *Suite Bergamasque*.

- Debussy was torn: On one hand, he really wanted the money; on the other hand, (writes Debussy scholar Paul Roberts): "Debussy's early piano style bears little relation to the works of his maturity, and he became loath to publish [the *Suite Bergamasque*] at all."

- Money and good sense won out. Debussy reworked the pieces, retitled two of them ("Promenade Sentimental" became "Clair de Lune"), and then handed the set over to the publisher. Had the set not been published, it might very well have suffered the fate of so many unpublished manuscripts: It might have been given away, lost, or just thrown out.

Important Terms

string quartet: A performing ensemble consisting of two violins, a viola, and a 'cello. (2) A musical composition written for that ensemble.

tone poem: Also called a symphonic poem. A one-movement orchestral genre that develops a poetic idea, suggests a scene, or creates a mood. The tone poem is generally associated with the romantic era.

The A-List

Lecture 24—Transcript

Welcome back to *The 23 Greatest Solo Piano Works*. This is Lecture 24. It is entitled The A-List.

Yes, I know this survey is called *The 23 Greatest Solo Piano Works*, and that if we count the nine short works examined in this lecture, we get a total of 31 piano works. But we're not going to count the works discussed in this lecture as nine, but rather, as one, for two reasons. The first is that I say so. The second is that unlike the other 22 works featured in this course, these nine are all relatively short and were composed for amateur pianists.

Please, as a reminder: the principal back story of this survey has been the technological development of the piano and the concurrent evolution of piano music that exploited its developing capabilities. What that means is that this course has primarily been about virtuosic piano music: music that pushes the capabilities of the piano and pianists to their limits. Consequently, to this point, this survey has excluded the sort of short, relatively easy piano works that are the mainstay of the pedagogic and amateur repertoire; works that are far more familiar to the general public than many (if not most) of the works featured in this survey. Accordingly, the works we will explore in this lecture represent –collectively—a "single" conceptual work: piano pieces intended primarily for amateurs. As such, the title of this lecture, The A-List, refers—with no disparagement implied—to "the amateur list."

Here's our game plan. We will survey the nine works in this lecture chronologically, from Mozart's Piano Sonata in C Major of 1788 to Debussy's *Clair de Lune* of 1890. After having stated the particulars of each piece—when and where it was composed, etc.—we will explore each piece from the point of view of a single and I trust most entertaining storyline.

Wolfgang Mozart: Piano Sonata in C Major, K. 545 (1788), Movement One

Storyline: Who says high art and pedagogy cannot coexist? My friends, we hear the opening of the first movement of Mozart's Piano Sonata in C Major. [**Piano performance:** Mozart, Piano Sonata in C Major, K. 545.] This sonata is the 16th of Mozart's 19 numbered piano sonatas. Mozart entered the work into his thematic catalog on June 26, 1788, when he was 32 years old. In the catalog, he described the piece as being "*eine kleine Klavier Sonate für Angfänger*" meaning "a little piano sonata for beginners." While it is the single best-known piano work by Mozart today, it was unknown in his lifetime, and wasn't published until 1805, 14 years after his death.

It is not unusual for composers to compose pedagogic music, and some composers built their entire careers around writing pedagogic music, Beethoven's student Carl Czerny, for example. Czerny wrote countless such works, many of which are used to torture students of the piano to this very day. (Talk about fecund: Czerny's final composition—poetically entitled "30 Studies for Left hand"—was published as Op. 861! Only death made him stop.)

Sometimes, great composers write pedagogic music as well. Johann Sebastian Bach wrote scads of it, including the two volumes of *The Well-Tempered Clavier.* Beethoven wrote some, including the so-called Two Easy Piano Sonatas of Op. 49. Clementi, Schumann, Tchaikovsky, Prokofiev, Stravinsky, and Bartók—among others—all composed significant works for students.

Which brings us to Mozart's gem of a sonata, a perfect example of the cliché that "big things come in small packages." The first movement is a crystal-clear sonata form, in which the essential pedagogic element—rising and falling scales—are heard during the modulating bridge and the development section. Mozart's principal themes are models of brevity, memorability, and elegance. Theme one is but four measures long and consists of just two phrases and 15 notes. But what a perfect set of 15 notes! **[Piano demonstration.]**

That might very well be the most succinct and memorable thematic melody ever composed, with enough rhythmic variety and harmonic interest to power a tune four times longer. Oh my goodness, if he were alive today, Mozart could make a fortune writing advertising jingles, although we pray he wouldn't have to. Truly, in Mozart's Piano Sonata in C Major K. 545, the highest of art and pedagogic utility coexist in perfect balance!

Ludwig van Beethoven: *Für Elise* (1810)

Storyline: Who the heck is Elise? *Für Elise* is cast as a rondo, which means that a principal theme—the rondo theme—returns periodically after various contrasting episodes. Along with the opening theme of Beethoven's Symphony No. 5 [**piano demonstration**] and the "Ode to Joy Theme" from the Symphony No. 9 [**piano demonstration**] the rondo theme of *Für Elise* is the most famous melody Beethoven ever composed. [**Piano performance:** Beethoven, *Für Elise*.]

Für Elise is rather more prosaically known as "Bagatelle No. 25 in A Minor, WoO 59." "Bagatelle" means, literally, "a trifle." A musical bagatelle, then, is a short piece of music—usually for piano—of a light and entertaining character. "Without opus" is a catalog assembled in the 1950s listing all of Beethoven's works that were not published with an opus number.

Für Elise was first published in 1867, 40 years after Beethoven's death. The manuscript had been discovered by a German music scholar named Ludwig Nohl, whose claim to historical fame was this discovery. According to Nohl, Beethoven's manuscript was inscribed "For Elise on 27 April as a memento from L. v. Beethoven." Nohl hand copied Beethoven's manuscript, and it was Nohl's copy that became the basis for the published version of the piece. And while preliminary sketches for *Für Elise* survive to this day, the manuscript from which Nohl made his copy has since been lost.

While there was no year in Beethoven's dedicatory inscription, it is generally believed—for reasons to be explained—that the piece was composed in 1810. However, lacking a year, and any further information regarding the dedicatee, we are left with a question as to who was Elise. The two principal candidates are a German soprano named Elisabeth Röckel and a rich, titled Austrian lady named Therese Malfatti. According to the German musicologist Klaus Kopitz, Elisabeth Röckel was part of Beethoven's inner circle around the year 1810 and might have gone by the nickname "Elise."

However, the general consensus is that Elise is Therese Malfatti. She was a competent musician, and based on surviving images, a dark-haired babe. Swept up in one of his periodic attacks of testosterone-induced passion, our

"Romeo van Beethoven" proposed to Therese in 1810, when she was 18 years old. Her rejection was immediate and absolute, and thus Beethoven was able to add Therese to that long list of aristocratic ladies who venerated him as a musician but were grossed out by him as a man.

So, the likely story is that *Für Elise* was composed as an offering for Therese during Beethoven's abortive courtship. As for the title, the speculation is that given Beethoven's nearly illegible handwriting, Nohl simply misread and then miscopied the inscription, turning *Für Therese* into *Für Elise*. As for why the original manuscript for *Für Elise* (the one Ludwig Nohl hand copied) wasn't discovered until the 1860s? Well, Therese Malfatti—or Baroness Therese von Droßdik, which was her married name—didn't die until 1851. The manuscript—as part of her private papers—did not turn up until after her death. She wouldn't have had the manuscript had she not been the dedicatee, so that's it: Therese Malfatti must be Elise!

Beethoven: *Minuet in G*, WoO 10, No. 2

Storyline: The think system. A little autobiography, please. My maternal grandmother was an actress named Nancy R. Pollock. She was known primarily for her work on and off Broadway, and among other shows she appeared in was: *Middle of the Night* with Edward G. Robinson (who I knew as "Uncle Eddie"); *Diamond Lil'* with Mae West; and Tennessee Williams's *Period of Adjustment.* She appeared in a number of movies as well, including *The Pawnbroker* with Rod Steiger; *The Last Angry Man* with Paul Muni; and a potboiler called *Go Naked in the World* with her pal Tony Franciosa, Ernest Borgnine, and the cone-breasted Gina Lollobrigida, whom my grandmother unkindly referred to as "the lump."

When she wasn't acting, she worked as a honcho for Actors' Equity, the labor union that represents American theatrical actors and stage managers. She could be a royal pain, and her fights with the producer David Merrick—who hated the union and did everything he could to bust it by importing non-Equity productions from London—were legendary.

Among her colleagues in Equity and one of her best friends was an actor who had achieved fame as a cowboy in B westerns named Robert Preston. Preston put the theatrical world on its ear when he starred as Professor Harold Hill in Meredith Willson's *The Music Man* in 1957 (for which Preston won a Tony) and then reprised the role in the movie in 1962. I was eight years old when I saw the movie and I loved it. I had just started taking piano lessons, and so—perhaps because Robert Preston was my grandma's friend (which was hecka cool beyond measure)—I was particularly enthralled by the think system.

In *The Music Man*, Professor Harold Hill (played by Preston) is a bogus music teacher. He teaching "method" is something called the think system: He tells his students that if they can think hard enough about a piece of music, they will actually be able to play it. The piece of music about which they are instructed to think is Beethoven's *Minuet in G*, WoO 10, No. 2. **[Piano performance:** Beethoven, Minuet in G.] I cannot hear that minuet without thinking about my grandmother, Robert Preston, my first piano lessons, and how I wish that the think system actually worked!

Schumann *Traumerei*, from *Kinderscenen* Op. 15 (1838)

Storyline: Joseph Stalin's funeral. In 1945, Schumann's *Traumerei*—which means "Dreaming"—was selected by some forgotten apparatchik at Radio Moscow to be played in the background during a moment of silence at 6:55 pm on May 8, 1945, in memory of the victims of the Soviet Union's war against Nazi Germany. Whoever that Radio Moscow functionary was, he has gained a measure of immortality for what was an inspired choice. Schumann's work evokes a mood of aching melancholy, loss, and nostalgia, a mood very different from that that would be evoked by the military or funeral music that might well have been chosen. Schumann's *Traumerei* was immediately embraced by the Soviet people, who felt in its sweetness and longing not just their own grief but a healing sense of peace as well.

Traumerei became the go-to piece played by Soviet military bands at World War II memorial ceremonies. To this day, it is played every hour on the hour at the massive war memorial at Mamayev Kurgan, the hill that dominates the city of Volgograd, formerly known as Stalingrad. It has been played 24/7 at St. Petersburg's Peskaryev Memorial Cemetery since it opened in 1960. It was even—according to the soprano Galina Vishnevskaya (the wife of 'cellist Mstislav Rostropovich)—performed at Stalin's funeral. **[Piano**

performance: Schumann, *Kinderscenen*, Op. 15, No. 7.] Fascinating, isn't it? That the music of a 19th-century German composer should become a memorial to the 26.6 million Soviets who lost their lives in a war against Germany. But really, it's just another example of the universal power of great art, which knows no boundaries or borders.

Mendelssohn *Spring Song*, Op. 62 No. 6 (1842)

Storyline: Cartoons. For many folks growing up in the United States in the 1930s, '40s, and '50s their first exposure to opera and concert music was not in an opera house or a concert hall but rather, through the cartoons that used to be played at movie houses before the featured movie. The repertoire of opera and concert music provided a huge, preexisting catalog of out-of-copyright music that could be used to accompany the new, synchronized-sound cartoons that were introduced the late 1920s.

No doubt the most famous of the many animated concert classics was Disney's *Fantasia* of 1940, which featured Stravinsky's *The Rite of Spring*, Mussorgsky's *Night on Bald Mountain*, and Paul Dukas's *The Sorcerer's Apprentice*. Another classical classic is Warner Bros.' 1957 *What's Opera, Doc?*, during which Elmer Fudd chases Bugs Bunny through various parodies of Richard Wagner's music dramas. The cartoon simultaneously achieves its comic apogee and musical perigee when Fudd, portraying the demi-god Siegfried, sings to the melody of *Ride of the Valkyries*: "Kill tha wabbit, kill tha wabbit, kill tha wabbit, kill tha wabbit." Oh yeah. (For our information, in 1994 *What's Opera, Doc?* was voted numbah one of the "50 Greatest Cartoons" by over 1,000 animation professionals.)

We can all wish we had a $20 for every time Franz Liszt's *Hungarian Rhapsody No. 2* was used in a cartoon. From Bugs Bunny to Tom and Jerry, Mickey Mouse to Woody the Woodpecker, the Liszt has gotten some major mileage. But to my estimation, the single most used of all concert works in the cartoon world is Felix Mendelssohn's *Song Without Words* Op. 62 No. 6 of 1842, also known as "Spring Song." [**Piano performance:** *Song Without Words* Op. 62 No. 6.]

The first cartoon to use the "Spring Song" in its soundtrack was released in 1931. Appropriately entitled "Mendelssohn's Spring Song," it was directed by Cy Young (who went on to big-time fame at Disney) and animated by Lillian Freedman. It features various small critters—a family of birds, a butterfly, amorous spiders, a caterpillar, and a frog—all cavorting to the music. At Warner Bros, the legendary team of cartoonist Tex Avery (who created—among other characters—Bugs Bunny, Porky Pig, and Daffy Duck) and his music director Carl Stalling used the "Spring Song" as a sort of *leitmotif* throughout their cartoons. Idyllic, out-of-doors scenes were almost inevitably accompanied by the "Spring Song," and many of the hunting sequences featuring Elmer Fudd use the "Spring Song" as well. How would Mendelssohn have felt about all of this? Well, given his own talents as a visual artist, we'd like to think that he would be amused. But in fact, he'd probably start singing, "Kill tha cartoonist, kill tha cartoonist ..."

Frédéric Chopin: *Minute Waltz* (Waltz in D-flat major, Op. 64, No. 1) (1847)

Storyline: Should we be watching the clock? OK, I will grant that it is theoretically possible to play the notes of Chopin's Op. 64, No. 1 waltz in one minute. However, not a one of us will grant that such a mach-3 sprint can constitute anything resembling a musical performance or anything approaching the Chopin's artistic intent. Let's hear a performance by Magdalina Melkonyan, one that clocks in at something more than a minute. [**Piano performance:** Chopin, Waltz in D-flat Major, Op. 64, No. 1.]

So, if the piece wasn't intended to be played in a minute, why is it called "The Minute Waltz"? It's a case of an epic mispronunciation! Here's the story. The piece was known as the "small" or "miniscule" waltz almost from the moment of its publication in 1847 by the Leipzig-based house of Breitkopf & Härtel. An early English edition entitled the piece "The Minute Waltz"; "minute", as in small or brief, not "minute," as in 60 seconds. Boy oh boy, talk about the damage that can be done by accenting the wrong syllable of a word! Confirmation comes from the pianist and professor of piano Dr. Maurice Hinson. In his book *The Pianist's Dictionary*, published by Indiana University Press, Hinson writes: "The piece bears an erroneous nickname since the story long associated with this nickname presumes the pianist is supposed to play the piece in one minute. The word min-Nute [actually] means small or little waltz."

As a matter of fact, the waltz actually does have a legitimate, Chopin-sanctioned nickname, and that nickname is "Waltz of the Little Dog." This nickname was bestowed on the waltz by none other than Chopin's main squeeze, the writer George Sand (whose birth name was Amantine Dupin). The little dog in question was George Sand's pooch Marquis, and its title was inspired by Marquis's proclivity to chase his own tail.

Rubinstein: Melody in F (1852)

Storyline: George Gershwin falls in love. Background: Anton Rubinstein lived from 1829 to 1894. He was one of the most important Russian musicians of the 19th century, a pianist, conductor and educator of the highest renown. He founded the St. Petersburg Conservatory in 1862 and by doing so put Russia on the European musical map. As a pianist and educator, he founded what is now understood to be Russian School of pianism, a sort of piano playing informed by titanic technique and marked by expressive virility, vitality, and passion. As a composer and educator he taught a generation of young Russian composers, the most important of whom was his protégé, Peter Tchaikovsky.

As a composer, Anton Rubinstein put the "p" in prolific: He composed 20 operas, six symphonies, five piano concertos, two 'cello concertos and a violin concerto; numerous other orchestral works and tone poems; oratorios, a ballet, a copious number of songs and chamber works; and many, many works for solo piano. So ain't it just a nasty bit of irony that the only one of Rubinstein's works consistently heard outside of Russia today is his Melody in F, Op. 3, No. 1, a modest little piano piece written in 1852 when he was just 23 years old? Here's a bit of it, in all its songlike, if somewhat sappy glory: [**Piano performance:** Rubinstein, Melody in F.]

Modest though it may be, Rubinstein's Melody in F changed at least one life for the betterment of all humankind, a statement completely lacking in hyperbole. George Gershwin (or Jacob Gershowitz, as was his birth name) was born in Brooklyn, New York on September 26, 1898. He was a rough-and-tumble street kid who nevertheless harbored a love for music that he discovered at the age of six. He was strolling down 125th street in Manhattan (we presume in the company of an adult) when he stopped outside a penny arcade. Anton Rubinstein's Melody in F was playing on an automated piano, and George was riveted. He later remembered, "The peculiar jumps in the music held me rooted. To this very day, I can't hear the tune without picturing myself outside that arcade, standing there barefoot and in overalls, drinking it all in!" Gershwin—who died all too young at the age of 38—went on to write more great tunes in a shorter period of time than any other American-born composer before or since. And if we have Anton Rubinstein to even partially thank for that, well, then Rubinstein's compositional career will not have been in vain!

Dvořák: *Humoresque* (1894)

Storyline: Passengers will please refrain, from flushing toilets while the train, is standing in the station (I love you). We'll get back to that storyline in a moment. First, the particulars. Antonin Dvořák was born in 1841 and died in 1904. He was a compositional synthesist, who blended the melodic and rhythmic sensibilities of his native Czech music with a high-end Germanic compositional technique and the expressive palette of romanticism. The result is an irresistibly tuneful, technically polished, expressively powerful body of music. In his own lifetime, Dvořák was the single most popular composer of instrumental music on the planet.

It was Dvořák's international popularity and his reputation as a "nationalist" composer that led him to be hired—in 1892—as director of the National Conservatory of Music in New York City. In that 400th anniversary year of Columbus's first voyage to the Americas, the board of the Conservatory hoped that Dvořák—through his own example—would found an American school of composition, at a time when most American composers were doing their best to "be like Brahms."

Dvořák directed the National Conservatory for three years, until 1895. During his stay in the United States he composed some of his greatest music, including his Symphony in E Minor, known today as "The New World Symphony," the String Quartet in F Major (known as the "American

Quartet"), the String Quintet in E-Flat Major, and the 'Cello Concerto in B Minor. In 1894, Dvořák returned home to Bohemia for summer break. He carried with him a sketchbook filled with themes presumably inspired by his American experience. During that summer of 1894, he composed a set of eight humoresques based on these American themes. He completed the set on August 27, 1894 and it was published a few months later.

A humoresque is genre of light music characterized by a mood of fanciful humor. Dvořák's *Humoresques* are brilliant, none more so than number seven which is, according to the American music critic David Hurwitz, "probably the most famous small piano work ever written after Beethoven's *Für Elise*." Let's hear a bit of it. [**Piano performance:** Dvořák, *Humoresque* No. 7.]

On to our storyline. In Dvořák's day, passenger trains employed something called a hopper toilet: human waste was simply deposited on the tracks through what was basically a hole in the floor (euphemistically called a drop chute). In the United States, placards hung over the toilets that read: "Passengers will please refrain from flushing toilets while the train is standing in or passing through a station." Well, it didn't take long for some unknown wag to alter these words ever so slightly and append them to the melody of Dvořák's seventh humoresque:

> Passengers will please refrain
> From flushing toilets while the train
> Is standing in the station (I love you).
> We encourage constipation
> While the train is in the station,
> Moonlight always makes me think of you.

The verses continue; charity demands that I do not. For our information: In his autobiography, Supreme Court justice William O. Douglas claims that he and a fellow Yale Law School professor named Thurman Arnold first put those words to Dvořák's *Humoresque* during a trip on the New Haven Railroad in the 1930s. Sorry Judge; you might have been the longest serving justice in the history of the court, but "your" little ditty long predates the 1930s.

There's a great punch line here. Dvořák loved trains, and believed them to be humankind's single greatest creation. He was also just about the nicest, most down-to-earth major artist we'll ever meet. I have no doubt whatsoever that had he heard the ditty he would have screamed with laughter.

Claude Debussy: *Clair de Lune* (1890)

Storyline: How this piece might have been lost forever. I would ask a series of rhetorical questions: Who doesn't adore Debussy's *Clair de Lune*? Who is not captivated by this gentle, gauzy, *tres romantique* evocation of "moonlight," which is what *Clair de Lune* means? What sort of miserable misanthrope is not enthralled by this piece? Answer to the last question: in 1905, Clause Debussy his very self!

Here's the scoop. In 1890, the 28-year-old Debussy composed a set of four piano pieces which he entitled *Suite Bergamasque*. The third of the four pieces was a slow, atmospheric piece called *Promenade Sentimental*. Having completed the *Suite Bergamasque*, Debussy put it on the shelf, where it sat for 15 years, until 1905. In the 15 years between 1890 and 1905, Debussy went from being a relative unknown to a famous composer. By 1905, there was a big demand for Debussy's music, and so it was that the Paris-based publishing house of E. Fromont approached Debussy with a request to publish the *Suite Bergamasque*. Debussy was torn: on one hand, he really wanted the money; on the other hand (writes Debussy scholar Paul Roberts): "Debussy's early piano style bears little relation to the works of his maturity, and he became loath to publish [the *Suite Bergamasque*] at all."

For example, by 1905 Debussy had come to feel that the rippling, left-handed accompanimental arpeggios in the third piece of the set—entitled *Promenade Sentimental*—were cheap and anachronistic. (They do, today, evoke a sort of "cocktail piano" sensibility, though we can't really blame Debussy for that, given that the style of playing we call "cocktail" was still some fifty-plus years in the future.)

Anyway, money and good sense won out; Debussy reworked the pieces, retitled two of them (*Promenade Sentimental* became *Clair de Lune*), and then handed the set over to the publisher.

Had the set not been published, it might very well have suffered the fate of so many un-published manuscripts in a pre-photocopy age: it might have been given away, lost, or just thrown out.

Let's hear it in its entirety: Claude Debussy's *Clair de Lune*, from the *Suite Bergamasque*.

[**Piano performance:** Debussy, *Clair de Lune.*]

Conclusion: An Ode to the Piano

On Monday, July 30, 2012, a front-page article in The New York Times sent shivers up and down my spine. Entitled "For More Pianos, Last Note Is thud in the dump", the article described how increasing numbers of used pianos are being dumped, trashed, and turned into scrap and fire wood. It seems that many of the pianos manufactured during the first part of the twentieth century—during what was, numerically, the golden age of piano building— have reached their maximum life expectancy. The article also explained that pianos are being replaced in homes by that abomination called an "electronic keyboard", heaven help us all.

The front-page photo showed a warehouse filled with smashed pianos; the caption read:

> "a yellow loader with a claw in front scuttled in like a giant beetle, crushing keyboards, soundboards and cases into a pile."

Oh the pain; oh the humanity! That warehouse reminded me of a big game hunter's trophy room: everywhere death and the evisceration of once beautiful, living things.

And make no mistake about it: a piano is—while it is being played—a living thing, an extension of the body AND life force of the person caressing OR pounding its keys. A piano is made out of wood, metal, leather, and felt which expands and contracts the same way our bodies do. A piano's entire reason to be is to respond—in analog—to our bodies' motion in such a way as to create sound.

456

And what glorious sound. The piano is a one-person orchestra, an instrument that has been lavished with a repertoire that is the envy of every other instrument. From the keyboard music of Johann Sebastian Bach through the piano music of Beethoven, Chopin, Liszt, Schumann, Brahms, Rachmaninoff, Scriabin, Ives, Prokofiev, Bartók, Messiaen, Rzewski, and hundreds of other composer old and new, the repertoire of the piano spans a historical and expressive depth far beyond that of any other instrument.

If, according to the nineteenth century English essayist Walter Pater, "All art aspires to the condition of music", I would most humbly (if parochially!) suggest that "all instruments aspire to the condition of the piano".

Thank you.

Timeline

1722..................... Johann Sebastian Bach (1685–1750), *The Well-Tempered Clavier*, Book One

1741..................... Johann Sebastian Bach, *Goldberg Variations* (1741)

1784..................... Wolfgang Mozart (1756–1791), Piano Sonata in C Minor, K. 457

1788..................... Wolfgang Mozart, Piano Sonata in C Major, K. 545

1796..................... Ludwig van Beethoven (1770–1827), Minuet in G Major, WoO 10, No. 2

1806..................... Ludwig van Beethoven, Piano Sonata No. 23 in F Minor, Op. 57, *Appassionata*

1810..................... Ludwig van Beethoven, "Für Elise"

1823..................... Ludwig van Beethoven, *Diabelli Variations*, Op. 120

1828..................... Franz Schubert (1897–1828), Piano Sonata No. 21 in B-flat Major

1836..................... Frédéric Chopin (1810–1849), Ballade in G Minor, Op. 23

1838..................... Robert Schumann (1810–1856), *Kreisleriana*

1838..................... Robert Schumann "Traumerei," from *Kinderscenen*, Op. 15

1839..................... Frédéric Chopin, *Préludes*, Op. 28

1842.................... Felix Mendelssohn (1809–1847), "Spring Song,"
Op. 62, No. 6

1847.................... Frédéric Chopin, "Minute Waltz" (Waltz in D-flat Major,
Op. 64, No. 1)

1852.................... Anton Rubinstein (1829–1894), Melody in F

1853.................... Franz Liszt (1811–1881), Sonata in B Minor

1855.................... Franz Liszt, *Années de pèlerinage* (*Years of Pilgrimage*),
First Year

1858.................... Franz Liszt, *Années de pèlerinage* (*Years of Pilgrimage*),
Second Year

1861.................... Johannes Brahms (1833–1897), *Handel Variations*,
Op. 24

1874.................... Modest Mussorgsky (1839–1881), *Pictures at
an Exhibition*

1890.................... Claude Debussy (1862–1918), "Clair de Lune"

1893.................... Johannes Brahms, Six Pieces for Piano, Op. 118

1894.................... Antonin Dvořák (1841–1904), *Humoresques*, No. 7

1907.................... Alexander Scriabin (1872–1915), Piano Sonata No. 5 in
F-sharp Major, Op. 53

1909.................... Isaac Albéniz (1860–1909), *Iberia*

1910.................... Claude Debussy, *Préludes*, Book One

1911.................... Maurice Ravel (1875–1937), *Valses nobles et sentimentales*

Glossary

accent: The emphasis of certain notes over others.

accidental: A notational sign/symbol that modifies a pitch. *See also* **sharp, flat**, and **natural**.

adagio: Slow.

allegro: Fast.

andante: Moderately slow.

asymmetrical meter: Exhibits no particular repeated metric pattern.

atonal/atonality: Music lacking the sense of a central pitch, as opposed to tonal/tonality.

augmentation: The process of systematically extending the note values of a given melodic line.

bar: *See* **measure**.

bar lines: Notational device: two vertical lines that enclose a measure and are equivalent to one metric unit.

basso continuo: Those instruments in a baroque-era ensemble (typically a chord-producing instrument and a bass instrument) whose job it was to articulate with unerring clarity the bass line and play the harmonic progressions built atop the bass line.

beat: Smallest pulse to which we can comfortably move our bodies. *See also* **meter**.

cadence: A harmonic or melodic formula that occurs at the end of a phrase, section, or composition and conveys a momentary or permanent conclusion—in other words, a musical punctuation mark.

cadenza: Passage for solo instrument in an orchestral work, usually a concerto, designed to showcase the player's skills.

chord: Simultaneous sounding of three or more different pitches.

chromatic: A pitch that lies outside of whatever key area presently anchors a passage.

classical: Designation given to works of art of the 17th and 18th centuries, characterized by clear lines and balanced form.

closed cadence: Equivalent to a period or an exclamation mark; such a cadence ends on the tonic and gives a sense of rest and resolution.

coda: The closing few measures of a composition; usually not a part of the main theme groups of the standard form of a composition but a finishing theme added to the end to give the composition closure.

col legno: Striking the strings with the wood side of the bow.

compound meter: Any meter that features a triple subdivision within each beat.

concerto grosso: A multimovement work in which multiple soloists are accompanied by, and sometimes pitted against, the orchestra.

conjunct: Melodic contour that generally features steps between pitches; such a melody will usually sound smooth and controlled.

consonance: A musical entity or state that can be perceived as a point of rest.

deceptive/false cadence: Equivalent to a colon or semicolon; such a cadence brings resolution but not to the expected tonic harmony.

development: The second large part of a sonata form movement, during which the themes are developed in a generally unstable harmonic environment.

diminution: The process of systematically shortening the note values of a given melodic line.

disjunct: Melodic contour that generally features leaps between pitches; such a melody will usually sound jagged and jumpy.

dissonance: A musical entity or state of instability that seeks resolution to consonance.

dominant: Pitch and chord five pitches above a given tonic pitch/chord. The dominant harmony is the chord most closely related to the tonic chord in a given key; the dominant chord will almost always immediately precede an appearance of the tonic chord.

double exposition form: Sonata form adapted to the needs of a concerto.

double scherzo: A five-part form in which there are two middle B sections separated by three A sections: A–B–A–B–A.

dynamics: Degrees of loudness—e.g., piano (quiet), forte (loud)—indicated in a musical score.

elegy: A song expressing sorrow for one who has died.

enharmonic: Pitches that are identical in sound but with different spellings, depending on the key context, e.g., C-sharp and D-flat.

exposition: The first part of a sonata form, during which the principal themes are introduced.

expressionism: The contemporary art movement that celebrated inner emotional states as the highest truth.

fermata: Pause.

flat: Accidental (sign/symbol) placed to the left of a note indicating that the pitch should be lowered by a semitone.

frequency: Rate of vibration of a string, column of air, or other sound-producing body.

fugato: A fugal exposition inserted into a movement that is not otherwise a fugue.

fugue: Important baroque musical procedure in which a theme (or subject) is developed by means of various contrapuntal techniques.

functional harmony: Harmonic usage that was standardized and codified into a fully coherent system during the baroque period. This method is still used by modern arrangers and orchestrators. The basic concept used in functional harmony is the fact that all harmonic sounds used in music may be classified into three large groups. These groups derive their names from the three important roots of the traditional harmonic system: the tonic, the dominant, and the subdominant.

fundamental frequency: Rate of vibration of the full length of a sound-producing body and the sound created by that full-length vibration.

graded dynamics: Markings used to indicate a progressive increase in loudness or softness, respectively, crescendo (getting louder) or decrescendo/diminuendo (getting softer/quieter).

half step: *See* **semitone**.

harmony: The musical art (and science) of manipulating simultaneous pitches.

home key: Main key of a movement or composition. *See also* **key**.

homophonic texture/homophony: Texture in which one melodic line predominates; all other melodic material is heard as being secondary or accompanimental.

hymn: A religious song.

inclusive art: An art in which distinctions between popular, sacred, and concert music are immaterial when compared to its universal power to move and enlighten.

intermezzo: An instrumental interlude between the acts of a performance.

interval: Distance between two pitches, e.g., C–G (upward) equals a fifth.

inversion: Loosely applied to indicate a reversal in melodic direction. Harmonic inversion is a situation in which a chord tone other than the root is in the bass.

key: Collection of pitches that relate to a specific major or minor mode.

largo/lento: Very slow.

major: Modern term for Ionian mode; characterized by an intervallic profile of whole tone–whole tone–semitone–whole tone–whole tone–whole tone–semitone (symbolized as: T–T–S | T–T–T–S).

measure: Metric unit; space between two bar lines.

melody: Any succession of pitches.

meter: Group of beats organized in a regular rhythmic pattern and notated in music as a time signature.

minor: Modern term for Aeolian mode; characterized by an intervallic profile of whole tone–semitone–whole tone–whole tone–semitone–whole tone–whole tone (symbolized as T–S–T | T–S–T–T).

minuet: A dance of the 17th and 18th centuries, graceful and dignified, in moderately slow three-quarter time.

minuet and trio form: A three-part musical form consisting of a minuet ("A"), followed by a contrasting minuet ("B," called the trio), followed by a return to the original minuet ("A," called the da capo). Minuet and trio was the only baroque-era form to find its way into the instrumental music of the classical era.

modal ambiguity: Harmonic ambiguity, in which the main key is not clearly identified.

mode: A type of pitch collection (or scale).

modulation: The process of changing key during the course of a piece of music.

motive: Brief succession of pitches from which a melody grows through the processes of repetition, sequence, and transformation.

movement: Independent section within a larger work.

musical form: The manner in which a given movement of music is structured.

natural: Accidental (sign/symbol) placed to the left of a note, indicating that the note should not be sharpened or flattened; a white key on a keyboard.

note: A sound with three properties: a single, singable fundamental frequency; timbre; and duration.

open cadence: Equivalent to a comma; such a cadence pauses on the dominant harmony without resolving the tonic harmony, creating tension and the need to continue.

open form: A movement in which thematic ideas are introduced and immediately developed in a continuous sequence.

opus number: A number supplied by a publisher to indicate the order in which a composition (or set of compositions) is published.

orchestral unison: A technique by which multiple instruments simultaneously play the same pitch but in different registers (ranges).

ostinato: A brief melodic idea that is repeated over and over again.

overture: Music preceding an opera or play, often played as an independent concert piece.

pedal: A single pitch or harmony sustained or repeated for a period of time.

pitch: A sound with two properties: a single, singable fundamental frequency and timbre.

pizzicato: Plucking, rather than bowing, a stringed instrument.

polyphonic texture/polyphony: Texture consisting of two or more simultaneous melody lines of equal importance.

presto: Very fast.

recapitulation: The third large part of a sonata form movement, during which the themes return in their original order.

recitative: Operatic convention in which the lines are half sung, half spoken.

ritornello form: A refrain procedure in which a theme returns in part, called a fragmentary refrain, over the course of a movement. This form is among the most common of all baroque-era instrumental procedures.

rondo form: A classical-era form that sees a principal theme (the rondo theme) return like a refrain after various contrasting episodes.

scale: All the pitches inside a given octave, arranged stepwise so that there is no duplication. The names of the chords built on the scale steps are: tonic, supertonic, mediant, subdominant, dominant, submediant, and leading tone.

scherzo form: Meaning literally "I'm joking," scherzo is the designation Beethoven gave to his modified use of minuet and trio form.

semitone: Smallest interval in Western music; on the keyboard, the distance between a black key and a white key, as well as B–C and E–F.

sequence: Successive repetitions of a motive at different pitches; compositional technique for extending melodic ideas.

sharp: Accidental (sign/symbol) placed to the left of a note, indicating that the pitch should be raised by a semitone.

solo concerto: A multimovement work in which a single soloist is accompanied by, and sometimes pitted against, the orchestra.

sonata: Piece of music, typically in three or four movements, composed for a piano (piano sonata) or a piano plus one instrument (violin sonata, for instance).

sonata form: A classical-era formal process posited on the introduction, development, recapitulation, and reconciliation of multiple contrasting themes.

string quartet: A performing ensemble consisting of two violins, a viola, and a 'cello. (2) A musical composition written for that ensemble.

subject: The theme of a fugue.

suite: A concert work consisting of a collection of dances extracted from a longer ballet.

symphonic poem: Orchestral work in which the form is determined by the story being told.

symphony: A multimovement work composed for an orchestra.

syncopation: Displacement of the expected accent from a strong beat to a weak beat and vice versa.

tempo: Relative speed of a passage of music.

texture: Number of melodies present and the relationship between those melodies in a given segment of music; they include monophony, polyphony (counterpoint), heterophony, and homophony.

theme: Primary musical subject matter in a given section of music.

theme and variations form: A classical-era formal process that exhibits a systematically varied theme in a series of variations.

timbre: Tone color.

tonal/tonality: Sense that one pitch is central to a section of music, as opposed to atonal/atonality.

tone poem: Also called a symphonic poem. A one-movement orchestral genre that develops a poetic idea, suggests a scene, or creates a mood. The tone poem is generally associated with the romantic era.

tonic: Home pitch and chord of a piece of tonal music. Think of the term as being derived from "tonal center" (tonic). For example, if a movement is in C, the pitch C is the tonic pitch, and the harmony built on C is the tonic chord.

tonicization: The process of creating a temporary tonic by articulating a dominant-to-tonic progression of a key other than the one currently in use.

triad: A chord consisting of three different pitches built from some combination of major and/or minor thirds.

trio sonata: Baroque-era genre of chamber music consisting of two soprano instruments, a bass instrument, and a chord-producing instrument (called the continuo). The most common trio sonata instrumentation was two violins, a 'cello, and a harpsichord.

triple meter: Metrical pattern having three beats to a measure.

tune: Generally singable, memorable melody with a clear sense of beginning, middle, and end.

waltz: A dance of Austrian/Viennese origin in triple meter.

whole-tone collection: Divides the octave into six equal segments; a whole-tone scale ascends and descends by major seconds, or whole tones.

Bibliography

Brendel, Alfred. *Alfred Brendel on Music*. Chicago: A Capella, 2001.

————. *Music Sounded Out: Essays, Lectures, Interviews, Afterthoughts*. New York: Farrar, Straus, and Giroux, 1990.

Buelow, George. "Andreas Werckmeister." In *The New Grove Dictionary of Music and Musicians*. Vol. 15. London & New York: Macmillan, 1980.

Davidson, Michael. *The Classical Piano Sonata from Haydn to Prokofiev*. London: Kahn & Averill, 2004.

Faivre, Antoine. *Theosophy, Imagination, Tradition: Studies in Western Esotericism*. Albany: SUNY Press, 2000.

Fuller, Jake. *Waltz: History of Dance*. Accessed at http://www.centralhome.com/ballroomcountry/waltz.htm.

Glockemeier, Georg. *Zur Wiener Judenfrage*. Leipzig and Vienna: Verlag Günther, 1936.

Good, Edwin M. *Giraffes, Black Dragons, and Other Pianos*. 2nd ed. Stanford: Stanford University Press, 2001.

Grout, Donald, and Claude Palisca. *A History of Western Music*. 4th ed. New York: W. W. Norton, 1988.

Hildebrandt, Dieter. *Pianoforte: A Social History of the Piano*. Translated by Harriet Goodman. New York: George Braziller, 1985.

Hinson, Maurice. *The Pianist's Dictionary*. Bloomington: Indiana University Press, 2004.

Lamb, Andrew. "Waltz." In *The New Grove Dictionary of Music and Musicians*. Vol. 20. London & New York: Macmillan, 1980.

Layton, Robert, ed. *A Companion to the Concerto*. New York: Schirmer Books, 1988.

Machlis, Joseph. *Introduction to Contemporary Music*. 2nd ed. New York: W. W. Norton, 1979.

Palmer, R. R., and Joel Colton. *A History of the Modern World*. 6th ed. New York: Alfred A. Knopf, 1984.

Rimsky-Korsakov, Nikolai. *My Musical Life*. Translated by J. A. Joffe. London: Faber, 1989.

Salzman, Eric. *Twentieth-Century Music: An Introduction*. 4th ed. Upper Saddle River, NJ: Prentice Hall, 2002.

Schoenberg, Arnold. *Structural Functions of Harmony*. New York: W. W. Norton, 1969.

———. *Style and Idea*. Berkeley and Los Angeles: University of California Press, 1975.

Schonberg, Harold. *The Great Pianists*. New York: Simon and Schuster, 1963.

———. *The Great Pianists*. Revised and updated. New York: Fireside, 1987.

———. *The Lives of the Great Composers*. New York: W. W. Norton, 1970.

———. *The Lives of the Great Composers*. 3rd ed. New York: W. W. Norton, 1997.

Shapiro, Nat. *An Encyclopedia of Quotations about Music*. New York: Da Capo, 1985.

Shostakovich, Dmitri. *Testimony*. Edited by Solomon Volkov. New York: Harper and Row, 1979.

Siepmann, J. *The Piano: The Complete Illustrated Guide to the World's Most Popular Musical Instrument*. Milwaukee, WI: Hal Leonard & Carlton Books, 1996.

Slonimsky, Nicolas. *Lexicon of Musical Invective*. 2nd ed. Seattle and London: University of Washington Press, 1975.

Stasov, Vladimir. *Selected Essays on Music*. Translated by Florence Jonas. London: Barrie & Rockliff, 1968.

Strunk, Oliver, and Leo Treitler. *Source Readings in Music History*. New York: W. W. Norton, 1998.

Taruskin, Richard. *The Oxford History of Western Music*. Oxford and New York: Oxford University Press, 2005.

Tovey, Donald Francis. *Essays in Musical Analysis: Chamber Music*. Oxford: Oxford University Press, 1945.

Waissenberger, Robert, ed. *Vienna in the Biedermeier Era*. New York: Mallard Press, 1986.

Warburton, Ernest. "Johann Christian Bach." In *The New Grove Dictionary of Music and Musicians*. Vol. 1. London and New York: Macmillan, 1980.

Weiss, Piero, and Richard Taruskin. *Music in the Western World: A History in Documents*. New York: Schirmer Books, 1984.

Wolff, Konrad. *Masters of the Keyboard*. Bloomington: Indiana University Press, 1990.

Albéniz
Clark, Walter Aaron. *Isaac Albéniz: Portrait of a Romantic*. Oxford: Oxford University Press, 1999.

Johann Sebastian Bach

David, Hans, and Arthur Mendel. *The Bach Reader*. Rev. ed. New York: W. W. Norton, 1966.

Geck, Martin. *Johann Sebastian Bach: Life and Work*. Orlando, FL: Harcourt, Inc., 2006.

Mellers, Wilfrid. *Bach and the Dance of God*. London: Faber and Faber, 1980.

Wolff, Christoph. *Johann Sebastian Bach: The Learned Musician*. New York: W. W. Norton, 2000.

Woodward, Roger. "In Search of a Performance Practice." *The Well-Tempered Clavier*. Celestial Harmonies, 14281-2.

Beethoven

Cooper, Barry. *Beethoven and the Creative Process*. Oxford and New York: Clarendon Press, 1990.

Cooper, Martin. *Beethoven: The Last Decade*. London: Oxford University Press, 1970.

Czerny, Carl. *On the Proper Performance of All Beethoven's Works for the Piano*. Edited and with a commentary by Paul Badura-Skoda. Vienna: Universal Editions, 1970.

Kinderman, William. *Beethoven*. Berkeley and Los Angeles: University of California Press, 1995.

Lockwood, Lewis. *Beethoven: The Music and the Life*. New York: W. W. Norton, 2003.

Morris, Edmund. *Beethoven: The Universal Composer*. New York: Harper Collins, 2005.

Ratcliffe, Ronald. *Steinway*. San Francisco: Chronicle Books, 1989.

Scherman, Thomas, and Louis Biancolli, eds. *The Beethoven Companion.* Garden City: Doubleday, 1972.

Solomon, Maynard. *Beethoven.* 2nd rev. ed. New York: Schirmer Books, 1998.

———. *Late Beethoven.* Berkeley and Los Angeles: University of California Press, 2003.

Stravinsky, Igor, and Robert Craft. *Memories and Commentaries.* Berkeley and Los Angeles: University of California Press, 1981.

Tovey, Donald Francis. *A Companion to Beethoven's Pianoforte Sonatas.* London: Associated Board of the Royal Schools of Music, 1931.

———. *Beethoven.* London: Oxford University Press, 1944.

———. *Essays in Musical Analysis: Chamber Music.* Oxford: Oxford University Press, 1944.

Brahms

Holde, Artur. "Suppressed Passages in the Brahms-Joachim Correspondence, Published for the First Time." *The Musical Quarterly* 45, no. 3 (July 1959): 312–324.

Litzmann, Berthold. *Letters of Clara Schumann and Johannes Brahms.* Westport, CT: Hyperion Press, 1979.

MacDonald, Malcolm. *Brahms.* New York: Schirmer Books, 1990.

Matthews, Denis. *Brahms Piano Music.* London: BBC Publications, 1978.

May, Florence. *The Life of Brahms.* Neptune City, NJ: Paganiniana Publications, 1981.

Musgrave, Michael, ed. *The Cambridge Companion to Brahms.* Cambridge: Cambridge University Press, 1999.

Sisman, Elaine R. "Brahms and the Variation Canon." *19ᵗʰ-Century Music* 14, no. 2 (Autumn 1990): 132–153.

Swafford, Jan. *Johannes Brahms: A Biography*. New York: Alfred A. Knopf, 1997.

Chopin
Chopin, Frédéric. *Preludes, Op. 28: An Authoritative Score, Historical Background, Analysis, Views, and Comments*. Edited by Thomas Higgins. New York and London: W. W. Norton, 1973.

Gavoty, Bernard. *Frederic Chopin*. New York: Charles Scribner's Sons, 1977.

Samson, Jim, ed. *The Cambridge Companion to Chopin*. Cambridge: Cambridge University Press, 1992.

Szulc, Tad. *Chopin in Paris: The Life and Times of the Romantic Composer*. New York: Scribner, 1998.

Zamoyski, Adam. *Chopin: Prince of the Romantics*. London: Harper Press, 2011.

Copland
Copland, Aaron, and Vivian Perlis. *Copland: 1900 through 1942*. New York: St. Martin Press, 1984.

Copland, Aaron. *Copland on Music*. New York: W. W. Norton, 1960.

———. *The New Music: 1900–1960*. Revised and enlarged edition. New York: W. W. Norton, 1968.

Pollack, Howard. *Aaron Copland: The Life and Work of an Uncommon Man*. New York: Henry Holt and Company, 1999.

Debussy
Borgeaud, Henri, ed. *Correspondence de Claude Debussy et Pierre Louÿs (1893–1904)*. Paris: Librairie Jose Corti, 1945.

Debussy, Claude. *Debussy on Music*. Translated by Richard Langham Smith. New York: Alfred A. Knopf, 1977.

————. *Monsieur Croche: The Dilettante Hater*. New York: Lear Publishers, 1948.

Roberts, Paul. *Debussy*. London: Phaidon, 2008.

Tresize, Simon, ed. *The Cambridge Companion to Debussy*. Cambridge: Cambridge University Press, 2003.

Vallas, Léon. *Claude Debussy: His Life and Work*. New York: Dover, 1973.

Dvořák

Hurwitz, David. *Dvořák: Romantic Music's Most Versatile Genius*. New York: Hal Leonard Corporation, 2005.

Liszt

Hamilton, Kenneth. *Liszt: Sonata in B Minor*. Cambridge: Cambridge University Press, 1996.

Renaud, Lucie. Translated by Peter Christensen. *Liszt: Années de pèlerinage*. CD program note. Analekta, AN 2 9980. 2010.

Searle, Humphrey. "Franz Liszt." In *The New Grove Dictionary of Music and Musicians*. London and New York: Macmillan, 1980.

Walker, Alan. *Franz Liszt, Volume I: The Virtuoso Years (1811–1847)*. New York: Alfred A. Knopf, 1983.

Mozart

Abert, Hermann. *W. A. Mozart*. Translated by Stewart Spencer. New Haven and London: Yale University Press, 2007.

Broder, Nathan. "Mozart and the 'Clavier.'" In *The Creative World of Mozart*. Edited by Paul Henry Lang. New York: W. W. Norton, 1963.

Solomon, Maynard. *Mozart: A Life*. New York: HarperCollins, 1995.

Wolf, Eugene K. "The Rediscovered Autograph of Mozart's Fantasy and Sonata in C Minor, K. 475/457." *The Journal of Musicology* 10, no. 1 (Winter, 1992): 3–47.

Mussorgsky
Russ, Michael. *Mussorgsky:* Pictures at an Exhibition. Cambridge: Cambridge University Press, 1992.

Taruskin, Richard. *Mussorgsky*. Princeton: Princeton University Press, 1992.

Prokofiev
Berman, Boris. *Prokofiev's Piano Sonatas*. New Haven and London: Yale University Press, 2008.

Jaffé, Daniel. *Sergey Prokofiev*. London: Phaidon, 1998.

Robinson, Harlow. *Sergei Prokofiev*. New York: Viking, 1987.

Seroff, Victor. *Sergei Prokofiev: A Soviet Tragedy*. New York: Taplinger, 1979.

Rachmaninoff
Bertensson, Sergei, and Jay Leyda. *Sergei Rachmaninoff: A Lifetime in Music*. Bloomington and Indianapolis: Indiana University Press, 2001.

Von Riesemann, Oskar. *Rachmaninoff's Recollections*. New York: Macmillan, 1934.

Ravel
Benjamin, George. "Last Dance." In *The Musical Times*, 135 (July 1994): 432–435.

Goss, Madeline. *Bolero: The Life of Maurice Ravel*. New York: Tudor Publishing Company, 1940.

Mawer, Deborah, ed. *The Cambridge Companion to Ravel*. Cambridge: Cambridge University Press, 2000.

Nichols, Roger. *Ravel Remembered*. New York: W. W. Norton, 1987.

Roberts, Paul. *Reflections: The Piano Music of Maurice Ravel*. Milwaukee: Amadeus Press, 2012.

Roland-Manuel, Alexis. *Maurice Ravel*. New York: Dover Publications, 1972.

Schubert
McKay, Elizabeth Norman. *Franz Schubert: A Biography*. Oxford: Clarendon Press, 1997.

Newbould, Brian. *Schubert: The Music and the Man*. Berkeley and Los Angeles: University of California Press, 1999.

Wechsberg, Joseph. *Schubert: His Life, His Work, His Time*. New York: Rizzoli, 1977.

Schumann
Cooper, Frank. *Robert Schumann: Kreisleriana*. Program note. Cliburn Concerts, Van Cliburn Foundation. January 25, 1996.

Daverio, John. *Robert Schumann: Herald of a New Poetic Age*. Oxford and New York: Oxford University Press, 1997.

Litzmann, Berthold. *Clara Schumann: An Artist's Life*. Three vols. Leipzig: Breitkopf and Hartel, 1925.

Ostwald, Peter. *Schumann: The Inner Voices of a Musical Genius*. Boston: Northeastern University Press, 1985.

Pleasants, Henry. *The Musical World of Robert Schumann: A Selection of Schumann's Own Writings*. London: Victor Gollancz, Ltd., 1965.

Reich, Nancy B. *Clara Schumann: The Artist and the Woman*. Rev. ed. Ithaca and London: Cornell University Press, 2001.

Taylor, Ronald. *Robert Schumann: His life and Work*. New York: Universe Books, 1982.

Scriabin

Baker, James. *The Music of Alexander Scriabin*. New Haven: Yale University Press, 1986.

Bowers, Faubion. *Scriabin*. Two vols. Tokyo and Palo Alto: Kodansha International, 1969.

Macdonald, Hugh. "Alexander Scriabin." In *The New Grove Dictionary of Music and Musicians*. London and New York: Macmillan, 1980.

Selective Annotated Bibliography

This bibliography recommends books in three categories: the history of the piano, the history of pianism and pianists, and recommended biographies of the principal composers discussed in this course. Finally, don't miss the video recommendation at the end of the bibliography.

The Piano

Good, Edwin M. *Giraffes, Black Dragons, and Other Pianos.* 2nd ed. Palo Alto: Stanford University Press, 2001. Good's is the standard text on the technological development of the piano from its invention in 1700 to the present day. But much more, it is a superb social history of the piano and its ongoing impact on music in the Western world. Lavishly illustrated.

The Pianists

Schonberg, Harold. *The Great Pianists.* Revised and updated. New York: Fireside, 1987. Schonberg, famed music critic for *The New York Times,* was a true student of the pianist. Given that many of the greatest pianists discussed in this book are among the greatest composers of piano music, this book is not just about the development of piano playing but about the ongoing evolution of piano *music* as well.

The Composers

Albéniz
Clark, Walter Aaron. *Isaac Albéniz: Portrait of a Romantic.* Oxford University Press, 1999.

J. S. Bach
Wolff, Christoph. *Johann Sebastian Bach: The Learned Musician.* New York: W. W. Norton, 2000.

Beethoven
Solomon, Maynard. *Beethoven*. 2nd rev. ed. New York: Schirmer Books, 1998.

Brahms
Swafford, Jan. *Johannes Brahms: A Biography*. New York: Alfred A. Knopf, 1997.

Chopin
Zamoyski, Adam. *Chopin: Prince of the Romantics*. London: Harper Press, 2011.

Copland
Copland, Aaron, and Vivian Perlis. *Copland: 1900 through 1942*. New York: St. Martin Press, 1984.

Debussy
Vallas, Léon. *Claude Debussy: His Life and Work*. New York: Dover, 1973.

Liszt
Walker, Alan. *Franz Liszt, Volume I: The Virtuoso Years (1811–1847)*. New York: Alfred A. Knopf, 1983.

———. Franz Liszt, *Volume II: The Weimar Years (1848–1861)*. New York: Alfred A Knopf, 1989.

———. *Franz Liszt, Volume III: The Final Years (1861–1886)*. Ithaca: Cornell University Press, 1996.

Mozart
Solomon, Maynard. *Mozart: A Life*. New York: HarperCollins, 1995.

Mussorgsky
Taruskin, Richard. *Mussorgsky*. Princeton: Princeton University Press, 1992.

Prokofiev
Robinson, Harlow. *Sergei Prokofiev*. New York Viking, 1987.

Rachmaninoff

Bertensson, Sergei, and Jay Leyda. *Sergei Rachmaninoff: A Lifetime in Music*. Bloomington and Indianapolis: Indiana University Press, 2001.

Ravel

Roland-Manuel, Alexis. *Maurice Ravel*. New York: Dover Publications, 1972.

Schubert

Newbould, Brian. *Schubert: The Music and the Man*. Berkeley and Los Angeles: University of California Press, 1999.

Schumann

Daverio, John. *Robert Schumann: Herald of a New Poetic Age*. Oxford and New York: Oxford University Press, 1997.

Scriabin

Bowers, Faubion. *Scriabin*. Two volumes. Tokyo and Palo Alto: Kodansha International, 1969.

Video Recommendation

Note by Note: The Making of Steinway L1037 (2007). A wonderful, movie-length DVD. Product description: *Note by Note* follows the creation of a Steinway concert grand, L1037, from forest floor to concert hall. Each piano's journey is complex, spanning 12 months, 12,000 parts, 450 craftsmen, and countless hours of fine-tuned labor. Filmed in key Steinway locations, *Note by Note* is a loving celebration not just of craftsmanship, but of a dying breed of person who is deeply connected to working by hand. In the end, this is an ode to the most unexpected of unsung heroes. It reminds us how extraordinary the dialogue can be between an artist and an instrument crafted out of human hands but born of the materials of nature.

Music Credits

The following solo piano compositions (either full pieces or excerpts) were performed by Magdalina Melkonyan.

J. S. Bach, *The Well-Tempered Clavier*, Book One.

Beethoven, Piano Sonata No. 23 in F minor, Op. 57, *Appassionata*.

Beethoven, *Diabelli Variations*, Op. 120.

Schubert, Piano Sonata No. 21 in B-flat Major.

Chopin, *Préludes*, Op. 28.

Schumann, *Carnaval,* Op. 9, No. 11.

Schumann, *Kreisleriana*.

Liszt, *Années de pèlerinage* (*Years of Pilgrimmage*).

Brahms, Six Pieces for Piano, Op. 118.

Mussorgsky, *Pictures at an Exhibition*.

Debussy, *Préludes*, Book One, Nos. 1, 2, 3, 4, 7, and 8.

Debussy, *Préludes*, Book One, No. 10, "The Sunken Cathedral."

Mozart, Piano Sonata in C Major, K. 545.

Beethoven, *"Für Elise."*

Beethoven, Minuet in G, WoO 10, No. 2.

Rubinstein, Melody in F.

Chopin, Waltz in D-flat Major, Op. 64, No. 1.

Dvořák, *Humoresques*.

Mendelssohn, *Song without Words*, Op. 62, No. 6.

Debussy, "Clair de Lune."

Schumann, "Traumerei," from *Kinderscenen*, Op. 15.

The following solo piano compositions (either full pieces or excerpts) were performed by Woobin Park (www.woobinpark.com).

J. S. Bach, *Goldberg Variations*.

Mozart, Piano Sonata in C Minor, K. 457.

Chopin, Ballade in G Minor, Op. 23.

Liszt, Sonata in B Minor.

Ravel, *Valses nobles et sentimentales*, Nos. 1–8. Published by Universal Music Publishing Group.

Scriabin, Piano Sonata No. 5 in F-sharp Major, Op. 53.

Rachmaninoff, Études-tableaux, Op. 39. Published by Boosey and Hawkes.

Prokofiev, Piano Sonata No. 7 in B-flat Major, Op. 83. Published by G. Schirmer.

Liszt, *Hungarian Rhapsody* No. 2, S.244/2.

The following solo piano compositions (either full pieces or excerpts) were performed by Eun Joo Chung (www.eunjoochung.com).

Brahms, *Handel Variations*, Op. 24.

Copland, *Piano Variations*. Published by Boosey and Hawkes.

Beethoven, Sonata in C Minor, Op. 13.

Additional Music

Albéniz, *Iberia*. Performed by Nicholas Unwin. Recording courtesy of Chandos Records Ltd.

Beethoven, *Diabelli Variations*, Op. 120, Variation No. 1. Performed by Beth Levin. Recording courtesy of Centaur Records, Inc.

Chopin, *Préludes*, Op. 28, Nos. 2, 16, and 19. Performed by Louis Lortie. Recording courtesy of Chandos Records Ltd.

Rachmaninoff, Études-tableaux, Op. 33, No. 7 in E-flat major. Performed by Xiayin Wang. Published by Boosey and Hawkes. Recording courtesy of Chandos Records Ltd.

Wagner, *The Ride of the Valkyries*. Performed by the Apollo Symphony Orchestra. Courtesy of Music Loops.

"Copenhagen" from *New Orleans Jazz Volume 3*, courtesy of Ted Shafer, leader of Ted Shafer's Jelly Roll Jazz Band.

Notes

Notes